The SEARCH *for* KNOWLEDGE *and* UNDERSTANDING

ALSO BY MAXWELL BENNETT

Autonomic Neuromuscular Transmission

History of Cognitive Neuroscience
With Peter Hacker

History of the Synapse

The Idea of Consciousness: Synapses and the Mind

Neuroscience and Philosophy: Brain, Mind and Language
With Daniel Dennett, Peter Hacker and John Searle

Optimising Research and Development in Australia

Philosophical Foundations of Neuroscience
With Peter Hacker

Stress, Trauma and Synaptic Plasticity
With Jim Lagopoulos

Virginia Woolf and Neuropsychiatry

The SEARCH for KNOWLEDGE and UNDERSTANDING

Maxwell Bennett

THE UNIVERSITY OF SYDNEY

First published by the University of Sydney
© Maxwell Bennett 2019
© The University of Sydney 2019

Reproduction and communication for other purposes
Except as permitted under the Act, no part of this edition may be reproduced, stored in a retrieval system, or communicated in any form or by any means without prior written permission. All requests for reproduction or communication should be made to the University of Sydney at the address below:

Sydney University Press
Fisher Library F03
University of Sydney NSW 2006
AUSTRALIA
sup.info@sydney.edu.au
sydney.edu.au/sup

A catalogue record for this book is available from the National Library of Australia.

ISBN 9781742104492 paperback
ISBN 9781742104508 epub
ISBN 9781742104515 kindle

Front cover: carved bannister in the Quadrangle © The University of Sydney / Louise M. Cooper.
Back cover: sandstone arches in the Quadrangle © The University of Sydney.
Cover design by Miguel Yamin.

Contents

List of figures vii

List of plates xi

List of tables xii

Acknowledgements xiv

Foreword xv

Introduction xvii

History 1

1 Ancient Greek red-figure pottery: Arthur Dale Trendall 3

2 Medieval Icelandic sagas and poetry: Margaret Clunies Ross 27

3 Early Australian colonies and Federation: John Manning Ward 41

Jurisprudence 63

4 Protecting the common law from autocracy: Alice Erh-Soon Tay 65

5 Ensuring legal decisions reflect society's mores: Julius Stone 79

Economics 89

6 Identifying instabilities in financial institutions: Warren Pat Hogan 91

Philosophy 117

7 Truth, time and causality: Huw Price 119

8 Brain and mind: David Armstrong 137

9	Foundations of modern science: Stephen Gaukroger	147

Physics, engineering and astronomy — 159

10	Star magnitudes and the invention of the stellar interferometer: Robert Hanbury Brown	161
11	Radio signals from stars and the invention of the Mills Cross telescope: Bernard Mills	173
12	Radio signals from sunspots and the invention of the swept-lobe interferometer: Ruby Payne-Scott	183

Chemistry and geology — 199

13	Photosynthesis and the quantum mechanics of electron transfer: Noel S. Hush	201
14	Discovery of land masses in Antarctica and Precambrian fossils: Tannatt William Edgeworth David	215

Biology, epidemiology and mathematics — 231

15	Distribution and abundance of species: Louis Charles Birch	233
16	Biodiversity, the spread of diseases and mathematical predictions: Robert May	247
17	Malignant melanoma, rubella hearing loss and mathematical correlations: Henry Oliver Lancaster	263

Neuroscience, neurology and respiratory medicine — 279

18	Seeing the world in three dimensions depends on identified neural mechanisms: Peter Bishop	281
19	Delaying nerve degeneration, inherited diseases and multiple sclerosis: James McLeod	291
20	Asthma risk factors identified as allergens and genetic predispositions: Ann Janet Woolcock	299

Epilogue: Knowledge and understanding	311
References	315
Index	327

List of figures

Figure 1.1 Professor Arthur Dale Trendall at the Australian National University, 1963. — 4

Figure 1.2 Typical ears and hands. From Morelli's *Italian Painters*. — 7

Figure 1.3 Map of South Italy and Sicily showing principal find-spots for red-figure vases. — 11

Figure 2.1 Professor Margaret Clunies Ross in Uppsala, Sweden, 1987. — 28

Figure 2.2 Page from an 18th-century Icelandic manuscript. — 31

Figure 2.3 Illustrated page from a 14th-century manuscript of Snorri Sturluson's *Edda*. — 34

Figure 3.1 Professor John Manning Ward. — 42

Figure 3.2 W.C. Wentworth, painted by Richard Buckner. — 49

Figure 3.3 Henry George Grey, 3rd Earl Grey, by Caldesi, Blanford and Co. — 52

Figure 3.4 James Macarthur, watercolour on ivory miniature, c. 1820. — 58

Figure 4.1 Professor Alice Ehr-Soon Tay. — 66

Figure 5.1 Professor Julius Stone. — 80

Figure 5.2 Portrait of Julius Stone, created by Naomi Berns. — 83

Figure 5.3 Caricature of Julius Stone, drawn by Ulf Kaiser. — 86

Figure 6.1 Professor Warren Hogan, taken by the *Newcastle Morning Herald* on 16 December 1952. — 92

Figure 6.2 Annual growth of real non-farm GDP, seasonally adjusted, March quarter. — 100

Figure 6.3 Risk aversion graph A. — 101

Figure 6.4 Risk aversion graph B. — 102

Figure 6.5 Cumulative abnormal returns (CAR) – individual companies. — 106

Figure 6.6 Credit default swap. — 111

Figure 7.1 Professor Huw Price. 120

Figure 7.2 A damper. 129

Figure 7.3 An antidamper. 130

Figure 7.4 Using an anti-damper to produce a damper. 131

Figure 8.1 Professor David Armstrong answering questions at the Catholic University of Lublin in 1995. 138

Figure 8.2 David Armstrong, B.A., B Phil., 1959, by Clifton Pugh (1924–1990). 144

Figure 9.1 Professor Stephen Gaukroger at the University of Sydney. 148

Figure 9.2 Portrait of Francis Bacon, painted circa 1620 by an unknown painter. 150

Figure 9.3 Portrait of René Descartes (1596–1650), philosopher, copied from an original by Frans Hals. 154

Figure 10.1 Professor Robert Hanbury Brown. 162

Figure 10.2 The display used for metre-wave air interception radar. 164

Figure 10.3 The pilot's spot indicator of AI Mark V. 165

Figure 10.4 Diagram of a classical interferometer. 170

Figure 10.5 Diagram of an intensity interferometer. 171

Figure 11.1 Dr Bernard Mills, Sydney University, 1960. 174

Figure 11.2 Mills enjoying a moment with the then Australian Prime Minister, Sir Robert Menzies during the official opening ceremony for the Molonglo Observatory on 19th November 1965. 176

Figure 11.3 A close up view of the prototype Mills Cross at the Potts Hill field station. 178

Figure 11.4 The Mills Cross at the Fleurs field station. 179

Figure 11.5 Radio contours from the Sydney University Molonglo Sky Survey at 843 MHz overlaid on an optical image of the field from the UK Schmidt IIIaJ survey. 180

Figure 12.1 Ruby Payne-Scott at the Potts Hill Reservoir in 1948. 184

Figure 12.2 Diagram of the sun. 186

Figure 12.3 An optical image of one of the largest sunspots ever observed. 187

Figure 12.4 Correlations between the size of the optical image of sunspots and the power of the solar radio noise recorded on the same dates in October 1945. 189

Figure 12.5 A plot of the position of 100 MHz radiation and that of the correlated sunspot group during a solar rotation. 191

Figure 12.6 Diagram of the sea-cliff interferometer at Dover Heights. 193

List of figures

Figure 12.7 Radio astronomers at the 1952 International Assembly of the Union Radio Scientifique Internationale. 196

Figure 13.1 Professor Noel Hush. 202

Figure 13.2 The three isomers of C_3H_4, propyne, cyclopropene and allene. 207

Figure 13.3 The Creutz-Taube ion. 208

Figure 13.4 Sketch of a single 1,4-benzenedithiol molecule chemisorbed between two gold electrodes, and molecule orbitals depicting different conduction channels through the device. 211

Figure 13.5 A quinone. 213

Figure 14.1 Professor Tannatt William Edgeworth David. 216

Figure 14.2 David, with shouldered pick, and assistant Jack Rourke on 3 August 1886, looking pleased to have uncovered the Greta Coal Seam. 218

Figure 14.3 Map of the route to the South Magnetic Pole taken by David, Mawson and Mackay. 220

Figure 14.4 David, Mawson and Mackay at the South Magnetic Pole. 223

Figure 14.5 David's preliminary plot of the New South Wales section of the Geological Map of the Commonwealth of Australia. 228

Figure 14.6 'Famous Australians' 5c stamp. 229

Figure 15.1 Professor Louis Charles Birch. 234

Figure 15.2 The ecological web. 241

Figure 15.3 The envirogram of the European rabbit in Australia. 244

Figure 16.1 Robert McCredie May, Baron May of Oxford, by Norman McBeath. 248

Figure 16.2 The utilisation functions for various species. 250

Figure 16.3 The minimum eigenvalue of the stability matrix is plotted as a function of niche overlap, given by d/w for an n-species guild. 251

Figure 16.4 The closest niche overlap, d/w, consistent with community stability in a randomly varying environment. 252

Figure 16.5 Depiction of the 'phase space' of two species with populations x and y. 253

Figure 16.6 A typical form for the relationship between X_{t+1} and X_t described in the text. 256

Figure 16.7 Curves depicting the relation between X_{t+1} and X_t, and the population trajectory, X_t, as a function of generation time, t. 258

Figure 16.8 This figure illustrates some of the stable (continuous line) and unstable (broken line) fixed points of various periods that can arise by bifurcation processes. 259

Figure 17.1 Professor Henry Oliver Lancaster in 1978. 264

Figure 17.2 Pathologist (Major Henry Lancaster), 1944, by Nora Heysen. 266

Figure 17.3 A comparison of the mortality from melanoma in Australia, 1951 to 1953 with that in England and Wales, 1950 to 1953. 270

Figure 18.1 Professor Peter Bishop. 282

Figure 18.2 The optic nerves, composed of individual axons, from *Renati Des-Cartes Tractatus de homine et de formatione foetus quorum prior notis perpetuis Ludovici de La Forge, M.D., illustratur*, 1677. 284

Figure 18.3 Peter Bishop in the laboratory. 287

Figure 19.1 Professor James McLeod. 292

Figure 19.2 Charts of sensory findings in 4 patients with leprosy following nerve grafting, selected to illustrate quality of results obtained. 294

Figure 19.3 Effect of trains of impulses on the amplitude of compound nerve action potential of sciatic-tibial nerves of control and Trembler mouse. 297

Figure 20.1 Professor Ann Janet Woolcock. 300

Figure 20.2 A diagram of the bronchi, bronchioles and in the enlargement the lung parenchyma. 302

Figure 20.3 Ann Woolcock and Ruthven Blackburn performing an electrocardiograph on a villager in Pompomere, Eastern Highlands, Papua New Guinea. c. 1966. 303

Figure 20.4 Shape of histamine dose response curves. 306

List of plates

Plate 1.1 Athenian white ground lekythoi.

Plate 1.2 Bell krater attributed the painter of BM F57, depicting a satyr, a maenad and Dionysus reclining.

Plate 1.3 Paestan bell krater attributed to Python.

Plate 1.4 The Death of Niobe.

Plate 1.5 Bell krater BM F57, depicting Orestes, Electra and Chrysothemis.

Plate 1.6 Panathenaic amphora attributed to the Judgement Painter.

Plate 1.7 Pelike attributed to the Truro Painter.

Plate 1.8 The Arrival of Helen of Troy, attributed to the De Schulthess Painter.

Plate 10.1 A comparison between the resolution of radio telescope and an optical telescope, and a very large array (VLA) radio telescope image of two lobes, with material drawn towards a black hole.

List of tables

Table 6.1 Ratio of 'used' to 'installed' capital. 97

Table 6.2 Rate of growth of real non-farm gross domestic product. 98

Table 6.3 Systematic risk: banking and finance industries. 105

Table 12.1 Solar Radio Burst Classifications. 192

Table 15.1 The life table (for oviposition span) age-specific fecundity rates and the method of calculating the net reproduction rate (R_0) for *Calandra oryzae* at 29 degrees in wheat of 14 per cent moisture content. 239

Table 15.2 Showing the method of calculating r for *Calandra oryzae* at 29 degrees by trial and error substitution in the expression $\sum e^{7-rx} l_x m_x = 1097$. 240

Table 17.1 A comparison of cancer patient skin types. 269

Table 17.2 Mortality from melanoma in Australia. 271

Table 17.3 Ratio of number of new events in 6 years to number exposed to risk: by initial systolic blood pressure and serum cholesterol. 274

Table 17.4. Partition of chi-square. 277

In memory of my father

Acknowledgements

Each of the essays in this work has been read by one or more experts in the appropriate field, given below. I am tremendously grateful to each of them for the advice concerning each of the drafts. I am particularly indebted to Agata Mrva-Montoya and Chelsea Sutherland for their meticulous care in guiding the work to press. Because these essays cover a diverse range of disciplines, the effort required to edit and check references was prodigious. I was very lucky to have my friend of twenty years, Richard North, with his very considerable experience in this regard, offer his services. I shall not easily discharge the debt of gratitude I owe him. Finally I would like to thank the Provost of Sydney University, Stephen Garton, for asking me to write this work. It has been a wonderful intellectual adventure.

Tony Aspromourgos (Economics); Margaret Clunies Ross (English); Bogdan Dreher (Neuroscience); Lesley Farnell (Mathematics); Stephen Gaukroger (Philosophy); Bill Gibson (Mathematics); Richard Hunstead (Astronomy); Noel Hush (Chemistry); Stephen Leeder (Medicine); Paul Martin (Neuroscience); Don Melrose (Physics); James McLeod (Neurology); Mark McKenna (History); Phil McManus (Geosciences); Ross McPhedran (Physics); Ian McPhee (Archaeology); John Pollard (Neurology); Huw Price (Philosophy); Jeffrey Reimers (Chemistry); John Robinson (Mathematical Statistics); Wojciech Sadurski (Law); Stephen Simpson (Ecology); William Tango (Physics); Kevin Walton (Law).

Foreword

These days the talk is all about the importance of interdisciplinary research and education, although the nature of such work (and sometimes its value) is much debated. The best interdisciplinary endeavours, however, are grounded in deep disciplinary expertise. It is not knowing a little about a lot of things but the bringing together of expertise around shared questions and objects of inquiry that drives the best interdisciplinary work.

While new interdisciplinary enterprises are now more commonly formalised and funded initiatives, institutionally driven through policies and funding allocations, talking across boundaries is far from new. Many of the best scholars over the years have drawn stimulus from the broad scholarly communities in which they thrive.

There are few more exemplary scholars in this respect than Professor Max Bennett AO. Professor Bennett is an internationally renowned neuroscientist, and his list of scholarly awards and distinctions fills many pages. He is one of those researchers whose capacious intellect and curiosity have inclined him to reach out to scholars in other fields – in physiology and neuropsychiatry, and equally to important scholars in fields such as philosophy and the history of science. These important collaborations have led to path-breaking monographs such as *The Idea of Consciousness* and *The History of the Synapse*. Professor Bennett was doing modern interdisciplinary work well before academic administrators started to think it was an idea for our time.

There could be few better, then, to chart the history of his immediate intellectual culture. The University of Sydney has had the privilege of providing an intellectual home for Professor Bennett for the past 50 years. And in that time he has engaged with a wide network of colleagues across the disciplines, inside and outside the university. Sydney was able to provide a rich intellectual environment that nurtured not just Professor Bennett but many other scholars. Long regarded as one of the world's leading universities (modern ranking systems, despite their limitations, provide a mechanism for suggesting it is one of the top 100 in the world), one of Sydney's remarkable strengths is its intellectual breadth and depth. It has nurtured, along with Toronto and a few other notable institutions, more disciplines than most other institutions in the world. And this tradition has put the University of Sydney at the forefront of contemporary interdisciplinary endeavours, precisely because of its remarkable disciplinary breadth and depth.

In this intellectual climate, many scholars have thrived. Professor Bennett has now written this wonderful homage to a select few of his peers at Sydney. There were many to choose from, but his focus has been on crafting short but insightful intellectual biographies of a small sample of the great scholars that have worked at the University of Sydney over the past century, in medicine, the life sciences, the physical sciences and the humanities and social sciences. There are colleagues here who have transformed knowledge in their disciplines in profound ways. Collectively, we can see the wonders of having such a rich intellectual culture nurturing future generations.

Professor Bennett has written a beautiful account of how one scholarly community has thrived by nurturing scholars and giving them the intellectual freedom to pursue their passions. And he has demonstrated how such a community produces inestimable benefits to the world of scholarship and the wider community. Public institutions can produce public goods. This is why they deserve support.

Stephen Garton FAHA, FASSA, FRAHS
Provost and Deputy Vice-Chancellor
The University of Sydney

Introduction

My father, Adler Bercov, came from a Jewish family that migrated to Australia in order to escape persecution, first in Galaţi (Romania), where his grandfather died following a pogrom, and later in Palestine. Dad had to contend with the Great Depression, during which time his own father died at an early age. The Bercovs, like so many Jewish families, held education in the highest regard, but there were not many opportunities for my father to pursue his love of engineering and science. The paramount necessity was financial support for the family, so he left school at 14 to obtain gainful employment.

When I was born in Melbourne, just before the Second World War, the economic conditions of the nation were still grim. By the time Dad returned from military service in 1946, they remained in the doldrums but were improving. My schooling occurred when there was a continual upward trend in the nation's economy. I did not, of course, understand the basis of the Great Depression, or the reasons for the subsequent recovery, until I became a member of the academic staff at the University of Sydney 50 years ago, a position I still hold. There I got to know and become good friends with some of the wonderful scholars and researchers that appear in these essays. Among them was the pre-eminent economist Warren Hogan (Chapter 6), who showed me how the financial policies of many countries had gone awry in the 1930s and had effectively exacerbated and sustained the depression.

My father was determined that I would not be caught up in the financial hardships he had endured. So he told me, when I was 14, that I had to leave school and apply for a job as an electrical technician's apprentice in what was then called the Postmaster-General's Department (now Australia Post and Telstra). He thought that having passed the trivial entrance exam I would be guaranteed a job for life as a member of the public service, at the same time paying my way within the family. I remember crying when Dad left the room after delivering this blow. I felt a sense of dread that my friends who were continuing their education would know and understand things about the world that I never would.

Of course, I did not realise at the time that brilliant men and women, who subsequently became colleagues at Sydney, were also driven by an insatiable appetite to know and understand, including the great chemist Noel Hush (Chapter 13), who, at 94, can still be seen passing my office in the Quadrangle, the oldest building at any university in the nation, with a brisk and determined walk towards the cafeteria to have lunch. On some occasions this is with me, to discuss his latest publication on the quantum mechanics of molecules involved in some aspect of photosynthesis or to reminisce about his time in Manchester, arguing over differential equations with the inventor of the theory of the computer, that genius Alan Turing. But at 14 all of this was in the distant future as I began my apprenticeship.

It soon became apparent that my salary was sufficient not only to pay for board and lodging but also, on enquiry, the fees necessary to continue my education at night school. So after returning home from soldering wires, I would snatch a quick meal and make my way into the city of Melbourne to attend a commercial college for a few hours. On returning home, I would spend a couple of hours on further study, until about 2 am, allowing me about five hours sleep before again commencing apprenticeship activities.

One evening, just before my 16th birthday, I was browsing in a city bookshop while waiting for a tram when I came across a paperback called *A Handbook in the History of Philosophy*.[1] Wondering what philosophy was, I bought it. On reading some sections, I was immediately hooked by the subject. Among the short sketches given on dozens of distinguished and mostly deceased philosophers was one on Bertrand Russell, who, at 78, had just visited Melbourne, where he became embroiled in a very public controversy with the senior Catholic archbishop, Daniel Mannix. I sought out some of Russell's books and found they tended to fall into three categories: one, such as the two volumes with Alfred Whitehead, *Principia Mathematica*,[2] that I found impenetrable; another that I found light-weight, like *Marriage and Morals*;[3] and a third encompassing material like *The Autobiography of Bertrand Russell*,[4] in which he describes his labours over ten very concentrated years, with his Platonist colleague Whitehead, writing *Principia Mathematica* and, more particularly, how he quickly realised when tutoring the young Ludwig Wittgenstein in Cambridge that he was dealing with a genius whose influence in philosophy would surpass his own.

When I entered Melbourne University in 1958, through the good fortune of winning scholarships made available in the improved economy, I immediately started to attend lectures and tutorials in philosophy, although enrolled in electrical engineering according to the edicts of my father. The most brilliant lectures were given by David Armstrong, who soon departed for Sydney (Chapter 8), while fascinating tutorials were provided by a former student of Wittgenstein, Cameron Jackson. The pervasive influence of Wittgenstein's insights rubbed off on me, particularly when, some decades later, I came to write *Philosophical Foundations of Neuroscience*[5] with my colleague Peter Hacker. I was therefore delighted when the formidable philosopher Huw Price (Chapter 7) came to Sydney, bearing with him critical insights into the ideas of Wittgenstein.

To some extent, I managed to subvert my father's directives regarding engineering by founding an undergraduate group, pretentiously named the Athenian Society, which

---

1 Avey 1954.
2 Whitehead and Russell 1910–3.
3 Russell 1972.
4 Russell 1967–9.
5 Bennett and Hacker, 2003.

was concerned with philosophy, history and literature, and for which we would take turns to read papers each week and to invite academic luminaries for discussions.[6] The first of these was Manning Clark, who had just published the first volume of his *History of Australia*.[7] Meetings with him were often hilarious for he liked to drink on these occasions, making it difficult for me to reconcile his attempts at a highly serious prose style, in the spirit of Dostoyevsky, with this aspect of his personality. Later, when I met and got to know another senior historian of Australia at the University of Sydney, John Ward (Chapter 3), it was not at all difficult to see how such a conservative gentleman could write in a style that was dense with facts and insights, specifically avoiding speculation.

The Athenian Society was introduced to the history and philosophy of science by the controversial polyglot Frank Knopfelmacher, who emphasised a very different approach to the subject than Bertrand Russell, namely that found in Edwin Burtt's *The Metaphysical Foundations of Modern Science*.[8] Here we discovered details on the historical development of the physical sciences going back to Galileo and, more particularly, an elucidation of the assumptions used by these scientists in their research, either implicitly or explicitly. Subsequently, Stephen Gaukroger (Chapter 9) published even more careful descriptions of the attainments of giants such as Galileo and Descartes, analysing with unprecedented care the underpinnings of their contributions and then providing an unmatched vision of the evolution of science in a multi-volume study that bowled me over. Indeed, both Burtt and Gaukroger significantly informed my approach to the history of the neurosciences in my *History of the Synapse*[9] and *History of Cognitive Neuroscience* (with Peter Hacker).[10]

Two other figures who presented to our Athenian Society of undergraduates at Melbourne were the great legal scholar Zelman Cowen and Australia's pre-eminent poet, A.D. Hope. It was Cowen who alerted me to the fact that the finest mind in jurisprudence was Julius Stone (Chapter 5) in Sydney, who I had often heard on the radio when I was an adolescent, delivering his opinions in brilliant five-minute snippets, without then having identified who he was. When A.D. Hope came to talk, it was mostly about his recently published first collection of poems, *The Wandering Islands*,[11] and his love of Russian literature, in particular Tolstoy's *Anna Karenina*. He also mentioned to me his admiration for the Icelandic writer Gudmundur Kamban, particularly *The Virgin of Skalholt*.[12] Around the time I read this, I discovered that Kamban had also written in relation to the eminent Icelandic 12th-century poet Snorri Sturluson. It was then a pleasure to discover at Sydney that Margaret Clunies Ross (Chapter 2) was the leading expert on Snorri, and to read her beautiful studies on this fascinating man, the Shakespeare of the Scandinavian peoples.

---

6   McNaughton, 'The Athenian Society'.
7   Clark 1962.
8   Burtt 1954.
9   Bennett 2001.
10 Bennett and Hacker 2012.
11 Hope 1955.
12 Kamban 1935.

The issues that dominated discussions of the Athenian Society concerned the relationship between the mind and the brain, as well as consciousness. When I graduated in electrical engineering, having obeyed my father's instructions, I at last felt free to take up philosophy as an undergraduate. But now two matters dissuaded me from this course of action: one was whether someone with substantially lesser gifts than Wittgenstein could contribute in an original way to the subject; the other was a growing conviction, intensified by my readings on the history and philosophy of science, that the best way to proceed with these profound questions was to study the brain and at the same time maintain contact with senior philosophers. I did this by carrying out research on the nervous system for a PhD in the early 1960s in the Zoology Department at the University of Melbourne, during which time I serendipitously made some discoveries that, among other things, laid the foundations for a number of new drugs, including the major anti-thrombosis agent.[13]

But this was all an aside for me in my quest to unravel the mystery, as I saw it, of consciousness. At this time, John Eccles, a neuroscientist at the Australian National University who was well known for his interest in consciousness, having written extensively on the subject, had just won the Nobel Prize for his experimental studies on synapses in the brain, so he seemed the ideal person for me to join for post-doctoral research. However, on reading further literature on these subjects I found another Australian neuroscientist, not as famous as Eccles but carrying out exciting studies on synapses in the brain and writing on consciousness. This was Peter Bishop at Sydney University (Chapter 18), who had recently discovered the neurons in the brain that allow us to see in three dimensions. So I applied for a position as lecturer in his physiology department, where a wonderful array of neuroscientific questions were being researched, and was accepted.

The day I arrived at the university, I was taken to my office in the old medical school, directly opposite the Nicholson Museum in the Quadrangle, where I would carry out research for the next 40 years, not shifting until I founded the Brain and Mind Research Institute (now Centre).[14] However, on the day of my arrival I had to displace a researcher who had borrowed the room for the purposes of measuring the speed of propagation of electrical activity along the nerves of rats, all part of his investigations into the regeneration of axons after an injury. This was Jim McLeod (Chapter 19), who was destined to become Australia's senior neurologist.

After I had settled in at Sydney, I naturally sought out like-minded biologists who were interested in the mind–brain problem and consciousness. Charles Birch (Chapter 15), one of the world's leading ecologists, was readily identified through his prolific writings on the subject. We became good friends, talking and writing to each other until his death at 91. His deep spirituality was manifest both in his personality and in his books, for which he was awarded the very rich Templeton Prize honouring attempts to reconcile science with religion.

But he was not alone on campus in this regard. I came to identify similar attributes in my dear friend Robert Hanbury Brown (Chapter 10), one of the leading astronomers

---

13 Bennett 2013.
14 Bennett, 'Founding the Brain and Mind Research Institute'.

of the golden era of astronomy. His engineering ability, coupled with mathematical gifts, placed him at the forefront of radio astronomy. As I lacked such gifts, either in engineering or mathematics, I had to turn to others for guidance, particularly in the School of Mathematics, where I have carried out projects with wonderful colleagues since arriving in Sydney. There I met the remarkable Oliver Lancaster (Chapter 17), who used his significant ability in statistics to determine why some children are born deaf and why some of us contract malignant melanoma.

This short personal narrative does not mention all of the leading scholars and researchers included in these essays because in most cases they were deceased before I arrived at Sydney. Questions then arise as to the criteria for choosing the 20 considered here and to whom these essays are addressed. When the Provost, Stephen Garton, asked me to consider working on this project in addition to my research and teaching, I was taken aback, until I realised that in my 80th year, with 50 of them spent at Sydney,[15] I might be in a unique position to give an overview of the very significant intellectual accomplishments achieved at this, Australia's oldest university. The Provost had been present when I gave the 150th anniversary address on behalf of the university in 2002, at a dinner in MacLaurin Hall in the Quadrangle, on which occasion I spoke very briefly about the attainments of some of the scholars and researchers mentioned above. Now he was offering me the very exciting opportunity to probe the contributions of those that did some of their best research and scholarship at Sydney University, chosen on the basis that their contributions are of a very high order, as gauged by their peers, and only excluding those on staff at present. While quality is the principal criterion, I have also attempted to keep a balance between the disciplines. A comment should be made concerning the number of females represented in this collection compared with the number of males, a ratio of 1:5. This reflects the low number of females in the undergraduate population at the time when most of the males considered here were undergraduates. For instance, Ruby Payne-Scott (Chapter 12) was only the third woman to graduate in physics from the University of Sydney, reflecting an imbalance that no longer exists. Now over 55 per cent of undergraduates are female.

The essays I have written are variable in length, which does not reflect the importance of the subject or the contribution of those I am considering. I am also well aware that these essays do not constitute a continuous narrative, with an attractive central theme wrapped in an exciting story as was achieved by Robert Pirsig in *Zen and the Art of Motorcycle Maintenance: An Inquiry into Values*,[16] which stresses among other things that a university is not a collection of buildings, ancient or otherwise, but rather a centre of what one hopes are major intellectual accomplishments. I have attempted to show that Sydney is such a centre, in which great achievements have occurred in the gaining of new knowledge and understanding. This requires me to go deep into the accomplishments of my subjects, revealing the basis of their international reputations. Who then have I written for? Essentially, for those faculty members and alumni who would like to have a

---

15 It seems appropriate that I should now occupy the oldest office in any building on a university campus in Australia – in the beautiful East Wing of the Quadrangle, designed by Edmund Blackett in 1854. See https://bit.ly/2GxrjPj.

16 Pirsig 2006.

scholarly account of some of the marvellous contributions made by their university over the past century, irrespective of the discipline they were made in. However, the work is also an act of self-indulgence, for I have often puzzled over what the terms 'knowledge' and 'understanding' mean. I hoped that the present intellectual adventure would help me clarify the notion of 'understanding' as it holds in different disciplines, across the slices of experience and thought that we humans have divided the world into. Whether my father would have approved of my efforts, some 66 years after telling me I had to leave school and earn a living, is another matter.

History

1

Ancient Greek red-figure pottery: Arthur Dale Trendall

Challis Professor of Greek (1939–1954) and Archaeology (1948–1954); Curator of the Nicholson Museum of Antiquities. Trendall was pre-eminent in the scholarship of the red-figure pottery of Magna Graecia of the fifth and fourth centuries BC and is recognised as one of the greatest 20th-century historians of classical art.

The Nicholson Museum at Sydney University houses the largest collection of antiquities in the Southern Hemisphere. For nearly 40 years, my office and laboratory were located in the old medical school, facing this museum. My favourite pot in the museum – and worth a special visit – is an Athenian lekythos (the larger pot in Plate 1.1), which was used for storing oil as a funerary offering.[1] I have a particularly close association with this pot, which I have admired since first entering the university in 1968. One afternoon I observed through my office window that the ceiling adjacent to the museum was on fire. Upon rushing into the building I saw that the glass cases were being unlocked and the antiquities taken from them to the opposite side of the Quadrangle, to be placed on the platform of the Great Hall. I immediately participated in the evacuation, and was able to take the precious lekythos and other items, some in my pockets, to the hall. I resisted a very strong temptation to bypass the hall and return directly to my office with these beautiful objects!

I subsequently discovered that the best description of this lekythos was to be found in a relatively old handbook to the Museum, as follows:

> in the centre a stele crowned by acanthus leaves, to the left of which sits a girl in an attitude of pensive dejection. From the right, another girl approaches with a basket of offerings. Her hand seems to be dropping something into a tall, slender-necked vase

---

1 Lekythoi are narrow bodied pots with a handle attached to the neck, which has no pouring lips. They are used in funeral rites. Special mention should be made of these pots, because of the great beauty of their drawings on a white ground. The pots were filled with expensive aromatic oils and often placed beside the funeral pyre or in the grave itself, or even on the funeral pyre. The beauty of drawing is well exemplified by the Pekythos pot in the Nicholson Museum, attributed to the Triglyph Painter, identified by Beazley.

Figure 1.1 Professor Arthur Dale Trendall at the Australian National University, 1963. Photograph by W. Pedersen. National Archives of Australia: Australian News and Information Bureau, Canberra; A1200; L45315.

standing upon the stepped base of the stele – it is a loutrophoros, a vase especially associated with offerings to the dead. The drawing is free and spontaneous; the seated figure is particularly well represented and shows a grandeur and feeling not often found in the contemporary red-figure painting of the Meidias Painter and his circle.[2]

The handbook also provides a description of the smaller pot in Plate 1.1:

representing a boy and a girl standing beside a stele, crowned with a beautifully drawn palmette. The precision of the drawing, the colour of the cloaks, and the depth of feeling expressed in the downcast eyes of the two mourners mark the vase as the work of a skilled and sensitive painter.[3]

This was my introduction to Dale Trendall, who had written the handbook in 1945, when he was the curator of the museum, at which time he had developed a mastery of red-figure vases.

Trendall's devotion to the red-figure vases

Southern Italy, together with Sicily, was, for several hundred years, a colonial outpost of Athens, constituting the major part of what the Romans called Magna Graecia. Magna Graecia is now identified with the regions of Lucania (Basilicata), Apulia and Campania, and the islands of Sicily and Sardinia. Some of these regions had a dozen Greek colonies as early as the eighth century BC, with immigrants arriving from their homelands in Greece following a variety of events, such as famine and overpopulation, as well as to take advantage of new commercial opportunities. Once the colonies had been established for about 200 years, they began to produce pottery that was patterned with the red-figure technique. In the red-figure technique, the narrative and decoration are left the colour of the clay and turn red when fired. The figures are delineated by fine black lines, with the space around them painted a lustrous black, allowing a new freedom of composition and providing for innovation of draughtsmanship and presentation of the human body in every imaginable position. The figuration on these vases gives invaluable information concerning the myths subscribed to by the local populations, as well as their domestic and everyday life. Such red-figure pottery continued to be produced from the middle of the fifth century until the third century BC, offering unequalled insight into the culture of the people of Magna Graecia over 140 years.

Trendall devoted his life to the study of red-figure pottery of the Greek cities of Southern Italy and Sicily, providing details of their chronology and shape and, more particularly, their style and subject matter. This became 'a subject that he pursued with absolute devotion and undimmed enthusiasm for more than 60 years'.[4] Trendall once remarked that he had '20,000 loves, and they were all vases'.[5] Perhaps only he could have

---

2   Trendall 1945, 153.
3   Trendall 1945, 151.
4   McPhee 1998, 504.
5   McPhee 1998, 504.

brought the unique combination of analytical gifts, reflecting his mathematical powers, and sympathetic scholarship, for as he states:

> my colonial upbringing had perhaps given me a slight prejudice in favour of the Western Greek colonists and it enabled me to view some of their problems, as well as their attitude to the motherland, with a more sympathetic eye, and perhaps with even a greater understanding, than my English colleagues, who tended to look upon the ancient Greek world very much through the eyes of the Athenians, rather than those of the Syracusans or the Tarentines.[6]

Early life and study at Cambridge

Trendall was born in Glenmore, Auckland, in 1909 to a mother who was a local school teacher and a father who also taught, specialising in woodworking and associated technical drawings. Trendall soon showed his intellectual precociousness, becoming Dux of the King's School in Auckland at 15 and again at 16. During this period he wrote his first public essay, with the memorable title *The Furniture and Appurtenances of Heaven as Revealed to Wondering Mortals through the Medium of Hymns, A & M*. He then entered the University of Otago in Dunedin in 1926, some 36 years after another New Zealander of genius, Ernest Rutherford, of splitting the atom fame, entered the nearby University of Canterbury, at a time when New Zealand's population was less than one million! Trendall possessed superior gifts in mathematics and Latin, with the latter engendering an interest in the classics. When he attended the lectures of an inspirational professor of Greek, T.D. Adams, he dropped mathematics in favour of the classics, a choice that was to enrich his chosen subject enormously, as well as giving him great pleasure throughout his life.

Trendall gained a first class honours degree in Latin and was awarded a travelling fellowship to Trinity College in Cambridge, perhaps the most distinguished educational centre in the world. Although the college was very famous, it carried among the fellows a snobbish attitude to those from the antipodes. Trendall's supervisor, A.S.F. Gow, referred to him as 'another damned colonial'.[7] But Gow did one thing for Trendall that proved to be of inestimable value – in 1932 he introduced him to J.D. Beazley at Oxford, probably the greatest living classical archaeologist. Beazley's studies of Attic Greek vases from Athens and its immediate surroundings were monumental, partly because he was the leading exponent of the Morellian technique for identifying the painters of these vases.

The Morellian Technique

Giovanni Morelli (1816–1891) was a doctor of medicine (Switzerland and Germany) who taught anatomy at the University of Munich. Here he developed a forensic technique for identifying the painter responsible for a work of art. Morelli showed that details of

---

6 McPhee 1998, 504.
7 McPhee 1998, 503.

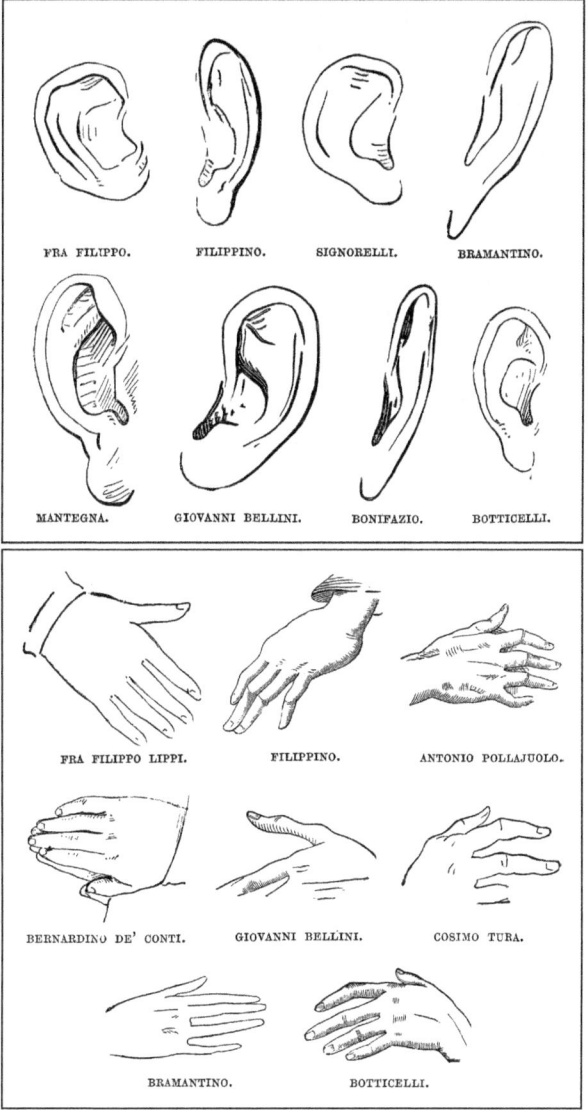

Figure 1.2 Typical ears and hands. From Morelli's *Italian Painters* (London: Murray, 1892).

figures in a painting, such as the hands of the principal figure and the folds of the ears of subsidiary figures, were rendered by mature artists in a formulistic way that characterised their developed style (see Figure 1.2). Such repeated detail of workmanship was shown to provide unequivocal evidence for the identity of the artist. Morelli discarded the obvious features of composition and subject matter in this detective work, hitherto taken to be sufficient to identify the artist, and focused on what had not been recognised – namely, that it was in the fine details of a composition, especially those concerning secondary figures, that the artist tended to fall back on formulistic presentations.

What became known as the Morellian technique is beautifully spelt out in his *Italian Masters in German Galleries* of 1883. Wind described this book as follows:

> This book looks different from those of any other writer on art. It is sprinkled with illustrations of fingers and ears, careful records of the characteristic trifles by which an artist gives himself away, as a criminal might be spotted by a fingerprint. Any art studied by Morelli begins to resemble a rogues' gallery.[8]

One of its greatest triumphs was to show that the 'Reclining Venus' held in the Dresden Gallery, heretofore thought to be a mere copy of the lost painting by Titian, was due to that other Venetian genius, Giorgione. The Morellian technique of connoisseurship was used to great effect, in terms of determining correct attributions as well as making large financial gains, by the master of Italian Renaissance painters Bernard Berenson around 1890. However, no one came as near to perfecting the technique as Beazley did in Oxford over a period of 20 years. His attribution of artists and schools responsible for the decoration of Attic pottery of the Archaic period gave a classification of the pottery in terms of the human, rather than in generalities, allowing him to follow the development of particular artists.

It was natural that Trendall, who had been greatly influenced by Beazley, should be imbued with the Morellian technique at an early stage in his career, while still in his 20s and composing his first monograph on Paestan pottery in 1936. His use of the technique to identify individual painters and stylistic groups is often accompanied by the details he used to determine the classifications. He was greatly assisted in this task by a phenomenal memory for the 20,000 or so pots he had studied. Like Morelli himself, Trendall had some spectacular successes. One of these was his prediction of the existence of a group of vase painters, none of whose vases had yet been found. This prediction was based on his ascertaining that the characteristics of some vases from South Italy and Sicily could not be attributed to influences from other schools in the region. This gap needed to be filled by an unknown school of painters identified by a style that Trendall explicitly spelt out. Amazingly, in 1970 a set of vases was discovered in the Lipari Islands (off the northern coast of Sicily) that corresponded to Trendall's prediction.

Background to red-figure pottery

Trendall's choice of subject was daring for at the time of his decision the vases of the Archaic Greek period (about the eighth century to the fifth century BC) championed by the brilliant Beazley, especially those of the Attic area, were of central scholarly interest, rather than the 'colonial' subject that Trendall had chosen. As he succinctly comments, the general attitude to the 'colonial' vases could be summed up as 'rather like Virgil's advice to Dante in regard to the lost souls outside the gate of hell, "non ragionan di lor, ma guarda e passa"' (let us not speak of them, best look and pass on).[9] Indeed, Trendall later admitted

---

8   Wind 1985, 40–1.
9   McPhee 1998, 504.

that the vessels of Magna Graecia did not constitute great art and once commented at the opening of an art exhibition: 'I have spent my life in the study of bad art.'[10] He set out for himself three specific tasks: first, to identify the main styles of red-figure vases of Magna Graecia; second, to determine the time course of development of these classical styles; and finally, through a stylistic analysis following the Morellian method, to identify the painters responsible for about 20,000 vases, including those that were now dispersed throughout the rest of the world.

It cannot be said, however, that Trendall had entered a virgin field of scholarship. Preceding him was François Lenormant, who had already begun the task of researching Magna Graecia in the period from 1879 to 1883. Furthermore, he was followed by another remarkable student of Beazley, Miss Noël Moon (later Mrs Noël Oakeshott). She had already published an inspirational paper in 1929 on South Italian pottery, which, together with Beazley's trail-blazing scholarship on Attic vases of the Archaic period, was to provide the core inspiration for Trendall's labours. Why had it taken so long for scholars to recognise this trove of antiquity in the South, leaving such a rich subject for Trendall's scholarship? The most likely reasons are that the area of Magna Graecia had been riven with malaria and brigandage, problems that were partly resolved by the establishment of a unified Italian government. There are, furthermore, few great Greek Doric temples to attract attention to the area of Southern Italy.

For what practical purpose did Trendall exert such labours over his lifetime studying red-figure pottery? The paintings on these Greek vases are a unique source of insights into the social and economic development of Magna Graecia for contemporary historians. Trendall placed the red-figure paintings into two major groups: those concerned with legend and myth and those concerned with everyday life. The former were of particular importance to the Greek colonies, isolated from their native land and from the heroic myths of the parent country. Trendall's task involved identifying the gods and their interventions in the everyday life of the colonies, as well as the actions of legendary figures such as Perseus, Jason, Theseus and Heracles, and those in the works of Homer, such as Agamemnon, Achilles and Menelaus. This group included vases depicting death, the cult of the dead and the afterlife, with images showing Persephone and Pluto in the palace of the underworld. Perhaps the most frequent class of presentation in the red-figure pottery are vases showing scenes from the theatre, indicating the importance of the stage in the cultural life of Magna Graecia. Greek tragedies, especially those by Euripides, figured prominently in these vase paintings. Greek mythology was also popular in theatrical presentations, with prominence given to Dionysus, the god of wine, the good life and the afterlife. It was therefore appropriate that scenes drawn from these myths should appear on vases celebrating the gods in a symposium or accompanying a deceased into the afterlife. These depictions of theatrical scenes on vases called for special attention, so Trendall collaborated with T.B.L. Webster in 1971 to produce the work *Illustrations of Greek Drama*.

The second of the major groups of red-figure images depict everyday scenes that show men wearing armour; athletes running, wrestling, riding and jumping; women in native costumes playing with dogs and birds, weaving and carrying out domestic duties;

---

10 Johnson, 'Trendall, Arthur Dale'.

and banquets and revelry. As the centuries passed many of these became unique to Magna Graecia, the style of red-figure pottery being quite distinct from that of the homeland. To what extent Trendall's prodigious labours may be said to be 'useful' was answered by one reviewer:

> Many scholars, like this writer, look to Apulian vase painting primarily for answers to questions of a general historical nature. Did the Tarentine adaptations of classical myths necessarily have a funerary tendency? What was the relationship between cult and tragedy in fourth century Apulia? Was the theater the primary medium for the transition of myths for the Tarentines, or did they rely equally on the epic and lyric traditions?[11]

Such scholars are dependent on Trendall's achievements.

The red-figured vases of Paestum

Trendall was particularly attracted, on his first visit to Magna Graecia, to the beauty of Lucania at the foot of Italy and, more specifically, to the city of Paestum, the major centre of ancient Greek culture in Lucania (see Figure 1.3). At the beginning of his career, he sketched, in the *The Journal of Hellenic Studies*, the very early period of Paestan pottery, before the much heralded and signed works of Isteis and Python from that region. As Trendall commented at this time, 'the problem of South Italian pottery is still rather a confused one, and this work is an attempt to put in order one of its more clearly defined fabrics'.[12] He later described one Paestan vase, which is now in the Nicholson Museum collection (see Plate 1.3), as:

> an excellent example of the style of Python ... The main design represents Dionysus with a woman seated below a window in which is framed a woman's head. The use of white and yellow for details and of red for some of the drapery is very characteristic; so are the two youths draped in cloaks with embattled borders who figure on the reverse of this vase, as they do with little variation on almost all the other vases of this group.[13]

Trendall took the position of Roman Scholar in classical studies at the British School of Athens in 1935 in order to study the red-figure vases from Paestum. This, as we have seen, was a choice of subject that was to have far-reaching consequences for his subsequent career. It led him to decide

> to make his life work the complete classification of the entire output of Italiote red-figured vases, a task that might well have daunted a scholar of less devoted tenacity.[14]

---

11   Keuls 1980, 111.
12   Oakeshott 1979, 4.
13   Trendall 1945, 147.
14   Oakeshott 1979, 4.

Figure 1.3 Map of South Italy and Sicily showing principal find-spots for red-figure vases. From *Red Figure Vases of South Italy and Sicily* by A.D. Trendall. © 1989 Thames and Hudson Ltd.

His study of the pottery of this area, when only 23, resulted in the monograph *Paestan Pottery: A Study of the Red-Figured Vases of Paestum*. This work considered all of the then 400 identified Paestan red-figure vases, and subjected each of them to the Morellian stylistic analysis championed by Beazley. However, it departed from Beazley with its own style of presentation; unlike his mentor, Trendall avoided austere and clinical presentation devoid of commentary and images. This work so impressed Beazley that he had Trendall elected to a fellowship of Trinity College Cambridge in 1937, at the young age of 28.

Over 50 years later, in 1987, Trendall published again on the fabric of Paestum in *The Red-Figured Vases of Paestum*, greatly enlarging the scope of his earlier work to include 2,000 vases, all treated with the same clarity, delicacy and detailed analysis as in his original work. This was his second last major contribution before he died in 1995.

The red-figure vases of Lucania, Campania and Sicily

Having described the fabric of the ancient Greek city of Paestum in Lucania in the 1930s, Trendall was at last able to turn, in the 1950s and 1960s, to the much larger task of identifying the individual painters and groups of artists responsible for the red-figure pottery in the remainder of Lucania, and in the regions of Campania and Sicily. His magisterial work, covering a period of 150 years, *The Red-Figured Vases of Lucania, Campania, and Sicily*, appeared in 1967 (with supplementary volumes in 1970, 1973 and 1983). It clearly attributed 6,500 vases to 250 painters and stylistic groups. Trendall's determinations have proved to be definitive over the half century since their publication, and are a testament to his scholarship and tireless capacity for applying the Morellian technique to reach unquestioned conclusions as to attribution. In this process he illuminated much of the culture of these ancient Greek colonies.

Challis Professor of Greek and curator of the Nicholson Museum of Antiquities

Trendall's *Paestan Pottery* had, as we have seen, laid the foundations for more ambitious projects on the red-figure pottery of Magna Graecia, and the auspicious offer in 1938 of the Chair of Greek at Sydney University – when Trendall was still only 29 years old – seemed to guarantee excellent prospects.

Trendall became curator of the Nicholson Museum of Antiquities at The University of Sydney (1939–1945) for which he acquired about 67 per cent or 33 of its collection of red-figure pots from Lucania, Campania, Paestum and Sicily. Furthermore, 80 per cent of the 49 pots were catalogued in his *The Red-Figured Vases of Lucania, Campania and Sicily*, as well as in *The Red-Figured Vases of Paestum*. Most importantly for the museum, Trendall wrote the *Handbook of the Nicholson Museum* in 1945. He noted that:

> Greek pottery, with its sober black and red colour-scheme, its economy of detail, its shorthand conventions such as a column for a building, a branch for an outdoor scene or a line of dots to represent broken ground, lacks the immediate appeal of Greek sculpture and may to some measure rank as an acquired taste.[15]

But, of course, this comment must be considered within the context that nearly all 'Greek sculptures' are not by the original sculptors such as Phidias and Polyclitus but are Roman copies, and so at best only reflect the hand of the masters. This was not case with the 20,000 pots that Trendall studied, where style, originality and composition directly reflected the hand of the practitioners, whose paintings revealed so much of the culture of their time.

The *Handbook of the Nicholson Museum* was not just a catalogue but a treasure trove of observations and historical insights, which remained unsurpassed as an introduction to red-figure pottery until his final summary of 1989, *Red Figure Vases of South Italy and Sicily*. Trendall directs our attention to a number of pots in the Museum, such as a

---

15 Trendall 1945, 94.

bell krater with Poseidon as subject, identified by the trident he holds, and Amymone ('blameless one'), who is gazing into his eyes. Also, a bell krater featuring Dionysus with a horned satyr, recognised by his horse tail and large ears; Dionysus holds a thyrsus (a kind of pine cone tipped wand), a symbol of fertility and hedonism. And a bell krater that depicts Pan, guardian of flocks, with legs of a goat, cloven hooves, shaggy hair and an erect member, dancing in a procession with a graphically nude female who is beating a tympanon (a small drum).

However, the red-figure vases of the museum were not given the kind of attention and formal study they needed until 2014. It was then that *Corpus Vasorum Antiquorum, Red Figure and Over-Painted Pottery of South Italy* by Michael Turner and Alexander Cambitoglou appeared. A single example from that work suffices to indicate the very high standard of the presentations:

> **Subject. The Death of Niobe** [see Plate 1.4]. The grieving Niobe stands in a naiskos turning to stone; as such she is dying. To the left, her father Tantalos kneels on the middle step of the building begging her not to die. He is supported by a naked young man who is dressed as a traveller wearing a pilos and a chlamys. To the right, seated on the top step of the naiskos is a young woman or girl, mourning. She and the young man are probably the two surviving children of Niobe … At the top right, Apollo, killer of Niobe's children, looks on. At the top left, a female figure looks on from behind a hillock. She is presumably Apollo's mother, the slighted Leto. In front of the naiskos is a selection of funerary offerings…
> **Comparanda.** For the composition of the scene, cf. the hydria attributed to the Libation Group, New York, Metropolitan Museum of Art 06.1021.230, LCS 411, no. 342, pl. 165.3, where the young man and woman are similarly positioned, one standing with a raised leg the other seated, either side of a funerary monument…
> **Attribution Date.** Libation Painter (Cambitoglou). 350–325 BC.[16]

War-time code breaking

There was a very important diversion of Trendall's labours as professor and curator shortly after he took up his Chair – Australia was at war with Japan. Given his analytical gifts, demonstrated by his precocious mathematical powers at an early age, as well as his exceptional talent with languages, shown by his fluency in Latin and Greek, he was singled out as a candidate for cryptography. Trendall was recruited in 1941 from the University of Sydney, together with senior mathematicians, when the Japanese military threat to Australia was rapidly reaching its climax. He and his colleagues were asked by the Chief of the Australian General Staff to join a signals intelligence organisation located in the Victoria Barracks in St Kilda Road, Melbourne. There he specialised in decrypting Japanese codes under the leadership of the very experienced Captain Eric Nave, work he carried out while still a professor of Greek at the University of Sydney and holding the rank of lieutenant colonel.

---

16 Turner and Cambitoglou 2014, 43–5.

He was then given his own group concerned with Japanese diplomatic traffic, while Nave's group concentrated on Japanese naval intercepts. Trendall worked both at the site of the intelligence organisation in the barracks and at a nearby boarding house in St Kilda Road, so that 'we could work for 30 hours each day,'[17] as his friend Sissons complained. This paid off handsomely as later in the year Trendall and his colleagues broke the Japanese cipher FUJI on a daily basis. This allowed his unit to send the deciphered messages immediately to London using the Australian Ultra System, a daily challenge that became a source of great pride. Furthermore, Trendall was primarily responsible for developing a cipher for use by Australian troops in the field, appropriately called TRENCODE, which 'if not unbreakable would have, even with heavy traffic, taken a long time to unravel'.[18]

Australian National University, Interim Council of Aboriginal Studies and Australian Humanities Research Council

Trendall found himself at the growing centre of Australian research, scholarship and political influence after leaving Sydney in 1953 to take up the position of Master at the new University House at the Australian National University. His friendship with Prime Minister Robert Menzies blossomed and was accompanied by his appointment in 1961 as head of the Interim Council of Aboriginal Studies, as well as Fellow of the new Australian Humanities Research Council. Trendall retired from the Australian National University after 16 years of service, concerned that his administrative load had detracted from his scholarly activities. He then took up an offer to be a resident fellow at the new La Trobe University near Melbourne. As he was notionally retired, there were no administrative chores. The fact that the university was still being built gave him a wonderful opportunity to personally design a very large apartment for himself in the new Menzies College. Much of this space was taken up by his massive library, the core of which was devoted to the pottery of Magna Graecia and included some 40,000 photos of these vases. His 'retirement' at La Trobe lasted more than 25 years, until his death at 86.

Apulia and collaboration with Alexander Cambitoglou

Apulia (see Figure 1.3) was first colonised by Mycenaean Greeks before the eighth century BC and was responsible for the largest production of red-figure pottery in Magna Graecia. It was natural that Trendall should turn to the study of this fabric after his work on Lucania, Campania and Sicily. About half of the 20,000 surviving red-figure specimens come from Apulia. Trendall collaborated on this massive project with Alexander Cambitoglou, whom he had encouraged to take up a position in the Department of Greek at Sydney University in 1961. The two met in Oxford in 1951, when they first shared their love of Apulian red-figure pottery. Cambitoglou had been trained by J.D.

---

17 Ball and Tamur 2013, 135.
18 Ball and Tamur 2013, 136.

Beazley, as Trendall had some 20 years before him. The results of this great partnership were such that, in the 'works co-authored by Trendall and Cambitoglou, the two hands cannot be distinguished and the end product bears the mark of excellence that distinguishes each author's publications'.[19]

Their collaboration on Apulian red-figure vases continued even after Cambitoglou had become Professor of Archaeology (1963–1989) and Curator of the Nicholson Museum (1963–2000), and Trendall had become Master of University House at the Australian National University and later 'retired' to La Trobe University. The collaboration produced three volumes that presented the shapes, subject matter and styles leading to the attributions of some 10,000 vases to about 370 painters and stylistic groups, with 1,300 pages and 400 plates altogether. The volumes were, in succession, *The Apulian Red-Figured Vase-Painters of the Plain Style*; *The Red-Figured Vases of Apulia, Volume 1* covering the later part of the fifth century to the middle of the fourth century BC, and including 3,500 vases; and *The Red-Figured Vases of Apulia, Volume 2* (1982) covering the period from about the middle of the fourth century to the beginning of the third century BC, and including some 6,000 vases. This latter volume showed how 'the baroque mystical-mythological style of Apulian pottery blossomed out and its iconographic symbolism became more fully codified'.[20] In addition, there were two supplements to *The Red-Figured Vases of Apulia* (one issued in 1983 and the other in 1992). It was altogether a tremendous achievement, some elements of which are sketched here.

Three main pottery schools of Apulia could be identified with tribes in the seventh to the third century BC: one that occupied northern Apulia (Daunian); another in central and western Apulia (Peucetian; from 650 to 500 BC); and finally, one in southern Apulia (Messapian; from 500 to 300 BC). Daunian pots mostly have a round-bottomed footless krater top with a plate-like rim and side handles. Decoration is geometric on the upper half of the vase, with panels isolated by vertical lines and filled with squares, triangles and lozenges. Peucetian pots, bowls, jugs and kraters are of two principal types, one painted in black and white and the other in red and black. The former frequently come with motifs of the swastika and the comb, as well as the festoon and the zigzag, with cross-hatched lozenges and a Maltese cross. Messapian pots are characterised by round, coin-like discs at the top and bottom and have simple geometric compositions. All of these pots are in the geometric style.

Ancient Taras (now Taranto),[21] the largest Greek colony, was the centre of Apulian vase production. These vases could be divided into two main styles: the plain and the ornate. As its name suggests, the plain style involved simple composition and was used for embellishing bell kraters in which up to four figures participate in a mythical narrative on the principal side, perhaps with warriors in battle dress and Dionysiac events. The other side shows cloaked youths, unaccompanied by any additional colouring. The ornate style, in contrast, was usually reserved for large vessels such as hydriai, lautrophoroi and amphorae of volute kraters that provided sufficient area on which to compose large

---

19 Keuls 1980, 111.
20 Keuls 1980, 112.
21 Taras was located adjacent to Messapia, on the southern coast. Unlike the three Lapygean tribes mentioned above, probably of Illyrian Greek origin, Taras was probably of Spartan origin. Taras had major wars with the Lapygeans and dates back earlier than the Lapygean tribes.

scenes with up to 20 floating figures, set in architectural structures rendered in simple perspective.[22] The neck and sides of these vases were frequently decorated with vegetal images, all coloured in rich white, reds and gold/yellows. Two common motifs emerged in the second half of the fourth century BC. First, a funerary tradition arose in which the vases were part of grave offerings and depicted scenes of the afterlife, the Assembly of the Gods, Heracles and the Trojan War, together with Aphrodisiac and Dionysiac scenes. The second common motif included more joyous scenes, showing weddings and erotic behaviour, with women's heads growing out of flowers or between tendrils.

Examples of the kind of detailed analysis that Trendall and Cambitoglou provided in their work in order to establish correct attributions are given below for three painters from the *Apulian Red-Figured Vase-Painters of the Plain Style* (1961):

> **The Painter of BM F57** [see Plate 1.5]. A glance at the London krater ... shows the relationship between this painter and his colleague, the Judgement Painter, especially in their treatment of the three-quarter face, the posing of the figures and the rendering of drapery. Here, however, the drawing is perhaps a little clumsier; note how the fold lines of the chiton over-run the breasts, and the squint which the artist has given to Electra.[23]

> **The Judgement Painter** [see Plate 1.6] is a clumsy artist. His drawing is of poor quality and the anatomical details of his nudes are carelessly treated. Note, for example, the left nipple of the seated warrior on the Brussels vase which is drawn out of its proper place, or his spear, which is drawn short to make room for the sash held by the woman behind him.[24]

> **The Truro Painter** [see Plate 1.7]. Most of [his] vases are small and bear representations of youths and women in conversation or pursuit scenes. His figures are mostly squat and their anatomy is often meticulously rendered. His youths have straggly hair. They often hold a palm leaf ... Their himation is often wrapped round one forearm and decorated with swastikas. The drapery of the women is often fussy, especially round the waist.[25]

Another example is taken from a later work, the Second Supplement to *The Red-Figured Vases of Apulia* (1992):

> **The De Schulthess Painter** [see Plate 1.8]. Three kraters (two of which are shown here) provide the core of the painter's *oeuvre*, and, when studied together, will be

---

22 Volute kraters are large vases with a volute or scroll at the top of the handle. Amphora vases are of various shapes but otherwise have two vertical handles. They were used for storing and transporting oils, wine, foodstuffs and therefore were the most common form of pottery. Hydria pots possess two horizontal handles for carrying and a vertical handle for pouring; they were principally used to store water. Loutrophoros pots are slim jars with elongated handles, most often used for storing water at weddings and funeral rites.
23 Cambitoglou and Trendall 1961, 30.
24 Cambitoglou and Trendall 1961, 29.
25 Cambitoglou and Trendall 1961, 68.

seen to be remarkably alike in shape, pattern-work, composition and drawing. All three have a mythological scene in two registers on the obverse, and on the reverse a stele surrounded by two youths and two women in a chiastic arrangement. On the neck of the obverse there is a band of bead-and-reel in added white above a broader one of swastika meanders alternating with enclosed squares in white on a black background, while on the reverse there is a wave pattern above, with black bead-and-reel, r.f. laurel, and a large central palmette-fan flanked by scrolls with smaller fans and drop-leaves.[26]

***

Trendall was without doubt the leading authority on the red-figure vases produced during the fifth and fourth centuries BC in the Greek colonies and native towns of South Italy and Sicily. Sir John Boardman, Britain's most distinguished historian of ancient Greek art, wrote that Trendall was 'one of the great classical art historians of [the 20th] century. ... His company and conversation shimmered with his delight in his work, and in the world around him.'[27] Eva Keuls, a recognised authority on Greek vase painting, stated that:

> the systematic framework for the study of Italiote pottery may be said to be the single-handed creation of A.D. Trendall. ... Prof. Trendall has dedicated to this goal a lifetime of study, his wide classical learning and a phenomenal expertise on styles and techniques of pottery painting.[28]

The 'In Memoriam' article to Trendall in the *Proceedings of the British Academy*, to which he was one of the few from the colonies elected to full membership, concluded:

> Dale Trendall believed absolutely in the value and joy of knowledge, and in the sharing of that knowledge with all who would listen. He was as much at home with the brash undergraduate as with the eminent scholar.[29]

Further reading

Cambitoglou, A., ed. *Studies in Honour of Arthur Dale Trendall.* Sydney: Sydney University Press, 1979.
Cambitoglou, A., and A.D. Trendall. *Apulian Red-Figured Vase-Painters of the Plain Style*. Rutland, VT: The Archaeological Institute of America, 1961.
Trendall, A.D. *Paestan Pottery: A Study of the Red-Figured Vases of Paestum.* London: Macmillan, 1936.
Trendall, A.D. *Handbook to the Nicholson Museum*. Glebe, NSW: Australasian Medical Publishing, 1945.

---

26 Trendall and Cambitoglou 1991, 133.
27 Boardman 1995.
28 Keuls 1980, 111.
29 McPhee 1998, 517.

Trendall, A.D. *Handbook to the Nicholson Museum*, 2nd ed. Glebe, NSW: Australasian Medical Publishing, 1948.

Trendall, A.D. *The Red-Figured Vases of Lucania, Campania and Sicily.* London: University of London, Institute of Classical Studies, 1983.

Trendall, A.D. *The Red-Figured Vases of Paestum.* London: British School at Rome, 1987.

Trendall, A.D. *Red Figure Vases of South Italy and Sicily.* London: Thames and Hudson, 1989.

Trendall, A.D., and A. Cambitoglou. *The Red-Figured Vases of Apulia, Volumes 1 and 2*. Oxford: Oxford University Press, 1982.

Trendall, A.D., and A. Cambitoglou. *First Supplement to 'The Red-Figured Vases of Apulia'.* London: University of London, Institute of Classical Studies, 1983.

Trendall, A.D., and A. Cambitoglou. *Second Supplement to 'The Red-Figured Vases of Apulia'.* London: University of London, Institute of Classical Studies, 1991.

Trendall, A.D., and T.B.L. Webster. *Illustrations of Greek Drama.* New York: Phaidon, 1971.

Turner, M., and A. Cambitoglou. *Corpus Vasorum Antiquorum, Red Figure and Over-Painted Pottery of South Italy.* Sydney: The Nicholson Museum, the University of Sydney, 2014.

Plate 1.1 Athenian white ground lekythoi. Left: attributed to the Painter of New York. Right: attributed to the Triglyph Painter. Nicholson Museum, the University of Sydney (NM41.2, NM41.3). Photographs courtesy of the Nicholson Museum.

Plate 1.2 Bell krater attributed the painter of BM F57, depicting a satyr, a maenad and Dionysus reclining. Civici Musei di Storia ed Arte di Trieste (S. 407).

Plate 1.3 Paestan bell krater attributed to Python. Nicholson Museum, the University of Sydney (NM42.2). Photograph courtesy of the Nicholson Museum.

Plate 1.4 The Death of Niobe. Nicholson Museum, the University of Sydney (NM71.1). Photograph courtesy of the Nicholson Museum.

Plate 1.5 Bell krater BM F57, depicting Orestes, Electra and Chrysothemis. © The Trustees of the British Museum. All rights reserved.

Plate 1.6 Panathenaic amphora attributed to the Judgement Painter. Royal Museums of Art and History, Brussels (R403). © RMAH.

Plate 1.7 Pelike attributed to the Truro Painter. Royal Cornwall Museum (TRURI: 1600.18). Reproduced with the kind permission of Cornwall Council and the Royal Institution of Cornwall.

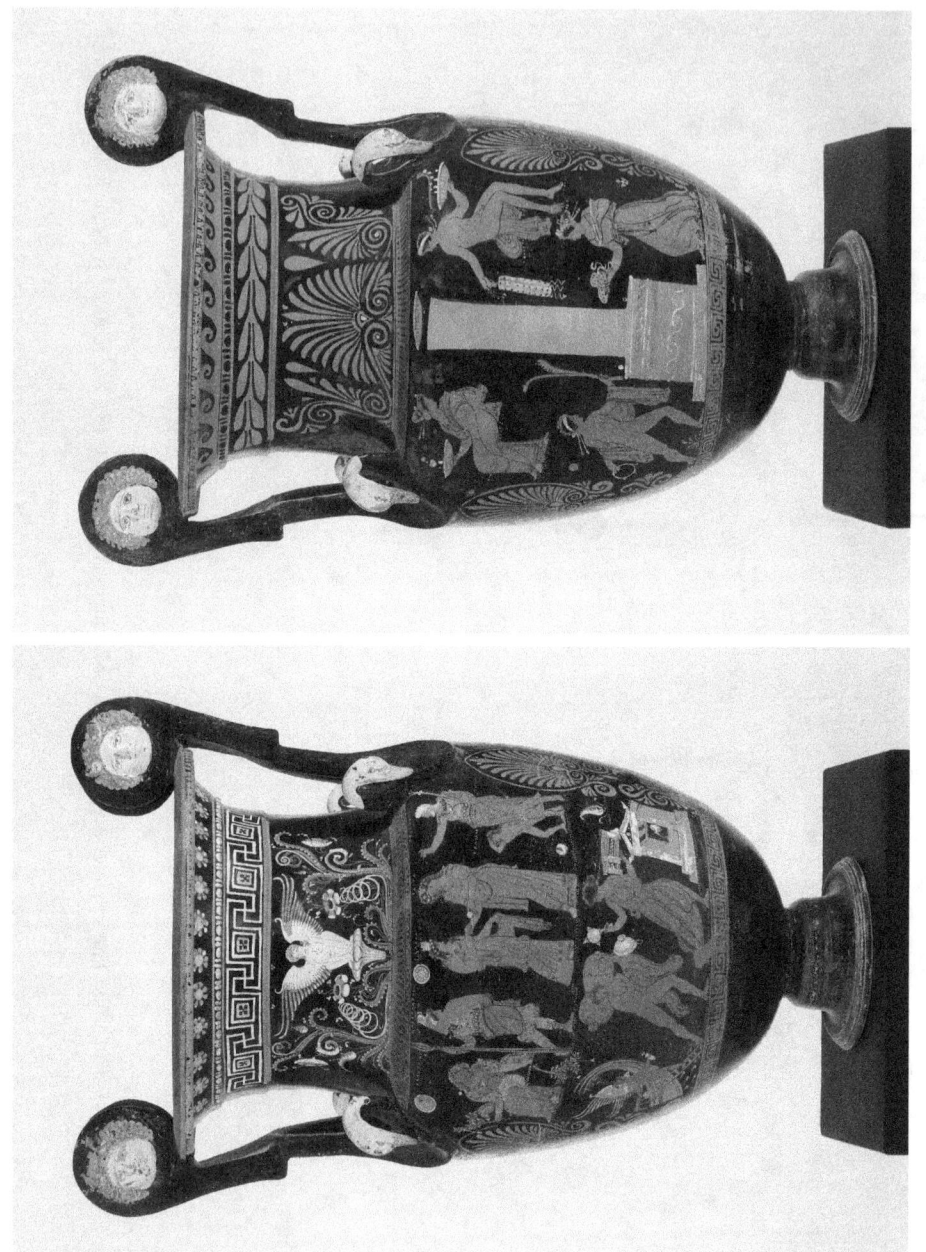

Plate 1.8 The Arrival of Helen of Troy, attributed to the De Schulthess Painter. Musée d'art et d'histoire (HR 0044). © Musées d'art et d'histoire, Ville de Genève.

2
Medieval Icelandic sagas and poetry: Margaret Clunies Ross

McCaughey Professor of English Language and Early English Literature (1990–2009). Clunies Ross is one of the world's foremost scholars of Old Norse–Icelandic and Anglo-Saxon studies as a consequence of her pioneering research on the sagas and poetry of the pre-Christian religions of the Scandinavian peoples.

What religions preceded Christianity in the West? The ancient Greek and Roman polytheistic religions, with their pantheons of gods, are well known. They are preserved, for example, in Homer's *Iliad* and *Odyssey*, as well as Virgil's *Aeneid*. The monotheistic religion of the Jews of the Levant is described in the Torah. What is not so well known is the polytheistic religion of the Germanic peoples (speakers of the Germanic languages, which include English, German, Dutch and the various Scandinavian languages) in pre-Christian times. This religion has reached popular appreciation in modern recreations and fantasy, for example, in the 19th-century operas of Richard Wagner and the 20th-century writing of Tolkien. But has the ancient Germanic religion been provided with the kind of scholarship offered long ago for the ancient religions of Greece and Rome? Such scholarship faces a daunting task for it requires identifying and analysing the pre-Christian culture of Iceland, located 1,500 km west of Norway in the North Atlantic. It is to the Icelandic people that we primarily owe the preservation of ancient Germanic culture, or at least of the version preserved in Scandinavian prose narratives and poetry. The University of Sydney is the home of one of the leading groups of scholars dedicated to medieval studies, led for several decades by Margaret Clunies Ross. Indeed,

> Foremost among scholarship over the last thirty years on the interaction between the historical forces and textual production in Old Norse-Icelandic literature is Margaret Clunies Ross's groundbreaking work on the significance of mythic paradigms in representing prevailing modes of thought in early Scandinavian society and the importance of Christian-Latin learning on the shaping of the written construction of Norse myth.[1]

---

1   Barnes 2007, 375.

Figure 2.1 Professor Margaret Clunies Ross in Uppsala, Sweden, 1987. Reproduced with permission from *Upsala Nya Tidning*.

Clunies Ross was born Margaret Tidemann on 24 April 1942 in Adelaide. She

> went to school at Walford Anglican School for Girls (still called Walford House when I first went there at the age of 4) from the ages of 4 to 16, and attended the University of Adelaide from 1959–62, where I enrolled in Arts and took a First Class Honours degree in English, graduating at the end of 1962 at the age of nearly 21.[2]

She recalled: 'When I was at school intelligent girls usually had to hide their brains under some cover or other. There were few bonus points to be gained among one's peers for cleverness or intellectual interests.'[3] When she commenced her second year at the University of Adelaide:

> It was my great good fortune that … just as I was entering the Honours stream, the department chose to restore its coverage of Old and Middle English. I won a George Murray Travelling Scholarship from the University of Adelaide in 1963 and took it up at the University of Oxford, where I studied Old Norse under Gabriel Turville-Petre, then the senior Old Norse scholar in the English-speaking world.[4]

Clunies Ross' subsequent contributions to Old Norse studies were so distinguished that she was made professor of English language and early English literature at the University of Sydney in 1990. This allowed her to create a centre for Old Norse-Icelandic and Anglo-Saxon studies.

Background to early Scandinavian religion

Cosmology in the old Nordic religion is structured around the concept of a 'Cosmological Tree', Yggdrasill, spanning nine worlds. The gods inhabited the heavenly realms of Asgard and Vanaheim; humanity inhabited Midgard, at the centre of the cosmos; giants, elves and dwarves inhabited Jotunheim, Alfheim and Svartalfheim respectively; and the goddess Hel dwelled in Hel. Travel between these worlds allowed the different beings to interact. The first humans, Ask and Embla, are said to have been animated from logs of driftwood by a trio of gods (rather akin to the God of the Torah breathing life into earth in order to create Adam). At death, humans may go to Hel, be chosen by the goddess Freyja to reside in her field, called Fólkvangr, be claimed by the goddess Rán if death occurs at sea, or, if they fall in battle, be taken by Valkyries to the martial hall of the god Odin.

In this rich cosmology, the sun, the moon and the Earth are conceptualised as animate beings – namely, Sol, Mani and Jord respectively. Elves and dwarves are not gods. They tend to possess opposite attributes; the elves are beautiful and radiant but the dwarves are not. The dwarves have special abilities and skills as craftsmen and are often associated with giants. Giants, who in contemporary times are often incorrectly thought of as very

---

2   Clunies Ross 1999, 2.
3   Clunies Ross 1999, 2.
4   Clunies Ross 1999, 2.

large beings, live in rocks and mountains and in cold northern regions, and challenge the gods. Valkyries and Norns are female beings who participate in the fates of humans.

Chief among the gods are Thor and Odin. Thor's popularity was paramount in the Viking era as he pursues the enemies of the gods and of humanity with his great hammer, Mjölnir. In contrast, Odin, residing in Valhalla, pursues knowledge and understanding throughout Yggdrasill and so is associated with wisdom and poetry. Extraordinarily, Odin's commitment is so great that he sacrifices one of his eyes in the Well of Urd, the ultimate source of wisdom, which is found below the world tree. The myths also involve many other gods and goddesses, including Frigg, the wife of Odin, who gives birth to Baldr, the god of light and favourite son of Odin, whose destiny is to die through the machinations of the evil Loki. It is Loki's pride and envy that leads him to fool the blind god Hodr into killing the innocent and much loved Baldr.

Old Norse refers to the languages of medieval Norway, the Norwegian colonies of Iceland, the Faroes, Orkney and Shetland, and other parts of the British Isles settled in the Viking age (around 800–1050). Most recorded texts from the medieval period are, however, in the Icelandic language. Vernacular Old Norse culture was dominated by three means of expression: sagas, often including poetry and conveyed in either an oral or written narrative; skaldic poetry delivered by court poets, or skalds, composed in a complex syllable-counting metre ornamented by alliteration and internal rhyme, and primarily concerned with the court; and Eddic poetry, which was simpler than skaldic, with alliterative verse, and principally concerned with mythology and heroes. Many of the highlights of these three forms are preserved, synthesised and analysed in Snorri Sturluson's classical 13th-century work *Edda*, a name that probably means 'art of poetry'.

The polytheistic religion that the first Icelandic settlers, under Ingólfur Arnarson, brought to Iceland in 874 had much in common with that found in all countries that spoke Germanic languages during the dominant Viking age. This is confirmed by the names of the gods and other supernatural beings described in the mythic stories passed down in oral traditions and appearing on objects discovered by archaeologists throughout all the Scandinavian countries. The written preservation of this great richness of myth and poetry probably began in Iceland in the 12th century, culminating in the work of Snorri Sturluson in the 13th century, although the great bulk of what was written has probably been lost. The fact that the saga narratives were written in the vernacular, using the Roman alphabet, made them readily available for oral presentation.

The *Edda* of Snorri Sturluson

Snorri Sturluson was the major figure responsible for preserving the Scandinavian oral traditions of religious myth and poetry. He was the 13th-century Icelandic scholar and patriot par excellence, living from 1179 to 1241 and so writing well after Iceland had accepted Christianity in 1000. His *Edda* (c. 1225) saved the Nordic oral traditions of the pre-Christian religion, expressed in poetry and poetics, from being discarded by the new religion of Christianity. The *Edda*, as a consequence of placing the myths of the pre-Christian period in a vernacular written tradition, preserved them for future generations. It shows command of narrative form that makes the myths and poetics readily accessible to

Figure 2.2 Page from an 18th-century Icelandic manuscript. Landsbókasafn Íslands–Háskólabókasafn, handrit.is, shelfmark: IB 299 4to.

the modern ear. Christianised classical models of ancient Greek and Roman mythology (in Latin) were now accompanied by the vernacular *Edda*, which was readily accessible to the Scandinavian people. Clunies Ross stated that the '*Edda*, probably meaning poetics, by the Icelandic chieftain Snorri Sturluson (1179–1241) is the single most important witness to our knowledge of pre-Christian myth in Scandinavia'.[5] She added:

> Without his work, our understanding of Old Norse myth and legend would be very meagre; without it modern recreations in fantasy literature (think Tolkien), film and other media could not have occurred.[6]

The *Edda* is a beautiful work of storytelling, poetry and poetics, and has such a brilliant didactic form that it could be recommended without much preparation to present-day students. It begins with a prologue, tracing the descent of the Norse gods from their beginning with the Trojans of Greece and ending some generations later with Odin arriving in Saxland (Germany), where he commences the royal line. Following the prologue, Snorri gives a detailed account of the identities and activities of the major gods in the Gylfaginning, otherwise called the 'Beguiling of Gylfi'. This section gives the story of Gylfi, king of Sweden, and his experiences when meeting a group of men who tell him stories about their gods. It provides an account of the formation of the world, together with its eventual destruction as a consequence of a battle between the gods and a collection of giants and other hostile beings at Ragnarok. The next section is the Skáldskaparmál (poetic diction or language of poetry), which consists of a discussion between the Norse sea god, Ægir, and the god of poetry, Bragi. In this section Scandinavian poetry, previously handed down through an oral tradition from pre-Christian times, is systematically analysed in terms of its complex references to the Norse gods and their activities, and, more specifically, its metre, rhythms and alliteration. These poems, composed by identified court poets who came to be known as skalds, were the principal source of Norse culture reaching back at least to the second half of the 9th century (the oldest Norse poem is Ragnarsdrápa, composed at this time, when Iceland was first settled). As poets to the kings and lords, the skalds were the principal means of preserving the history of their people through an oral tradition that, in particular, celebrated their masters. Most Norse verse in the Viking period came in skaldic or Eddic forms, and Snorri's *Edda* uses both.

The foundations of Snorri Sturluson's *Edda*

Clunies Ross' first great work, published in 1987, was *Skáldskaparmál: Snorri Sturluson's Ars Poetica and Medieval Theories of Language*. She commented: 'My interest in Snorri's *Edda* was and still is closely associated with my interest in the pre-Christian religion and mythology of Scandinavia.'[7] When Clunies Ross first came to Snorri's work, she found

---

5   Margaret Clunies Ross, unpublished autobiographical notes, 2016.
6   Margaret Clunies Ross, unpublished autobiographical notes, 2016.
7   Margaret Clunies Ross, unpublished autobiographical notes, 2016.

an integrated view of how native and foreign influences might have combined to produce Snorri's work (which survives in several versions) had not really emerged (in the 1970s and early 1980s). In the German speaking world, in particular, many scholars acknowledged that there were learned sections in Snorri's *Edda* but explained them as the work of one or more later interpolators (even though there is precious little manuscript evidence to support this idea). Thus a kind of split view of the *Edda* arose – native in its presentation of Norse myths while embroidered with fancy foreign learning around the edges.[8]

Furthermore, Clunies Ross found that in the standard editions of many Old Icelandic texts, for example that of Finnur Jónsson (1858–1934), there were:

> conjectural emendations when he could not make sense of the manuscript readings with which he was faced. In addition, he and many other earlier editors were happy to rearrange material in ways they felt were appropriate with little concern for the primary data.[9]

These confusions had to be corrected. In relation to Snorri's prologue, Clunies Ross stated:

> My 1987 book proposed that the prologue was far from being a learned add-on to the main part of the *Edda*, which presents first, an overview of the old mythology, and, second, analysis of the nature of Old Norse poetic language and metre.[10]

Indeed, Snorri had absorbed 'Latin philosophy and rhetorical and poetic theory', which 'exerted a sort of influence that might be labelled "learned" and viewed in terms of the history of ideas'.[11] Turning to Skáldskaparmál, Clunies Ross found that Snorri's *vernacular ars poetica* emerged from this work. Furthermore, she contrasted Olafr Thordarson's emphasis, in his *Third Grammatical Treatise*, on the formation of poetry in a Latin rhetorical tradition with that of his uncle Snorri through a 'comparative analysis of the technical terminology' used by Olafr, on the one hand, and Snorri, on the other.[12] Clunies Ross then set out to determine

> the likely background influences on the text in which Snorri saved old Norse mythology and poetics from the unknown, with his poetics from the older Eddas embedded in the narrative prose and his highlighting the skaldic art of the early masters, the chief poets, treated as the vernacular authorities as were Virgil and Horace, the classical Latin authorities.[13]

---

8 Margaret Clunies Ross, unpublished autobiographical notes, 2016.
9 Margaret Clunies Ross, unpublished autobiographical notes, 2016.
10 Margaret Clunies Ross, unpublished autobiographical notes, 2016.
11 Malm 2007, 305.
12 Raschella 2007, 351.
13 Margaret Clunies Ross, unpublished autobiographical notes, 2016.

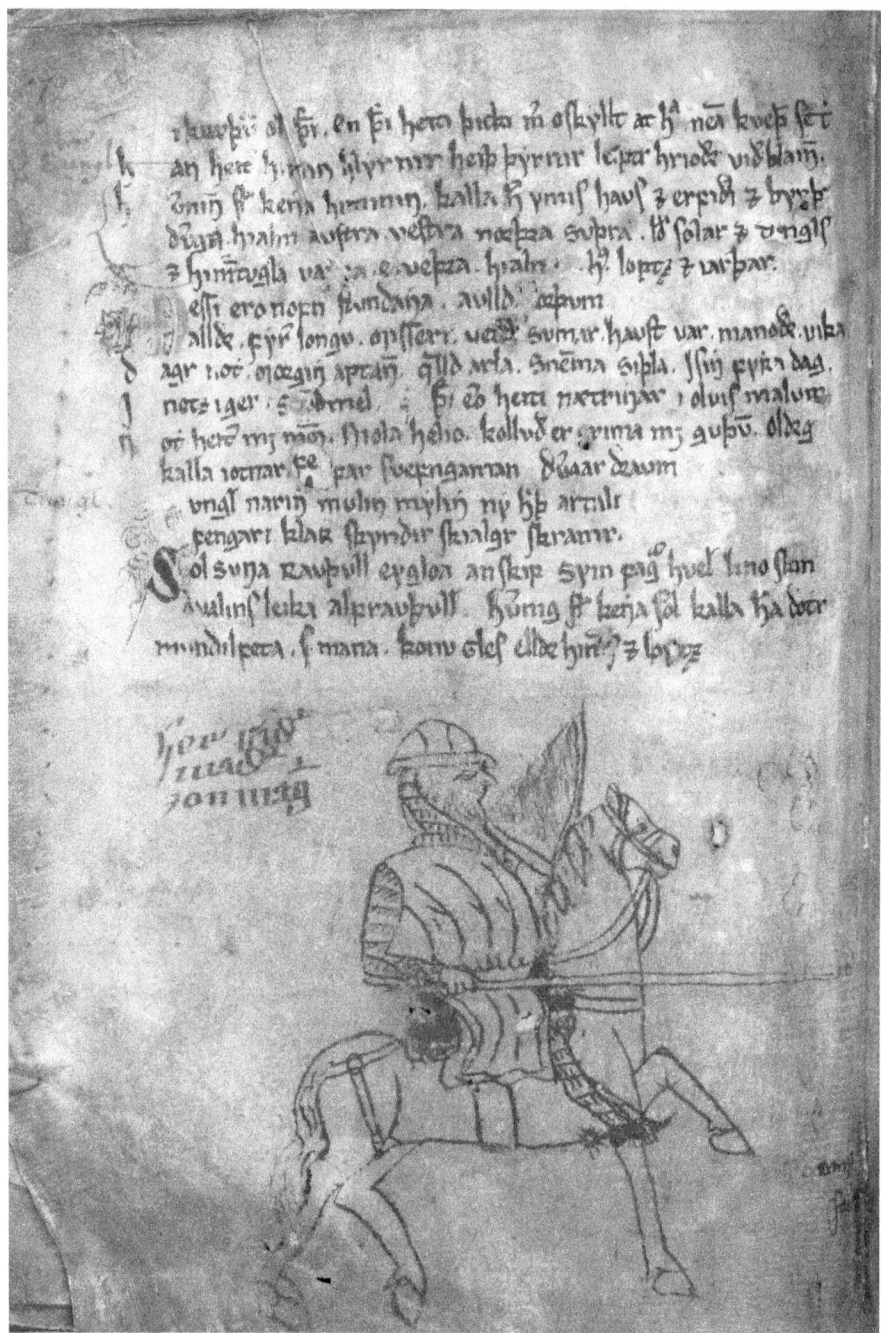

Figure 2.3 Illustrated page from a 14th-century manuscript of Snorri Sturluson's *Edda*. Uppsala universitetsbibliotek, alvin-portal.org, shelfmark: DG 11.

She continued:

> I argued that its presentation of the nature of pagan religions (the argument from mankind's five senses and the world's design) and the acceptance of euhemerism was the basis upon which Snorri's presentation of the beliefs and poetic language of the pre-Christian Scandinavians was founded, and that he set out to show, with examples, how pre-Christians conceptualised the world. This I argued was the basis of his arrangement of its subject matter. I demonstrated (and this has never been gainsaid) that the underlying structure of the *Edda* was modelled to some extent at least on the subjects usually treated in medieval Christian encyclopaedias, like that of Isidore of Seville, the point here being to demonstrate that the pagan world's understanding, as Snorri put it, led them to represent the world through the use of their senses without the benefit of the spiritual understanding that came from the Christian God.[14]

The Icelandic saga

For a period extending from a few decades after settlement until the time Iceland swore allegiance to the Norwegian king (930–1262), Icelandic society celebrated its unique structure and achievements in sagas – the Icelandic word for something said, a narrative. This occurred first as an oral tradition and later in written text, meant to be delivered in a performance context for entertainment as well as education and instruction. This literary form has been compared with the modern novel as it narrates a chronologically ordered sequence of events. However, in contrast to the novel, sagas may have several distinct but interrelated stories that are in sequence, some of which may be abruptly dropped from the saga when, for instance, a particular participant is no longer required (this is made explicit by the narrator). Furthermore, considerable parts of the saga may constitute poetry, rather than prose. Also, the saga does not have a stream of consciousness or internal monologue associated with the characters, but rather allows a person's character or personality to emerge through their actions. There are more than 100 medieval Icelandic sagas, of which the majority did not exist in manuscript form before the 13th century. Clunies Ross and her fellow scholars have shown that they fall into several subgroups:

- Sagas of the Old Time, also called Fornaldarsögur, relate to a period before the settlement of Iceland (around 874). They are concerned with the pagan time in the Scandinavian countries, principally Norway, although they were first written in about the 13th century. Their age is attested to by Viking poetry containing some of the sagas' stories. Such sagas may include beings from the nine worlds of Yggdrasill, with humans playing an important role, often going about their normal business of harvesting, herding cattle and fishing while interacting with dwarves, giants and gods such as Odin. The Christian world in which these sagas were documented would probably regard them as a form of history, whereas for pre-Christians of the old religion they were contemporary events.

---

14 Margaret Clunies Ross, unpublished autobiographical notes, 2016.

- Family Sagas, also called Sagas of Icelanders, were first written, like most other sagas, in about the 13th century. They attempted to trace ancestral continuity of the major Icelandic families all the way back to the period of the old religion, so they incorporated myths connecting their Norwegian forebears to the gods. These sagas are primarily about major disagreements between powerful families, and how they are resolved or lead to conflict, fighting and sometimes being outlawed from the community.
- Contemporary Sagas, called Samtíðarsögur, involve histories of struggles and political intrigue between the major families in the different districts of Iceland: the northern district (the Ásbirningar); the west fjords (the Vatnsfirðingar); the western district (Sturlungar); and the southern districts (the Oddaverjar, the Haukdælir and Svínfellingar).
- Kings' Sagas are primarily biographies of the kings of Norway, stretching from prehistoric times to the 14th century. Originally written by Norwegians, they were soon incorporated into the unique saga form by Icelanders, with embedded skaldic poetry that formed an oral tradition over several hundreds of years.
- Sagas of Knights, also called Riddarasögur, an Old Norse term for sagas of courtly settings. They were originally in Anglo-Norman, Latin and French vernaculars, concerned with kingship, courtly love and chivalry around the time of the legendary King Arthur of Britain. They are therefore mostly concerned with knights and nobles that are not of Scandinavian origin and take place in early Christian court settings. It was the Norwegian King Haakon Haakonsson who promoted the translation of these romances from their original vernacular to Norwegian.

Njáls Saga is the most famous literary achievement of the saga tradition – indeed, probably of all Nordic literature. Njál was one of the first to convert to Christianity after it was declared the religion of Iceland by the Althing in 1000.

At the beginning of saga writing in the late 12th century, the pagan myths served as templates for the relationships between members of different social strata in Iceland. As Clunies Ross stated:

> There were many purposes for which writers of Old Icelandic literature employed conceptual schemas that involved myth. ... My own recent work ... demonstrates the importance of mythic schemas in the presentation of such topics as the settlement of Iceland, the inheritance of family talents, the conceptualization of Icelandic history, and development of a range of subclasses of a dominant medieval Icelandic literary form, the saga.[15]

Clunies Ross showed that in such sagas

> there is comparability between the often-repeated stand-offs between gods and giants and the behaving of feuding factions of chieftains and their supporters in thirteenth-century Iceland. Again, the condition of negative reciprocity ... in which the gods and

---

15 Clunies Ross 2000, 121.

giants conduct their relationships, and the strategies of treachery, theft and deception they characteristically adopt to maintain their positions, or seek to improve them, are reminiscent of many of the behaviour patterns represented in saga literature as characterising Icelanders from the age of settlement and the commonwealth period.[16]

She also showed that

> the 'building blocks' of the saga genre … include stock scenes, stock descriptions, action patterns, particular narrative segments that join one episode to another, specific combinations of motifs used to characterise certain character types, who are represented as acting in typical ways, and a range of kinds of background knowledge about the saga world that would have been conventional wisdom for the medieval saga audience, but that the modern reader has to learn.[17]

Clunies Ross has shown that Icelandic sagas do not each consist of a single mode (such as realistic, fantastic, comic, satiric, ironic, etc.). Rather, they

> often display a 'mixed modality', by which I meant that sagas switch more easily between a realistic and non-realistic mode than much modern writing has done, especially before the advent of postmodernist literary genres.[18]

She added: 'Most modern studies of the Icelandic saga have neglected the genre's literary mode and have consequently been ill at ease with the combination of modalities sagas often display.'[19]

Prolonged Echoes

Clunies Ross has stated that she regards the two volumes of *Prolonged Echoes*,[20] the first especially, as her most important individual contribution to the field of Old Norse-Icelandic studies.[21]

> I began to think, during the late 1980s and early 1990s, of how modern scholarship could make overall sense of what has come down to us in the medieval sources about Old Norse myths. Given that they have been recorded mainly in Icelandic texts, I thought it probable that they must still have had meaning for Icelanders, notwithstanding the latter's Christian perspective on life. My idea was to analyse the extant corpus of Old Norse myths as a whole, drawing on all extant sources and referring as much as possible to modern archaeological finds from the Viking age,

---

16 Clunies Ross 2000, 122.
17 Clunies Ross 2010, 49.
18 Clunies Ross 2010, 96.
19 Clunies Ross 2010, 96.
20 Clunies Ross 1994; Clunies Ross 1998.
21 Margaret Clunies Ross, unpublished autobiographical notes, 2016.

which have been considerable. Above all, though, I drew on some of the insights of recent anthropology to discover patterns of social structures that emerged from mythic narratives that were, on the face of it, about a whole range of disparate and often bizarre subjects.[22]

This she achieved. As one critic observed:

> In the two volumes of her *Prolonged Echoes* she gives us a remarkable analysis of the mental world of Old Norse myths, their relation to social structures, and how they continue to echo in the prose works of the thirteenth century.[23]

In Volume One, Clunies Ross shows that Old Norse mythology can be regarded in its entirety as a struggle between the gods and the giants, reflecting opposition within a hierarchical social order embedded in a complex symbolic system. She attempts

> to move away from the study of individual myths and individual texts as discrete entities without much connection with the rest of the mythic system, towards a kind of analysis that respects individual myths but sees their meanings in a larger textual and contextual frame. ... We need to ask, further, how this pattern fits into the general social structure attributed to the supernatural world of gods and giants and what general semiotic significance the various categories of beings and their actions carry in the Norse mythic corpus as a whole.[24]

One senior scholar commented that this is 'the best modern treatment of the mythology ... Clunies Ross knows the scholarship intimately and has masterful analytical skills'.[25]

In Volume Two of *Prolonged Echoes*, Clunies Ross discloses a unique insight into the sagas – that the myths are of a genealogical bent in order to support the social establishment's elitist claims. The sagas were commissioned by important laymen in Iceland as a means for them to project their importance and power. Myths associated with the settlement of Iceland legitimised land-taking by families and served as a defence against counter claims. Myths also substantiated ancestral claims to specific talents in legal, medical, religious and poetic professions. Clunies Ross

> extends the familiar notion that templates derived from heroic narrations were immanent in medieval Icelandic literature so as to make parallel claims for the inherited mythology. Sometimes invoked consciously, sometimes merely latent, myths maintain their status as powerful cognitive tools throughout the period when this literature took shape ... The volume establishes that the sagas have a special place within European literature of the middle ages. She shows that the sagas are not constituted of individual genres as thought previously, but rather of a single genre, which may be considered to have subcategories. Her scholarship shows that the

---

22 Margaret Clunies Ross, unpublished autobiographical notes, 2016.
23 Tulinius 2007, 49.
24 Clunies Ross 1994, 17.
25 Lindow 2001, 337–8.

separate sagas may be considered as occupying different places in a shared historical timeline. This continuity can be observed in the successive legendary sagas, kings' sagas, family sagas, sagas of Icelanders and the contemporary sagas. In addition, they are all synthesised from both fantastic and realistic modes, that is they possess a multimodal character.[26]

***

The history of the early Icelanders is truly remarkable, from the beginnings of settlement in 874, which required the establishment of a new social order, to the creation of a new legal and political framework that became centred in the first democratic parliament, the Althing, in 930. These Icelanders held to the old religion of the Scandinavian countries, with its myths related in the sagas as well as Eddic and skaldic poetry. The edict of the Althing to accept Christianity in 1000 occurred in the commonwealth period (930–1262). There was then no need for conversion of individual Icelanders or clans, which would inevitably have involved conflict between those adhering to the old religion and those subscribing to Christianity. The resulting smooth transition had the immense advantage of allowing the old myths to be secularised and removed from necessary identification with belief in the old religion. In this way they were renewed and rejuvenated within Christianity without, for instance, the necessity of disregarding Odin and the other gods.

Clunies Ross has shown how this came about and how the myths were preserved in a way that did not challenge Christianity. She has shown how it was argued after 1000 that the myths included clear signs of an early recognition of Christian beliefs. Although these signs were crude and somewhat opaque, they were taken as worthy precursors of the new religion. Clunies Ross has stressed how significant social forces were at play to hasten this re-reading of the old beliefs. It was the Icelandic chieftains who saw the necessity of supporting an accommodation between the old and the new, given that the former provided them with much of their legitimacy. Hence, for example, the sagas had to be preserved to support their legitimacy but re-interpreted to accommodate Christianity. In the commonwealth period, society's structure was mirrored in the mythic relationships between the gods and other supernatural beings, and these had to be accommodated in the new religion. For example, in the Landnámabók story the chieftain Thormodr was the law-speaker in the Althing at the time it adopted Christianity. This was appropriate as his father was shown in this narrative to be a man of purity and goodness in a Christian sense. Another example is the story of Allsherjargoði, who held the senior priestly position in the Althing at the time of its adoption of Christianity, and whose ancestral family was endowed with Christian virtues well before 1000.

The Icelanders succeeded in the daunting task of both maintaining the content of the old myths, sagas and poetry and transmitting them so they would not only survive but harmonise with the new religion. Their success in doing so was their most remarkable achievement, accomplished through 'self-identification as the custodians of their own and all Scandinavia's traditional history and culture'.[27] This 'self-identification' was not

---

26 Poole 2001, 162.
27 Clunies Ross 2000, 117.

passive; they made a conscious effort to become a centre of scholarship for Europe, with their skalds travelling the continent, absorbing and noting the literature, myths and poetry of other lands before returning to Iceland. As a consequence, the commonwealth in the 12th and 13th centuries saw an astonishing new literature, which successfully preserved the old culture by re-interpreting it in the context of the newly arrived Christian beliefs.

Clunies Ross' ambition to identify and understand the pre-Christian religion and mythology of Scandinavia and of the early Germanic peoples was fulfilled through profound scholarship.

Further reading

Clunies Ross, M. *Prolonged Echoes. Old Norse Myths in Medieval Northern Society. Volume 1: The Myths*. Odense, DK: Odense University Press, 1994.

Clunies Ross, M. *Prolonged Echoes. Old Norse Myths in Medieval Northern Society. Volume 2: The Reception of Norse Myths in Medieval Iceland*. Odense, DK: Odense University Press, 1998.

Clunies Ross, M., ed. *Old Norse Myths, Literature and Society*. Odense, DK: University Press of Southern Denmark, 2003.

3
Early Australian colonies and Federation: John Manning Ward

Challis Professor of History (1948–1979). Ward is recognised as the pre-eminent historian on the policies and actions of the Colonial Office with respect to the British colonies of the Pacific in the 19th century. The detailed elucidation of these policies and their modification and execution provided the basis for understanding how the colonies of Australia became self-governing and formed a federation.

In 1972, when I had carried out research and teaching at Sydney University for over four years, I applied for promotion to reader, the best academic position for those devoted to research as it relieved one of administrative duties and much teaching. In order to obtain this promotion, I had to be interviewed by the chairman of the Academic Board. I was informed that he would come to my research office in the basement of the old medical school. I was rather concerned about this for I knew he would have to make his way through some fearful smells, emanating from the nearby morgue and the rodent animal facility – hardly conducive to him being well disposed at the interview. I was therefore surprised when a smiling middle-aged gentleman wearing a three-piece tweed suit entered my office and gently proceeded to ask a few questions. This was John Ward, the Challis Professor of History, who I got to know quite well in succeeding years. He became Vice-Chancellor the year I was awarded a first Centre of Excellence by the federal government, amounting to several million dollars, which required some supervision from senior university officers. However, the main basis for our friendship was a love of history, envisaged in my *History of the Synapse* and *History of Cognitive Neuroscience* (with Peter Hacker) and his series of historical works on the evolution of the Australian colonies towards a federation. What follows then is an attempt to bring these great works of Ward together in such a way as to highlight each of his novel ideas concerning this evolution.

John Manning Ward was born in 1919 at Burwood, Sydney, the son of a commercial traveller, Alexander Ward, and his wife, Mildred Boughay (née Davis). John Ward and his two siblings were raised as Presbyterians and went to Fort Street High School, noted for training future scholars. He won a public exhibition to Sydney University's Faculty of Arts in 1936, at 17. There he studied English and History under (Sir) Stephen Roberts, graduating with first class honours and the University Medal in history in 1939, at the

Figure 3.1 Professor John Manning Ward. Photograph from the University of Sydney Archives (G77_1_0633).

outbreak of the Second World War. Deafness precluded him joining the services, so he lectured in history at the University of Sydney while working for the retired premier of New South Wales and reading law. He was called to the bar as a barrister in 1948 and succeeded Roberts as Challis Professor of History at the early age of 29. This legal training, together with the 'tough-minded and analytic approach to history'[1] that he had learned from Roberts, provided Ward with the necessary skills to become the pre-eminent historian of colonial history. He displayed 'a deeply informed view about the evolving imperial connections, and [Australia's] transformation from colony to nation'.[2] Ward studied the workings of the Colonial Office in depth and was able to show, in six books, that many of the 'grand themes' that previous historians had discerned in the evolution of Australian governance were not based in fact. Here we trace the narrative Ward offers in his books and identify several unique ideas that emerged from his scholarship.

Minimal intervention

At the beginning of the 19th century, the governor of New South Wales, under the guidance of the Colonial Office, was responsible for an extensive group of islands in the Pacific, including New Zealand, Fiji and Tonga, with the latter over 3,500 km from Sydney. The native inhabitants of these islands,[3] of Polynesian origin, had occupied them for generations and spoke Polynesian languages, which have strong similarities, especially in vocabularies. Ward argued that the Colonial Office did not wish to annex these islands, but rather pursued a policy of recognising native sovereignty, such as that of Tahiti under the rule of Pomare in 1827 and of the Maori in 1840 under the Treaty of Waitangi. The Colonial Office thought that such recognition would help them to guide pre-colonial native 'governments' in such a way as to maintain the trade between them as well as with their parent colony, and restrict the more reprehensible behaviour of whites on the islands, at a minimal cost to Great Britain. Ward was the first to explain this policy, which he called 'minimal intervention'.

The number of Maori in New Zealand when the British arrived around 1800 was about 120,000. In Australia at this time there were about 800,000 Aboriginal people, spread out over a land mass about 30 times greater than New Zealand. In 1800, Maori was the language spoken among the dozens of tribes or tribal groupings, called iwi, on both the North and South Islands, whereas in Australia at this time there were about 250 languages and a similar number of Aboriginal peoples or social groupings. Over several hundred years, tribal warfare among the Maori, in order to maintain the integrity of their tribes, had honed their military skills. About 50 British could be found in the islands at the end of the 18th century, mostly whalers and sealers. They needed to come to terms with an indigenous

---

1   Schreuder, Fletcher and Hutchinson 2001, xiv.
2   Schreuder and Fletcher 2001, vii.
3   The word 'natives' is frequently used in Ward's books. In contemporary times this is perceived as a racist term. In modern usage, more appropriate descriptions are 'Aboriginal peoples' or 'Torres Strait Islander peoples'. The word 'native' is only used in this essay in order to keep to the letter of Ward's narratives.

Polynesian population infused with tribal customs and capable of uniform confrontation with foreigners, facilitated by use of a common language. As Ward commented, the Maoris were 'a quite proud and warlike people' and 'could not be relegated to obscurity in the same way as the aboriginals of Australia'.[4]

At first, the Maori welcomed the white whalers and sealers and those trading in other commodities, together with escaped convicts and castaways, and assisted them by cutting timber for their ships. But this state of coexistence deteriorated as the white men showed no consideration for the customs or spiritual beliefs of the indigenous population. Furthermore, they inadvertently brought with them typhoid, pneumonia, influenza, tuberculosis, measles and venereal diseases, which, over just a few decades, reduced the Maori population from about 120,000 to 80,000. Brutal fighting ensued, necessitating intervention by the New South Wales governor. In 1809, he placed justices of the peace on many of the islands, but without police or military support for their decisions, scandalous behaviour continued, particularly in New Zealand. As a consequence, in 1817 an act of parliament determined that murders and acts of manslaughter '"not within His Majesty's dominions, nor subject to any European state or power, nor within the territory of the United States of America" should be cognizable "in any of His Majesty's islands, plantations, colonies," etc. as though they were offenses committed on the high seas under 46 Geo. III, c. 54'.[5] This statute determined that such offences could be tried on any of His Majesty's islands. The bond that Governor Macquarie issued specifically declared that 'natives of all the said islands are under the protection of His Majesty'.[6]

Despite these proclamations and warnings, the relationship between Maori and whites continued to deteriorate, often resulting in severe injuries to the Maori. The Colonial Office appointed residents (senior to justices of the peace) on some of the islands and stressed that the authority of New Zealand resided with the hereditary chiefs and heads of tribes. A 'Declaration of Independence' in 1835 attempted to persuade the chiefs to assert their right to New Zealand. This provided explicit evidence that Great Britain had a protective attitude to the Maori, with no intent of annexing the islands. This was not only an attitude of benevolence to the Maori. The Colonial Office thought, Ward argued, that the islands could be best managed by recognising the sovereignty of their indigenous people and entering into diplomatic and protective relations with these people. This would allow the British to police the wild white elements in these societies that, through their acts, brought disgrace on the Empire, and at the same time encourage trade unhindered by violence. The attitude of the Colonial Office was popular with the commercial classes in Britain, for they only 'regarded the Empire from a profit and loss point of view'.[7]

Ward showed that the policy of minimal intervention was not sustainable. Violent clashes between the Maori and whites continued, and the Colonial Office decided that they must intervene again. They sent out Captain William Hobson with direct orders to protect the Maori, not by annexation of the islands, but through negotiations with the Maori tribal chiefs, who were treated as sovereign rulers. The Maori were to be given

---

4   Ward 1966, 50.
5   Ward, *British Policy in the South Pacific*, 1976, 40.
6   Ward, *British Policy in the South Pacific*, 1976, 37.
7   Ward, *British Policy in the South Pacific*, 1976, 43.

possession over lands and fisheries under guarantee by the British government, together with the new rights and privileges they would receive as British subjects. The treaty was to incorporate a ruling that Maori land could only be sold by them to the Crown, although it might then be acquired from the Crown by appropriate settlers. These considerations were ratified in the Treaty of Waitangi on 6 February 1840, signed by chiefs of the North Island and the British. It stated that 'the chiefs ... cede to Her Majesty the Queen of England absolutely and without reservation all the rights and powers of sovereignty which the ... chiefs ... exercise or possess'.[8] Such civilised arrangements did not last. Some resented the arrangement and sought to buy land directly from different Maori chiefs. A major dispute broke out in 1843 with the chiefs Te Rauparaha and Te Rangihaeata. They challenged the sale of their Wairau lands, and when 21 British arrived to take possession, they were massacred. Such chaos had to be settled once and for all by the Colonial Office. They sent out George Grey in late 1845 with a large military attachment that intimidated Maori and whites alike, virtually ending the conflict. All land sales henceforth were placed firmly in the hands of the Crown. Calm was restored and mostly held up to the time of removal of the responsibilities for New Zealand from the governor of New South Wales and annexation of the islands by the British with the granting of a constitution to New Zealand. This constitution provided for a legislature and general assembly but reserved to the Crown the right to support the laws and customs of the Maori and to sell their lands. Minimal intervention was then abandoned.

Ward argued, contrary to widely held belief, that the history of the Colonial Office in the first half of the 19th century was one of protective benevolence towards the native populations – exemplified by their treatment of the Maori – and not one of aggressive colonisation. However, the different attitudes of the Colonial Office to the First Nation peoples of New Zealand and Australia requires explanation. The explanation Ward offered was, essentially, that the Aboriginal peoples were 'relegated to obscurity'[9] as a consequence of their lack of war-like qualities, presumably together with their relatively low density over the continent and the difficulty of coordinating the actions of peoples with more than 250 languages. We now know that they were not 'easily brushed aside' and that the consequences for our First Nation peoples were profound.

Anomalous societies

The colonies of Newfoundland and New South Wales were granted self-government[10] relatively late, compared with other colonies of the Empire. Ward showed that this was because the Colonial Office regarded these colonies as unfit for such government as they were what he called 'anomalous societies'.

The Colonial Office at 13 and 14 Downing Street, close to the prime minister's office at number 10, exerted immense influence over the British colonies between 1840 and

---

8   Ward, *British Policy in the South Pacific*, 1976, 77.
9   Ward 1966, 50.
10 Self-government refers to an elected government that reaches decisions without reference to a colonial power (in some cases it might be elected by an elite class).

1860. During this time, free trade began and the colonies were guided towards elected or responsible government.[11] Earl Grey was the head of the office between 1846 and 1852, during which time he proceeded, with some alacrity, to introduce a free trade policy for all the colonies and, in particular, to shepherd many of them to responsible government. Such government was granted to the colonies of Canada, Nova Scotia, New Brunswick and Prince Edward Island during Grey's tenure or shortly after his retirement. But he held back from promoting such representative government[12] in the colony of Newfoundland and in the antipodes. Although the colony of Newfoundland had experienced very little convict transportation, it was nevertheless riven with strife, largely arising from the aggressive attitudes of the appointed Protestant mercantilists in the council towards the Catholics in the elected assembly. In the colony of New South Wales, the strife arose between exclusivists, who had no taint of a convict past, and the emancipated convicts. The Colonial Office did not regard the political maturity of these anomalous societies to be sufficient for any form of representative government. Law and order in Newfoundland in the early part of the 19th century was directed in a crude way by the captains of fishing vessels, so that the country did not even have colonial status until 1824. When elections were eventually allowed in 1832, there were riots, accompanied by arson and bloodshed, supporting the anomalous society designation.

In 1819, W.C. Wentworth of New South Wales, the son of a convict mother, published his *Statistical, Historical and Political Description of the Colony of New South Wales and Its Dependent Settlements in Van Diemen's Land* (with a particular enumeration of the advantages these colonies have to offer for emigration and their superiority, in many aspects, over those possessed by the United States of America). The book painted a rosy picture of the colony, as the title implies, but also displayed a deep hatred of the exclusivists, indicating the continuing feud between emancipists and exclusivists at this time. However, the wealthy exclusivists and emancipists had, by the 1830s, realised the advantages of joining forces in some common causes. The colony had become relatively rich with the success of the wool industry and, indeed, of trade in general. This necessitated the recruitment of labour, preferably through emigration, rather than transportation. Both exclusivists and emancipists also saw the need for protection against the increase in squatters. The maturing relationship between these two groups, together with the May 1840 Order in Council in Britain stopping transportation to New South Wales, paved the way for self-government. Nevertheless, Grey still held that the colonies of Australia and New Zealand lacked the political maturity and experience necessary for an advanced political system. The outlook of the Secretary of State for War and the Colonies changed in 1852, when Grey was replaced by the Duke of Newcastle, who occupied the post until 1854. The Duke determined that the executive governments in the antipodes should be made responsible to elected legislatures. New South Wales did not escape the opprobrium of being an anomalous society unfit for responsible government until 1856, when such government was granted.

---

11   Responsible government is a political principle requiring that governments and members of parliament must be accountable for their actions (e.g. government to parliament, parliament to the people).
12   Representative government is generally a government that represents the people through elections.

Self-government imposed

Ward was the first historian to 'look into the tortuous course that history actually took' in the colonies towards gaining self-government.[13] *He contrasts this with 'how much less difficult it has been to attribute the coming of responsible government to Durham, or, like J. S. Mill, to Durham and his associates jointly with the triumph of free trade'.*[14] *Perhaps it was the authority of J. S. Mill, who, in 1861, argued that Britain 'always felt under a certain degree of obligation to bestow on ... her outlying populations ... representative institutions formed in imitation of her own'.*[15] *However the evolution of representative government in the colonies and in Great Britain differed greatly. Ward showed that self-government in the colony of New South Wales was largely imposed by the Colonial Office, rather than won through a struggle for independence.*

Free trade

J.S. Mill argued that Britain had been held to a mercantilist policy as a means of ensuring subordination of the colonies. When free trade was adopted by Great Britain in the 1840s as 'a policy of such universal wisdom',[16] it greatly loosened the disciplinary grip that Britain had heretofore exercised over the colonies. The Colonial Office, under Lord John Russell between 1839 and 1841, and later under Earl Grey between 1846 and 1852, thought of the colonies as belonging to a free trade empire of commercial partners. It followed that any attempts by the colonies to introduce tariffs, such as those between the eastern seaboard colonies of Australia, and between the colonies of Canada, were disallowed by the Colonial Office. Although the introduction of free trade released the colonies from direct disciplinary action by Great Britain, it did not release them from fiscal control. Indeed, Grey thought that such policies needed regulation to save the colonies from their natural tendency to fall back into protectionism and to earning income from tariffs. The granting of self-government was qualified by these considerations. Ward showed that responsible government evolved in the colonies under the direction of the Colonial Office, rather than, as Mill would have it, the colonies, freed from mercantilist restrictions, suddenly bursting forth with demands for responsible government.

The Durham Report

Lord Durham was made governor general of the Canadian provinces in January 1838 and was sent out to prevent the provinces from breaking away from Great Britain – or even joining France – as well as to relax the considerable antipathies directed toward Great Britain. The Colonial Office suggested that one way of achieving this would be to introduce a federal body that could act as a buffer between the provinces and Great Britain. Instead, Durham's ostentatious behaviour so offended the Canadians that he was recalled just before rebellion broke out. Instead of showing contrition when he returned in disgrace, Durham declared his work in Canada a triumph and published an

---

13   Ward, *Colonial Self-Government*, 1976, 65.
14   Ward, *Colonial Self-Government*, 1976, 65.
15   Ward, *Colonial Self-Government*, 1976, 1.
16   Ward, *Colonial Self-Government*, 1976, 235.

essay of no official status called 'Report on the Affairs of British North America'. In this he emphasised the importance of making the executive councils responsible to the legislatures as in Great Britain and of distinguishing between colonial matters and those of imperial concern requiring the authority of the Colonial Office. He claimed that the implementation of these suggestions would keep the Canadian provinces in the British Empire.

The Durham Report has been hailed by historians and social commentators as the beginning of the evolution of responsible government throughout the colonies in British North America (the future Canada) and later in the antipodes. J.S. Mill, for example, argued that the Durham Report made free trade possible by laying down the liberal path that Britain's Colonial Office subsequently followed. The heads of the Colonial Office had then simply acted on the mature suggestions of the Durham Report. Ward argued, however, that 'Durham caught the tide of history, with a broad, bold outline of policies long agitated by other men'.[17] The Durham Report was then largely irrelevant to the Colonial Office. The kind of self-government granted to the British North American colonies was determined by changing ideas about the colonies, on the one hand, and about the British Constitution itself, on the other. The report was, as Ward commented,

> a mere auxiliary of change, more remarkable to historians as a landmark, and, in [the 20th] century, as a guide to colonies seeking what was formerly called dominion status, than it was to contemporaries as an influence on policy making in Britain.[18]

Exclusivist versus emancipist

Until about 1840, when transportation to the colonies of New South Wales and Victoria ceased, the political complexities of New South Wales mostly involved exclusivists and emancipists. Exclusivists, a wealthy, mostly landed class, wished any representative government to reflect their position at the top of a hierarchy. Emancipists, who had arrived as convicts, served their time and then achieved such success that they had been able to acquire property, thought they should have the same rights as the exclusivists. It was not until the late 1830s that these two land-owning classes saw the advantage of joining forces in dialogue with the Colonial Office over powers concerning land policy, finance, public appointments, immigration and the cessation of transportation. As a consequence of these discussions, the Colonial Office enlarged the legislative council established in 1824, allowing a large proportion (24/36) to be elected and reducing the proportion nominated by the Crown. The franchise was given to the property-owning electorate so that emancipists were no longer excluded. Effectively, a property-owning legislature was voted in by a property-owning electorate. These property owners were primarily a conservative group as seat distribution greatly favoured rural areas over urban ones.

Having obtained a legislature that reflected the landed classes, irrespective of their origins, the next task was to obtain a transfer of power over colonial activities from the Colonial Office to the landed classes of New South Wales. To this end, a committee consisting of powerful figures such as James Macarthur and W.C. Wentworth determined

---

17 Ward, *Colonial Self-Government*, 1976, 65.
18 Ward, *Colonial Self-Government*, 1976, 3.

Figure 3.2 W.C. Wentworth, painted by Richard Buckner. Parliament of New South Wales (Accession: A2004). © State of New South Wales through the Parliament of New South Wales.

that the transfer of powers should be effected and colonial activities should be placed under the control of the old exclusivists. The Colonial Office decided that the executive would be brought within the purview of the legislature, which could now make laws for the colonial judicial system. It also lowered the qualifications of voters so that squatters who had acquired land on leasehold could be enfranchised. These significant changes to what had once been considered an 'anomalous society' were certainly not what Macarthur had advocated, coming largely at the initiative of a Colonial Office concerned that the colony should move towards a truly representative government. Running in parallel with these changes was the granting of a constitution to New Zealand in 1852, the removal of the Port Phillip District from the colony of New South Wales to become the colony of Victoria in July 1851 and the formation of the new colony of Queensland in 1859. The legislature of New South Wales had, by 1860, assumed prime responsibility for a land mass that could be identified with present New South Wales. Ward stated that

> the transition from the groping, reactionary uncertainty of 1837 to the generous recognition of full self-government (with responsible ministries and elected legislatures) as the panacea of discontent in colonies of settlement was the most important change in British colonial policy during the nineteenth century.[19]

Grey had introduced into the Colonial Office the liberal idea that executive councils in the colonies should be aligned with the policies of the legislatures and appointed by them as ministers, taking on the form of constitutional conventions found in Great Britain. Grey's attitudes to government in the colonies greatly relieved friction between the Canadian colonies, which were demanding a constitution, and Great Britain. This wish was soon granted to them, as we have seen. The lack of consistent and coherent pressures from the antipodean colonies for representative self-government, which Grey interpreted as want of political maturity, delayed the conferring of constitutions in the South Pacific. This immaturity was manifest in the established property classes seeking a form of self-government that maintained, or even extended, the existing power structure that was so much to their benefit. So the Colonial Office, under the Duke of Newcastle, had to force the issue. A dispatch on 4 August 1853 to the governments of New South Wales, Victoria and South Australia stated that 'the new constitutions, which were being drafted in every colony, ought to contain adequate provision for full responsible government';[20] this dispatch was sent out even though there had been no demand for such government.

When responsible government was introduced in New South Wales, the ministries were of short duration, to some extent supporting Grey's thoughts concerning the political immaturity of the colony. On the other hand, the quality and importance of the numerous bills that passed through the legislature, and the significant figures that led the ministries, made for a remarkably productive period of government, during which major political parties began to emerge, promoting more stable periods of governance. Indeed, manhood suffrage was admitted to the vote via ballot for the legislature in 1858, leading Great Britain in 'maturity' by ten years.

---

19 Ward 1966, 74.
20 Ward 1966, 84.

Federation avoided

Ward showed that 50 years before federation was achieved by the Australian colonies, the Colonial Office, led by Earl Grey, attempted to bring the colonies together in a union to promote 'efficiencies', particularly in relation to the introduction of free trade. This failed for three reasons: the colonies considered it highly irregular of Grey not to consult them in the drafting of such a proposal; the colonies thought they could negotiate among themselves without needing a union; and most importantly, the colonies were in an uproar over Grey's attempt to re-introduce convict transportation some ten years after it had been prohibited. As Ward argued, federation was not achieved in the 1850s because the man who proposed it, Grey, unnecessarily offended the parties he wanted to join in union.

Earl Grey's period at the Colonial Office, from 1846 to 1852, was perhaps its most active period during the 19th century. This was the time when Britain began the transition to free trade and initiated forms of self-governance for many of its colonies. In a place such as Australia, with several colonies in immediate juxtaposition, the promotion of free trade between them, together with the granting of self-government, was never going to be easy; such freedoms naturally lead to the introduction of tariffs to enhance income. Grey's Colonial Office proposed a solution for this conundrum – namely, what the colonial secretary Edward Thompson called an 'inter-colonial legislature',[21] formed through a federal union of the colonies. This, it was suggested, would provide a means of dialogue concerning the elimination of tariffs between the colonies leading to a collective increase in their efficiency. Grey argued for such a union on the basis of his 'conviction that there were common interests upon certain subjects among these different colonies which would require almost immediately to be considered by some common authority'.[22] However, Grey had not consulted the Australian colonies about the formulation of his proposal, so when it reached the colonies in 1850 there was no interest in, let alone enthusiasm for, such a union. Grey's argument was that important efficiencies could be introduced where common interest existed, for instance, in tariffs, railroads, beacons, roads, gold regulations and postage. But the colonists thought these efficiencies could be reached through dialogue, considering each 'common interest' one at a time, without the complexities of developing and running an imposed union.

The attempt to re-introduce transportation

After much effort, the colony of New South Wales won an Order in Council in 1840 to abolish transportation. It was then particularly galling when Grey attempted to re-introduce transportation to New South Wales in 1848 in order to alleviate the over-crowding of jails in Great Britain. Grey's order named New South Wales, Van Diemen's Land (Tasmania), Norfolk Island and the Cape Colony as lands to which felons could henceforth be sent from Great Britain. This order aroused tremendous controversy and resentment in all the Australian colonies, including those such as South Australia that had never received convicts. The colonies felt that a united front was called for, so on

---

21 Ward 1958, 74.
22 Ward 1958, 174.

Figure 3.3 Henry George Grey, 3rd Earl Grey, by Caldesi, Blanford and Co. © National Portrait Gallery, London.

16 September 1850 6,000 people gathered in Barrack Square in Sydney. At this event speakers heavily criticised the New South Wales legislative assembly for not sending a forceful note to the Colonial Office rejecting Grey's proposal. A petition was signed, with a ratio of 70 to 1 against transportation, and sent to the legislative assembly. They responded immediately, and on 1 October a letter was sent to Grey through the effective governor general, Fitzroy, stating that 'no more convicts ought, under any conditions, be sent to any part of this colony'.[23] An Association for the Prevention of the Revival of Transportation was then established in Sydney. Melbourne followed, creating the Australasian League for the Abolition of Transportation in February 1851. The league sent delegates to New South Wales to negotiate a united front, with the result that the association was dissolved, allowing the league to represent the colonies to Grey and the Colonial Office. South Australia and New Zealand then joined the league, although neither had ever had convicts. The feeling was that transportation to any one colony meant transportation to them all.

The large rally in Sydney and the sentiments subsequently expressed by the New South Wales legislative council forced Grey's hand; he decided not to send any more convicts to New South Wales 'for the time being'.[24] The 'time being' was extended to 'for good' when the sentiments of all the colonies, including South Australia and New Zealand, were subsequently expressed. The tide of opinion in the United Kingdom had also turned against the inhumane practice of transportation. The matter was settled with a dispatch from the Colonial Office in December 1852, stating that the Secretary had no problem agreeing to a 'wish so generally and so forcibly expressed by the colonialists of Australia'.[25]

An interesting question is why did the legislative council of New South Wales drag its feet in opposing Grey's re-introduction of transportation, leaving mass rallies to express the feelings of the colony? It seems that the legislative council was divided on the issue because a strong minority in the council saw the advantages that cheap convict labour offered in relation to working land holdings. So a resolution carried in the council as early as 1 June 1849, that Her Majesty be approached to revoke the Order in Council of 1848, was not acted on. It took public action and coordinated inter-colonial activity to stop Grey.

The efficiency argument for a union

After the battle over transportation had been won, the next serious issue that called for unified effort concerned trade tariffs between the colonies at a time when free trade in the Empire was being almost universally enacted. In the Australian colonies, the principal problem concerned tariffs being applied by New South Wales and Victoria across their common border at the Murray River. There was also hostility between New South Wales, Victoria and South Australia as a consequence of the complexity of tariff payments between them. At this time, Tasmania placed tariffs on tobacco from New South Wales. New South Wales responded by placing tariffs on grain from Tasmania. In general, high duties on other goods were exercised on trade between these two colonies. Tariffs on the

---

23   Ward 1958, 204.
24   Ward 1958, 201.
25   Ward 1958, 214.

same goods differed considerably between the colonies, all of which sought to maximise their income from this source of revenue. The growing independence of the legislative councils of New South Wales, Victoria and South Australia from the Colonial Office almost ensured that income from tariffs would be optimised, to the detriment of free trade. This necessitated the erection of customs houses for each of the colonies along their common borders. Although the *Australian Colonies Government Act* of 1850 prohibited differential duties between colonies, it did not force free trade.

The 'efficiencies' that Grey sought were essentially those obtained by the introduction of free trade. He thought this could be realised through a federal union of the colonies of Australia. However, the colonies saw the solution to these tariff conundrums as simply requiring sensible resolutions between individual colonies, without the necessity of establishing something as complex as a federation. To this end, in 1855 the New South Wales Executive Council decided on free trade with Victoria across the Murray, as well as on equal division of the customs collections made by South Australia on behalf of New South Wales and Victoria between these two colonies. The free trade proclamations of New South Wales and Victoria both occurred in October 1855 and took effect the following month.

Tentative steps towards a union

Ward did not think that the transient union of activity involved in opposing Grey on transportation had a direct effect on later movements to form a federal union in Australia. There is no evidence that the impulse for federation can be thought of as a consequence of the formation of the anti-transportation league. Nevertheless, the inter-colonial unity of purpose displayed in thwarting the initiatives of the Colonial Office did show the usefulness of colonial synergy of activity and may be said to have laid the groundwork for union without pushing towards it. There was neither a strong nationalistic spirit nor any doubt about the ties between the colonies and Great Britain. The colonies certainly did not want to form a republic. There were no attempts to widen the function of the anti-transportation league or to organise the working classes to push for more universal franchise and a liberal constitution.

One might have thought that the Eureka Stockade rebellion on the goldfields of Victoria in 1854 would have led to a demand for an independent republic of Australia, but it did not. The discovery of gold in Victoria and New South Wales led to a great influx of new immigrants of diverse origins and brought unexpected wealth to these colonies, causing substantial changes to society, industry and trade after 1852. However, this was not accompanied by a substantial push for union in these colonies. In fact, it made it more difficult to see how colonies such as South Australia that did not benefit from enhanced gold income could be incorporated into a union with colonies that did.

Tentative steps were made in 1853 towards the establishment of a general assembly, with representatives from each of the colonies, as envisaged in the *Australian Colonies Government Act* of 1850. At the same time, members of the Victorian Legislative Council expressed the hope that the British government might revisit the proposal for some kind of general assembly. In 1853, the lower house in Victoria expressed the opinion that 'the establishment of a system of mutual action and cooperation among' the colonies would be worthwhile and that while we wish to continue members of the British Empire we must not forget also that we are colonists of the Australian branch of the British Empire and, as there are many subjects of mutual interest to the different Australian colonies, in my opinion some provision ought be made for their confederation.[26]

However, this proposition was not developed further.

The synergies of action of the colonies in rejecting the return of transportation and removing tariffs between them led to consideration of other matters that needed a uniform solution across colonies, such as lighthouses in Bass Strait and the erection of a telegraph line between Adelaide and Melbourne. But the solutions to these problems were determined by negotiations, such as those in the Second Border Convention for the Murray Trade (1857–1858). While these transactions were often rather tortuous, they did not require the introduction of a federal union.

Federation without nationalism

Ward comments that the debate concerning federation in the 1890s 'was on whether and how the role of the state should be extended in social and economic matters',[27] not on any form of fervent Australian nationalism. Although no single factor determined the outcome, agreement on the role of the state, which followed the liberal idea of accepting state interventions that had blossomed in New South Wales in the 1890s, played a prominent role. Such interventions included, for example, the 'proposed powers over marriage, divorce and the family'.[28] Ward argued that a federal constitution was achieved through an interplay of ideas between colonial conservatives, liberals and labour, in which the conservatives appeared to have won, although the succeeding half century showed they had not.

Working and lower middle class people migrated from Great Britain in large numbers from the 1830s onward. Given that there were no barriers to their advancement and no hereditary aristocracy, these migrants became supporters of property and of civil order to protect it, anticipating that they might become owners themselves someday. The discovery of gold in Victoria and New South Wales accelerated this immigration, which, together with the success of pastoral activities, helped transform 'a sordid, predominantly convict and ex-convict society of 1830 ... out of all recognition' by 1860.[29] The British population of the colonies consisted of about 30 per cent Irish. They were able to set about developing a Catholic school system without any serious resistance from the Protestant churches, reflecting the extent to which the colony had become largely tolerant and secular. By 1868, the non-indigenous population was about 1,540,000. The greatest number (671,300) lived in Victoria, which had experienced the greatest of all the gold

---

26 Ward 1958, 341.
27 Ward 2001, 129.
28 Ward 2001, 138.
29 Ward 2001, 15.

discoveries, with much smaller numbers (463,000) in New South Wales. About this time, the population had the greatest per capita real product of any country in the world.

The family was universally considered to be the social and economic unit upon which the stability of the colonies rested. The comparative wealth of the colonies of Victoria and New South Wales led to great expectations. Liberal conservatives such as James Macarthur saw change with continuity as a guiding principle, while still adhering to English legal, moral and social codes that protected the family and property.[30] Obligations due to rank and privilege were not emphasised by liberal conservatives. Colonial society had come to believe, by the 1870s, that some form of federation was inevitable, a sentiment that was expressed in the major newspapers. It was not political leadership that encouraged the colonies to move towards federation so much as the colonialists drifting in this direction.

In the 1880s and 1890s, the colonial conservatives, liberals and labour had very different ideas concerning the role of the state in controlling economic and social affairs. They were also divided on whether such control required a federal parliament or could be carried out by the existing colonial legislatures, or both? There was general agreement over currency, tariffs, external relations, defence, immigration and maritime services, as well as ports and telegraphs, to which marriage, company law, banking, insurance and patents might be added. Businessmen, bankers and politicians were aware of the administrative complexities arising across the colonies in many of these areas. The conservatives lent their weight to matters that gave individuals unfettered freedom to pursue their goals, calling on Social Darwinism – self-development through competitive individualism – to bolster their case. But this claim was turned against them by the liberals, who asked where in Australia such unfettered individualism and free markets had shaped society.

The conservatives had powerful voices supporting their stance on the protection of individual freedom, as well as on economic matters. Edmund Barton of New South Wales, who had a highly successful career in politics and law and a reputation for tolerance, was destined to be the first prime minister of the Commonwealth and later a justice of the High Court. The Victorians had Alfred Deakin, who was also of exceptionally high standing. These conservatives were confronted by equally gifted liberals, such as the Irish-born Victorian barrister and politician George Higinbotham, who was destined to become the first Chief Justice of the High Court. George Reid, an outstanding liberal from New South Wales and its premier from 1890 to 1898, sought to preserve in the new constitution clauses that would maintain the social stability won over decades by the liberals and, in some cases, liberal conservatives such as James Macarthur. David Syme in Victoria sought to protect and expand the liberal legislation in that colony, which was even more progressive than in New South Wales. All these fine leaders argued and fought throughout the federation conventions of the 1890s, determined that their advocacy of conservative or liberal claims on the constitution would win the day. When the referendum took place across the colonies in 1899 and 1900, 60 per cent of the 983,000 eligible voters took part in the then voluntary vote (about the average turnout for an election), with a large margin of 72 per cent voting yes. The constitution of this new federation largely reflected

---

30 Ward 2001, 43.

the conservative stance. It was meant to be a kind of treaty between all-powerful states, with only limited and highly delineated powers passing to the Commonwealth, leaving the states supreme. It only emerged much later that the largely conservative framers of the constitution had not drafted their intentions carefully enough; within 50 years the Commonwealth came to dominate the government of Australia.

How did this come about? The 19th-century political leaders, who had become skilled at framing and developing colonial constitutions, were faced with novel challenges in drafting a Commonwealth constitution. Particularly challenging, as Ward pointed out, was the choice of appropriate British and American precedents to fashion a uniquely Australian constitution, developed for antipodean conditions. The Commonwealth was given full power over pensions and taxation concurrently with the states, but, importantly, granted preference when Commonwealth and states conflicted. This had enormous impact when the Commonwealth became the principal revenue collector halfway through the 20th century. Likewise, the growth in the industrial power of the commonwealth was unforeseen by the framers of the constitution. The drafting also delivered a High Court with a conservative edge, which the liberals had tried to avoid.

Special drafting seemed to be required in order to preserve the social homogeneity of a British society transplanted to the antipodes; this became known as the White Australia Policy. The argument that social homogeneity was a necessary requirement for maintaining a stable society in Australia, which had been blessed with freedom from strife for a century, ignored the Aboriginal peoples. The constitution then became, in part, a racial document – the stain of which has still not worn off – consolidating a view of Australia as a Caucasian people embedded in Asia. The claim that parts of the constitution are racial does not arise from a misinterpretation of the intentions of the founding fathers, who sought a homogeneous society. The first prime minister, Edmund Barton, and the future governor general, Isaac Isaacs, 'described the coloured races as intrinsically inferior to whites'.[31]

James Macarthur

A personal narrative that brings to life the period leading up to the establishment of representative government in NSW, during which Australia's first university was founded at Sydney, is provided by Ward's study of the leading liberal conservative in the colony at that time, James Macarthur. Consideration of his views helps identify the main political forces at play in the colony, particularly during the controversies accompanying the cessation of transportation and the introduction of manhood suffrage.

Colonial conservatism, liberal conservatism and liberalism

The conservatives of Great Britain held to the principle that land-owning men of wealth formed an elite class, which, together with their sovereign and some very senior officials, should constitute the social and political authority of the Kingdom and the Empire. Conservatives in the colonies held much the same view, transplanting the hierarchy to

---

31 Ward 2001, 124.

Figure 3.4 James Macarthur, watercolour on ivory miniature, c. 1820. State Library of New South Wales (IE1556289).

a pastoral society with a ready source of cheap labour, consisting of convicts or slaves. Indeed, like their counterparts in Great Britain, the colonial conservatives held a deep suspicion of democracy and certainly of manhood suffrage.

After the middle of the 19th century, liberal conservatism in New South Wales placed the usual emphasis on land ownership for the privileged class at the top of the social hierarchy, but now leavened with the expectation that that class was well-educated and, in particular, committed to the well-being of society as a whole. The claims of privilege for the propertied classes came with commitment to the belief that every citizen had a claim to justice, education and civil rights. This would ensure a stable society, with morality and the family forming the foundation. There is no doubt in New South Wales that James Macarthur subscribed to these values, especially as he grew more mature in his role as a senior member of the Legislative Council and adviser to the Colonial Office in Great Britain. Macarthur's father John, founder of the Australian wool industry, was a conservative who, together with his wife Elizabeth (née Veale), brought James up to be a conservative.

Liberals, like liberal conservatives, placed emphasis on property, different levels of wealth, family, personal liberty, law, social stability, constitutional government, freedom of religious practice and, particularly, education. They departed from liberal conservatives in their support of manhood suffrage and of a legislature that was representative not only of the propertied and wealthy classes but of all enfranchised people. Here Macarthur certainly could not be counted as a liberal. His conservative upbringing imbued a deep suspicion of an uneducated class possessing the power to elect. He could not see how enfranchising such a class would bring about a stable and evolving society.

Political allegiances and the end of transportation

In the late 1840s, the Legislative Council of New South Wales had been split as to the re-introduction of transportation of convicts, with the conservatives and some liberal conservatives seeing the need for cheap labour to work their pastoral properties. This was strongly opposed by the liberals and, to some extent, the radicals, who stressed the moral evil of a decision that returned the colony to the days of penal servitude. Macarthur attempted to find a middle ground, on the one hand supporting the cessation of transportation and on the other arguing that exiles from Great Britain should be accepted.

As noted, the liberals organised a meeting of 6,000 people in Barrack Square in 1850 to protest Grey's attempt to re-introduce transportation. Macarthur, somewhat intemperately, described the speakers as 'cowardly, canting and selfish',[32] a description that helped drive a wedge between the liberals and the liberal conservatives, hindering cooperation on other issues, at least while transportation remained a serious problem. So the alliance that Macarthur had sought between liberals and liberal conservatives on entering the New South Wales legislative council in 1848 was thwarted by his own actions.

Manhood suffrage

Ward argued that there was unanimity among conservatives, liberal conservatives, liberals and even the few radicals in 1856 that the colony of New South Wales should have complete control over its lands and revenues and possess a civil service modelled on that of Great Britain. Macarthur sought to lead the liberal conservatives and some liberals to obtain the kind of independence from Great Britain that he envisaged would involve a form of limited representative government, as well as the transfer of senior officials from imperial to colonial control. But the idea of representation based on manhood suffrage, rather than following the interests he represented, was anathema to him, as it was, of course, to the conservatives. The constitutional bill for New South Wales was passed in 1853, and the inauguration of responsible government occurred two and a half years later, in 1856. At this time, manhood suffrage had not been implemented, although those eligible to vote were now represented by an increased number of members in the

---

32   Ward 1981, 161.

Legislative Council (making a total of 36). These members included 12 pastoralists or farmers and nine businessmen, manufacturers or merchants, with the remainder being judges, professional men or retired civil servants. This council was hardly representative of the people. Macarthur was exultant over this outcome, which he saw as a vindication of his liberal conservative vision for the colonies' first 'responsible and reform ministry'.[33]

The blossoming of Macarthur's liberal conservatism is shown in his advocacy of a public education system in the colony. As Macarthur matured he determined that the lower classes could, through education, be part of forming a true democracy. To this end, he and his wife Emily provided schools on their Camden estate. He was also a fervent supporter of higher education, becoming a founder of the Australian colonies' first university in Sydney in 1852 and an original fellow of its Senate. Another foundation member of the Senate was Macarthur's close friend Sir Charles Nicholson, who brought many archaeological treasures to the colony, which are now housed in the beautiful museum named after him at Sydney University (see Chapter 1). It was in the company of such men that Macarthur consolidated his view of the need to further culture and higher education in the colony. He made public his support for manhood suffrage once universal education had been implemented in the Legislative Assembly of 1858.

Macarthur, coming from landed gentry with a large income and possessing an excellent education as a consequence of receiving private tutoring, including from his conservative father, was expected to continue in the conservative tradition. That was not to be. By the 1840s, he saw himself more as a Whig than a Tory; if the latter label applied at all, it would have to be qualified by the adjective 'reform'. In 1843, he declared at an election meeting that he was not a Tory but a moderate conservative. In 1856, after New South Wales had acquired representative government, Macarthur pondered his contribution to this outcome and how close he had come to being identified as a liberal – and, indeed, that he was truly a liberal conservative. At that time, Governor Denison commented that 'no one ... could reasonably suspect the liberal conservative Macarthur of having any personal end to serve that was not consistent with the good of New South Wales'.[34]

***

The considerable length of this essay is necessary to illustrate Ward's depth of scholarship and his narrative power and originality. The latter is evident in the four concepts examined here: 'minimal intervention', 'anomalous societies', 'self-government imposed' and 'federation avoided'. Ward showed that there was no rising nationalism in the Australian colonies forcing ties with Great Britain to be severed and independence gained, as had occurred in the former colonies of the United States. No grand theme emerges from our 19th-century history to stir the emotions. Rather, the colonies followed a tortuous route that slowly led to their federation. Ward also showed that the constitutional document signed in 1901 reflects the conservative nature of our peoples, or, at least, the liberal conservative bent that we have followed. Like his hero James Macarthur, Ward was a

---

33   Ward 1981, 218.
34   Ward 1981, 202.

liberal conservative. That sat well with the University of Sydney, to which Ward and Macarthur were such significant servants, at its founding and over one hundred years later, during considerable periods of growth. The university community felt a great sense of shock and loss when John, his wife and his daughter were killed in a train crash just after he retired on completing more than 50 years as a student, scholar and Vice-Chancellor.

Further reading

Ward, J.M. *Earl Grey and the Australian Colonies, 1846–1857: A Study of Self-Government and Self-Interest.* Carlton, VIC: Melbourne University Press, 1958.

Ward, J.M. *Empire in the Antipodes: The British in Australasia, 1840–1860.* London: Edward Arnold, 1966.

Ward, J.M. *British Policy in the South Pacific, 1786–1893: A Study of British Policy in the South Pacific Islands Prior to the Establishment of Governments by the Great Powers.* Westport, CT: Greenwood Press, 1976.

Ward, J.M. *Colonial Self-Government: The British Experience, 1759–1856.* London: Macmillan, 1976.

Ward, J.M. *James Macarthur, Colonial Conservative, 1798–1867.* Sydney: Sydney University Press, 1981.

Ward, J.M. *The State and the People: Australian Federation and Nation-Making 1870–1901.* Edited by D.M. Schreuder, B.H. Fletcher and R. Hutchinson. Annandale, NSW: The Federation Press, 2001.

Jurisprudence

4
Protecting the common law from autocracy: Alice Erh-Soon Tay

Challis Professor of Jurisprudence (1975–2001). A leading scholar on human rights and the common law, Tay sought to protect the law from the encroachment of modern society seeking 'quick and efficient' administrative resolution of contractual disputes, through a comparative analysis of legal systems. She considered all of this within a broader framework of the dangers posed by the development of autocratic systems of law, supported by her rich knowledge of the evolution of communist legal systems, especially in China.

I found it inspiring to see the diminutive figure of Alice Tay on campus, walking determinedly to a meeting, and to know that here was the embodiment of human rights in Australia – the President of the Human Rights and Equal Opportunity Commission and the leading scholar on the protection of our common law. An important part of the respect she received originated from her unique combination of analytical gifts, wedded to a profound knowledge of the legal systems of China and Russia.

Tay was born in Singapore in 1934, one of six siblings, to parents from Guangdong province in Southern China. Her father, a clerk for an Australian water-pipe company, maintained strong ties with China. At ten, she attended Raffles Girls' School, where her intellectual abilities soon displayed themselves. She won a prize that took her to leading academic schools in the United States for three months, with the prospect of going on to Yale or Harvard. Instead she went to London to study law at the Inns of Court. On completing her legal studies, she returned to Singapore and was admitted to the Singapore Bar in 1957, where she practised criminal law. At the early age of 25, Tay took up an appointment in the law department at the University of Malaya in Singapore. She left two years later to carry out studies for a PhD in the Research School of Social Sciences at the Australian National University (ANU) and was awarded a PhD in 1965 for her thesis on the 'Concept of Possession in the Common Law'. This was followed by an exchange scholarship to Russia in 1965–1966 that led to a deep interest in the Russian law and state, which she shared with her future husband, the eminent Russian scholar Eugene Kamenka. By the time she returned to ANU, Tay had become committed to a life dedicated to human rights, not only in the West but also in the communist countries of China and Russia. This is reflected in her subsequent publications over eight years at ANU.

Figure 4.1 Professor Alice Ehr-Soon Tay. Photograph from the University of Sydney Archives (G3_224_1378).

In 1975, she took up the Challis Chair of Jurisprudence at the University of Sydney following the retirement of the formidable Julius Stone (Chapter 5). While at Sydney, she was President of the Australian Human Rights and Equal Opportunity Commission (1998–2003) and a part-time Commissioner of the Australian Law Reform Commission (ALRC) (1982–1987), where she was responsible for, among other matters, enquiries into the recognition of Aboriginal customary laws (ALRC 31, 1986), privacy (ALRC 22, 1983), contempt (ALRC 35, 1987) and matrimonial property (ALRC 39, 1987).

Throughout her period as a Challis professor, Tay's scholarly commitment to human rights was primarily apparent in her determination to preserve what she referred to as the marvel of the common law. This took the form of a comparative analysis of the law through consideration of what she called the

> three great paradigms of social ideology, social organization, law and administration – each of them representing a complex but potentially coherent view of man, social institutions and their place in society. These paradigms we call the *Gemeinschaft* or organic communal–familial, the *Gesellschaft* or contractual commercial–individualistic, and the bureaucratic–administrative paradigms[1]

to which she later added the domination–submission paradigm. Tay's contribution to each of these concepts and their relationships is spelt out in this essay. How the paradigms facilitate the analysis of legal systems and their origins is considered in the context of the communist laws of the USSR and China, on which Tay had become a particular expert. Finally, I summarise the main object of Tay's human rights commitment – namely, to protect the integrity of the common law – an objective that she met by comparing the results of applying the four paradigms to the common law and to the laws of communist states, which frequently decline into merely a facade of law.

Gemeinschaft and Gesellschaft paradigms

In sociological theories, motivation, or the will, is divided into the natural and the rational in order to account for why people do what they do in a social setting. At its most rudimentary, the natural will is taken as elemental, belonging to deep levels of an individual's psychology and manifesting itself in unreflective, naive and emotional volition. The rational will, on the other hand, involves rational deliberations concerning the actions one may take, based on a perception of one's own best interests. At a more sophisticated level, the natural and rational wills are considered to act synergistically. German sociologist Ferdinand Tönnies wrote: 'Indeed, intellect in natural will attains its fruition in the creative, formative, and artistic ability and works and in the spirit of genius.'[2]

Tönnies' great work *Gemeinschaft und Gesellschaft*,[3] often translated as community and society, was the original template Tay used when considering and writing on human

---

1 Kamenka and Tay, 'Social Traditions', 1980, 7.
2 Tönnies 1955, 17.
3 Tönnies 1887.

rights and the law. Tönnies identified the *Gemeinschaft* as all kinds of social groups in which the natural will is the predominant guiding force; the *Gesellschaft* included those social groups associated with and dominated by rational procedures. In the *Gemeinschaft* life is regarded in a closed, cohesive and organic grouping, as occurs in the family. In the *Gesellschaft* the life of a large grouping is considered, such as that of a society regulated by rules, mechanical procedures and plans, as well as methodologies concerned with persuasion, all in order to obtain material goods and wealth.

The organic and personal emphasis in the *Gemeinschaft* may involve larger groupings than the family, as manifest, for example, in religious communities. Once these communities enter into formal grouping for the purposes of interacting with other groups in a larger society, they manifest as *Gesellschafts*; however, this does not deprive them of their *Gemeinschaft* status. Strong *Gemeinschafts* have traditionally been found in rural communities, where people live together in close and lasting relationships. In strong *Gesellschafts* the relationships are transitory in comparison. Tönnies' emphasis on sustained friendship and kinship in the *Gemeinschaft*, in contrast with the fragmentary, superficial and mechanical nature of the *Gesellschaft*, reflects the state of 19th-century German society. The feudal systems crumbling before the growth of large-scale industrial cities was manifest and lent itself to the stark contrast that Tönnies drew between organic and mechanical societies. He stressed that there was a tendency to idealise the *Gemeinschaft*, with its intimate and deep relationships, and forget that such a lifestyle can easily be manipulated into irrational enthusiasm and populism. He compared this with the great strides made in the area of human rights in the *Gesellschaft*, accompanied by the realisation that deep levels of economic and physical deprivation in a society are unacceptable.

The concept of man in the *Gesellschaft* as possessing powers of rationality as a consequence of acquiring language – and hence a moral status, as highlighted by Kant – leads to the framing of laws enshrining human rights and powers, which become the embodiment of freedom. Tay argued that the diverse aims of individuals within society emphasise the importance of 'formal procedure, impartiality, adjudicative justice, precise legal provisions and definitions, and the rationality and predictability of legal administration'.[4] At the heart of the *Gesellschaft* is the notion of contracts between persons; when disagreements between the parties occur, it is the identification and clarification of the essential points at issue that is highlighted. This is in contrast to the *Gemeinschaft*, where the emphasis is on the traditional relationships between parties and general social harmony, without exact formulations of how this may come about.

The *Gesellschaft* makes a clear distinction between public and private, civil and criminal, and between law and administration. It helped free society from restrictions emphasised by the *Gemeinschaft* that are based on religious status and the communalisation of family and government within a hierarchical setting, which typified feudalism before the Industrial Revolution. Tönnies hoped that eventually a society would emerge that took the best of the *Gemeinschaft* and the *Gesellschaft*, eliminating hierarchy and inequality from the former and overburdened, mechanical and inhumane legal strictures from the latter.

---

4   Kamenka and Tay, 'Social Traditions', 1980, 17.

The bureaucratic–administrative and domination–submission paradigms

While using Tönnies' *Gemeinschaft* and *Gesellschaft* template to understand the legal system of a particular society, Tay found the need to use a social grouping dominated by a new paradigm – namely, the bureaucratic–administrative type introduced by the sociologist Max Weber. While *Gesellschaft* law takes as its foundation the free and rational individual, with rights limited only by those of other individuals, and the *Gemeinschaft* centres on the organic community, the bureaucratic–administrative considers human persons of minor interest. Instead, it focuses on rules and public policy. The concept of the bureaucratic–administrative society and legal system highlighted by Tay was required to accommodate the vastly increased reach of bureaucracies in the 20th century, compared with those at the time Tönnies wrote the first edition of *Gemeinschaft und Gesellschaft*. Tay warned repeatedly that if the law under the *Gesellschaft* is weakened or curtailed by the *Gemeinschaft*, or by a bureaucratic–administrative emphasis, so that the *Gesellschaft* becomes merely another form of policy and regulation, then the resultant failure of legal ideology will expose man to a less humane society.

Western democracies are, at present, best described as following a mixture of the *Gemeinschaft*, *Gesellschaft* and bureaucratic–administrative paradigms. This raises the question of which of these paradigms should predominate; is there one approach that is morally superior to the others, or should we aim for an optimal mix? According to Tay and Kamenka: 'The real question of our times is not how to pass from one model to another, but how to promote and maintain an optimal mix of the three.'[5] The distinction between most of the socialist countries and civil law countries of the European continent, on the one hand, and the common law countries, on the other, is that the former, although *Gesellschaft* systems, are based on a code, rather than case law procedures, inevitably leading to the bureaucratisation of the law.

Tay also brings to our attention another paradigm that has unfortunately been predominant in the 20th century, one she called domination–submission.

> Domination–submission ... is clearly extra-legal and supra-legal in that it neither implies nor requires a structured system of regulation incorporating certain values ... it can, to some extent, live above or within all of them [the Gemeinschaft, Gesellschaft and bureaucratic–administrative], modifying or shaping the conditions in which they operate. ... In communist countries, including China, the domination–submission relation has been institutionalized ... in the doctrine of the leading role and historical infallibility of the communist party.[6]

Impoverishment of the *Gesellschaft* in the Soviet Union

Justice could not arise from communist law in the Soviet Union because it was concerned with 'the will of the state', which was placed beyond reach of persons and of lawyers. Law

---

5 Tay and Kamenka, 'Editors' Introduction', 1980, 26.
6 Kamenka and Tay, 'Social Traditions', 1980, 22.

then became almost the sole province of the bureaucratic–administrative system, with its tendency to morph into a system of domination–submission. This morphing is made explicit by consideration of the Soviet Union's constitution of 1936, which guaranteed freedom of speech, assembly and the press, as well as the right to gather for the purposes of public demonstrations. It elevated the humanity of the person, providing freedom of conscience and of religion. It held the promise that these would be protected by an independent judiciary, with lawyers appearing in open and protected trials. However,

> the most important civil rights and freedoms (speech, freedom of assembly, street demonstrations, religious worship and privacy) are granted only to be exercised in conformity with the interests of the working people and for the purpose of strengthening the socialist system.[7]

This required a vast bureaucratic–administrative structure, divorced from both the *Gemeinschaft* and the *Gesellschaft*, but with strong links to a domination–submission system that led, through its coercive methods, to the deaths of over a tenth of the Russian population – more than the number that were killed by Germany in the Second World War. The communist state and the party's interests were paramount in the all-powerful bureaucratic–administrative structure, leaving no room for adjudication between persons. As Tay put it,

> the failure of communist law as a system of justice lay primarily in the longstanding communist insistence that the law was the will of the state which could not be legitimately contested by citizens or lawyers.[8]

Although the *Gesellschaft* seemed to be strongly represented in the freedoms mentioned, this was, of course, mere lip service for propaganda purposes. There were no legal structures in place, no *Gesellschaft* that could have fulfilled claims to justice and freedom in the courts.

Impoverishment of the *Gemeinschaft* in China

Tay shows that between the Second National Conference on Judicial Work in China, held in 1953, and the Eighth National Congress of the Communist Party of China in 1956, there occurred the only serious attempt to put in place a formal regulatory structure, with strong bureaucratic–administrative procedures coupled with weak *Gesellschaft* legal requirements. This was dramatically dismantled following a speech by Mao 'On the Correct Handling of Contradictions among the People', on 27 February 1957, before the Supreme State Conference. Mao identified two types of social contradictions under socialism: contradictions between the people and their enemies, and contradictions among the people themselves. According to Tay,

---

7   Tay, 'Marxism, Socialism and Human Rights', 1978, 111.
8   Kamenka and Tay 1993, 159.

the former contradiction rests on a basic conflict of interest linked with class and property position; confronted by this contradiction, faced by the enemies of the people, law becomes a weapon of suppression, an instrument of dictatorship which is by definition non-benevolent, violent and entitled to exceed proper limits to crush the enemy, who is to be deprived of all legal or constitutional rights.[9]

This speech led to an abrupt end to any *Gesellschaft* concept of the law, and, indeed, to the bureaucratic–administrative system when it came to consideration of the enemies of the people, namely, those associated with class and property, for whom domination–submission and terror were to be the violent methods of their elimination.

On the other hand, a form of *Gemeinschaft* was given support for the people in general, with the development of methods of persuasion to settle disagreements among themselves. This was congenial to the Chinese people for, as Tay comments,

traditional Chinese justice is 'parental' rather than 'adjudicative' justice, oriented toward situations rather than individual rights, toward settlement of disputes rather than definition of claims. ... it is the law of a *Gemeinschaft* and not of a *Gesellschaft*; it is based on the primacy of traditional social relationships and not on the primacy of the right- and duty-bearing individual, social ties rather than contractual obligations.[10]

The function of the courts was seen to involve popular participation in order to carry out their traditional role of mediation and conciliation, rather than any *Gesellschaft* legal procedure. In his speech, Mao said:

contradictions 'among the people' are based on differences of occupation and social location; there are contradictions within the working class, within the peasantry, within the intelligentsia, between all three of these and even between the Government and the People ... These latter contradictions, however, all conceal an underlying unity of interests; they are non-antagonistic contradictions. They should therefore be resolved benevolently through mediation and conciliation according to the 'dialectical' principle of 'unity–criticism–unity'.[11]

Mao then placed further emphasis on *Gemeinschaft* procedures with respect to alleviating differences between the people. Traditional social relations were emphasised again, and the *Gesellschaft* of rights-bearing persons was downplayed, if not eliminated. Mao's speech was followed by enhanced participation of the people in *Gemeinschaft* activities. This emphasis on *Gemeinschaft* procedures was further highlighted following the economic failure of the Great Leap Forward between 1957 and 1965, with additional enhancement of participation by the people in informal rather than legal deliberations. Towards the end of this period, in 1964, Ts'ao Tzu-tan commented in *On the Relationship between Crime and Class Struggle* that

---

9   Tay 1976, 414.
10 Tay 1969, 156.
11 Tay 1976, 414.

criminal phenomena in socialist States are also the manifestation of class struggle. The difference between this and crime in exploitative States is that a fundamental change has occurred in the class nature of crime. Because classes, class struggle and the possibility of capitalist restoration still exist during the stage of transition, there is a need for the socialist State to use the declaration of crime to struggle against behaviour that seriously endangers the interests of the State and people.[12]

Ts'ao Tzu-tan emphasises Mao's idea of the eradication of the propertied class through domination–submission and terror.

The Great Leap Forward was followed by the Great Proletarian Cultural Revolution (1966–1969), which amounted to consolidation of a form of *Gemeinschaft*, with populism and revolutionary emotion running high, leading once more to domination–submission and terror. One is reminded of the extent to which an unbridled *Gemeinschaft* can lead to terror when contemplating the uninhibited *Gemeinschaft* of Puritan New England, which resulted in the Salem witch hunts. Mao's declaration led to excesses in the form of legal requirements in a manipulated *Gemeinschaft* allowing the expropriation of land and property through terror engendered by trials, resulting in the destruction of those deemed enemies of the state. Mao's *Gemeinschaft* also eliminated security for all those participating in and guiding the Cultural Revolution, for the only foundation upon which these activities could find legitimacy was the leader himself, not the law. The formation of conciliation committees during the Cultural Revolution seemed, on the surface, to be fully in accordance with the *Gemeinschaft* concept. But these were not committees to settle disagreements among the people; rather, they were committees concerned with political indoctrination on behalf of the revolution's leaders, ultimately resting on Mao's authority. This led to the formation of institutions that infiltrated all aspects of human activity, resulting in immense pressure being placed on regularising the behaviour of individuals comprising the population of 800 million. Tay concluded that 'the People's Republic of China [came] closer to George Orwell's *1984* than either Nazi Germany or the USSR'.[13]

The common law: a *Gesellschaft* complemented by *Gemeinschaft* elements

In *Law and Society*, Tay suggested that

> nobody who has studied the history of the common law in England and in the English-speaking world can fail to marvel at the way it has been shaped to take into account and to facilitate change, to enable man to do, in an orderly and responsible way, what has never been done before.[14]

So Tay extolled the central aim of her scholarship – namely, to protect the great legal traditions of the common law *Gesellschaft* from displacement by the *Gemeinschaft* and the bureaucratic–administrative paradigms. Her intent was to protect the flexibility and

---

12 Tay 1976, 415.
13 Tay 1976, 422.
14 Tay, 'Law, the Citizen and the State', 1978, 3.

non-restrictive openness of the common law from becoming merely a civil law review process and to ensure people before courts are considered only in the context of the matter of concern, unrelated to privilege or status. Tay emphasised that the marvel of the common law lies in it being a prime example of a *Gesellschaft* system with some modification by important elements of the *Gemeinschaft*, such as family, morality and the concept of the reasonable man.

The glory of the common law reports is that they are pre-eminently human narratives – the people in them have quirks and character, and they play out their lives in particular social settings. A person before the courts is assumed to have free will, to exercise choices. Mental or physical diseases are only taken into account as possible grounds for mitigation of sentencing. They are not considered, as much contemporary neurolaw would have it, as patients to be cured. Tay emphatically rejected the idea of a society that treats all people before the courts as patients to be cured and not as agents to be judged. She commented that she

> would not care to live [in that society]. It would turn the whole world into a gigantic mental hospital in which the doctors would be the law, and in which each individual doctor, as in Stalin's Russia or Mao's China, would himself be a potential patient.[15]

The common law reports contain an unparalleled history of the development of current legal precepts, ideals, concepts, norms and techniques, embedded in the concrete evaluation of real, identifiable individuals, living out their lives in an identifiable society. The accumulation of knowledge pertinent to the consideration of a particular case and the introduction of new principles can only be paralleled by science, with its accumulation of facts relating to specific theories or understandings, the latter being modified in the face of novel observations, to arrive at even more credible theories for future experimentation.

Tay held that in order to understand the common law one needs to realise that it is a tradition based on three major principles. The first concerns the independence of the courts and judges in carrying out the rule-governed and predictable procedures of the law. The second concerns the notion of a person, or persons, before the courts, considered as possessing a moral status, exercising free will and taking responsibility for their actions, which can only be set aside, in part, by conditions or circumstances that may call for mitigation. The third requires that each person is considered as an individual before the law – one not to be dishonoured as to their rights, especially with regards to property. Nevertheless, Tay stressed that

> legal justice, as it is often called, is far more in the actual practice of the Common Law than the application of abstract, procedural canons of fairness and impartiality. Without these, it is true, there is nothing, but by themselves they could hardly ever lead to a decision.[16]

---

15 Tay, 'Law, the Citizen and the State', 1978, 9.
16 Tay 1979, 93.

This is reflected in the fact that there is very little reference to justice, conceived of in the abstract, in the histories of the English common law. Rather, justice is what is done in the common law, without the need for further philosophical consideration. Tay emphasised that even Lord Denning, the senior judge most prone to giving judgements with minimal reference to authority, thus elevating his judgements to pronouncements of new principles, commented that

> when you set out on this road, you must remember that there are two great objects to be achieved: one is to see that the laws are just; the other that they are justly administered. Both are important, but of the two, the more important is that the law should be justly administered. It is no use having just laws if they are administered unfairly by bad judges or corrupt lawyers. ... [A] country cannot long tolerate a legal system which does not give a fair trial.[17]

Weakening of the *Gesellschaft* through the media and the internet

A good deal of the concern of critics of the common law *Gesellschaft* resides in their wish to resurrect a simpler, more organic community of the past, as in the *Gemeinschaft* paradigm. As mentioned, Tay argued that judicious modifications of the *Gesellschaft* by elements of the *Gemeinschaft* have always been a singular strength of the common law. She commented that

> the classical *Gesellschaft* paradigm of law is faced with a revitalization and extension of *Gemeinschaft* and bureaucratic–administrative conceptions of law that conflict, in important ways, with the *Gesellschaft* values, procedures and conceptual system.[18]

This conflict that must be resolved in favour of the present notion of the common law.

The massive effects of the media and the internet on the expression and guidance of the emotions of the populous, promoting irrational attitudes to solutions of inherently complex problems, highlights the worst features of the *Gemeinschaft*. Dishonesty, showmanship and selfishness come to dominate what was once an attempt at considered and thoughtful opinion. Justice, as Tay commented

> will not long survive in a society in which *Gesellschaft* procedures, laws and freedoms have become weak or in which the language people use is no longer the carrier of *Gesellschaft* conceptions and ideals.[19]

Recent political events in the United States of America show how extraordinarily prescient Tay was in issuing these warnings.

---

17 Tay 1979, 84
18 Tay and Kamenka, 'New Legal Areas', 1980, 256.
19 Kamenka and Tay, '"Transforming" the Law', 1980, 107.

Weakening of the *Gesellschaft* through excess regulation and arbitration

Tay saw serious loss of the *Gesellschaft* in the common law of Australia through the extension of bureaucratic–administrative processes, warning that

> in the broadest sense of the word 'law', there is a constant proliferation today, in Australia as elsewhere, of law and laws. More and more areas of social life come under the control or regulation of the State and its agencies; the laws and regulations connected with these may, in some departments of social and economic life, be moving away from technical and formalistic distinctions but they are nonetheless constantly increasing in number and complexity. Above all, they are losing the universality associated with a system of *Gesellschaft* law; they are no longer general rules of behaviour but detailed regulations for specific circumstances.[20]

An example of this is the extent to which the law of torts, concerned with harms arising between individuals, has been extended to place major liabilities on those responsible for poor structures, manufactured goods, etc.

The weakening of the *Gesellschaft* in the common law of Australia is especially evident in the context of the *Family Law Act 1975* and its interpretation by the Family Court. Section 49(1) of the act states that 'an application under this Act by a party to a marriage for a decree of dissolution of the marriage shall be based on the ground that the marriage has broken down irretrievably.'[21] Tay observed that the law of divorce appeared to be taken from the law of contract, 'which sees marriage as a system of reciprocal rights and duties and matrimonial "wrongs" as "breaches" of that contract and "grounds" for discharge'.[22] This was evident, she wrote, in the act being interpreted by Justice Raymond Watson, who helped to draft it, as 'dispensing with the notion of parties and putting the court into the position of conducting an inquiry'.[23] In this context, Justice Watson understandably regarded his role as 'more in the nature of an inquiry and an inquisition, followed by an arbitration.'[24] Contrary to this opinion, the High Court of Australia, in *R v Watson; Ex parte Armstrong*,[25] blocked Watson from continuing with the case because of his failure to adhere to the adversarial method, asserting that the duty of a judge was to carry this out judicially.[26] This confirmed Tay's view that the

> law is being asked to shift its attention from adjudicating between 'private' interests after they are already in conflict to securing and regulating the conduct of social affairs in the name of the social good, and within the adjudicative area to substitute quick *ad hoc* 'justice' for rule-bound 'technicality', the equities of the fireside for legal precept, technique and precedent.[27]

---

20 Tay and Kamenka, 'New Legal Areas', 1980, 247.
21 Tay and Kamenka, 'New Legal Areas', 1980, 253.
22 Tay and Kamenka, 'New Legal Areas', 1980, 253.
23 Tay and Kamenka, 'New Legal Areas', 1980, 254.
24 Tay and Kamenka, 'New Legal Areas', 1980, 254.
25 *R v Watson; Ex parte Armstrong* (1976) 136 CLR 248.
26 Tay and Kamenka, 'New Legal Areas', 1980, 254.

Tay powerfully argued that while rapid changes in society necessitate that the law is flexible and capable of dealing with new activities in appropriate ways, it is very important to resist any diminution of the great legal tradition of the common law. Until the *Gesellschaft* of the common law, modified in certain ways by elements of the *Gemeinschaft*, is supplanted by an as yet unspecified new methodology, it must be protected. The adjudicative processes of the common law cannot be replaced, for reasons of economy and efficiency, by *ad hoc* rule-bound codes without destroying the most unique and valuable system of law that man has conceived. This amounts to a call to be on guard concerning the encroachment of bureaucratic–administrative rules and procedures on the *Gesellschaft* of the common law.

Protecting the common law

The common law, manifested in law reports dating back to the 13th century, has developed a unique code-free emphasis on the rights of the individual, protected in concrete circumstances by the courts and by precedent. However, Tay noted,

> the increasing inability of the *Gesellschaft* paradigm to cope with inequalities of power, education and understanding ... are leading to a marked development of public law globally at the expense of private law, and of *Gemeinschaft* and bureaucratic–administrative structures and procedures at the expense of Gesellschaft structures and procedures.[28]

The moral is that the *Gesellschaft* of the common law can be an object of attack for those arguing for the less formal and more apparently humane procedures that seem to exist in the *Gemeinschaft*. But the 20th-century story of Chinese society indicates how this can degenerate into the domination–submission paradigm. On the other hand, emphasis on bureaucratic–administrative structures may seem harmless at first as they are being fashioned to cope with more numerous and complex rules than can be dealt with in the law of the *Gesellschaft*. However, this path may eventually lead to the degeneration of the *Gesellschaft* into a domination–submission society under the guidance of a malevolent figure who rules by terror, as happened in the Soviet Union. In either case, any human society may be subjugated to domination–submission for, as Tay's meticulous scholarship shows, there are many paths within and emanating from the *Gemeinschaft und Gesellschaft* that ultimately lead to domination–submission and terror. Tay called for eternal vigilance on behalf of the best guardian of our human rights – the common law.

***

It is understandable that China should figure large in Tay's considerations, given that she spent her first 25 years in Singapore. Her interest in Russia was nurtured by her

---

27 Kamenka and Tay, 'Socialism, Anarchism and Law', 1978, 51.
28 Tay and Kamenka 1985, 249.

husband and frequent co-author, the political philosopher and Marxist scholar Eugene Kamenka. Tay's knowledge of these legal systems, together with the template laid down by Ferdinand Tönnies in *Gemeinschaft und Gesellschaft*, provided her with the tools needed to sharply delineate the challenges we are meeting and will continue to meet in preserving our human rights through the common law.

Further reading

Kamenka, E., and A.E. Tay. 'Socialism, Anarchism and Law.' In *Law and Society: The Crisis in Legal Ideals*, edited by E. Kamenka, R. Brown and A.E. Tay, 49–80. London: Edward Arnold, 1978.

Kamenka, E., and A.E. Tay. 'Social Traditions, Legal Traditions.' In *Law and Social Control*, edited by E. Kamenka and A.E. Tay, 3–26. London: Edward Arnold, 1980.

Kamenka, E., and A.E. Tay. '"Transforming" the Law, "Steering" Society.' In *Law and Social Control*, edited by E. Kamenka and A.E. Tay, 105–16. London: Edward Arnold, 1980.

Tay, A.E. 'Law in Communist China Part I.' *Sydney Law Review* 6, no. 2 (1969): 153–72.

Tay, A.E. 'Smash Permanent Rules: China as a Model for the Future.' *Sydney Law Review* 7 (1976): 400–23.

Tay, A.E. 'Law, the Citizen and the State.' In *Law and Society: The Crisis in Legal Ideals*, edited by E. Kamenka, R. Brown and A.E. Tay, 1–17. London: Edward Arnold, 1978.

Tay, A.E. 'Marxism, Socialism and Human Rights.' In *Human Rights*, edited by E. Kamenka and A.E. Tay, 104–12. London: Edward Arnold, 1978.

Tay, A.E. 'The Sense of Justice in the Common Law.' In *Justice*, edited by E. Kamenka and A.E. Tay, 79–96. London: Edward Arnold, 1979.

Tay, A.E., and E. Kamenka. 'New Legal Areas, New Legal Attitudes.' In *Law Making in Australia*, edited by E. Kamenka and A.E. Tay, 247–62. London: Edward Arnold, 1980.

Tay, A.E., and E. Kamenka. 'Marxism, Socialism and the Theory of Law.' *Columbia Journal of Transnational Law* 23, no. 2 (1985): 217–49.

5
Ensuring legal decisions reflect society's mores: Julius Stone

Challis Professor of Jurisprudence and International Law (1942–1972). Stone was recognised as one of the foremost philosophers of law for some decades as a consequence of his great scholarship, which led many judges to reach their decisions in the light of the morals and mores of society, rather than in the context of strict legal formalism.

From 1942 to 1963, at about 5 minutes to 7 pm, before the ABC news on the radio, Julius Stone would comment on world affairs, alternating in this spot with the Chancellor of the University of Sydney, Sir Hermann Black.[1] As a boy of 14, I listened with fascination to these broadcasts, as did another young boy who was destined to be a justice of the High Court of Australia and a jurist of international fame, Michael Kirby. I did not realise that these comments were coming from a professor of jurisprudence, for the term meant nothing to me. Now I know that the word 'jurisprudence' comes from the Latin *juris prudentia*, the first word meaning law and the second knowledge or skill. The two main sets of problems that jurisprudence is concerned with are those arising within the practice of the law and the legal structure in which it is embedded, on the one hand, and the relationship between these and the society in which they operate, on the other.

Julius Stone came from a Lithuanian Jewish immigrant family that, at the end of the 19th century, had settled in Leeds, where his father was a cabinet maker and where he was born in 1907. His brilliance as a scholar was revealed at Oxford and later at Harvard, where he was appointed as a lecturer. At Harvard he came under the influence of the great American jurist Roscoe Pound. Pound rejected the analytical–philosophical approach to jurisprudence with its detailed verbal analysis. Instead, he championed sociological jurisprudence, which holds that the law needs to be continually reformed in light of changes in society. Sociological jurisprudence is then a study of the workings of legal institutions and the interplay of these with society. It refines our knowledge of how a society shapes the evolving law, and of how economic, social and political conditions impact on the developing law. Pound held to a concept of justice that provided 'such an adjustment of relations and ordering of conduct as will make the goods of existence …

---

1   See Stone 2014.

Figure 5.1 Professor Julius Stone. National Archives of Australia (SP1011/1, 4353.5).

go round as far as possible with the least friction and waste'.[2] It is the role of the law to adjudicate between conflicting claims as to these goods and of justice to show how this might be achieved. Stone accepted this form of jurisprudence, viewing formal legal reasoning as secondary to the requirements of resolving and relaxing conflicts between competing interests.

---

2   Pound 1942, 64–5.

5 Julius Stone

Schools of thought in jurisprudence can be roughly divided into three classes. 'Natural law' claims that the foundations of law are found in human nature – that is, in morality – which places limits on how far the legislature can go in creating new laws and which, through reasoning, gives rise to the regard in which the law is held. 'Legal positivists' oppose natural law advocates, arguing that the foundations of law are found in a social compact unrelated to morality. 'Legal realism' holds to the idea that the law is nothing more than what those engaged in this discipline – namely, legislators, judges and barristers – want to make it. Stone held that moral considerations were at the core of correct standards of judicial judgement; in this he followed his mentor Pound. Such judgements involved balancing different and often conflicting interests. Consideration of ' balancing tests' became more dominant among Australian judges after the Second World War. Stone insisted that moral considerations were central to such tests.

Stone was appointed Challis Professor of Law at Sydney University in 1942 and began to write *The Province and Function of Law*, which immediately identified him as an exceptionally talented scholar of jurisprudence. This work was referred to as 'the best general introduction to jurisprudence that has yet appeared in the English language' by F.S. Cohen in the *Yale Law Journal* in 1949.[3]

The trilogy

Stone's great trilogy consisted of the volumes *Legal Systems and Lawyers' Reasonings*, *Human Law and Human Justice* and *Social Dimensions of Law and Justice*. These reflect his contributions to jurisprudence in the categories of the analytical, the normative and the sociological respectively. In the first of these, concerned with the analytical, Stone developed a sustained criticism through detailed scrutiny of the pretence by legal positivists that they were following an analytical procedure of logical argument; this, they claimed, made their judgements immune to criticism on the grounds of legal activism (see also 'Judgements and illusory reference'). Stone pointed out that it is impossible to see how the common law could have developed if the positivists were correct and the law was independent of social mores and conventions. He asked: 'How can it be that a judge with a creative attitude can produce change within a framework of binding precedent or statutory expression?'[4]

Stone considered the normative in his *Human Law and Human Justice*. In this work, he gives a detailed description of how ideas of justice evolved in societies during different periods with differing social and economic conditions. From Hebrew and Greek ideas of justice through to the present era, with its emphasis on pragmatism, he discerned historically developed precepts that he called enclaves of justice. He stated that 'social arrangements must leave everyone free to form and assert his own interests, treating every adult sane person as morally autonomous'.[5] Stone argued that the

---

[3] Cohen 1949, 177.
[4] Stone 1964, 233.
[5] Stone 1965, 332.

> irreducible minimum requirement of legal justice is ... that society shall be so organised that men's felt wants can be freely expressed ... the law shall protect that expression, and provide it with the channels through which it can compete effectively.[6]

He claimed that

> while justice as a normative entity transcends human history in the sense that men's aspirations to move by its light seem irrepressible even through eras of the greatest darkness, the approach to understanding justice must still be through history itself.[7]

> ... even when justice ... is seen as transcending men's ideas about it in any given time and place, it still represents, like those ideas, an emanation and a striving *from*, but also a creature *of*, particular situations in time and space.[8]

So 'it is not given to any generation of men to complete the tasks of human improvement and redemption; but no generation is free, either, to desist from them'.[9] Striving for a transcendent justice is therefore, Stone claims, innate but ultimately unobtainable.

The final volume of the trilogy, *Social Dimensions of Law and Justice*, sets up Stone's focus on sociological jurisprudence – the study of law in its application and functioning in a society so as to address conflicting interests. This involves first identifying the various interest groups making claims; second, ascertaining to what degree they should be supported; third, making specific the legal concepts, precepts and mechanisms that can be utilised once these claims have been identified; and finally, identifying any restrictions that impede the law in supporting these interests, of securing them within the system of the law itself. Above all, Stone sought to optimise these elements in the context of freedom of expression, which he suggested should

> 'approach nearer absoluteness than perhaps any other single claim', principally because they are a vital prerequisite to the formulation of human demands, as well as fundamental to the proper development of democratic political institutions.[10]

He went on to argue that only through protection by the law of freedom of expression can human wants and desires be expressed and gain political recognition.[11]

Judgements and illusory reference

Stone used the phrase 'categories of illusory reference' to refer to judgements in which judges claim to have reached their decisions on the basis of some legal proposition under

---

6 Stone 1946, 785.
7 Stone 1946, 546.
8 Stone 1946, 796.
9 Stone 1965, 355.
10 Aroney 2008, 122.
11 Stone 1946, 794.

Figure 5.2 Portrait of Julius Stone, created by Naomi Berns. Reproduced with permission from Naomi Berns.

which consideration of the facts of the case seemed to lead inexorably to a particular conclusion. Such judges suggest that their conclusions have been reached by logical necessity from a legal premise and do not acknowledge the free choice, in the first place, of the premise itself. In this way, the judicial decision to apply a particular premise is obscured by such illusory references, concealing the actual choice made. In contrast, Stone argued for greater transparency in the decisions made by judges, urging them to make explicit their reasons for choosing particular legal premises and for exercising their opportunity to broaden or narrow the precedents in play. Stone identified seven different categories of illusory reference, of which three will be highlighted here. First, the category of 'competing reference', in which a particular set of facts can be considered within two or more legal formulations, each of which have different consequences, leaving it to the discretion of the judge which formulation will be acted on. Second, that of 'the single category of competing versions of reference', in which a single legal rule, with a particular label, has been given subtly different expressions by different judges. In this case, different applications of the rule transpire depending on which version is chosen, although each is under the same label, leaving the choice to the judge's discretion. Third, the category of 'meaningless reference', in which reasonably close attention to the legal rule being used shows that it is without meaning at all as the basis of the decision made.

Stone suggested that these illusory references mask the fact that judges are continually faced with 'leeways of choice', which should be made explicit and, indeed, without which the law would not evolve. The adherence of some judges to legal formalism, a commitment to the literal expression of legal material, is then a subterfuge that hides the reasons for their decisions behind different categories of illusory reference. However, Stone argued, by exercising and making explicit their value choices, together with their reasons for making these choices, the law will become more rather than less rational. Often this will require adjustments of conflicting interests in a value-specific context.

Most judges in Australia after the Second World War held to the declarative theory of the law, in which their role was merely to declare the law within a framework of strict legalism. This was championed at that time by the great Chief Justice Sir Owen Dixon, who strongly supported a form of legal positivism in which, Stone suggested, the evaluative aspects of a judgement are marked by illusory reference. The courts, in particular the High Court, thus failed to address the question of whether a law under consideration could be justified as an appropriate way to reach a legitimate goal. Judges did not, in fact, follow the declarative principle of believing in the bizarre notion that the law had survived unaltered since time immemorial, and that all they had to do was declare it and apply it to the facts of the case at hand. However, they promulgated a view of judicial activity in which no judicial creativity had a hand. Stone argued that the historical facts show that judges do, in fact, make law, although this action is concealed. He appealed to judges to make this explicit in their judgements. It should be emphasised, however, that Stone was not calling for support of judicial whims or unbounded judicial creativity, for he had a strong commitment to the rule of law. Rather, he was calling for the abandonment of 'inscrutable fiat[s] of judgment'[12] used by judges favouring the declarative doctrine.

Stone's influence on judgements

Stone's criticism of legal positivism, influenced by Pound, had a great effect on judges in Australia. After the Second World War, when his great works were widely read in judicial circles, judgements began to be formulated along the lines Stone advocated. This was particularly the case in relation to his criticisms of the declarative theory, such as those manifest in illusory reference, which were taken on board by a new generation of justices, many of whom had been students of Stone's at Sydney University. Even in the area of substantive legal analysis, Stone's influence was felt: in *Dawson v The Queen* even the arch legal formalist Sir Owen Dixon approvingly quoted Stone in relation to 'profound obscurities' of the law,[13] and in *Hall v Braybrook* Justice Kitto quoted Stone in relation to whether the prior convictions of an accused should be made explicit in the special context of the accused having commented on a witness for the prosecution.[14]

The gradual loosening of the ties that judges had to the declaratory principle, as occurred in the 1970s, was accompanied by more frequent quoting of Stone's articles and books, particularly by High Court Justices Murphy and Aickin. In *Jaensch v Coffey*, Justice Deane referred to Stone's criticism of the growth of the law of negligence.[15] Justice Murphy, in *Jackson v Harrison*, noted the 'defects in the concept of duty of care which had been exposed by ... Stone'.[16] In *Gala v Preston*, Justice Toohey confirmed the explanation of how the *ratio decidendi*[17] is found in the court according to the

---

12 Aroney 2008, 133.
13 *Dawson v The Queen* (1961) 106 CLR 1, quoted in Kirby 1997, 243.
14 *Hall v Braybrook* (1956) 95 CLR 620, 657; Kirby 1997, 243.
15 *Jaensch v Coffey* [1984] HCA 52.
16 *Jackson v Harrison* [1978] HCA 17.
17 The point in a case that determines the judgement.

method preferred by Stone.[18] Several of Stone's former students identified difficulties before them as falling into Stone's 'categories of competing reference' (see *Waterford v Commonwealth*)[19] and 'categories of indeterminate reference' (see *McGinty v Western Australia*).[20] The many important judgements decided in the High Court during Sir Anthony Mason's tenure as Chief Justice are understood in light of Stone's jurisprudence, especially the free speech cases in the 1990s. Stone's influence during this period extended not only over legal education and scholarship, but also to the highest practitioners of law in Australia.

Stone's work *Legal Control of International Conflict* came at a time of extraordinary growth in the consensual view of international law – that is, international law based on the consent of the states. Justice Michael Kirby referred to the challenges that Stone offered his students in this area of jurisprudence, challenges that were to become 'abiding interests' in Kirby's life.[21] Indeed, Kirby commented: 'Little did I suspect then that Public International Law would come to be of acute practical importance to me in a number of activities for the United Nations.'[22] One might, in particular, point out Kirby's recent United Nations Commission Report on the appalling treatment of the people of North Korea by the dictatorship there, a report with far-reaching ramifications for the legal responsibility of autocrats and their possible indictment before international courts.

Jurisprudence in the second half of the 20th century

Stone's influence, and, in particular, his criticisms of legal positivism, came to be less recognised following the rejuvenation of the analytical tradition in jurisprudence with the publication of H.L.A. Hart's *The Concept of Law* in Oxford in 1961. This followed in the wake of Ludwig Wittgenstein's influential work *Philosophical Investigations*, published posthumously in 1953. This volume greatly affected Hart, and he placed emphasis on connective analysis of language, in this case touching on justice and the law. Stone dismissed this as simply a 'linguistically-based contribution to jurisprudential study' and as 'derivative or terminological or inconsequential'.[23] One could not find a greater contrast in Stone and Hart's styles of thought than that exemplified in their texts. On the one hand, Stone was an encyclopaedist, bringing together vast amounts of judicial opinion to support a particular view – namely, that of the law as a complex operation embedded in society and facilitating different functions of that society. Hart, on the other hand, working in the tradition of analytical philosophy, wrote an intellectually dense and relatively short book. In so doing, he revived legal positivism, especially through his argument that the power of the law resides in its function of imposing and conferring rules. This is not to say that Stone did not copiously refer in his works to other scholars working in the fields of linguistics, epistemology, logic, etc. However, the theoretical basis of these scholars'

---

18 *Gala v Preston* [1991] HCA 18.
19 *Waterford v The Commonwealth of Australia* [1987] HCA 25.
20 *James Andrew McGinty and Others v The State of Western Australia* [1996] HCA 48.
21 Kirby 1997, 240.
22 Kirby 1997, 240.
23 Quoted in Hutchinson, 'The Province of Jurisprudence'.

Figure 5.3 Caricature of Julius Stone, drawn by Ulf Kaiser. This sketch appeared in *The Australian* in 1992, with a review by Gordon Hawkins of a biography of Julius Stone by Leonie Star. Reproduced with permission from Ulf Kaiser.

work was open to criticism and therefore so were Stone's contributions. Gradually Hart's arguments won the day and those expressed in Stone's three great volumes began to appear outdated. This was accelerated by the publication of Rawls' *Theory of Justice* in 1971, which had an enormous influence and, indeed, shifted the debate to entirely new areas from those contemplated by either Stone or Hart. The debate in relation to considering justice as involving an individual in the context of their social role and the common good is ongoing.

***

Stone dominated the discipline of jurisprudence for more than two decades while a Challis professor at the University of Sydney. During that time, because of the depth of his scholarly work, he moved the emphasis of judgements from strict legalism to consideration of the mores and morals of contemporary society. This had far-reaching consequences, not only for the courts of Australia, but also for international deliberations at this time.

Further Reading

Stone, J. *The Province and Function of Law: Law as Logic, Justice and Social Control – A Study in Jurisprudence*. Sydney: Associated General Publications, 1946.
Stone, J. *Legal System and Lawyers' Reasonings*. Stanford: Stanford University Press, 1964.
Stone, J. *Human Law and Human Justice.* Stanford: Stanford University Press, 1965.
Stone, J. *Social Dimensions of Law and Justice.* Sydney: Maitland Publications, 1966.

Economics

6
Identifying instabilities in financial institutions: Warren Pat Hogan

Professor of Economics (1968–1998). Hogan is recognised for his introduction of quantitative methods and analytical modelling of economic phenomena, which allowed him to establish rigorous criteria for risk management in financial institutions, expose the inadequate foundations of financial policies and identify the need for enhanced regulation of banks, both national and international, without which recession, depression and a Global Financial Crisis like that of 2008 might once more be upon us.

In October 2002, I was asked to give the Sesquicentenary Lecture on behalf of the University at the dinner celebrating its anniversary in MacLaurin Hall, in the Quadrangle. I took advantage of the occasion to ask the then vice-chancellor, Gavin Brown, if he would help me financially with developing the Brain and Mind Research Institute, dedicated to the amelioration of diseases of the brain and mind. He did so handsomely, to the order of several million dollars, but I then needed to raise close to $80 million to complete the project. This required putting in place a foundation of community leaders, who were ultimately successful in acquiring the funding. They were a remarkable group; among them was Warren Hogan, together with a famous previous Chair of the Reserve Bank of Australia, Robert Johnston. I soon realised how true the comment made by Professor Tony Aspromourgos was: 'Hogan had a formidable intellect and an equally formidable personality',[1] both of which he used to great effect in ensuring that funds would be forthcoming for the new institute. But more particularly, I became aware that he held very high ethical standards – a level of integrity that made it clear why, among economists, 'Warren Hogan remains our policy "conscience". This is the mark of a valuable legacy; this is the mark of a great economist'.[2] The importance of Hogan's legacy is emphasised by the 2019 Royal Commission into the management and ethics of our banking system.

Hogan was born in 1929 in Papakura, New Zealand, the second of two sons of Patrick Hogan and Ivy Kate (née Saunders). He went to the University of Auckland, where he acquired a Bachelor of Arts in 1950 and a MA in 1952, at which time he married

---

1 Aspromourgos 2010, 291.
2 Laker 2013.

Figure 6.1 Professor Warren Hogan, taken by the *Newcastle Morning Herald* on 16 December 1952. Newcastle Region Library (104 002132). Reproduced with permission from the City of Newcastle.

fellow economics student Ialene (née Stretton). Hogan's arrival at university in the 1940s was propitious. During the Second World War, the great philosopher Karl Popper took refuge from Nazi Germany with an appointment to the University of Canterbury in New Zealand, where he wrote the monumental work *The Open Society and Its Enemies*. He exerted considerable influence over men of brilliance in New Zealand at that time, such as the future Nobel Prize winning neuroscientist Sir John Eccles and the economist Colin Simkin, both of whom he guided towards optimising quantitative methods in their respective disciplines. Simkin taught Hogan when he was a brilliant undergraduate at the University of Auckland and instilled in him the importance of quantitative economics, a novel commitment in Australasia at a time when economics was largely taught in isolation from quantitative analysis and economic statistics.

After graduating, Hogan spent three years carrying out research at the Reserve Bank of New Zealand, where he produced the first set of balances of foreign payment accounts that followed the recommendations of the International Monetary Fund. His success at the Reserve Bank led to him being awarded a PhD research scholarship at the Australian National University, towards the end of which, in 1959, he was made a lecturer at Newcastle University College. Six years later, he became a professor. This meteoric rise was followed, three years later, by appointment as professor of economics at the University of Sydney, a post he held for 30 years.

Hogan was noted, during his tenure at Sydney University, for the rigour of his analytical and quantitative methods, which inspired many future economists of note, such as the governor of the Reserve Bank of Australia Glenn Stevens. During this time, it could no longer be said that Australia lagged behind in the application of quantitative and statistical methods in economics. Economist John Laker noted that Hogan's

> contributions serve as a continuing challenge to policymakers to seek rigour in their economic analysis, to acknowledge the powerful driving forces in financial markets, efficient or otherwise, and to understand the consequences of policy interventions in the world of the second-best.[3]

Hogan was able to say, towards the end of his academic career, that

> Australia has had the good fortune of an independent agency pronouncing on trade and protection issues. The contributions from professional economists in these developments I judge to have been substantial. Economists brought rigour to the theoretical and empirical analyses of issues, while those close to government had great influence on the ultimate outcomes.[4]

Yet he cautioned that the emphasis on the quantitative might have gone too far:

> The way the mathematisation of economics has gone as well as the statistical aspects has brought a shift in purpose to the study of the discipline. Emphases on technique

---

3   Laker 2013.
4   Lodewijks 2007, 455.

and so on may have been overstated compared with thinking about basic issues. ... Having always been quite a supporter for quantitative economics, I do get worried by the ways in which the mathematics and the statistics can capture individual's attention for the elegance of the instrument itself rather than for wanting to use it for gaining insights ... Yet the greater worry is the failure to attract to economics the type of person whose interests lie in policy and market spheres but is repelled by intellectual and professional rigidities.[5]

Here we trace three principal themes in Hogan's work that illustrate how he applied quantitative methods and modelling to elucidate important principles but refrained from using mathematics when the use of such instruments would only oversimplify complex issues. Hogan's earliest contribution in the theme of government policy, in the late 1960s, provided quantitative techniques for estimating whether a then developing nation like Pakistan was underutilising the productive capacity of its manufacturing industry, a serious question in relation to maximising the use of existing resources in a relatively poor country. Ten years later, Hogan contributed further to this theme, showing that the economic data available to the Australian government at the time of formulating the annual national budget was seriously flawed and introducing the felicitous phrase 'the quicksands of policy making'.[6] This analysis did not require mathematics, but rather a comparison of cleverly conceived tables of data. A second theme that concerned Hogan was the viability of financial institutions: can the risks they take be regulated to improve their stability without making them an unattractive investment? Furthermore, is it possible to predict that a financial institution is likely, at some time in the future, to go bankrupt or at least require considerable restructuring? Hogan produced answers to these questions through astute mathematical modelling. In a final theme, Hogan considered the extent to which financial institutions sought to maximise their profits using methods that avoid regulation and minimise risk by selling it on to larger institutions. Careful probing of the procedures used to achieve these aims required no mathematisation and pointed out the advantages and pitfalls of such approaches, which went unheeded and contributed to the Global Financial Crisis that occurred in 2008, the ramifications of which are still with us.

Government policy

Capacity utilisation

Capacity utilisation is a measure of the extent to which an enterprise, be it a company or a nation, utilises the productive capacity it possesses, compared with what it could achieve if it were fully utilised. Excess productive capacity is a measure of capacity utilisation. Hogan determined the capacity utilisation of the manufacturing industries of Pakistan in 1968, less than 20 years after the nation-state had been founded, and recommended how excess capacity could be righted.[7] The nation's poor capacity utilisation had been

---

5   Lodewijks 2007, 459.
6   Hogan 1979.
7   Hogan 1968.

attributed, up until the time of Hogan's study, to the vicissitudes of aid provided to Pakistan and the low level of foreign exchange, neither of which, he showed, explained the problem. Rather, he identified it as arising from the poor technical and managerial skills of those in administration, their adoption of inappropriate foreign technologies and their misidentification of the skills training necessary in the existing workforce.

Hogan found that a central problem in determining capacity utilisation in Pakistan was the lack of quantitative data needed to provide accurate estimates. The data that was available indicated a significant amount of idle plant. He soon discerned that many industries had developed production capacities that were considerably in excess of the availability of the resources necessary to employ these capacities. This, in turn, could be attributed to the lack of success in promoting the growth of the economy at the national level. The question then had to be considered: is the concept of 'productive capacity' really worthwhile in a developing country like Pakistan, when examining the potential and realised productivity of a sector such as manufacturing? For example, this concept does not take into account value added to a product in the production line, which might be considerable even though the final output is the same and so then is the productive capacity. Hogan argued that further consideration should also be given to heterogeneity in the utilisation of different processes in a plant; it might not be feasible for the output of a particular process to be maximised, so the problem becomes one of obtaining equilibrium between the various processes to maximise their joint capacity. Furthermore, it is generally not possible to equate productive capacity to the technical efficacy of machines, as is possible, for example, with a petroleum refinery. Such engineering measures of capacity, in terms of the ratio of actual output per unit of time to the maximum units machines could produce in that time, might not be appropriate in some industries. Alternatively, an economic measure in which output is measured against the possible increase in output up to the point where the cost of the product begins to rise may be appropriate.

There are militating factors for poor capacity utilisation in Pakistan, such as shortages of imported spare parts and raw materials, incorrect predictions concerning the rate of sales of products, leadin to poor investments, and the poor quality of professional administrative and skilled employees, as noted. All of these factors lead to the expectation that there will be very high levels of excess production capacity in a newly emerging country. A major worry was that the inefficiencies were chronic to the system and not just a transient phenomenon arising from the then relatively recent founding of Pakistan.

Of importance are possible delays in bringing a plant into production, particularly when a country's manufacturing industry is rapidly expanding, as was the case in developing Pakistan. Delays can be caused by, for example, an inadequate electricity supply. Hogan considered that the appearance of excess capacity arising from delays in establishing new plant, especially of a high-tech nature, is of such importance that he developed the idea of apparent excess capacity, expressed in analytical terms as follows:

> With the expansion of manufacturing into the more technologically complex industries the length of time taken to run-in plant is certain to increase. ... This phenomenon will contribute to the *appearance* of excess capacity. And it will be most marked in those sectors where the growth rate is highest. In the simplest case, let m

be the average life of capital, *r* the cumulative rate of growth of gross investment; *I* is annual gross investment, *K* is the gross capital stock, *x* is the period after completion of the investment outlay and before the plant is in full production, so that $x < m$ and *K'* is the gross capital stock embracing only those investments in full operation. Then the position is:

$$I = e^{rt} \tag{1}$$

$$K = \int_{t-m}^{t} I\,dt = \frac{e^{rt}(1 - e^{-rm})}{r} \tag{2}$$

$$K' = \int_{t-m}^{t-x} I\,dt = \frac{e^{rt}(e^{-rx} - e^{-rm})}{r} \tag{3}$$

$$\frac{K'}{K} = \frac{e^{-rx} - e^{-rm}}{1 - e^{-rm}} \tag{4}$$

With $x < m$ and $r > 0$ then $e^{-rx} < 1$. Thus the ratio of the capital in production to the capital 'installed' shown in equation 4 is less than one. And the ratio will diminish with increases in the rate of growth of investment, *r*, and the running-in period, *x*. In Table [6.1] a series of values for this ratio is shown for a range of estimates of the growth of investment, average life and the running-in period. As the rate of growth of gross investment has been high in the manufacturing sector in Pakistan, the values of the ratio applicable in this instance are on the right-hand side of Table [6.1]. Even where the length of the 'running-in' period *x* is short, and in the context of this most simplified hypothesis, the value would probably be between $x = ½$ and $x = 1$. This suggests possibilities for a good measure of apparent excess capacity.[8]

So the extent of unused productive capacity in Pakistan's manufacturing industry due to apparent excess capacity (given by *K'/K* above) is not conclusive. Hogan commented that 'some criticisms of the performance recorded by manufacturing industries in less developed countries may be misplaced if they associate under utilization of productive capacity with shortages of factor inputs'[9] (that is, inputs required to produce an output, such as manufactured goods).

Quicksands of policy making

Hogan emphasised that relatively little attention had been given to the collection of data and the determination of its quality, compared with that given to the development of new models to guide economic policy. He analysed the quality of the information available to policy makers at the time of formulating federal budgets. As he put it,

---

8   Hogan 1968, 42.
9   Hogan 1969, 184.

		Percentage rate of growth of gross investment							
		1	3	5	18	10	13	15	20
x=½	m=10	.9476	.9425	.9373	.9288	.9228	.9135	.9083	.8899
	m=20	.9725	.9670	.9610	.9509	.9436	.9320	.9250	.9068
	m=30	.9808	.9749	.9682	.9569	.9487	.9358	.9279	.9083
x=1	m=10	.8954	.8860	.8761	.8604	.8495	.8324	.8207	.7904
	m=20	.9451	.9345	.9228	.9037	.8942	.8683	.8534	.8153
	m=30	.9616	.9502	.9372	.9154	.9037	.8756	.8591	.8183
x=2	m=10	.7917	.7753	.7582	.7315	.7132	.6853	.6664	.6187
	m=20	.8908	.8709	.8495	.8147	.7904	.7527	.7272	.6642
	m=30	.9236	.9019	.8775	.8374	.8092	.7663	.7379	.6695
x=3	m=10	.6895	.6679	.6460	.6125	.5900	.5561	.5336	.4782
	m=20	.8370	.8092	.7796	.7327	.7003	.6512	.6186	.5404
	m=30	.8859	.8550	.8207	.7653	.7272	.6704	.6336	.5477

Table 6.1 Ratio of 'used' to 'installed' capital = K'/K. From W.P. Hogan, 'Capacity Creation and Utilisation in Pakistan Manufacturing Industry,' *Australian Economic Papers* 7, no. 10 (1968), published by John Wiley and Sons Australia Ltd. © Flinders University and University of Adelaide and John Wiley & Sons Australia Ltd.

> The concern is not with an analysis of what might have been, given all the advantages of hindsight ... Those responsible for major decisions cannot enjoy any scope for 'jobbling backwards'.[10]

What information was available at the time decisions were made? How good was, and is, that information?

With these questions in mind, Hogan examined the quality of the data available on domestic economic performance in Australia around five months before the announcement of the budget. He analysed the annual growth of non-farm gross domestic product (GDP) from 1969–70 to 1977–78 based on the June quarter prior to the budget in the fiscal year when the budget was brought down (see Table 6.2). This table also gives the estimates for the GDP in the particular fiscal year of interest one year and two years later, as well as several years later, as indicated by the columns. In so doing the table reveals the directions taken by the economy, with very interesting repercussions. There are dramatic differences in evaluation of the GDP and the pre-budget quarter as data improves for a particular fiscal year over the time. Hogan pointed out that the decline in GDP predicted at the time of the 1971–72 budget (2.87 per cent, compared with 4.41

---

10 Hogan 1979, 384.

	Initial estimates (1)	Estimates provided 1 year later (2)	Estimates provided 2 years later (3)	Latest available estimates (4)
1969–70	6.85	6.85†	6.99	7.19
1970–71	4.41	4.53	4.46	4.83
1971–72	2.87	2.89	3.71	3.95
1972–73	5.22	5.58	6.42	6.29
1973–74	5.46	5.69	5.95	5.94
1974–75	−2.62	−1.17	−0.15	0.14‡
1975–76	0.82	1.96	2.43*	2.41*
1976–77	3.53	4.23*	–	3.85*
1977–78	1.80*	–	–	1.86*

Table 6.2 Rate of growth of real non-farm gross domestic product (per cent). From W.P. Hogan, 'Quicksands of Policy Making,' *Australian Economic Papers* 18, no. 33 (1979), published by John Wiley and Sons Australia Ltd. © Flinders University and University of Adelaide and John Wiley and Sons Australia Ltd.

† Constant price estimates were published initially for June quarter 1971 on a 1966–67 base. Hence the estimates for 1970–71 are listed as the same in columns 1 and 2.

* Based upon the revised 1974–75 constant price base.

‡ Constant 1974–75 price series appears to show a rise of 1.04 per cent; linking problems between the old and new series suggest a need for caution when interpretting that calculation.

per cent in the previous fiscal year) turned out to have been grossly exaggerated; the latest available estimate for the 1971–72 fiscal year was 3.95 per cent, more than one percentage point greater than the initial estimate. The predicted GDP of −2.62 per cent for the 1974–75 budget, an historically very severe decline compared with the 1973–74 initial estimates of 5.46 per cent, was actually much milder, at 0.14 per cent, as the latest available estimate shows (Table 6.2), amounting to only a minor stagnation.

Indeed, a glance at Table 6.2 shows that there was consistent failure to gauge the gains in the economy for each of the nine fiscal years considered, particularly 1974–75. Hogan commented: 'The extent of these adaptations is startling; all too clearly the foundations of measurement are based upon shifting sands.'[11] The unreliability of the initial estimates, which, in most cases, do not predict the outcome in later years and so do not reflect the real gains in the economy, has considerable implications for policies involving determinations of employment, productivity estimates and economic activity. The table shows that consideration should be given to the economic data in the context of the time at which it was gathered, or, as Hogan put it,

---

11   Hogan 1979, 385.

the application of economic policies has to be taken in the context of the time as it is then perceived. What is clear is the uncertainty as to what has taken place in the economy during immediate past quarters and the even greater uncertainty as to what the position is at the time critical policy measures are being explored and then determined.[12]

Hogan observed a very interesting trend in revisions of the kind given in Table 6.2 over 10 to 13 quarterly measures of non-farm GDP, following the initial estimates. Figure 6.2 shows the estimates for successive March quarters and indicates that in most cases there is a downward movement in the first revisions, followed by an upward movement in later revisions of the initial estimates, giving U-shaped curves. Whether the series of revisions of the initial estimates will reach a steady state cannot be predicted from either the average or the latest revisions. Such an inconclusive determination leaves the economic policy maker in a quandary as to exactly what econometric model will be useful, given the inherent unreliability of economic data available at the time of preparation of the budget. The implications of these difficulties in determining the real rate of growth for planning for employment expansion, the cost of wages versus that of capital equipment and the cost of wages as a share of GDP are evident.

Identifying and reducing risk in financial institutions

In his 2013 Hogan Memorial Lecture, John Laker talked about the 'attributes and insights of a great economist, and his enduring contributions to academia and public policy'.[13] He went on: 'Hogan had a clear conceptual framework for analysing arguments for financial regulation, whether through direct controls or prudential regulation.'[14] With regard to banking regulation, Hogan's first major contribution was to assess 'the impact of two periods of major change in the regulatory environment – an easing of direct controls in late 1960 and a substantial re-tightening in mid-1975'.[15] He 'found that bank risk fell when regulation was applied more intensively'.[16] As regards prudential controls, Hogan noted that the adoption of a more formal prudential supervisory framework by the Reserve Bank of Australia in the mid-1980s was not accompanied by a reasoned account supporting such controls. In particular, the central concerns of protecting small depositors and providing payment services were misplaced, especially given that such transactional services were, by then, provided by other financial institutions. Instead, Hogan argued that prudential control should concentrate on three issues: first, the role of the Reserve Bank of Australia as a lender of last resort in order to guarantee the stability of the banking system; second, that banks provide sufficient information for the market to make judgements on their performance, leading to the introduction of some form of discipline in the banking system; and finally, that the best way of protecting small depositors involves developing

---

12 Hogan 1979, 389.
13 Laker 2013.
14 Laker 2013.
15 Laker 2013.
16 Laker 2013.

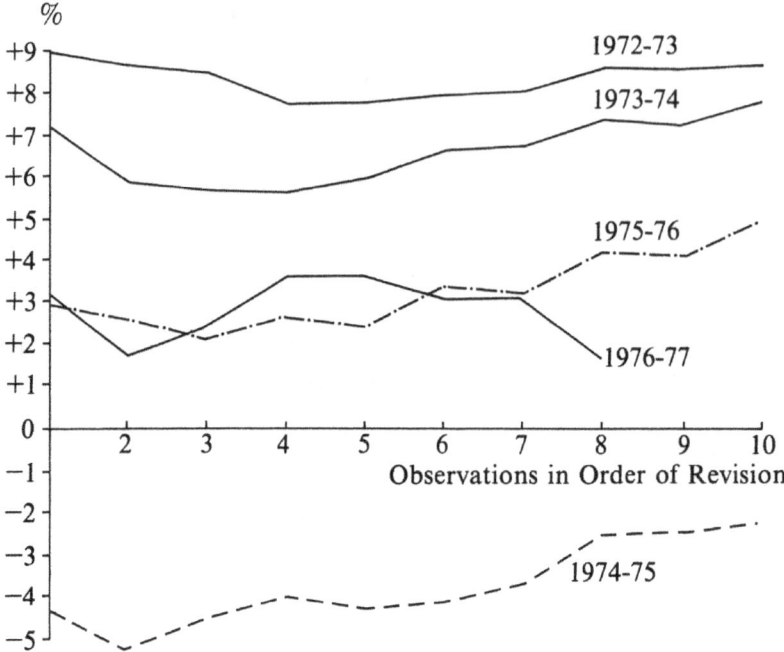

Figure 6.2 Annual growth of real non-farm GDP, seasonally adjusted, March quarter. From W.P. Hogan, 'Quicksands of Policy Making,' *Australian Economic Papers* 18, no. 33 (1979): 385, published by John Wiley and Sons Australia Ltd. © Flinders University and University of Adelaide and John Wiley and Sons Australia Ltd.

an insurance scheme that offers a limited deposit guarantee. Hogan used quantitative arguments to establish that increased bank regulation can reduce risk and that evaluation of a bank's performance over time by the market provides a good indication of the bank's viability.

Capital adequacy

Capital adequacy refers to the minimum amount of capital that a bank or other financial institution must retain, as determined by a financial regulator, in order to ensure that the bank or institution does not enter into excessive leverage that could lead to it becoming insolvent. 'Capital requirements' are often confused with 'reserve requirements' (the proportion of an institution's assets that must be held as liquid assets or cash). In this context, Hogan and Ian Sharpe from UNSW examined the effects on banks of changes in the minimum percentage of all deposit accounts that they were required to hold as cash (the Statutory Reserve Deposit or SRD). Increases in SRD over 20 years were shown to result in decreases in returns to shareholders of banks, whereas decreases in SRD increased their returns. So changes in SRD policy act indirectly as a tax on shareholders or as a subsidy.

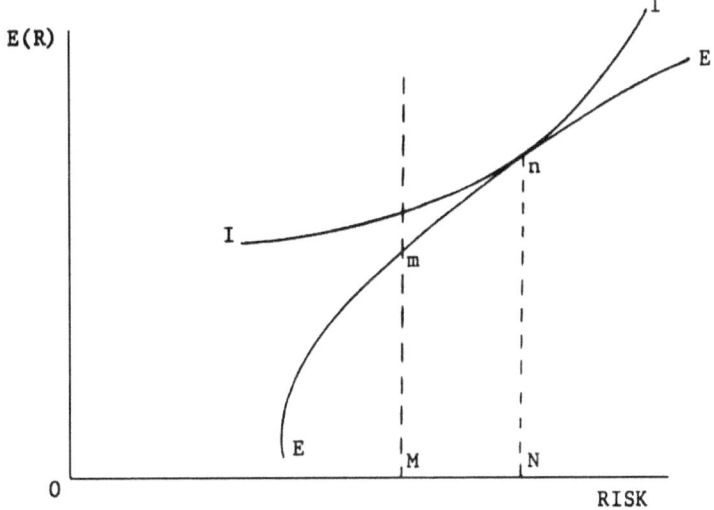

Figure 6.3 Risk aversion graph A. From W.P. Hogan and I.G. Sharpe, 'Regulation, Risk and the Pricing of Australian Bank Shares 1957–1976,' *Economic Record* 60, no. 1 (1984), published by John Wiley and Sons Ltd. © The Economic Society of Australia.

Systematic risk

What are the risks associated with sudden changes in banking regulation, such as the relaxation of regulations in Australia in November 1960 and the re-introduction of controls in July 1975? Hogan and Sharpe showed that there was a substantial increase in systematic risk following the 1960 relaxation and a decrease in such risk following the re-introduction in 1975.[17] So regulation reduces risk. In developing this theme they considered the scenario illustrated in Figure 6.3. Here are graphed a bank's efficient portfolio opportunities against risk (that is, the highest returns for a defined level of risk, given by the *EE* curve on the graph), as well as the expected returns on the portfolio against risk (given by the *II* curve), which naturally increase sharply with risk. The two curves cross at point *n*, which gives the optimal expected returns – that is, the return is maximised and the risk minimised. However, the regulatory authority might consider the risk at *N* far too high and require the institution to work within the risk to the left of *M*.

The institution may be able to avoid the uncertainty of risk by exerting market power, as illustrated in Figure 6.4. *EcEc* and *IcIc* in Figure 6.4 are the same as *EE* and *II* in Figure 6.3, but an *EmEm* curve is introduced in Figure 6.4. This curve provides for the market power of the firm and thus lies above the *EcEc* curve, reflecting the high returns for such a firm, above those of competitors that do not have such power. The steeper slope of *ImIm*, compared with that of *IcIc*, reflects the risk aversion of a firm with a large market share

---

17 Hogan and Sharpe 1984.

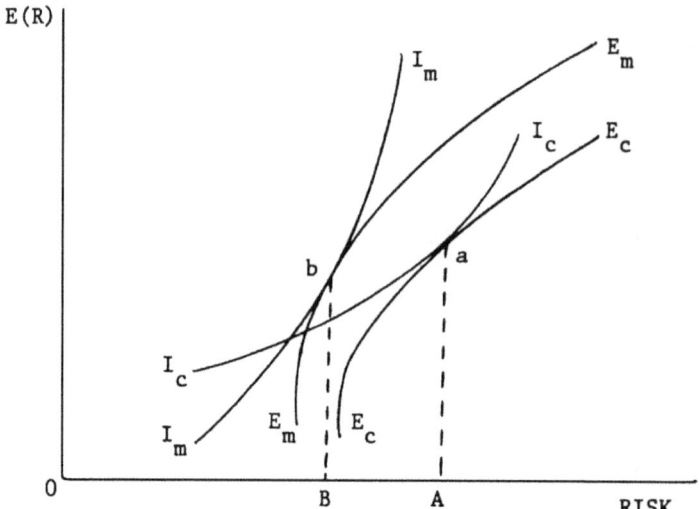

Figure 6.4 Risk aversion graph B. From W.P. Hogan and I.G. Sharpe, 'Regulation, Risk and the Pricing of Australian Bank Shares 1957–1976,' *Economic Record* 60, no. 1 (1984), published by John Wiley and Sons Ltd. © The Economic Society of Australia.

– that is, with major market power. The optimal portfolio of such a firm may then have lower risk for the same anticipated profit as a firm without such market power.

These graphs show that market power confers on a company reduced risk for the same level of profits as a company without such power. So if regulatory restraints on bank competition are lessened, there may be increased systematic risk in the banking sector. However, the opposite may be the case in some circumstances. For example, if the regulatory authority exerts direct banking controls over portfolios that may be held or places limitations on interest rates for deposits, there may be abrupt changes in the extent of deposits in banks and other financial institutions, causing instability and increased risk. Other effects of such regulatory control may include inefficient investment by banks in enlarging their numbers of branches. All in all, changes in a bank's risk–expected return curve (*II* in Figure 6.3) compared with their efficient portfolio opportunities (*EE* in Figure 6.3) may place the bank in a higher risk regime.

These considerations indicate the complexity of determining the relationship between regulation and risk, which can only be untangled by a quantitative analysis that Hogan and Sharpe supplied.[18] They first defined a measure of systematic bank risk as β_{it}, given in equation 1 as

$$\beta_{it} = \hat{a}_i + \beta_i RM_t + \hat{e}_{it} \qquad (1)$$

---

18 Hogan and Sharpe 1984, 38–41.

where RM_t is the return on the market portfolio during a period t, $â_i$ is a constant and $ê_{it}$ is a normally distributed error term with an expected value of zero. A dummy variable technique is then used to determine whether considerable changes in β – that is, in systematic risk – are related to regulatory change. A dummy variable (D) is one that takes on a value of zero or one to allow for a categorical change that would be anticipated to change the results. The introduction of dummy variables into the equations allows for determination of the degree to which β changes with particular regulatory changes (see Table 6.3).

The effects of the regulatory changes in November 1960 and July 1975 on systematic risk (β) are then analysed; the results given in Table 6.3. For the 1960 change, the dummy variables D_1 and D_2 are used in relation to equation 1, where R_i is the return of the bank i, as follows:

$$R_i = c + \left(\beta + D_1 \gamma_1 + D_2 \gamma_2 \right) RM \qquad (2)$$

$$R_i = c + \beta RM + RMD_1 \gamma_1 + RMD_2 \gamma_2 \qquad (3)$$

D_1 here and in Table 6.3 takes on a value of one from 1960(10; i.e. October) to 1972(02; i.e. February) and zero otherwise. D_2 equals one from 1959(10) to 1960(10) and zero otherwise, and is introduced to allow for a measure of the very severe banking controls over the period from 1959(10) to 1960(10) and their implications for systematic risk. It follows that for the period from 1957(02) to 1959(09), systematic risk is $(\beta + \gamma_1)$. For 1959(10) to 1960(10), systematic risk is $(\beta + \gamma_1 + \gamma_2)$. For 1960(11) to 1964(12), systematic risk is β.

Table 6.3 shows that γ_1 indicated increased systematic risk in relation to the deregulated circumstances of 1960(11) to 1964(12), following the introduction of this environment in November 1960. The regulatory controls were stricter from 1959(10) to 1960(10), requiring the introduction of a dummy variable D_2 with coefficient γ_2, as already noted. Determination of the values of γ_2 and γ_1 shows that systematic risk during this period $(\beta + \gamma_1 + \gamma_2)$ was relatively small, indicating a decrease in systematic risk with the introduction of regulatory controls. Table 6.3 then shows that there is an inverse relationship between systematic risk in banks and the extent of regulatory control, a very important principle for the stability of the banking sector. But to what extent can one arrive at a quantitative measure of the likelihood of instability occurring?

Stability and failure

Examination systems for banks and financial intermediaries attempt to ascertain problems that may lead to insolvency using a study of different components of each institution's activities. Such reviews normally involve analysis and judgements concerning the institution's liquidity, capital adequacy, management quality and structure. But ascertaining these, primarily using accountancy-based practices, does not generally reveal the institution's market value. An alternative approach is to analyse market information as a pointer to potential failure – a then controversial idea that Hogan and his colleagues attempted to place on a firm foundation, at least for Australian financial conditions.[19] Their work showed that a financial institution's share market returns over time provide a good

---

[19] Hogan and Sharpe 1988.

indication of abnormal performance indicative of possible failure, or at least of the need for restructuring. This can be observed empirically using a 'backward cumulative abnormal return series' (see Appendix).[20]

Hogan and his colleagues identified six financial institutions in Australia, among the 329 listed on the Sydney stock exchange, that either failed or required re-organisation between 1965 and 1980. Figure 6.5 gives the results for these six institutions, together with 90 per cent confidence intervals for a one-tailed test of the null hypothesis that the cumulative standard (backward) abnormal return (CSAR; see Appendix) series is significantly negative. A large, near vertical increase or decrease in the plot in Figure 6.5 for one of the six institutions indicates that a large negative or positive return occurred in that month. The figure also shows that if a relatively short period of six months is taken for the backward cumulation, then four of the six institutions that failed show statistically abnormal (negative) returns. However, none are significantly abnormal if the horizon timeline is extended to 24 months.

The most likely explanation for the lack of a significant negative CSAR for the Bank of Adelaide, one of the institutions that was re-organised, is that the perception of investors (the public) was that they would be bailed out by the government if the trading bank failed. No explanation is forthcoming as to why another failed institution, Associated Securities, did not show a negative CSAR. Nevertheless, with four out of the six failures clearly showing significant negative CSARs, and a plausible explanation as to why the fifth did not, there is a clear case for tracking the CSAR of financial institutions over time as part of the system in place for regular examination of banks and financial intermediaries.

Prudential themes

Prudential supervision refers to the regulation of financial enterprises or entities in order to contain risk and ensure appropriate capital is held. In Australia, since 1998, this has been carried out by the Australian Prudential Regulation Authority (APRA). However, at the time Hogan and Sharpe[21] provided their insights into prudential supervision it was largely carried out by the Reserve Bank of Australia (RBA), together with the Australian Financial Institutions Commission (AFIC) and the Insurance and Superannuation Commission (ISC). The analysis of the regulatory framework and procedures used by examiners of financial institutions offered by Hogan and Sharpe is now applicable to APRA.

Hogan and Sharpe's main objective was to clarify, criticise and make recommendations concerning the supervision of Australian banks. They concluded that there was 'a lack of clarity in specifying effective means to secure the main objectives of prudential regulation, especially system stability' and that 'banking legislation is not attuned to contemporary arrangements in the financial services sector'.[22] This was especially concerning in relation to possible runs on banks, and the availability of suitable and comprehensive information on a bank's financial state and the policies followed by its directors. Hogan and Sharpe stressed the need for quality information that would allow markets to make judgements on a bank's performance and risk management.

---

20   Hogan and Sharpe 1988, 45–50.
21   Hogan and Sharpe 1990.
22   Hogan and Sharpe 1990, 143.

Reg. #	Sample	Dependent variable	Independent variables							R^{-2}	D-W	S.E.E.
			Constant	RM	D1.RM	D2.RM	D3.RM	D4.RM	D5.RM			
1	1957(02)–1964(12)	R Bank	.0024 (.84)+	1.082 (8.43)	−.462 (2.48)	−.503 (2.18)				.456	1.94	.024
2	1957(02)–1964(12)	R Finance	−.0034 (1.01)	1.299 (8.62)	−.132 (.54)	−.240 (.82)			.987 (2.93)	.613	2.07	.029
3	1957(02)–*1964(12)	R Bank	.0054 (1.69)	1.050 (8.00)	−.495 (2.60)					.460	2.09	.025
4	1970(01)–1976(12)	R Bank	.0037 (.85)	1.092 (7.61)			.677 (3.59)	−.487 (2.01)		.774	1.96	.038
5	1970(01)–1976(12)	R Finance	.0005 (.10)	1.267 (8.16)			372 (1.82)	−.077 (.29)		.754	1.86	.041

Table 6.3 Systematic risk: banking and finance industries. From W.P. Hogan and I.G. Sharpe, 'Regulation, Risk and the Pricing of Australian Bank Shares 1957–1976,' *Economic Record* 60, no. 1 (1984), published by John Wiley and Sons Ltd. © The Economic Society of Australia.

+ *t* statistics in parentheses.
* Sample excludes 1959(10)–1960(10).

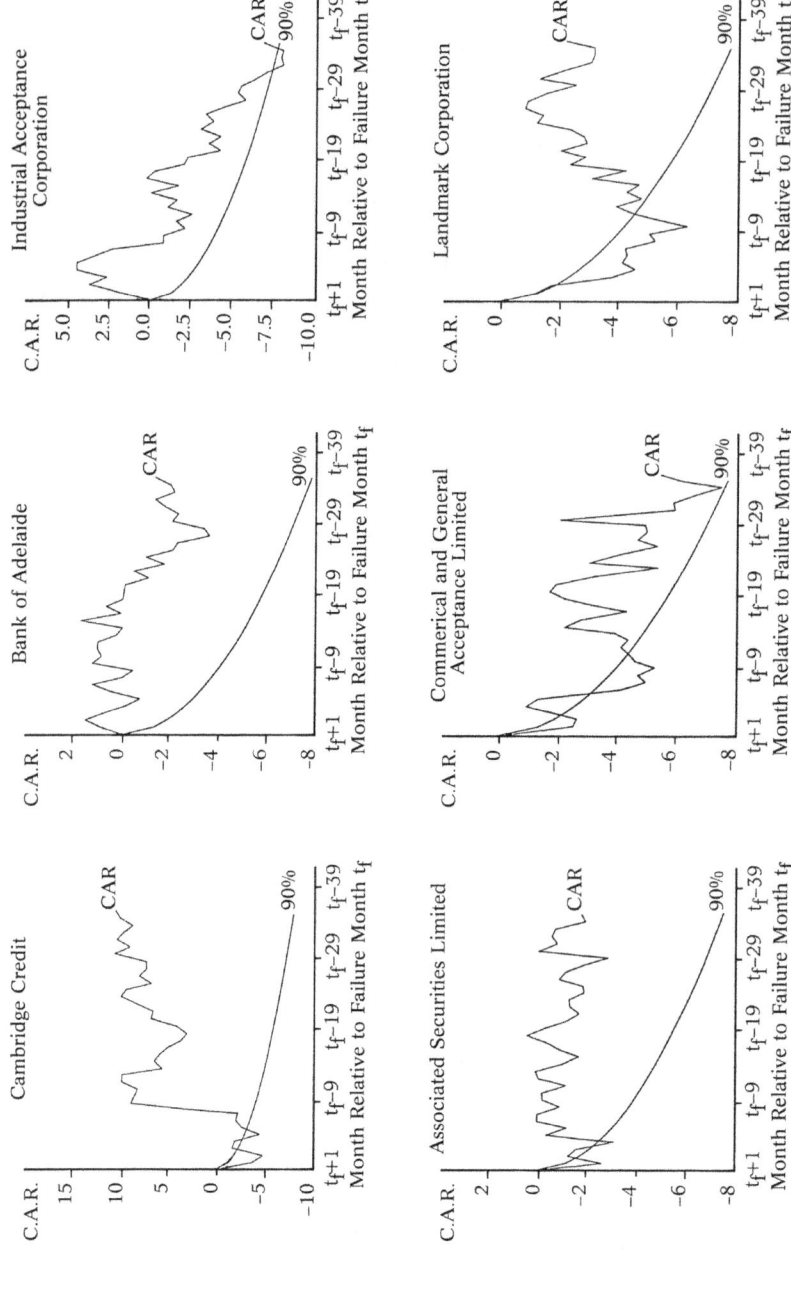

Figure 6.5 Cumulative abnormal returns (CAR) – individual companies. From W.P. Hogan and I.G. Sharpe, 'Market Information and Potential Insolvency of Australian Financial Institutions,' *Australian Economic Papers* 27, no. 50 (1988), published by John Wiley and Sons Australia Ltd. © Flinders University and University of Adelaide and John Wiley and Sons Australia Ltd.

They identified certain key issues for prudential supervision that should be enacted in any new legislation, and emphasised that new legislation should have as its key priority the stability of the banking system and not the protection of depositors. In contrast, the chairman of the Reserve Bank of Australia, R.A. Johnston, stated that the objective of prudential supervision 'is particularly to maintain ... the stability of the financial system as a whole and to protect the interests of bank depositors'.[23] Later, Johnston stated,

> the special status of banks, as institutions which provide the community with important payment services and are safe havens for small investors is warranted and must be supported – but not underwritten – by a system of prudential supervision.[24]

However, Hogan and Sharpe argued that the view that banks uniquely provided transaction services through deposits was misplaced.[25] The claim that prudential supervision has a major role in protecting small investors and depositors is not supported, whereas the importance of stability is clear. The failure of one bank can lead to runs and withdrawals of cash from other banks, and the transfer of deposits to perceived stronger banks, leading to severe instability in the sector.

The main role of the central bank, they argued, is to limit such instabilities, which endanger the whole sector. To this end, two regulatory strategies were recommended. First, the removal of cash from the banking system must be offset by the injection of liquidity into the system through, for example, providing loans as a lender of last resort. Second, depositors must be provided with a guarantee against certain forms of loss if a bank becomes insolvent. Ideally, the availability of appropriate information to determine the extent of a bank's exposure to risk, together with relatively inexpensive transactions so as to diversify portfolios, allows markets to make appropriate evaluations and adjustments. However, the poor availability of such information and the high cost of transactions restricts accurate evaluations by investors, as well as the affordability of transactions for those that are relatively poor.

Hogan and Sharpe suggested that the following should be implemented in any new legislation. First, 'the proposed amendments to the Banking Act should target prudential policy to the objective of maintaining the stability of the banking system, rather than on depositor protection.';[26] this requires streamlining information and improving its accessibility, as well as removing the complexities introduced by the high cost of transactions. Second, penalties for noncompliance with the regulations should be scaled against the size of the offending bank. Third, sophisticated analysis of the extent to which a bank is exposed to risk, with concomitant capital requirements, should be spelt out. Fourth, the cost of depositor protection should be related to the risk taken by the bank; if these are not explicitly related then banks will be tempted to take increased risks without invoking such cost, which becomes a moral hazard problem. Finally, an appropriate policy for the closure of banks should be implemented, given the considerable seriousness of market perceptions of the extent of risk that a bank may accrue before

---

23 Johnston 1985, 7.
24 Johnston 1986, 5.
25 Hogan and Sharpe 1990.
26 Hogan and Sharpe 1990, 130.

such action is taken. This involves determining the net worth of a bank through market value accounting methods, which should be part of any monitoring mechanism; allied to this, an objective threshold should be determined at which closure or reconstruction is implemented before a bank's market value reaches zero. It was widely recognised that new legislation implementing these suggestions would make a major contribution to identifying and reducing risk in financial institutions.

The consequences of avoiding financial regulation and selling off risk

The final theme in the life's work of this great economist is very topical; it touches on financial procedures or instruments that were devised to pass on risk between banks, and how banks and other financial institutions developed schemes whereby they could largely bypass the control of local regulatory authorities, at least for international transactions. These initiatives are now taken to have played a significant role in the Global Financial Crisis that unfolded so dramatically in 2008. This crisis narrowly avoided developing into another Great Depression (the Great Depression lasted for more than a decade, from 1929, and caused great hardship for much of humanity). Hogan and Ivor Frank Pearce first examined, some decades before the GFC, the relatively regulatory-free environment created by the development and use of what became known as the Eurodollar, and identified the risks associated with it.[27] Later, Hogan and his colleague Jonathan Batten from the University of Western Sydney gave prescient warnings concerning the more recent and spectacular rise of an instrument called credit derivatives, by which a financial institution could apparently avoid risk – an instrument that has had a spectacular fall following the GFC.[28]

The Incredible Eurodollar

Following the Bretton Woods Economic Agreement between nation-states, presided over by the economic genius Maynard Keynes after the ruinous circumstances of the Great Depression and the Second World War, the exchange rates of national currencies were pegged to the United States dollar. The US dollar, in turn, was fixed to the price of gold, at the value of 35 US dollars per ounce. Adjustments of exchange rates were under the guidance of the International Monetary Fund (IMF). This system held for some 25 years, until the early 1970s, when the US abandoned pegging its currency to gold and other nations started floating their currencies against the US dollar. Another concept that grew rapidly around this time was the Eurodollar, the name given to deposits in banks outside of the US that are denominated in US dollars and so do not fall under the regulatory authority of the Federal Reserve, placing them in a relatively regulatory-free environment. Trade in Eurodollars began in the 1950s, when countries wished to obtain greater interest rates on their dollar reserves in the US and so sought out European banks that would pay higher interest if the dollars were deposited with them. Such banks, in turn, sought customers that wished to borrow such dollars at a higher interest rate. They were successful in doing

---

27 Hogan and Pearce 1982.
28 Batten and Hogan 2002.

so, establishing the Eurodollar as a currency in global finance. European banks borrowed funds held in New York and lent them to European companies involved in foreign trade with conversion of these US dollars to the local currency of the nation in which the company was located, thus avoiding foreign exchange regulations by the supervising national authorities. The rate of growth of the Eurodollar is indicated by the fact that the Bank of International Settlements, owned by over 60 central banks in different countries, held about two trillion US dollars in 1984; by 2011 the holding had grown to about 32 trillion US dollars, indicating an enormous increase in the comparatively unregulated market of the Eurodollar.

In their book *The Incredible Eurodollar*, Hogan and Pearce set out how the Eurodollar market operated. The book is primarily concerned with the role of financial institutions mediating between borrowers and savers at the international level – that is, between countries. They state that 'financial intermediaries live upon imbalances'[29] and, in so doing at the international level, decrease the pressure on individual countries to make adjustments for imbalances in their current accounts. That is, such intermediaries facilitate the transfer of funds from savers to borrowers, as well as the reverse. In this scheme, savers believe they have the security of a very large global bank, which they assume makes their money safe, even though they have no knowledge of the borrower or, indeed, of the regulatory regime of the country in which the borrower resides. Hogan and Pearce contradict this assumption and emphasise that, unlike local currency transactions, those involving Eurodollars do not have support from a lender of last resort. Eurobanks, at the time, could access marks or francs or pounds from their respective national banks, but in times of crisis there was no guarantee that these currencies could easily be exchanged for US dollars. This limitation was central to the unfolding of the Global Financial Crisis in 2008. The need to borrow dollars to support US dollar denominated holdings in Europe drove applications to central banks for such funding. These banks then had to enter into agreements with the US Federal Reserve to exchange local currencies for US dollars. But in a time of crisis such swaps might not be readily forthcoming. In 1982, *The Incredible Eurodollar* warned of the possibility of a crisis – one which indeed unfolded some 25 years later – pointing out how financing between different national entities could produce financial chaos. However, it did not pinpoint the extent to which a high-deficit country could both instigate major risk and export it to other countries, as was the case with the US.

Hogan and Pearce concluded that lending nations must have saved what they lend, for giving away printed money that has not been secured by goods will not work in the long run (it cheats everybody). What is lent is ultimately goods not money. When the lender seeks underwriting, this should be in the form of long-term bonds and not liquidity. On the other hand, the borrower must plan over time to generate trade surpluses to pay the debt. Given this is the case, the means should be promoted by which balances are restored in real trade and the 'newly discovered liquidity-creating machinery', involving the recycling of funds 'which have already been spent so that they might be spent again' (a procedure that brings joy to politicians, who plan in their national budgets to provide more to the community than the community can itself produce), is abolished.[30] Hogan and

---

29 Hogan and Pearce 1982, 60.

Pearce point out that the very large increase in the price of crude oil in the 1980s forced many European and other countries into a balance-of-payments crisis, which Eurobanks accommodated. This meant that these international lenders accumulated high levels of debt, which was concentrated in just a few countries, leading to very considerable risk.

Hogan and Pearce emphasised that the financial intermediaries involved in Eurodollar transactions carry not only the usual risks associated with particular portfolios, but also the fluctuating activities of the foreign exchange markets. They were prescient in pointing out that liquefying deposits in such intermediaries can only occur if there is already access to US dollars through exchange with the currency of the intermediary. Any run on this exchange might be met with resistance, leading to sudden changes in exchange rates and even failure of the conversion to take place, a central theme in the Global Financial Crisis of 2008. There is no alternative to the requirement of a stable reserve currency, which is entirely missing in the mostly regulatory-free environment of the Eurodollar. In this regard, Hogan and Pearce quoted the 1949 annual report of the Bundesbank:

> Pressures to diversify foreign exchange holdings will probably not ease until the United States durably succeeds in achieving better equilibrium in its balance of payments – the principal source of international liquidity in the past – and in stabilising the dollar in the foreign exchange markets so as to make it sufficiently attractive for investable funds again.[31]

This has still not occurred. Glenn Stevens, former governor of the Reserve Bank of Australia, summarised his perspective with the sage comment that

> in Hogan and Pearce's book, financial institutions and their behaviour were seen as central to the build-up of imbalances. But they are in one sense merely facilitating flows of capital that are reflective of other phenomena, resulting from the collective behaviour of the actors in surplus and deficit countries.[32]

So the development of suitable regulatory guidance for financial institutions is important, but attempting to understand their behaviour and other elements in the 'real economy' is crucial.

Credit derivatives

Credit risk occurs when a borrower's ability to pay off debt declines. This is reflected in the fact that the borrower is then required to pay more if the old contract is up for renewal or further funding is negotiated. Concomitantly, the lender will be exposed to higher risk for the same financial benefit, as well as a decline in the quality of their asset portfolio. Credit derivatives are a means of managing the risk associated with asset portfolios through the use, for example, of credit default swaps to transfer risk. They exist as financial contracts, most of which involve three parties – a borrowing party, a lender,

---

30 Hogan and Pearce 1982, 11.
31 Hogan and Pearce 1982, 104.
32 Stevens 2011.

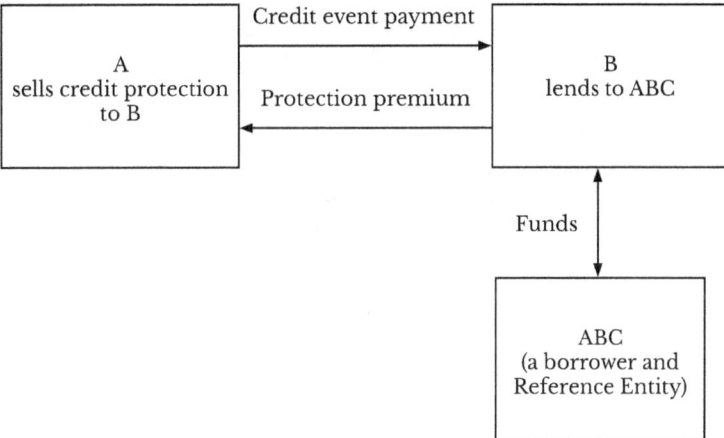

Figure 6.6 Credit default swap. This figure illustrates the relationships between counterparties in a credit (default) swap. Initially, B (a bank) lends to ABC (a corporation). Later, B decides to buy protection against credit risk from A (typically A is an investment style bank). In the event of default or another specified credit event, then A (the seller) pays B (the buyer) the credit event payment (the principal less recovery costs). Reprinted from Batten and Hogan 2002, with permission from Elsevier.

which is usually a bank, and a seller of protection (see Figure 6.6). Thus, a credit default swap is a means (or 'instrument') by which a bank lending to an organisation can decrease or eliminate the loan's credit risk.

Credit derivatives, such as credit default swaps, offer a means of preserving the quality of the portfolio and reducing risk (see Figure 6.6). In the past, the classical methods of managing risk were for a bank (*B*) to retain sufficient levels of capital in reserves or equities to meet losses by customers (*ABC*s), and to make sure that such loans were of a suitable size and number to ensure diversification over many *ABC*s. The first method requires that certain amounts of capital be held in a non-productive capacity, a problem that could be solved with the introduction of credit derivatives. Another important advantage of credit derivatives is that they provide a highly flexible means of alleviating risk associated with concentration in the loan portfolio. If *B* believes there is excessive concentration in its loan portfolio, credit default swaps allow it to buy protection (from a seller of protection, *A*) to effectively sell off the credit risk due to such concentration.

Hogan and his colleague Jonathan Batten offered the following example (see Figure 6.6): *B* wishes to acquire protection from *A* for its loan to organisation *ABC*.[33] The cost of buying this protection is set with respect to what is called a reference asset, which might be the value of a market bond. Lender *B*, the protection buyer, pays a quarterly fee to the

---

33   Batten and Hogan 2002.

protection seller, *A*, at an interest rate expressed in basis points (each basis point equals 0.01 per cent interest), which might be regarded as payment of a premium to maintain the protection, with larger premiums being paid by smaller companies. If the reference bond defaults, the protection seller pays the value of the bond to the buyer of the protection and the buyer transfers ownership of the bond to the seller, as spelt out in Figure 6.6.

If *B* has put up poor assets (of *ABC*) for a credit default swap, then a higher fee will be charged by *A*. A number of specific 'events' may be stated in the contract for determining the threshold at which payment from A to B takes place; for example, if the bond fell by 15 per cent. The sum of this payment would be reduced by the recovery value of selling the assets for which the protection was purchased. Specifying an 'event' that triggers payment from A to B is critically important for the success and stability of credit derivative markets. Of importance to B, the credit default swap allows B to move the risk from its asset portfolio, so that it is no longer on the bank's books. Not only is credit risk removed from the bank's books, its capital requirements are also reduced. Batten and Hogan pointed out that at the time of writing their paper, in 2002, an

> absence of a commonly shared interpretation of what constitutes an event, or sets of events, impair[ed] the transferability of financial instruments in an over-the-counter market and inhibit[ed] the inauguration of exchange-traded activities.[34]

Some of these 'events' may be identified, such as bankruptcy (in which ABC is unable to pay its debts) or a downgrade in credit rating.

Thus, credit derivatives provide a means of transferring credit risk involved in loans in such a way that the risk can be managed separately from the loan and, indeed, traded independently of the original asset owner. They allow the management of liquidity in asset portfolios, as well as of the risk involved in the concentration of portfolio assets. As noted, Batten and Hogan warned that there are regulatory concerns about credit derivatives, particularly their risk management and pricing. Concerns were also highlighted around the paucity of information provided to the original borrower (*ABC*) regarding the extent to which their credit risk had been passed on by the lender (*B*). A key question at this time is to what extent did these credit derivatives contribute to the Global Financial Crisis of 2008? Ten years later, it is still not clear what role derivatives, such as credit default swaps, played in this crisis.[35] There is an evident need for ongoing analytical untangling, of the kind pioneered in Australia by Hogan, of the processes in play between financial institutions, both national and international.

***

When Hogan was asked to identify the central issue involved in the maintenance of stability and efficiency in financial markets, he did not emphasise quantitative methods, as might be expected, but ethics. Towards the end of his life, he commented that 'matters of personal and professional integrity are vital.'[36] He went on to say:

---

34   Batten and Hogan 2002, 261.
35   Gil, Gonzalez, Agra and Santomil 2015.

However effective internal systems are for checking conduct, if a person is sufficiently motivated and malign, methods to get around procedures at least for some short period of time can be devised. Issues of recruitment in terms of quality have to be matched by testing for integrity. Searching out people who are brazen in the ways in which they approach their conduct in markets is vital. This rests entirely on management and the capacity of management to identify these characteristics. Personal accountability and responsibility can never be lost from sight by bank management; issues about integrity of people are part and parcel of this responsibility.[37]

John Laker observed that Hogan 'had a strong sense of professional ethics and propriety and understood the vital importance of personal integrity and accountability to financial institutions'.[38] At the time of writing, our major Australian banks have had the integrity of many of their officers put to serious question, resulting in a Royal Commission, a reminder of the importance of 'integrity' as the core consideration for financial institutions.

Appendix

Systematic risk, or β_j, is given by the following equation:

$$\beta_j = \frac{Cov(R_{it}, RM_t)}{Var(RM_t)}$$

where R_{it} is the return of the financial institution i in period t; RM_t is the corresponding return on the market portfolio, the Cov (R_{it}, RM_t) is the covariance of returns on the institutions i and market portfolio, and Var (RM_t) is the variance of the market return. The failure month – that is, the month during which the institution is liquidated or begins reconstruction – is t_f, where f denotes failure. The intention is to determine the abnormal returns for a period of 35 months prior to t_f.[39]

In the Tth month before the failure month, the abnormal return is given as AR_{fT}, so

$$AR_{fT} = R_{fT} - RC_{fT}, \; T = (t_f - 35), (t_f - 34), \ldots, (t_f) \tag{1}$$

where R_{fT} is the return of the institution f in the Tth month prior to the failure month and RC_{fT} is the return on a portfolio of financial institutions that did not fail. The systematic risk of failure of an institution, β_f, is then obtained from the least squares regression to the time series data over a 60 month period that includes $(t_f - 95)$ to $(t_f - 36)$, for the market model

$$R_{ft} = a_f + \beta_f RM_t, \; t = (t_f - 95), (t_f - 94), \ldots, (t_f - 36), f = 1, 2, \ldots, F \tag{2}$$

---

36 Aspromourgos 2010, 291.
37 Aspromourgos 2010, 291.
38 Laker 2013.
39 Gross, Hogan and Sharpe 1988, 47.

A control portfolio having a systematic risk equivalent to that of the failed institution is then obtained as follows. First determine the systematic risk for each non-failed institution n from

$$R_{nt} = a_n + \beta_n RM_t, \; t = (t_f - 95), (t_f - 94), \ldots, (t_f - 36), n = 1, 2, \ldots, N \quad (3)$$

Each of these institutions are then ranked according to the value of β_n and the entire portfolio of these control institutions is divided into two portfolios, the half with the highest β_n (denoted H) and the half with the lowest β_n (denoted L). The values of β_H and β_L are then determined by averaging the β_n of the securities belonging to each of the portfolios.

Using a weighting, w_f, giving the proportion of the total portfolio invested in the various securities, so weighting the β_H and β_L portfolios, we obtain a portfolio with β equal to that of the failed institution, i.e.

$$B_f = w_f \beta_H + (1 - w_f) \beta_L, \; f = 1, 2, \ldots, F \quad (4)$$

$$w_f = \frac{\beta_f - \beta_L}{\beta_H - \beta_L}, \; f = 1, 2, \ldots, F \quad (5)$$

In other words, in this case the control portfolio is made up of a proportion w_f of the high β_H portfolio and $(1 - w_f)$ of the low β_L portfolio.

The return on the control portfolio is then given by:

$$RC_{fT'} = w_f R_{HT'} + (1 - w_f) R_{LT'}, \; T' = (t_f - 95), (t_f - 94), \ldots, (t_f) \quad (6)$$

The abnormal returns for failed institution f in month T' prior to failure are then calculated from equation 1, for $T' = (t_j - 95), (t_j - 94), \ldots, (t_f)$. The abnormal return series may be standardised by dividing each observation by the estimated standard deviation of the series for the $(t_f - 95)$ to $(t_f - 36)$ period, giving the standardized abnormal return (SAR) series, where

$$SAR_{fT'} = \frac{AR_{fT'}}{\sigma(AR_f)}, \; T' = (t_f - 95), (t_f - 94), \ldots, (t_f) \quad (7)$$

$$\sigma(AR_f) = \left(\frac{1}{59} \sum_{t = t_f - 95}^{t_f - 36} (AR_{ft})^2 \right)^{\frac{1}{2}} \quad (8)$$

One can now take this to develop a cumulative standard (backward) abnormal return (CSAR) for failed institution f, for $T_0 = t_f, (t_f - 1), \ldots, (t_f - 35)$:

$$CSAR_{fT_0} = \sum_{T' = t_f - T_0}^{t_f} SAR_{fT'}, \; f = 1, 2, \ldots, F \quad (9)$$

Under suitable statistical restrictions, the standard deviation for $CSAR_{fT}$ is

$$\sigma\left(CSAR_{fT_0}\right) = \sqrt{(T_0 - t_f)} \qquad (10)$$

A 'tailed t-test' may then be used to determine if the $CSAR_{fT_0}$ is significantly negative to support the argument that failed institutions or those needing reconstruction show abnormal returns in the preceding months as suggested (see Figure 6.5).[40]

---

40   After Gross, Hogan and Sharpe 1988.

Philosophy

7
Truth, time and causality: Huw Price

Challis Professor of Philosophy (2002–2012). A foremost pragmatic philosopher, Price's arguments concerning the concepts of truth, time and causality greatly clarified their meanings and in doing so provided important practical insights for both the natural and social sciences.

Huw Price established a Centre for Time in the university Quadrangle in 2002, not 100 metres away from the old medical school, where I was writing my book *Philosophical Foundations of Neuroscience* with Peter Hacker.[1] Very unfortunately, I did not realise this, and so I missed out on the critical considerations this great pragmatist could have offered, especially as many of the arguments we separately developed drew on the profound insights of that genius Ludwig Wittgenstein.

Price was born in Oxford in 1953 and came to Australia at the age of 13, already showing a precocious interest in science by attending the university's International Science School three years later, aged 16. Hoping to become an astronomer, he carried out undergraduate studies at the Australian National University. But he soon got caught up in mathematics and philosophy – as had so many great philosophers before him – graduating with a double honours degree in these subjects. He then proceeded to carry out postgraduate work in mathematics and philosophy, first at Oxford and then Cambridge. He took up an academic position at Sydney University in 1989, where, in the subsequent 23 years, he established himself as the leading philosophical pragmatist. Price became Challis Professor of Philosophy in 2002, a while after David Armstrong (Chapter 8) held that position, but offering a very different view of the world.

The development of Price's pragmatism took place mostly while he was at Sydney before becoming Bertrand Russell Professor of Philosophy at Cambridge. This pragmatism is evident in his first major work, concerned with truth, in which he suggests that a main role of this concept is to encourage debate over issues, with the eventual resolution of disagreements through clarification of the issues involved. In his work on representationalism, Price argued that it is not possible to divide statements into two

---

1   Bennett and Hacker 2012.

Figure 7.1 Professor Huw Price. Reproduced with permission from the Leverhulme Centre for the Future of Intelligence.

distinct categories: those of a descriptive nature subserving science and others, such as those involving values and morals. Rather, all are subject to the kind of language game analysis introduced by Ludwig Wittgenstein. Perhaps the work of Price's that has generated the greatest interest is that on the asymmetry of time, researched in his Centre for Time at the University of Sydney, which suggests that there are no objective criteria for arguing that time flows from past to present to future. This work naturally fed into his consideration of causality, in which he argued that causes do not objectively have to precede effects, a conclusion that is, at first, very surprising. This essay considers Price's contributions to each of these subjects in turn – truth, representationalism, time and causality – primarily as reflected in his major books.

7 Huw Price

Truth

Non-factualism and language games

Price drew out the meaning of the word 'non-factualism' (not concerning statements of fact), with the following anecdote:

> The Prime Minister might say for example that the Soviets have the best possible system of government, with the exception of all the rest. An emotivist [non-factualist] would interpret the remark as an expression of the PM's own political preferences, of her marked antipathy to the Soviet state, rather than as a factual claim in comparative political theory.[2]

Hence the term 'non-factualism' is appropriately applied to the PM's view. However, statements such as the PM's are often thought of as fact-stating or descriptive as a consequence of the form they take, rather than looking at the way they figure in linguistic practice. When examining the normal use of a word or phrase in linguistic practice, an explanatory non-factual approach is often found to be appropriate. The main alternative is that offered by analysis, often using logical, conceptual and even mathematical techniques. Price rejected this approach, favouring the explanatory method, requiring study of the 'function of talk about truth'.[3] He seeks to give an explanatory account of the notion of truth through consideration of the part it plays in normal linguistic discourse, rather than attempting to identify any substantial properties it might have.

Price showed that consideration of the idea of a 'social class' would, at first, seem to be ripe for analytical investigation revealing the intrinsic differences between members belonging to different classes. He showed that this merely leads to a re-description of the original problem – namely, what are social classes? In contrast, the explanatory method leads to revealing insights into social classes. The rejection of an analytical consideration of truth follows many similarly unsuccessful attempts to identify the properties of truth through analysis. Price searched for the functional role of truth in our linguistic practices, a role that asks 'not what these terms [such as truth and assertion] refer to, but rather what they do for us (and hence why we might have developed them)'.[4] He arrived at the conclusion that they are, as we shall see, 'social construct[s], rather than ... natural feature[s] of the world.'[5]

The explanatory approach frequently employs Wittgenstein's concept of the 'language game', 'consisting of language and the actions into which it is woven.'[6] The complexity of the language game is apparent when naming something, a procedure that is far more difficult than just putting a label on something in a museum. Wittgenstein stressed that what is called 'ostensive definition' – namely, pointing at something and naming it, as if one were putting a label on it – is not possible until one knows the role of the labelled word in the language

---

2 Price 1989, 1.
3 Rice 1990, 302.
4 Price 1989, 132.
5 Price 1989, 132.
6 Wittgenstein 1953, 5.

in general. Price goes further than Wittgenstein's emphasis on 'descriptions of our practices which dissolve the apparent need for explanation'[7] by asking 'how our vocabularies come to be, and for what they are useful'.[8] Price ventures to ask pragmatically, given the plurality of ways in which we talk when using a particular term, to what extent does its particular function promote our community?

Price recommended that when considering an entity X, the first question to ask is not whether it belongs somewhere in the natural order, subject to scientific enquiry, but rather how does the community talk and think about it? Wittgenstein stressed that a community has a multitude of language games, so Price is asking how X is dealt with in some of these games. If an answer is forthcoming, then there is no reason to posit X as part of the natural order. If one goes about the enquiry in the opposite way, asking first if X is part of nature, then a trap might occur – since object naturalism presupposes how representationalism works, it subscribes to a particular theory of language without taking on board how the different language games give meaning to the words used. One must start the enquiry into X from within subject naturalism, enquiring as to how language works.

Price stated that 'my main claim is that we have not understood truth until we understand its role in the game we currently play'.[9] When we obtain such insights through this approach, through consideration of the language games in which truth participates, we find that the linguistic use of truth confers behavioural advantages, a point that may be considered in evolutionary terms as a benefit to the community that uses truth. This is not to say the explanatory approach develops a theory of truth, for this would be the intention of an analytically based approach, which Price rejected. He averred that

> we need to step backwards, asking not why truth matters but why it matters that ordinary speakers should think that it matters. We need to enquire what purpose could be served by our ordinary conviction that there is an end to enquiry.[10]

So 'we need to examine the game rather than the goal'.[11] The failure of a naturalistic or scientific analysis to illuminate the notions of truth and belief leaves the task to non-factualism, which Price revealed offers 'a system of incentive'[12] to enter reasoned debate that has a prospective outcome and an agreed-on position.

Agreements, disagreements and the role of truth

A conclusion of Price's explanatory account is that true and false are terms that's main function is

> to encourage a useful form of linguistic behaviour, namely reasoned argument, ... [which] can be expected to have a beneficial effect on the behavioural dispositions of individual speakers ... [by helping] to ensure that as individuals we hold and

---

7   Beasley 2015, 575.
8   Beasley 2015, 575.
9   Price 2003, 190.
10 Price 1989, 214.
11 Price 1989, 215.
12 Price 1989, 207.

act on attitudes that reflect, to some extent, the combined wisdom of our linguistic community.[13]

The functional role of the word truth is then to promote reasoned argument in linguistic disputes, which can lead to beneficial effects through a more harmonious linguistic community. The attractiveness of this non-factualist explanatory approach to truth can be contrasted with the sterile analytical approach of consigning, for example, truth values to sentences that do not provide insights into truth and, indeed, are probably not applicable at all.

Price stressed that the normal linguistic use of terms involving questions, requests and commands does not alone have the effect of leading to consensus in arguments and disagreements. Rather, the incentive that leads the parties to strive for agreement is revealed in dispute behaviour, through the effort to reach an internal criterion – namely, truth. The participants in the reasoned disagreement have a belief in truth, which is the principal incentive for their striving for the behavioural success of reaching agreement. As Price put it, 'unless we take truth as something to be aimed at, we will be given no incentive to argue by the claim that one of our utterances lacks it.'[14]

Price distinguished between three different classes of disagreements between parties: those that are substantial, implying that one of the parties must be wrong; those that are insubstantial, indicating that neither are wrong; and those in which disagreements start off as substantial and then become insubstantial. Price commented:

> I shall say that in such a case the initial disagreement *evaporates* or becomes *insubstantial*. A disagreement is *substantial* so long as the parties concerned regard each other as mistaken, and evaporates when such evaluations are no longer felt to be appropriate.[15]

On the other hand, disagreements involving factual judgements are substantial and are not given to evaporating.

The role of truth in assertoric and probabilistic statements

Assertoric sentences assert that something either is or is not the case. One proposal concerning truth in relation to such statements is that a person's assertion is right or wrong depending on its truth or falsity, so assertoric statements may be bearers of a truth value (right or wrong). This approach presupposes a notion of truth that does not seem to apply to assertoric sentences. What does apply is a notion of truth as an encouragement to linguistic argument, not as a property of linguistic entities. The same notion applies to probabilistic judgements. Price suggested that a non-factualist account of probability draws on the extent of its generating rational argument leading to provisional conclusions, so that 'probabilistic judgement is a species of intrinsically "non-final" judgement'.[16]

---

13 Price 1989, 145.
14 Price 1989, 207.
15 Price 1989, 161.
16 Price 1989, 165.

Price then emphasised the important functional role of truth as the principal incentive in rational argument attempting to reach agreement, leading to the development of a linguistic community. This functional notion of truth offers cognitive science a very useful alternative to the complexities of non-naturalistic accounts, and naturalistic ones that, by their very structure, lead to intractable reductionism and a form of representationalism founded in metaphysics.

The search for truth leads to favourable behavioural dispositions

A class of mental states whose utility, or behavioural manifestation, is much the same within a linguistic community led Price to hypothesise the Same Boat Property (SBP). If a member of the community has a mental state that possesses the SBP, so will all members of the community, as they all share the same boat. Price illuminated the SBP further:

> I emphasized the importance of the SBP ... only in virtue of which can it be true that if two people hold conflicting commitments, then one of them is likely to be behaviourally disadvantaged. Without the SBP there would be no reason to encourage agreement, and hence none to treat disagreement in evaluative terms – as an indication that someone has made a *mistake*.[17]

Price suggested that within a community that has the SBP there are some placed at a behavioural disadvantage that can only be alleviated through argument. For instance, two parties that start from a different set of relevant facts might be considered as each belonging to a different boat. Their disagreement cannot be alleviated through argument, but if the mistaken facts are identified, then the two parties come to reside in the same boat and possess the same SBP, and disagreements can be resolved through rational argument.

Price suggested that biological insights into the origins of morality, based on the view that the acceptance of a particular value system by a group confers an evolutionary advantage through regulation or guidance of their behaviour, could be used for other folk psychological terms. The SBP of a group with similar mental attitudes might place them at an evolutionary advantage due to their use of rational argument to reach agreement based on their collective experiences – that is, the experiences of the whole community and not only of an individual within it. Truth's principal function is to encourage dispute and rational argument within the community, with the ultimate benefit of agreement based on a wide body of experience, considered in a large variety of interpretations. When a party argues for the truth of their statement, they appear to be appealing to an external standard. Price showed that such a view may be held within the community, but his explanatory approach to the function of truth in the language game shows that it is not an external standard, but rather an internal perspective. It is this internal perspective that drives rational argument and subsequent agreement to the benefit of communities possessing the SBP.

Price suggested that our behavioural dispositions in relation to truth are such that we commit to the idea that truth is the end point of our enquiries and judgements. That is not to say that reaching a consensus in reasoned argument necessarily leads to behavioural

---

17 Price 1989, 159.

advantages; liabilities can be generated by errors in frames of reference, beliefs and even facts. Indeed, there is no necessary correlation between behavioural advantages and truth, especially when the behavioural advantages will only be revealed in the long term. Price argued that nevertheless

> disputes can be expected to have a beneficial effect on the behavioural dispositions of individual speakers. They help to ensure that as individuals we hold and act on attitudes that reflect, to some extent, the combined wisdom of our linguistic community.[18]

Truth and argument: their relationship

Price offers a unique hypothesis concerning the role of truth (and falsity) in ordinary use, which he summarises as follows:

> I shall propose that we explain it in functional and evolutionary terms. The main idea will be that in virtue of the normativity of truth and falsity, speakers are encouraged to resolve disagreements. This has long-term survival advantages. On the whole, it improves the behavioural commitments with which language users meet the world. As I said earlier, this is not intended to be an analysis of truth. It is a genealogical theory, an explanation as to why a language community might come to possess such a notion.[19]

Price set out to show how truth functions in particular language games, and by doing so illuminated its use and meaning. Price then regarded truth as a kind of myth: 'We thus regard truth as a "mythical" goal of enquiry, whose popularity is to be accounted for in terms of the benefits of subscribing to such a myth.'[20] The principal benefit is that the myth engenders rational arguments whose goal is to reach a consensus that ultimately benefits the linguistic community, which is sustained and evolves as a consequence of such benefits.

Naturalism and representationalism

Price suggests that the central issues of philosophical pragmatism,[21] of which he is a leading exponent, are naturalism and anti-representationalism.

Subject naturalism

Naturalism in philosophy is the view that science studies all that there is, so that all knowledge comes from scientific enquiry. Price called this view 'object naturalism'. What

---

18 Price 1989, 145.
19 Price 1989, 15.
20 Price 1989, 150.
21 Philosophical pragmatism holds that the meaning of a proposition is to be found in its satisfactory use, its practical outcomes.

Price called 'placement problems' arise when an attempt is made to place particular objects or properties (such as truth, meaning, number, probability and causation) in a world considered solely in object naturalistic terms. Representationalists' accounts carry 'the assumption that the linguistic items in question "stand for" or "represent" something non-linguistic'.[22] If one holds to object naturalism, then the placement problem appears to be dealt with using terms such as those above when they are taken as representations, conceived of as metaphysically substantive relations. However, as Price commented,

> If all reality is ultimately natural reality, how are we to 'place' moral facts, mathematical facts, meaning facts, and so on? How are we to locate topics of these kinds within a naturalistic framework, thus conceived?[23]

Price suggested that such an attempt be abandoned, for 'there is no need to try to squeeze the problem cases into naturalistic clothing'.[24] This is because placement problems actually arise in the contexts of a great variety of linguistic behaviours, and these behaviours are what is required to be elucidated.

Price adopted the phrase 'subject naturalism' to describe the task that seeks to provide an account of values, ethics, truth, causality etc. and of how we come to use procedures in our ' language games' that lead to placement problems. Subject naturalism is pragmatic in as much as it seeks to determine both the function of our vocabularies and how they came to be be of benefit to our communities. In doing so, it recruits anthropology to its service. Because subject naturalism studies of the use of our vocabularies in language games, avoiding the metaphysical pitfalls of representationalism, it must encompass scientific statements that are necessarily couched in language. So object naturalism is subservient to subject naturalism.

Object naturalists must turn to subject naturalism for an understanding of representational terms like probability and truth. Without the subject naturalist's understanding of the functional role of these words in the language games that science plays, object naturalists are left with a heft of metaphysical terms. So subject naturalism strengthens object naturalism by removing the necessity of simply designating many representations as metaphysical. Subject naturalism then solves the placement problem for object naturalism. The solution of placement problems – for example, those that arise in the attempt to place consciousness, meaning and values in a naturalistic setting – seems to be an impossible task from an object naturalist perspective. However, these terms represent tasks with well-defined procedures or solutions from a subject naturalist point of view. In subject naturalism, they are not taken as properties or objects in the natural world, but rather as arising in language games, in forms of linguistic behaviour. The pragmatic task of the subject naturalist is then to ascertain the function of the word in a set of language games (or behaviours) and how the word might have come about (a form of scientific anthropology) in such a way as to promote the viability and practices of the community that gave rise to it.

---

22 Price 2013, 9.
23 Price 2013, 6.
24 Price 2013, 6.

i-Representation

Semantics cannot be explained in terms of representations. Rather, an account of assertions and judgements can be made by placing them in the role of 'premises and conclusions in inferences', which function as 'a coordination device for social creatures, whose welfare depends on collaborative action. ... [Assertoric language] helps to reduce differences among the behavioural dispositions, or other variable aspects of speakers' situations on which such action depends'.[25] Price commented that this function provides an explanation of 'how there come to be statements with particular contents',[26] without any need for representationalist accounts. These accounts should be abandoned and replaced by consideration of the relationship between different behaviours, without the need to develop special metaphysical categories, as representationalism requires. Different behaviours are explicated in terms of the different language games we play, for example, in discussing causality. Considering the talk and context in which an entity under consideration is used reveals the functions of the entity in linguistic behaviour. Price distinguished between two forms of representation, which he referred to as e-representation and i-representation, and suggested that conflating the two leads to classical representation and object naturalism. Price commented that

> I distinguish two nodes, or 'attractors', for the notion of representation, as it figures in contemporary philosophy. One node ('i-representation') emphasises position in an inferential or functional network, the other ('e-representation') stresses correlation with an aspect of an external environment.[27]

e-Representation mostly involves tracking objects or properties in the natural world through, for example, covariance. This is largely a scientific enterprise – taking a measurement with a device that is then said to reflect the condition of some aspect of the environment. For example, the recordings of a barometer and atmospheric pressure. The representing device (the needle of the gauge) changes in parallel with changes in the system being represented (barometric pressure). This covariance may come to be considered as reflecting a causal relationship. Indeed, in much of biology the representing system is taken to represent some environmental or external condition as a consequence of covariance – hence it is an e-representation (for example, the potential fluctuations recorded by an electrode from a neuron in the brain are taken to e-represent a vertical contrast). Such environmental tracking is paramount in science but is of no use in explaining normative concepts such as value.

Price claimed that i-representations are required even for statements in the natural sciences (and so subsume e-representations). i-Representations play functional roles that are central to language games involving asking for and giving reasons, in the context of standards that are commonly adhered to. i-Representation then emphasises the functional roles of representations, particularly in some cognitive language games (concerned with the knowledge and understanding of things). Price illustrated the diversity of i-representations

---

25 Price 2013, 49.
26 Price 2013, 41.
27 Price 2013, 45.

by considering probability, causation and truth. Probability arises because we must make decisions under conditions of uncertainty. As a community we have devised a collective method for reaching consensus under such uncertainty through debate. This leads to consolidation of our beliefs about probability, strengthening our cohesion as a community. Causation, on the other hand, is different from probability in as much as it stresses the capacity of an individual to act as an agent that intervenes in their environment and, in so doing, provides outcomes with certain probabilities, considered by the agent as indicating a causal relationship (see 'Causality'). Truth arises in language games of giving and asking for reasons, with participants collectively attaching themselves to agreed-upon community standards (see 'Truth'). As Price commented,

> in my view, the most illuminating route to a pragmatic theory of truth is to see it as associated with this kind of in-game externality – as a normative constraint, external to any individual speaker, to which speakers necessarily take themselves to be subject, in playing the game of giving and asking for reasons.[28]

In all three cases, a person is taking practical steps to implement procedures that allow them to participate in the language games that play such an important role in their life and the life of the community.

The role of i-representations in the assertoric language game might involve beliefs about truth, probability, causation, numbers, etc., with none of these corresponding to anything in the world, but rather carrying out a functional role in the language game. The assertoric language game achieves this through individuals in a community justifying the assertions they make, giving reasons and asking for reasons within the dialogue of the community, and so reducing differences among their behavioural dispositions.

The arrow of time

Consider waves in a pond spreading from where a pebble has been dropped. The energy transferred from the pebble to the water is propogated by means of waves, a mechanism called radiation. The frequency of observing large outgoing waves from the site of pebble's impact with the water (say, at the middle of the pond) is very great compared with that of seeing the opposite – namely, a large number of small waves generated from the sides of the pond and converging on the middle. Next consider electromagnetic waves in relation to an antenna. Again, outgoing (retarded) waves carry energy from the antenna in the form of concentric waves, to be dispersed over a wide area. Incoming (advanced) waves converging on the antenna are not observed. James Clerk Maxwell derived the equations for electromagnetic waves, which, like all fundamental physical laws, are symmetrical – that is, they predict that both retarded and advanced radiation will occur. There is then an apparent contradiction between the symmetrical laws of physics and the asymmetry observed in nature between the occurrence of retarded and advanced waves. The problem is that, on the one hand, the laws of physics describe both a process

---

28 Price 2013, 37.

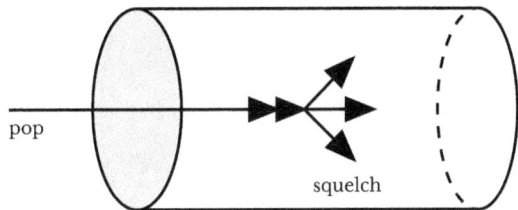

Figure 7.2 A damper. Reprinted from Price 2006, with permission from Elsevier.

and its reverse; on the other hand, these processes exhibit temporal asymmetry. Why then is the physical world asymmetric in time? Or as Price put it: 'How is it possible to derive the asymmetric world we find around us from the symmetric laws we find in physics?'[29]

An analogical model for retarded radiation

In considering the origins of asymmetry, in which retarded radiation is greatly favoured over advanced radiation in a universe governed by the symmetrical laws of physics, Price introduced the analogical model of what he called 'dampers' and 'anti-dampers'.[30] A damper consists of a tub (or hollow cylinder of gas), one end of which allows fast Newtonian particles to penetrate (but not slow ones). If a fast particle penetrates the wall, it will very likely collide with a gas particle, which will, in turn, collide with other particles so that the energy of the penetrating particle is spread among all the gas particles, raising the temperature of the gas slightly. Price called the penetrating particle a 'pop', the subsequent collisions that spread the energy a 'squelch', and the tub, pop and squelch collectively a 'damper' (Figure 7.2).

Now consider a 'time reversed damper', as in Figure 7.3. Here a group of colliding gas particles in the tub sufficiently increase the momentum of one particle so that it penetrates the end of the tub – an unusual event but one that can occur – producing an 'anti-pop' from this 'anti-squelch', so we now have an 'anti-damper' consisting of tub, anti-pop and anti-squelch (Figure 7.3). Price then set up a damper and an anti-damper facing each other, as in Figure 7.4. Now, when a low probability of occurrence event such as an anti-squelch takes place in an anti-damper, the emerging anti-pop enters the damper, becoming a pop and giving rise to a squelch. In this isolated system, the squelches will equal the anti-squelches, so the extent of dampering is the same as that of anti-dampering and there is no temporal bias. However, there are clearly a lot more dampers in the real world than anti-dampers, giving rise to a temporal bias. So how did this come about?

Price showed that the particle analogical model provides the argument for a wave analogical model. In the latter case, the dampers are replaced by tubs of water. In one tub, a buoy is thrown in, producing concentric waves of outgoing (retarded) ripples with

---

29 Price 1996, 94.
30 Price 2006.

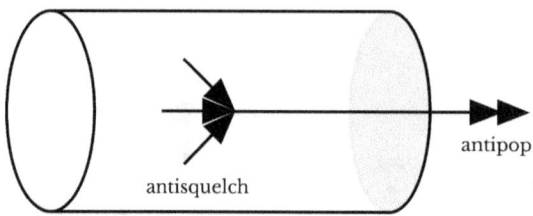

Figure 7.3 An antidamper. Reprinted from Price 2006, with permission from Elsevier.

the kinetic energy of the thrown buoy dissipated at the edges of the tub. Alternatively, incoming small concentric waves can come from the sides of the tub, meet in the middle and throw a buoy out of the tub. If the two tubs (damper and anti-damper) are juxtaposed to each other, then occasionally a buoy ejected from one tub will land in the other tub, exchanging energy between the tubs. At equilibrium we would expect, as in the particle case in Figure 7.4, a symmetry between the tub (damper) and anti-tub (anti-damper), with incoming waves propelling buoys out equal to outgoing waves in response to a buoy coming in. The symmetry in the wave model is maintained, as it was in the particle case. Again, the question arises: why, in this example, are there more tubs than anti-tubs in the world?

The radiative arrow of time

Price answered this question by suggesting that it is because of the large number of what he called 'kicks', or additions of energy, not large anti-kicks, or subtractions of energy, that occur in the world, 'explained by the thermodynamic nature of the environment'.[31] It is not then any temporal asymmetry of the physical laws that gives rise to an excess of emitters (dampers) over absorbers (anti-dampers), but the environment provided by the universe we live in, which favours the former over the latter. As Price put it:

> the lesson of the [two-tub] argument is that the observed asymmetry of radiation depends on an asymmetry in the environment in which wave media are embedded: the asymmetry is that the environment supplies large 'kicks' in one time-sense but not in the other. In our ordinary time-sense, it adds large amounts of energy to the media ('all in one go' – in a coherent way, in other words) much more frequently than it subtracts or removes large amounts of energy, in a similar coherent fashion.[32]

Where do these large additions of energy come from? The reason dampers are common in the real world is that there are a number of high-temperature sources of particles in our vicinity; for example, a star like our sun (in the vicinity of the damper in the analogical model in Figure 7.4). So the dampers are given a very large advantage

---

31 Price 2006.
32 Price 2006.

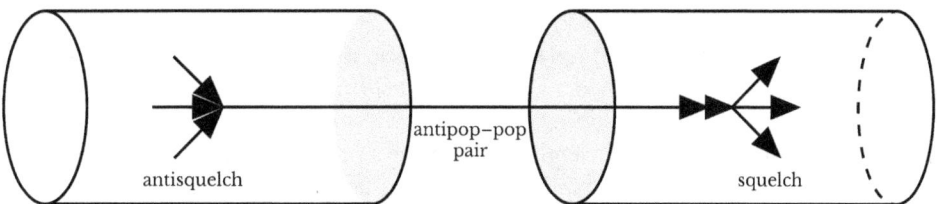

Figure 7.4 Using an anti-damper to produce a damper. Reprinted from Price 2006, with permission from Elsevier.

over the anti-dampers, with relatively large numbers of particles penetrating the damper tub and leading to squelches. On the other hand, there is an absence of anti-sources or anti-stars (made of anti-matter, for which there is no evidence at this point) that would enhance the number of anti-dampers – that is, the number of anti-pops – and so reduce the apparent time asymmetry. If these hot sources (stars) were eliminated, the temporal asymmetry would be removed.

Why do stars predominate over anti-stars at this time? Price suggested that the answer to this question comes from a consideration of entropy, which was very low at the beginning of the universe and then increased so that at this time we have a great number of stars. He stated:

> This is simply the most likely thing to happen, given the combination of the time-symmetric Boltzmann probabilities and the single low-entropy restriction in the past. This 'boundary condition' is time-asymmetric, as far as we know, but it is the only time asymmetry in play, according to Boltzmann's approach[33]

which also gave us the Second Law of Thermodynamics.[34] What constituted this low-entropy boundary condition? After the Big Bang, there existed both matter and fields, with a density and pressure that were fairly uniform (constituting a hot soup at thermal equilibrium), together with very high gravitational energy. So there existed a very low gravitational entropy (low probability that a state could exist consisting of uniform matter and fields together with a very high gravitational potential energy). This meant that the initial state of the universe was one of very low entropy.[35] The universe then followed the Boltzmann time-symmetric probabilities.[36] The gravitational potential exerted its force, eventually leading to the clumping of the hot soup into stars, present in a cold space environment in an expanding universe and so moving away from the initial thermal equilibrium. Price then reached the surprising conclusion that the origin of the great predominance of retarded radiation over advanced radiation that we now observe is to be found in the conditions of the early universe. This then determines the time asymmetry.

---

33 Price 2006.
34 See Cercignani 1988.
35 North 2003, 15.
36 Price 2002.

Causality

How do we come to make causal judgements and use causal concepts in a bare world of associations between events, called a Humean world? Price suggested that:

> In essence, this would be a scientific account of a particular aspect of human linguistic and cognitive practice, explaining its origins in terms of certain characteristics of ourselves, as structures embedded in time in a particular way.[37]

Such an account would need to determine first how our deliberations lead to interpretations in terms of cause and effect. Second, how does the temporal asymmetry of causes being taken as preceding effects (rather than, say, the other way around) come about? That is, why is there an emphasis on actions in the future being contingent on those in the past? Finally, is there an objective basis for this temporal asymmetry?

The perspectival aspect of our deliberations on causality

The concept of causation, the development of indispensable causal laws, arises from deliberation on the nature of the world. What facts concerning the workings of the world are used in the development of these causal laws depends on a deliberative process. This process is, in turn, dependent on the perspective of the deliberating agent. Price held to a view that 'begins with deliberation, and sees causal judgements as projections and idealizations of judgements made from the agent's perspective'.[38] This is not to denigrate such judgements, for they are often 'an indispensable construct for coping with the situation we find ourselves in, as enquirers and especially as agents'.[39] Price identified several factors that contribute to this perspectival view. The first perspectival contingency arises from the fact that

> deliberation is epistemically constrained, in several ways – it depends on both knowledge and ignorance, and these epistemic factors are contingencies, whose limits may well vary from agent to agent. Hence causal judgements are correspondingly perspectival: they are necessarily 'situated', relative to some implicit boundaries to the knowledge and ignorance of the agent concerned.[40]

A boundary that is generally not taken into account concerns the factors determining the agent's own actions in deliberating.

A second perspectival contingency, closely allied to the first, is that even in a deterministic world we have to work with probabilities, for we are ignorant of the totality of causal facts that should be considered in our deliberations following our interventions in the environment (see 'i-Representation'). We need probabilistic ideas because we are not in the position of an omniscient person, sometimes referred to as a Laplacian god, who

---

37 Price 2007, 253.
38 Price 2007, 286.
39 Price 2007, 290.
40 Price 2007, 282.

can have complete knowledge of the present state of things and deterministically predict the future. Also, the advantage of a probabilistic theory of causality, Price argued, 'is the fact that it avoids the problem of spurious causes'.[41]

A third perspectival consideration concerns the temporal characteristics of the deliberative process leading to considerations of causation, which Price introduced by means of the following story, involving what he called the Stargate Doughnut.

> Imagine a photon, p, which spends billions of years in intergalactic space as it travels from one distant galaxy, $Gpast$, to another, $Gfuture$. At some point in between, at a time t, it passes through the central aperture in a tiny doughnut-shaped object, which happens to be spinning on a transverse axis, somewhere in deep space. As this doughnut spins, it periodically occludes the path the photon takes from $Gpast$ to $Gfuture$, and hence acts as what we could call a 'stargate'. At t, however, the gate is open, and the path is unobstructed.
> Consider the following counterfactuals:
> Proposition 1: If the Stargate Doughnut had been closed at time t, the photon p would not have been absorbed at $Gfuture$.
> Proposition 2: If the Stargate Doughnut had been closed at time t, the photon p would not have been emitted at $Gpast$.
> We take Proposition 1 to be true, and Proposition 2 to be false. Accordingly, we take the orientation of the stargate to be a cause of the *later* position of the photon, but not the *earlier* position of the photon. What is the source of this time-asymmetry?[42]

Consideration of the Stargate Doughnut illustrates 'the typical perspective we have as deliberating agents – the perspective we bring to the situation, quite unconsciously, when we think about manipulating the stargate'.[43]

The idea of a past, present and future is generally recognised as arising from our own temporal viewpoint, not from some objective viewpoint (of a Laplacian god, for instance). Our deliberations are normally future directed. A final perspectival consideration concerns how it is that, as deliberating agents, we consider cause and effect to occur in temporal sequence, obeying an arrow of time that points into the future. This temporal asymmetry, in which causes lead to effects in the future, rather than effects leading to causes, reflects the asymmetry of 'our own temporal orientation, as physical structures embedded in time'.[44] The time asymmetry of our deliberations can be explained in terms of such asymmetries in our environment and constitution. As Price argued (see 'The radiative arrow of time'), the arrow of time is determined by the entropy gradient initiated shortly after the Big Bang, which established a very low entropy condition that has been increasing in the universe ever since. Our deliberations take the direction of the entropy gradient, towards what we call the future. An inverse situation, in which the entropy gradient is reversed due to, say, a very high entropy condition immediately after the Big Bang, would provide a reverse arrow of time. Then our causal arguments would look to

---

41 Price 2007, 281.
42 Price 2007, 266.
43 Price 2007, 267.
44 Price 2007, 278.

the future for events or conditions that lead to conditions in the present, reversing the direction of causation. Our viewpoint concerning the past and future is then not objective but perspectival.

In summary, explanations in science come overwhelmingly in causal terms; the main aim of science is to describe particular phenomena in these terms. Science is then, by necessity, perspectival. As noted, Price canvassed a number of factors contributing to our perspectival view of causality. He stated:

> the perspectivalist project is itself scientific – it treats the use of causal concepts as an aspect of human behaviour and psychology, and sets out to provide an explanation, in the same scientific spirit in which we might investigate the emotions, say, or vision.[45]

He went on:

> According to the perspectival view, causal reasoning too depends on the standpoint of creatures engaged in a certain kind of journey ... a journey in which – *from the epistemic standpoint of the creatures themselves* – their choices determine what path they take through a tree of forking possibilities.[46]

The forking branches are provided by a combination of causal laws and insights taken at a particular time and from a particular perspectival viewpoint. This project amounts to taking the Humean world, in which only laws of association (not causality) exist, and investigating how we come to theorise about it in causal ways. Causation 'is a way of thinking about the world that we need because we are not gods'.[47] Price's project amounted to deliberating on the perspectival view of our causal notions, as well as the process of coming to such notions in the first place.

***

Price provided significant insights into the foundations of quantum mechanics, arising from his work on the asymmetry of time in the context of cause and effect. In this work, he put to use relatively simple models, such as the damper and the Stargate Doughnut, to explore and offer solutions to various quantum mechanical conundrums, such as what Einstein called 'spooky action at a distance'.[48]

Price's deliberations and conclusions may be compared with those of a previous holder of the Challis Chair of Philosophy, David Armstrong (Chapter 8). Armstrong's materialism is in direct contrast to Price's considerations on representationalism, which emphasise that it is not possible for the descriptive statements of science to be considered as distinct from non-descriptive statements and to be free from analysis in the context of the language games they participate in. Readers are encouraged to study the original

---

45 Price 2007, 289.
46 Price 2007, 265.
47 Price 2007, 284.
48 Price 2012.

works of these two great philosophers and to use their own critical capacities to decide whether they would like to delve further into the ideas of Armstrong or Price.

Further reading

Price, H. *Facts and the Function of Truth.* Oxford: Basil Blackwell, 1989.
Price, H. *Time's Arrow and Archimedes' Point.* Oxford: Oxford University Press, 1996.
Price, H. 'Boltzmann's Time Bomb.' *The British Journal for the Philosophy of Science* 53, no. 1 (2002): 83–119.
Price, H. 'Truth as Convenient Friction.' *Journal of Philosophy* 100, no. 4 (2003): 167–90.
Price, H. 'Recent Work on the Arrow of Radiation.' *Studies in History and Philosophy of Science Part B – Studies in History and Philosophy of Modern Physics* 37, no. 3 (2006): 498–527.
Price, H. 'Causal Perspectivalism.' In *Causation, Physics and the Constitution of Reality*, edited by H. Price and R. Corry, 250–92, Oxford: Clarendon Press, 2007.
Price, H. 'Does Time-Symmetry Imply Retrocausality? How the Quantum World Says "Maybe".' *Studies in History and Philosophy of Science Part B – Studies in History and Philosophy of Modern Physics* 43, no. 2 (2012): 75–83.
Price, H. *Expressivism, Pragmatism and Representationalism.* Cambridge, UK: Cambridge University Press, 2013.

8
Brain and mind: David Armstrong

Challis Professor of Philosophy (1964–1992). Recognised as the leading materialist philosopher of his generation, Armstrong argued that all that exists can be explained by physics, so that, for example, the mind is identical to the brain.

I attended some of David Armstrong's lectures at Melbourne University when he was a senior lecturer in philosophy and I was an undergraduate in electrical engineering. The clarity and forcefulness with which he expressed his arguments was maintained after his subsequent appointment as Challis Professor of Philosophy at Sydney University in 1964, as I can attest after attending his lectures once more when I moved to Sydney some four years later.

Armstrong was born in Melbourne in 1926, into a family with some distinguished academics, such as his grandfather, the anthropologist Robert Marett, who served as rector of Exeter College in Oxford between 1928 and 1943. At the end of the Second World War, during which Armstrong served in the Royal Australian Navy, he became an undergraduate in philosophy at the University of Sydney. He was awarded a university medal in 1950 and then went on to his grandfather's college to complete a DPhil at Oxford. During this time he was exposed to the then dominant theme in Western philosophy – namely, ordinary language or analytical philosophy. Great philosophers such as J.L. Austin and Gilbert Ryle, the latter famous for his work *The Ghost in the Machine*, were the major figures at Oxford, and the genius of Ludwig Wittgenstein at Cambridge was made manifest once more with the publication of *Philosophical Investigations* in 1953. One would have thought that a young antipodean would be bowled over by the teachings of these eminent philosophers, with their emphasis on the analysis of language, but this was not the case with Armstrong. He never accepted 'that analysis alone could be the whole of philosophy',[1] and, indeed, he 'listened with some incredulity that such matter could be of philosophical interest'.[2] Even when Armstrong returned to Australia in 1960 to complete a PhD under one of Wittgenstein's former students, Alan Cameron

---

1 Irvine 2014.
2 Mumford 2007, 16.

Figure 8.1 Professor David Armstrong answering questions at the Catholic University of Lublin in 1995. Reproduced with permission from the Armstrong family.

Jackson, he was not persuaded that the precision of Oxford analysis was the be-all and end-all of philosophy. He considered it important, but he wanted to pursue the subjects of philosophical psychology, mind, perception, epistemology and metaphysics.

Physicalism informs naturalism

Armstrong became famous for the arguments he provided in relation to physicalism, naturalism and especially materialism. By physicalism he meant that the universe contains particulars (things) that exist in a single space-time system and are governed by the laws of physics. In this context, he endorsed the thesis that:

> (1) The world contains nothing but particulars [things], having properties [universals] and related to each other. (2) The world is nothing but a single spatio-temporal system. (3) The world is completely described in terms of (completed) physics.[3]

Given this physical stance, Armstrong rejected things that are not identifiable as physical things. He gave physicalism tremendous reach, claiming that phenomena normally falling under the purview of the biological, chemical and social are ultimately described by physics. His theory of knowledge and his theory of being are grounded in physics.[4] Minds, spirits, numbers, propositions and values, if not reduced to the physical, are not particulars, so Armstrong rejected them from further consideration. This also holds for Plato's Forms (such as Justice and Squareness). It follows that Armstrong saw philosophy as a working partner with science, in particular physics, a view shared by the great American philosopher Quine and in complete contrast to that of Wittgenstein, who held that philosophy's main job involves removal of conceptual confusions, whether in physics, psychology or sociology – that is, whether in the physical or moral sciences. It seemed to Armstrong that physicalism no longer needed much defence; alternative scenarios, such as the concept of creationism, provided little credible account of the world, and its things, properties and causal relations, compared with that provided by physics.

Given his commitment to physicalism, Armstrong's naturalism involved rejection of any extra-natural or supernatural things or particulars, such as angels or God. He set himself the 'objective to give an account of possibilities that are in no way otherworldly',[5] so he was committed to showing that the concepts of universals (properties of particulars), numbers, minds and propositions could be given a naturalistic account. This account rejects the *a priori* arguments of such great philosophers as Leibniz and Bradley concerning the nature of reality, with a thorough commitment to the *a posteriori* – that is, to the view that only empirical science, specifically physics, can provide the properties of particulars and their causal interrelations. Given the role of physics, it follows that metaphysics is constrained by the *a posteriori*, rather than having an *a priori* role in guiding physics.

---

3   Armstrong 1978, 126.
4   In other words, he claims that physics provides the foundations for epistemology and metaphysics.
5   Armstrong 1989, 3.

Materialism identifies the mind with the brain

Armstrong rejected the idea of a 'mind' as conceived, for example, by Plato and Descartes. He considered it impossible that something that exists in space-time (a material thing) can interact with something that does not exist in space-time (an immaterial thing). This argument goes back to Aristotle's rejection of Plato's concept of an immaterial soul. Somewhat ironically, Armstrong used Plato's Eleatic Principle, which states that if a thing has no power, then it cannot affect other things, so even though it may exist, we have no reason to think that it does. Any claim that the mind can affect material things although it cannot be affected by these things, fails, according to Armstrong, as he believes it fails this principle.

Armstrong claimed that some find the idea that our minds can be identified with the workings of our brains objectionable because introspection does not give us access to these workings. Much of the activity of our brain is not accessible to us, he averred, but is involved in myriad processes that do not enter our minds. In order to illustrate such a possibility, Armstrong introduced the tale of the ' headless woman magic trick'. In this illusion, a woman is placed on a stage against a black background, suitably lit. Unbeknown to the audience, a black cloth is placed over her head, so to the audience it appears that she has no head. Members of the audience may correctly comment that 'I cannot perceive that the woman has a head' or make the illegitimate comment 'I perceive that the woman has no head'. This, Armstrong argued, is equivalent to introspecting, failing to discover the physical states of our minds and incorrectly concluding that minds are non-physical. We tend to make the illegitimate shift from 'We are not introspectively aware that mental processes are brain processes' to 'We are introspectively aware that mental processes are not brain processes'.[6]

Armstrong held to what is called the type/type identity theory – that, for instance, if a person believes that today is Friday or the pot is on the stove, then there is a particular brain state that is active at that time. The question then arises as to whether a different person, when holding the same belief, must have the same brain state. Armstrong suggested that there is a probability that the brain state is the same, but this is not to be considered a necessary condition. If it is not necessary, then the argument has shifted from type/type identity to what is called token/token identity. In this case, there is a family of alike brain states that are associated with a particular belief – for example, that one is in pain – with different members of this family present in different individuals that exclaim that they are 'in pain'. But what of the brain states of individuals of different species that show by their behaviour that they are in pain? Armstrong suggested it is not necessary that such a family of brain states exists across species. It might be that another family of brain states is applicable when members of a different species show by their behaviour that they are in pain.

The great Oxford philosopher Gilbert Ryle claimed that all the evidence we have for human capacities is provided by their behaviour, so he rejected the concept of mind, understood as involving 'inner' experiences. Armstrong rejected this as nonsense in his *Materialist Theory of Mind*. He argued that we have direct experience of the mind, and we do not need to fall back on supernatural things to accept this, for different states of the mind are simply different states of the brain, of the workings of our nervous system.

---

6   Armstrong, 'An Intellectual Autobiography: Part II', 71.

Ryle's behaviourism suggests that for each stimulus one experiences, there is a specific behavioural manifestation; it excludes dispositions or states that mediate between the stimulus and the behavioural manifestation. These are accepted by Armstrong for 'the concept of a mental state is the concept of the state of the person apt for the production of certain sorts of behaviour'.[7] All dispositions are states of the central nervous system and so are central states. It follows that, for a particular sensory input, the tendency for a specific motor behavioural output is determined by one's disposition, which is set by a third category of brain function – namely, the central state. Neuroscience would attribute this central state to the association cortex. Armstrong suggested that the central state theory meets four criteria that must be met or satisfied for any theory of mind: first, it provides for the unity of mind and body; second, it accounts for causal interactions between mind and body; third, it provides that each individual has a unique mind; and finally, it accounts for inner mental states.

But what of consciousness, a major concern of contemporary philosophy and neuroscience? Armstrong does not regard understanding consciousness as presenting any obstacles to a materialist interpretation of the mind:

> I suggest that consciousness is no more than awareness (perception) of inner mental states by the person whose states they are. If this is so, then consciousness is simply a further mental state, a state 'directed' towards the original inner states.[8]

Materialism identifies intention with the workings of the brain

In 1874, Brentano famously claimed that a key distinction could be made between the mental and the physical. This was based on the observation that the former has the power to be directed towards, to point out and to be about something, and that these are the properties of mental states. The mind has the capacity to be about something other than the person whose mind it is, a capacity missing from inanimate things. So when I am jealous, I am jealous of someone; when I believe X, I believe a proposition or statement X; when I am brave, I show courage in the face of the enemy. These are examples of intentionality. The essential problem is how mental states show intentionality. That is, how are they directed towards the intentional object, which, in the above examples, might be a person or a proposition? Armstrong strove to give a naturalistic account of how intentionality arises.

An intentional state is manifest in purposive behaviour, such as when I move towards something, like walking up to a dog and patting it. Armstrong argued that such intentionality can be considered to be a brain state between the reception of information (say, perceiving the dog) and the overt motor performance manifest in our behaviour (walking towards and patting it). He suggested that intention and perception need to be understood together – we form a belief and gain knowledge through perception, and this disposes us to act in certain ways, which results in purposive behaviour. A disposition of

---

7 Mumford 2007, 136.
8 Armstrong 1968, 94.

the mental state is then a particular brain state that can lead to intentional behaviour. For example, the brain state connoting my intention to raise my arm, an intention that I claim is responsible for my moving my arm, is a state hidden from me. It is the neural workings of the brain that result in this disposition, intermediate between perception and purposive behaviour.

Armstrong's 'dispositional' view of mental states presents his solution to the problem of intentionality. He regarded the dispositional view of mental states as essential for providing an 'inner mental life'. Intentions and beliefs are dispositions; they are tendencies for particular outcomes in specific circumstances. Dispositions play a central part in Armstrong's *A Materialist Theory of Mind*. To have a disposition is to be in a mental state that, in the appropriate circumstances, causes a behavioural manifestation. The workings of some parts of our brains, hidden from introspection, may dispose us to behave in certain ways, to believe in certain things. These dispositions need not manifest in our behaviour, such as motor action, unless the appropriate circumstances arise, ascertained through perception and sensations. In neuroscientific terms, the circumstances are determined in the sensory cortices, the behaviour by the motor cortex and the dispositions in the association cortex.

Perception as a belief

Armstrong read a paper in 1962, shortly after completing his PhD under Alan Cameron Jackson in Melbourne, that influenced him profoundly: *Philosophy and the Scientific Image of Man* by Wilfrid Sellars, which drew out the distinction between the 'manifest image' of the world as it appears to our senses (sometimes somewhat derisively referred to as 'folk psychology') and the 'scientific image' that is gradually being articulated. Armstrong later wrote: 'This stuck in my mind and has been in my mind ever since and I have worked with that.'[9] Most philosophers before Armstrong held to the view that these two images could be reconciled by considering that things (particulars) in the world – which one only really knows through physics – are not what we directly experience with our senses. However, these things do give rise to representations of some kind in our brains, for example, the activity of certain neural networks. Audaciously, Armstrong did not accept this view; neither did Wittgenstein, for quite different reasons. Instead, Armstrong defends direct realism – namely, that our perceptions allow us to be directly acquainted with things.

Armstrong claimed that the things (objects) we perceive and the sensible qualities (e.g. colour) we are aware of are the same things that are the objects of study in physics. This is the direct realist stance – namely, that these things are not just representations in the brain. Physics tells us that these things are made of atoms, with their own particular waves or particles separated by space, a description that does not involve sensations such as colour. How then does one reconcile the 'manifest image' with the 'scientific image'? This is a profound problem, one that Armstrong described as *the problem of science*.

---

9 Mumford 2007, 136.

The answer that he propounded for this problem hinges on the concept of belief. Beliefs, Armstrong averred, are to be identified with 'particular type[s] of causally efficacious brain state[s]' that can commit us to an intentional action and so are the causes of behaviour.[10] Beliefs are brain states that are associated with dispositions – namely, brain states that incline us to a particular behaviour, an intentional behaviour, following perception of a state of affairs. If one experiences an illusion then the belief is clearly false, and we are in error. Such an error occurs in attributing colour to an object, for colour is an illusion. We do not perceive colours; rather, we misperceive them. It is true to say that the colour of grass is green, under normal conditions of illumination, to a normal observer. But, although this is a true report of our experience, it is a misperception.

Armstrong held to direct realism that proposes that physical things and their qualities are directly apprehended by perception. They are not then ideas or sense impressions or sense data, triggered somehow by the thing, that is then used to provide a representation of the thing in the brain. Rather, we have direct perception of physical reality, which we can use to gain knowledge of that reality.

Caveats

Perhaps the two main issues that Armstrong confronted in his philosophy concern the irreducible nature of sensible qualities, such as colours, and the apparent non-physical nature of intentionality. He seems satisfied with his solution to the latter problem, in terms of dispositions and their reflecting states of the brain, which are neither associated with perception nor motor activity. On the other hand, he is completely dissatisfied with the solution he offers for the existence of sensible qualities, sometimes referred to as secondary qualities, in contrast to the primary qualities measured in physics, such as dimensions and weight. Such secondary qualities, Armstrong suggested, may be considered as a subject of ordinary language discourse; we have held that blood is red since time immemorial. But now science has described blood in terms that do not involve colour, so we know our belief in red is not correct. He conceded, however, that this discovery does not require us to drop the concept that 'blood is red' but to continue to use it as an everyday concept, with the proviso that physics has shown it to be incorrect – a false belief. Such false beliefs hold for the sensible qualities of objects, rather than the true primary qualities that are supplied by the physical scientist. However, he remained dissatisfied with this demarcation between primary and secondary qualities; the splitting up of qualities between the physical discourse of the sciences and the 'folk psychology' of everyday discourse. This disquiet revolved around the word 'substantial'. How, he asked, can a thing be 'substantial' in the world and only possess primary qualities provided by the physical sciences? Just what these 'extra' qualities might be, he did not know. This realisation that something else is needed undermines Armstrong's appeal to direct realism, to empiricism and, most importantly, to his naturalism.

***

---

10   Irvine 2014.

The Search for Knowledge and Understanding

Figure 8.2 *David Armstrong, B.A., B Phil.*, 1959, by Clifton Pugh (1924–1990). Oil on masonite. Collection: National Portrait Gallery, Canberra. Gift of Jennifer Armstrong, 2018; donated through the Australian Government's Cultural Gifts Program. Reproduced with permission from the Pugh family.

Armstrong proposes that for any truth, there must be a 'truthmaker', some observation about the world that makes the truth true. The truthmaker relates to the relevant physical facts in the world, without any linguistic analysis being relevant.

> I really have no time for linguistic idealism on the playing down of truth. What I certainly do not like is the denial of truth, the notion of truth and objectivity. I believe that science and mathematics get us to objective truth.[11]

Armstrong stated:

> You know that terrible bores sweep over the philosophical world, in particular the world of analytical philosophy. One of them was the private language argument, which I characterise as the bore of the 50s (Wittgenstein). Then there was the indeterminacy of translation (Quine) which was more or less the bore of the 60s or the 70s.[12]

Armstrong's physicalism, 'if not quite the received wisdom of the age, has been so remarkably influential that it is hard to imagine it having greater impact'.[13] However, it is not only his contribution to philosophical doctrine that is important, but also his 'admirable contribution to the style in which we philosophize ... Armstrong's philosophical writings are examples of how to discuss the hardest questions in philosophy without sacrificing the kind of clarity that makes progress possible'.[14] 'The impact of all this has been two generations of philosophers, following his lead as much as that of any other single figure, engaged in the revival of metaphysical philosophy. A matchless legacy.'[15]

Towards the end of his life, Armstrong commented that

> I think of myself as in the Christian and Jewish tradition, and in the tradition of Greece. Matthew Arnold thought of Hebraism and Hellenism as twin poles of Western culture. I see myself as a person in the stream within that culture, and I think it may perhaps be the best tradition of thought and life that has so far been evolved.[16]

Finally, he stated:

> I have the greatest respect for ... [religion]. I think it may be the thing that many people need, and it enshrines many truths about life. But I do not think it is actually true. ... In some metaphorical and symbolic way, I think it grasps at the truth.[17]

This passion for the truth made Armstrong's 'place in our philosophical and intellectual life ... cherished and unforgettable'.[18]

---

11 Mumford 2007, 127.
12 Chrucky, 'An Interview with Professor David Armstrong'.
13 Irvine 2014, 39.
14 Bacon, Campbell and Reinhardt 1993, ix.
15 Campbell 2014.
16 Chrucky, 'An Interview with Professor David Armstrong'.
17 Chrucky, 'An Interview with Professor David Armstrong'.
18 Bacon, Campbell and Reinhardt 1993, x.

Further reading

Armstrong, D.M. *Perception and the Physical World*. London: Routledge and Kegan Paul, 1961.
Armstrong, D.M. *A Materialist Theory of the Mind*. London: Routledge and Kegan Paul; New York: Humanities Press, 1968.
Armstrong, D.M. *Belief, Truth and Knowledge*. London: Cambridge University Press, 1973.
Armstrong, D.M. *Nominalism and Realism, Volume 1: Universals and Scientific Realism*. Cambridge: Cambridge University Press, 1978.
Armstrong, D.M. *The Nature of Mind and Other Essays*. St. Lucia: University of Queensland Press, 1980.
Armstrong, D.M. 'An Intellectual Autobiography.' *Quadrant* 27, no. 1–2, (1983): 98–102.
Armstrong, D.M. 'An Intellectual Autobiography: Part II.' *Quadrant* 27, no. 3 (1983): 68–78.
Armstrong, D.M. *A Combinational Theory of Possibility*. Cambridge; New York: Cambridge University Press, 1989.
Armstrong, D.M. *Truth and Truthmakers*. Cambridge; New York: Cambridge University Press, 2004.
Bogdan, R.J., ed. *D.M. Armstrong*. Dordrecht, NL: D. Reidel Publishing Company, 1984.
Mumford, S. *David Armstrong*. Stocksfield, UK: Acumen, 2007.

9
Foundations of modern science: Stephen Gaukroger

Professor of History of Philosophy and History of Science (1999–2015). Gaukroger is one of the world's leading historians of science and philosophy as a consequence of his scholarship on Descartes and Bacon, as well as his magisterial three-volume study Science and the Shaping of Modernity. *Together these works have shaped debate on the origins and development of modern science.*

In my first year as an undergraduate in electrical engineering, I was directed to the building in which physics was taught and researched on the campus of Melbourne University. The large glass doors at the entrance were emblazoned with a coat of arms and the words 'Natural Philosophy'. I thought I must have been misdirected, for this could not be the physics department. When reassured that it was, I became curious as to how Natural Philosophy could be the name for a physics department. On making further enquiries, I was told to read the short monograph by Burtt *The Metaphysical Foundations of Modern Science*. I was greatly impressed by this work, not only because it sketched the origins of physics as a branch of philosophy, but also because it showed that physics had a history and that the subject was based on certain assumptions that curtailed the reach of its explanatory power. It was a great good fortune for me personally that Sydney University was able to recruit Stephen Gaukroger, probably the foremost historian and philosopher of science. His monumental works provide new insights into the evolution of the scientific enterprise.

Gaukroger was born in 1950 in the industrial cotton town of Oldham in the north of England. His English father was a pattern maker in the aircraft industry, and his Irish immigrant mother was a bookkeeper. On leaving school, Gaukroger worked a number of jobs. He was a factory worker, a labourer on a building site, a shop assistant and a civil servant. Concerned by a range of intellectual questions, he enrolled in philosophy at Birkbeck College at the University of London. There his intellectual gifts were quickly recognised. He subsequently went to Cambridge, where he came under the influence of his PhD supervisor, Gerd Buchdahl, probably then the foremost historian on the interdependence of science and philosophy through his work *Metaphysics and the Philosophy of Science. The Classical Origins: Descartes to Kant*. So began Gaukroger's interest in Descartes, manifest in his showing that Descartes was a formative figure not

Figure 9.1 Professor Stephen Gaukroger at the University of Sydney. Photograph by Sarah Lorien. © Sydney University Press.

only in philosophy, but also in mechanics, optics and physiology. This led Gaukroger to question the origins of the enduring scientific culture in the West. Such a culture had not been sustained in Sung/Ming-dynasty China or in Arab-Islamic cultures that had achieved significant scientific developments well before the West. Understanding the origins of the sustained growth of the scientific culture in the West called for a detailed description and analysis of this growth and, especially, of how it involved study of the interaction of science and philosophy over 500 years. Gaukroger's fascinating three volume study, under the general title *Science and the Shaping of Modernity*, provides answers to these questions.

Natural philosophy in the 13th and 14th centuries was concerned with the philosophical study of the physical in nature and the cosmos, and, as such, was an important subject within philosophy in universities, especially that of Paris. The subject greatly expanded following the insights of Galileo, Descartes and Newton in the 17th century. Indeed, Newton's great work of 1687 was called *Mathematical Principles of Natural Philosophy*, a rare first edition of which can be viewed in the University of Sydney's Fisher Library. During the 17th century, natural philosophy became a major discipline in its own right. It was not until the 19th century, with the emergence of the discipline of biology, that the phrase ' natural philosophy' came to refer to physics alone. The Latin word 'scientia', meaning knowledge, was then brought into play in the late 19th century as 'science', a term that embraced all the physical and new biological disciplines.

9 Stephen Gaukroger

Establishing the persona of a natural philosopher in the 16th century

Gaukroger suggested that Plato's formative account of philosophy, in its contrast between genuine philosophy and sophism, shaped a persona for the philosopher, establishing the idea that what marks out the philosopher from the sophist is not the ability to argue a point, but rather what may be identified as 'intellectual honesty', which Plato described as using argument to discover truth, rather than simply argument for argument's sake. Francis Bacon (1561–1626), in the spirit of Plato, rejected the procedures of scholastic disputation, with its emphasis on winning arguments in universities, and sought to show that obtaining new knowledge should be the goal of the natural philosopher. In this spirit, he castigated the guilds and the universities, the former for prohibiting the dissemination of their techniques outside the guild and the latter for restricting access of those outside the universities to new knowledge through the use of obscure language. With this kind of emphasis, Bacon began to shape the *persona* of the natural philosopher in the early-modern period, as Gaukroger showed in *Francis Bacon and the Transformation of Early-Modern Philosophy*. Bacon went on to round off this new persona by emphasising a life of engagement in the world of affairs, rather than isolated contemplation of eternal truths. The search for truth, unfettered by argumentative disputation, was ultimately a search for useful products made available by the search for truth. This was to become the dominant persona of the natural philosopher. Gaukroger showed that

> Bacon constructed a new persona for the natural philosopher by pitting individual contemplation against the communal/productive. This was a revolutionary change in ethos, and stands as the basis for scientific practice as it was to subsequently develop.[1]

Establishing a bridge between Aristotelian and early-modern science

Nevertheless, Gaukroger showed that Bacon, unlike Descartes and Galileo, made no significant contribution to physical theory. Indeed, he was the last defender of a geocentric astronomy (one in which the planets move around the Earth), a defence he based on physical rather than astronomical grounds. In many respects, Bacon was an unreconstructed Aristotelian, despite contrary claims that he was an originator of the scientific method. Nevertheless, Bacon's Aristotelianism had an interesting aspect to it. He subscribed to the idea that matter had inherent potentialities and tendencies, as argued by Aristotle, but departed from him by suggesting that these tendencies could be found in the microscopic constituents of matter. This idea created the possibility of reductionism – that is, of using Aristotelian potentialities and tendencies of matter to probe down into the physical causes of these phenomena at the microscopic level. Bacon then conceived of natural philosophy, or science, as we now call it, as an experimental means to probe down from the manifest Aristotelian properties of matter to their underlying causes. This was the beginning of a form of micro-corpuscularism that was to play a central role in Descartes' scientific method in the following century.

---

1   Gaukroger, personal communication.

The Search for Knowledge and Understanding

Figure 9.2 Portrait of Francis Bacon, painted circa 1620 by an unknown painter. Royal Łazienki Museum, Warsaw (LKr 896). Reproduced with permission from the Royal Łazienki Museum.

The failure of 16th-century eliminative induction

Although Bacon's reductionism had no hope of succeeding as a consequence of starting out with Aristotelian notions concerning matter, he did lay claim to a method of practising science that would deliver not only new knowledge, but also practical applications (that is, useful knowledge). Furthermore, it would have the advantage of disciplining the human mind and avoiding exaggeration and error. This method involved making experimental observations and then forming inferences from these facts – a process of induction, or, more specifically, what Bacon called ' eliminative induction'. In this way, first principles are arrived at by inferences from our experiences. These principles are then used to infer the design of new experiments. Bacon went on:

> But even this is not enough, for even when this is done, still the understanding, if left to itself and its own spontaneous movements, is incompetent and unfit to form axioms, unless it be directed and guarded. Therefore ... we must use *Induction*, true and legitimate induction, which is the very key of interpretation.[2]

However, Bacon's much heralded 'eliminative induction' did not provide a sure-fire method of discovery at all. As Gaukroger pointed out:

> Indeed the two great triumphs of mathematical physics in the first half of the seventeenth century – Galileo's establishment of the law of falling bodies and Descartes' establishment of the angle at which colours are formed when white light is refracted through a raindrop – can be seen in terms of an eliminative procedure; but once we examine these cases a little more closely, it becomes clear that eliminative induction is really playing, and can only play, a very minor role.[3]

Bacon's really important and lasting contribution in the 16th century, which Gaukroger identified in *Francis Bacon and the Transformation of Early-Modern Philosophy*, was to successfully develop and effectively proselytise a new persona for the natural philosopher.

Descartes and the emergence of a new natural philosophy in the 17th century

The break from Aristotelian natural philosophy to what can now be discerned as the beginning of modern science came at the start of the 17th century, with the work of Galileo and Descartes. Gaukroger showed how this came about, in Descartes' case, in *Descartes, An Intellectual Biography* and *Descartes' System of Natural Philosophy*. In particular, he revealed how natural philosophical considerations led to the metaphysical ideas of Descartes' Principia, as well as to his immensely influential concept of the mind.

Descartes is shown to have developed his physical concepts, in the first instance, through (surprisingly) natural philosophical considerations of hydrostatic mechanisms. In this he attempted to 'combine a geometrical representation of a problem with a micromechanical model of it'.[4] This came to constitute Descartes' concept of an explanation in natural philosophy. He emphasised hydrostatics because that area of physical enquiry was developed to the extent of offering 'comprehensive quantitative expression'

---

2 Gaukroger 2001, 142.
3 Gaukroger 2001, 150.
4 Gaukroger 1995, 89.

that was 'rigorous' and 'mathematically developed'.[5] This is beautifully illustrated in Gaukroger's intellectual biography in terms of Descartes' detailed microscopic description of the mechanical forces exerted by water that are involved in the solution of various problems in hydrostatics. Gaukroger provided a specific example in relation to Descartes postulating the existence of a ' plenum' – that is, the idea that the cosmos is completely filled with matter in which material particles of various sizes simply circulate. This idea was necessary in order for Descartes to argue that the planets move around the sun. His hydrostatic solution is that

> a region of matter will ... be able to move when contiguous matter in the direction of its motion ('in front of it'), and contiguous matter in the opposite direction ('behind it'), also move in the direction of its motion, and when the same conditions hold for these contiguous pieces of matter, so that in the end a continuous loop or ring of matter is displaced.[6]

He argued that 'all the motions that occur in the world are in some way circular'.[7] It follows that

> the planets move around the sun because they are carried around in a rotating fluid, namely the plenum, which finds an equilibrium between upwardly directed centrifugal forces and the heavier matter pressing inwards.[8]

In this way, heliocentrism arises from mechanistic concepts of matter and the laws of motion, which are open to quantitative elaboration and testing, in contrast to Aristotelian explanations in terms of potentialities and tendencies, which are not.

Descartes also offered metaphysical arguments against the existence of empty space in his *Principia*. Scholars believed that these provided the reason for his asserting the existence of a plenum. Gaukroger showed that this was not the case. The long-held belief that Descartes proceeded to his natural philosophy through foundations provided by his metaphysics and epistemology is incorrect. Rather, it was the other way around; natural philosophy was constitutive of his thinking in both metaphysics and epistemology. They could be placed on a firm basis through the emerging mechanical worldview in his natural philosophy.

Descartes' identification of the mind

Gaukroger illuminated how Descartes arrived at his concept of mind, which had a paramount effect on future philosophical and scholarly approaches to the subject and, indeed, on Western society to this day. Descartes sought to identify what cognitive activities are clearly corporeal – involving a body, as possessed by both humans and

---

5   Gaukroger 1995, 256.
6   Gaukroger 1995, 234.
7   Gaukroger 1995, 234.
8   Gaukroger, personal communication.

animals. He did this through careful and extensive exploration of the contrast between human and animal cognition, using the new methods of natural philosophy. One can then consider what additional cognitive abilities are possessed by humans as a consequence of them alone having a rational mind, illuminating an answer to the question what does it mean to be human?

Descartes asserted that the material substance of the bodies of humans and animals is open to mathematical enquiry:

> For I frankly admit that I know of no material substance other than that which is divisible, has shape, and can move in every possible way, and this the geometers call quantity and take as the object of their demonstrations.[9]

He went on to say that 'all the phenomena of nature are explained thereby, and demonstrations concerning them which are certain can be given'.[10] So understanding the bodies of animals and humans involves the application of geometrical principles. In contrast, the pursuit of mathematical physics of the kind that Descartes carried out in his physical and cosmological theories is a distinctly rational process. It is, Descartes averred, not to be found in bodies, for

> when I looked to see what functions would occur in such a body, I found exactly those that occur within us without reflecting upon them, and hence have no contribution from our soul: that is, from the part of us, distinct from the body, whose nature, as I have said, is simply to think. These functions are just those in which animals that lack reason may be said to resemble us. But I could find none of the functions which, because they depend on thought, are the only ones that belong to us men; though I found these later, as soon as I supposed that God created a rational soul and joined it to the body in the way I have described.[11]

Gaukroger argued that, on Descartes' account, what marks out human beings from animals is not their perceptual states as such, but the fact that they can 'stand back' from them and make judgements about them, something animals cannot do. In animals, both the cognitive and affective states are modular – that is, fragmented into largely isolated components – whereas in human beings they are brought together in the 'self', giving us a unified mental life that is totally lacking in animals, which may then be considered mere automata.

The new natural philosophy sustained by the emergence of a scientific culture in the 13th century

In *The Emergence of a Scientific Culture*, the first of volume in his *Science and the Shaping of Modernity*, Gaukroger stated that the Church was not opposed to science (natural philosophy) as such, as is often thought, but, through its earlier embrace of Aristotelianism,

---

9   Gaukroger 2002, 67.
10 Gaukroger 2002, 67.
11 Gaukroger 2002, 217.

Figure 9.3 Portrait of René Descartes (1596–1650), philosopher, copied from an original by Frans Hals (1581/5–1666). Musée du Louvre, Paris (INV1317). © RMN-Grand Palais (musée du Louvre)/Tony Querrec.

saw science as the key to understanding the natural realm. Other civilisations had produced great insights into natural phenomena, such as those in mathematics and astronomy in 10th-century Baghdad and those emerging from the Maragheh Observatory in 13th-century Persia. Practical inventiveness was greatest in the Sung and Ming dynasties in China, which produced mechanical clocks, movable type and seismographs that predated developments in the West by at least a couple of centuries. Why were these outbursts of creativity not sustained? Gaukroger showed that the intellectual framework provided by the Church in the West was the scaffold upon which the scientific enterprise could be consolidated and allowed to flourish from the 13th century until the end of the 18th century. It was then that the cognitive domain of science claimed to be able to dismantle the scaffold itself – the very armature that had allowed it to be consolidated in the first place – in the process assimilating all cognitive values to scientific ones.

So a scientific culture did not suddenly arise in partnership with the new natural philosophy in the early 17th century, but rather emerged in the 13th century, at the time of the Church's dominance in matters philosophical and theological. The Church is generally pictured as antagonistic to the scientific enterprise, whereas Gaukroger showed that the introduction of Christianised Aristotelianism in the 13th century put natural philosophy in a dominant position, which it retained. However, to the extent that we associate the scientific revolution with a set of novel technical achievements, it made a clean break with what went before. Christianised Aristotelianism established natural philosophy as a major cultural force, although it provided no basis for a scientific understanding of the world.

The debate between Christianity and natural philosophy was intensified in the West by an 11th century decree of Pope Gregory VII, called *Dictatus Papae*, in which he asserted papal supremacy over the entire Western Church and declared the Church's independence from secular control. But the Church was not the only corporation formed in the wake of this decree. In the succeeding century, the students of the stadium at Bologna formed another corporation, a 'university', in order to secure exemption from municipal taxation. It was universities that were to provide the physical settings for the emergence of a scientific culture.

The rediscovery of Aristotle's manuscripts in the 11th century and the formation of universities in the 12th century led to unparalleled intellectual ferment in the West. This was for two reasons. One was that Aristotle had indicated a possible procedure for gaining new knowledge: first, take note of observed events relating to the physical phenomenon of interest, then develop first principles from these observations that allow an account to be made of the behaviour in such a way that it may be predicted in a variety of circumstances. So in astronomy one might first accrue tables of data of the positions of heavenly bodies, allowing for a mathematical description that can be used in future determinations of the positions of these bodies. This does not, however, provide a method for discovery, something that Bacon also unsuccessfully attempted at the beginning of the 17th century. The other way in which Aristotle contributed to the intellectual excitement in the emerging universities of the 12th century concerns theology. His work indicated that there was more than one way of investigating basic questions, such as could anything like a soul exist after the degeneration of the body? The Aristotelian approach to these questions was in terms of natural philosophy, and the results conflicted with Christian dogma. The problem was reconciling conclusions obtained via very different routes. The 13th century Italian theologian and philosopher Thomas Aquinas thought metaphysics could bridge the two and provide a neutral arbiter. In *The Emergence of a Scientific Culture*, Gaukroger showed that, even though it became clear in the 16th century that Aquinas' own Aristotelian solution did not work, his conception of the bridging role of metaphysics influenced early-modern approaches to dealing with the problem of different sources of understanding.

The failure of the new natural philosophy to account for observations emerging in chemistry, electricity and physiology

In *The Emergence of a Scientific Culture*, Gaukroger explored in detail how Aristotle's naturalism, in which the 'ultimate constituents of the natural world' were to be found in 'immanent powers or principles', gave way to what might be called 'corpuscularism', in which the natural world was seen as reducible to inert atoms, in the scientific revolution of the early 17th century.[12] In the second volume of *Science and the Shaping of Modernity*, devoted to the *Collapse of Mechanism and the Rise of Sensibility*, Gaukroger showed that both corpuscularism and mechanics in general, which had been so successful in the early 17th century, failed. By the early 18th century, there were many areas of experimental investigation that could not fall under the reductive forms of explanation required by mechanics and micro-corpuscularism. These included phenomena found in electricity, chemistry and especially physiology.

The matter theory that underlay micro-corpuscularism gave way to a new form of matter theory in the 18th century. By 1750, the rational mechanics of the old mechanistic matter theory was replaced by a range of more localised forms of explanation. The matter theory underlying chemistry, for example, made no essential reference to micro-corpuscularism. The intrinsic active powers of the matter of some organs, such as the capacity of muscle to contract with a force well beyond that of a slight initiating force, fell well beyond the grasp of the mechanics of the old matter theory. A gulf arose between the increasing mathematical sophistication of rational mechanics and the proliferating realms of chemistry, electricity and physiology, which required very different forms of explanation. There was no single discipline providing a model for the emerging forms of natural philosophy. Nevertheless, a rear-guard action occurred in which great mathematicians such as Euler continued to pursue ever more esoteric forms of mechanics in the conviction that mechanical explanation could eventually be extended to any physical phenomenon. Gaukroger commented that this 'reduction was no more than a promissory note, and indeed little more than a bluff'[13] when it came to physiology, electricity, chemistry and gravitation.

Natural philosophers' attempt to extrapolate their methods to the cognitive domains

Volume 1 of Gaukroger's *Science and the Shaping of Modernity* showed how science gained standing as a legitimate form of enquiry in the 13th century and how the nature of science was transformed in the 17th century with the rejection of Aristotelian forms of explanation in favour of mechanical, atomistic ones.

In Volume 2, Gaukroger showed that the success of this explanatory model collapsed in the 18th century, as it proved fruitless in the new domains of chemistry, electricity and physiology. No single form of explanation was envisaged that could accommodate all these disciplines, so each developed its own distinct forms of enquiry.

---

12 Gaukroger 2006, 108.
13 Gaukroger 2010, 149.

These were all physical disciplines, however, and, as Gaukroger set out to show in Volume 3, the problems were compounded in the middle decades of the 18th century, when it began to be considered that the controversies raging in humanistic disciplines – such as law, history, political theory and ethics – could be resolved by pursuing them as empirical studies, following the model of the natural sciences. This was a process of 'naturalisation of the human', a naturalisation that covered all aspects of human behaviour. Among the main forms of naturalisation that Gaukroger identified are: the medicalisation of human psychological faculties; the development of a 'philosophical anthropology' that studied the ways in which different languages reflect different mentalities; the use of comparative anatomy to mark out distinctively human features; and the use of collective or aggregate properties of human beings to illuminate the behaviour of individuals.

A crucial feature of this naturalisation, Gaukroger showed, is the extent to which historical evidence plays a central role in the empirical resources that are drawn upon. One of the most contentious forms of naturalisation, for example, is that of religion. The naturalisation of Christianity that emerged from the late decades of the 18th century onwards was a historicisation of Christianity. Gaukroger showed that such an approach was very different from the French Enlightenment attempt to subject religion to the dictates of reason, which failed because the appeal of religion lies in its ability to 'come to terms with the world' through fears, desires, raw beliefs, anxieties and goals, so that a simple reduction to reason fails to engage with what is at stake.[14]

The only form of naturalisation that faced up to these questions was 'philosophical anthropology', particularly as developed in the writings of Schiller. He provided a non-reductionist account of how we interact in the world in ways that can only be described in a non-propositional way, involving aspirations, desires, anxieties and fears, which religion had heretofore come to terms with. In this way, he naturalised the range of human experience that, up to that time, had been explained by mythology and religion. He did this by appealing neither to religion nor to reductive mechanical strategies, but rather through what became known as an aesthetic model of man. Schiller was able to do this in *On the Aesthetic Education of Man* by harmonising the rational with sensibility through aesthetics. It should be emphasised that the bridging principle afforded by aesthetics was not metaphysical, involving a 'deeper reality', but rather an imperative – a regulative principle. It involved highlighting the importance of feelings and desires in sensibility and showing how these were brought together with rationality in aesthetics. No such bridging principle was available in natural philosophy, for feelings and desires were beyond its purview. Nor was it available to religion, for the natural realm was also beyond its purview. Rather, Schiller argued, one must shift the entire conceptual framework and turn to aesthetic perception in order to ultimately discover our unity and integrity as human beings.

***

Gaukroger has been a pre-eminent figure in the history of philosophy and science for nearly two decades while professor of these subjects at the University of Sydney, offering readers of his work 'a wealth of insight and a feast of intelligent, provocative thinking and

---

14 Gaukroger 2016, 305.

interpretation'.[15] His contribution amounts to an extended essay on what it means to be human, given the extent to which our present culture is suffused with science.

> The core problem he has perceptively and courageously set out to solve is how science moved from a marginal cultural phenomenon wherever it came into being at all, to the cultural center it has come to occupy in the Western world.[16]

Gaukroger's considerations are a major departure from the approach taken by most historians who, with the very large number of resources now at their disposal, prefer to remain in the sinecure of their particular historical period and not reflect on the implications of their work for present culture. Gaukroger's scholarship is 'detailed and profound'[17] and places in perspective the claims made on behalf of science, outside its purview, by contemporary philosophers as well as scientists.

Further reading

Burtt, E.A. *The Metaphysical Foundations of Modern Science*. London: Kegan Paul, 1925.
Gaukroger, S. *Descartes, An Intellectual Biography*. Oxford: Clarendon Press, 1995.
Gaukroger, S. *Francis Bacon and the Transformation of Early-Modern Philosophy*. Cambridge, UK: Cambridge University Press, 2001.
Gaukroger, S. *Descartes' System of Natural Philosophy*. Cambridge, UK; New York: Cambridge University Press, 2002.
Gaukroger, S. *The Emergence of a Scientific Culture: Science and the Shaping of Modernity*. Oxford: Clarendon Press, 2006.
Gaukroger, S. *The Collapse of Mechanism and the Rise of Sensibility: Science and the Shaping of Modernity, 1680–1760*. Oxford: Oxford University Press, 2010.
Gaukroger, S. *The Natural and the Human: Science and the Shaping of Modernity, 1739–1841*. Oxford: Oxford University Press, 2016.

---

15 Shank 2017, 1679.
16 Cohen 2013, 24.
17 Smith 2005, 62.

Physics, engineering and astronomy

10
Star magnitudes and the invention of the stellar interferometer: Robert Hanbury Brown

Professor of Physics (1962–1981). Hanbury Brown invented the stellar intensity interferometer, gave the first dimensions of a star and went on to map the angular size of more than 30 stars. All of this was accomplished after playing a leading role in the development of airborne radar during the Second World War.

In 1986, the Australian Academy of Science asked me to organise a symposium on 'Science and Society'. As Robert Hanbury Brown, a University of Sydney physicist whom I did not know at the time, had just written a wonderful book called *The Wisdom of Science: Its Relevance to Culture and Religion*, it was imperative that I persuade him to lead the symposium. Thereafter I got to know him very well, to appreciate his deep spiritual values and to learn first-hand of his remarkable life. The word 'boffin' was first used by Robert Watson-Watt, the pioneer of radar, to describe Hanbury Brown as he went about his radar detection work in the United Kingdom during the Second World War.

I have departed from the format of most of the other essays in this collection, laying great stress on the boffin's contributions before he took up the position of professor of physics at Sydney University. These constitute such a *Boy's Own Annual* story that I could not resist giving them attention. At any rate, without such a narrative it would not be possible to appreciate what Hanbury Brown achieved at Narrabri while professor of physics at Sydney.

Hanbury Brown arrived in Sydney aged 45, having had a precocious career, first as a young man in the development of radar before and during the Second World War (1936–45), and then as a major figure in the development of radio astronomy. He used intensity interferometry to measure the angular diameter of stars with an accuracy of about one per cent, allowing the apparent brightness and luminosity of the stars to be deduced. In addition, he gave the orbits of binary stars. Hanbury Brown was responsible for the delineation of many of the sources of radio waves in the universe, some of which could be aligned with stars previously identified using light. In particular, he played a major role in the identification of the most distant, and therefore oldest, observable objects in the universe – quasars, or 'quasi-stellar objects'. His work made a major contribution to cosmology, leading to new techniques for proving the origin, evolution and dynamics of the structures that make up the universe.

Figure 10.1 Professor Robert Hanbury Brown. Reproduced with permission from the Hanbury Brown family.

Hanbury Brown was a born electrical engineer, taking a first class degree in the subject from Brighton Technical College in 1935. He then completed a PhD at Imperial College London, concerned with valves, the electrical forerunner of transistors. It was during this time, he later recalled, that he found himself describing

> how a triode worked to an elderly gentleman who showed polite interest when Sir Henry [Tizard, rector of Imperial College] appeared and told me that I had been explaining the principle of the triode to Sir Ambrose Fleming the inventor of the thermionic valve![1]

Unbeknown to Hanbury Brown at this time, thermionic valves were being considered in the design of devices that became radar. The concept of radar was suggested by Robert Watson-Watt, who, in 1935, provided the UK's Committee for the Scientific Study of Air Defence, composed of future Nobel Prize winners such as Patrick Blackett and A.V. Hill, with a secret memorandum entitled *Detection and Location of Aircraft by Radiometrics*. Its central proposal was to build an aircraft detection system in preparation for a war with Germany.

Towards the end of his undergraduate studies, in August 1936, Hanbury Brown was asked to join a very secret project being carried out in the beautiful grounds and buildings of Bawdsey Manor, without any precise specification of what the project was about. At 21, Hanbury Brown was already recognised as an exceptionally talented electrical engineer, and he was clearly being persuaded to join an electronics project involving preparation for the coming war. In fact, the project was to develop radar, and as he later recounted, 'no one who worked at Bawdsey in those early days will ever forget the place. It was magical'.[2] This was the case not only because of its beautiful location on the Suffolk coast, but also because of the intellectual talent that had been gathered there. The group assembled at Bawdsey was given the task of implementing Watson-Watt's plans, under conditions of extreme secrecy. They were required to design and implement a system for detecting enemy aircraft as they approached the English coast. The sense of urgency was enhanced by a visit from Sir Winston Churchill, who commented to Hanbury Brown 'how very important it was to have something which could "smell out" enemy bombers'.[3]

Radar for airborne interception

In order to convert land-based detection methods for use on an aircraft for air interception, Hanbury Brown had four receiving antennae aerials mounted on an aircraft. The actual signals obtained with this aerial array appeared on two cathode-ray oscilloscope tubes mounted in the aircraft, one devoted to the azimuth[4] and the other to elevation. The time

---

1 Hanbury Brown 1991, 3.
2 Hanbury Brown 1991, 4.
3 Hanbury Brown 1991, 28.
4 In spherical coordinates, the perpendicular projection onto a reference plane of a vector from the origin to a particular point provides an angle between the projection and a reference vector, called the azimuth.

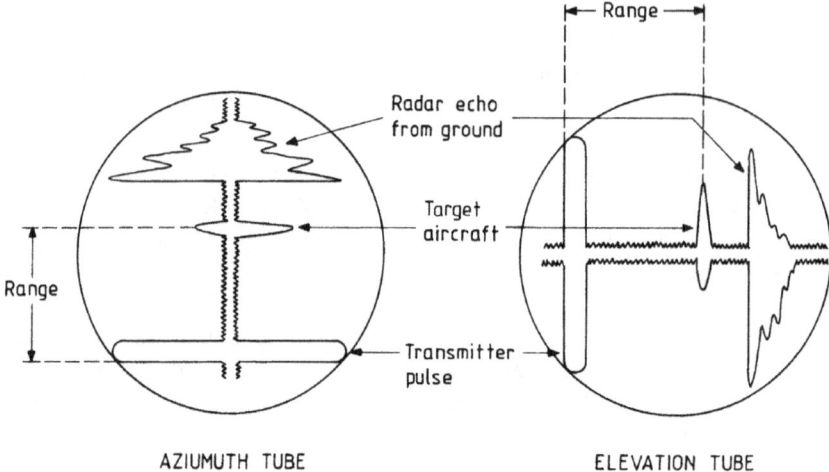

Figure 10.2 The display used for metre-wave air interception radar. The left-hand (azimuth) cathode-ray tube shows that the target aircraft is off to the right of the fighter; the right-hand (elevation) tube shows that the target is above the fighter. From R. Hanbury Brown, *Boffin: A Personal Story of the Early Days of Radar, Radio Astronomy and Quantum Optics* (New York: Taylor and Francis, 1991); new edition published by the Radio Society of Great Britain in 2016. Reproduced with permission from the Hanbury Brown family.

base for the azimuth tube was vertical, with the signals from the two aerials devoted to the azimuth shown to the right and left of the vertical time base (see Figure 10.2). The time base for the elevation tube was horizontal, with the signals from the two aerials devoted to elevation shown above and below the horizontal line (see Figure 10.2). In Figure 10.2, the azimuth tube indicates that the target aircraft is off to the right of the fighter and the elevation tube shows that it is above the fighter.

The whole radar system was operational on 9 June 1939, with war beginning three months later, on 1 September. Hanbury Brown was a pivotal figure in ensuring that airborne interception provided by radar was available during the aerial Battle of Britain. By October 1940, he had introduced a new version of airborne interception with a greatly simplified display on the cathode-ray tubes for estimating the location of the target relative to the fighter, giving both the distance (range) and direction (above/below), as shown in Figure 10.3. This airborne interception radar led the world as an operational system. It was small and light (less than 90 kilograms), and had a range of about 305 kilometres. Its development was accelerated by future Nobel Prize winners Alan Hodgkin (neuroscience) and John Kendrew (chemistry) joining the group. The result was that about 50 enemy aircraft were shot down by night fighters and 40 by land-based guns in April 1941. During the following month, 100 were shot down by night fighters and 30 by guns, following introduction of the air-interception Mark IV. So the proportion of radar-assisted downings compared to downings by land-based guns increased from 56 per cent to 77 per cent in a month.

The development of air to surface vessel radar, primarily required to detect submarines from aircraft, was urgent in 1940 in order to protect the Atlantic shipping routes,

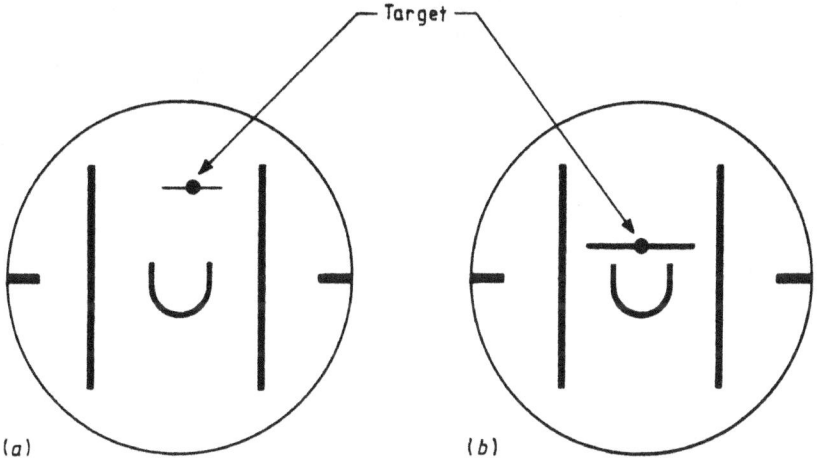

Figure 10.3 The pilot's spot indicator of AI Mark V: (a) target at 5000 feet range, above the fighter and slightly to the right and (b) target at 1000 feet range, above the fighter and dead ahead. From R. Hanbury Brown, *Boffin: A Personal Story of the Early Days of Radar, Radio Astronomy and Quantum Optics* (New York: Taylor and Francis, 1991); new edition published by the Radio Society of Great Britain in 2016. Reproduced with permission from the Hanbury Brown family.

which brought vital supplies to the United Kingdom from the United States. To meet this challenge, Hanbury Brown designed a high-gain sideways-looking aerial array that he attached to the long, box-like fuselage of a Whitley aircraft. The development of the SV Mark II achieved the required result, with all that meant for the supply of food and armaments to the British people, who, at this stage, stood alone before Hitler's armies, which had already conquered most of continental Europe.

Hanbury Brown had a serious accident at this time. During a test flight of an airborne interception device, his oxygen supply failed at high altitude, leaving him unconscious. He was subsequently in hospital for three months and was left with permanent hearing loss. Nevertheless, he was able to push on at this time, providing a mathematical explanation for why a fighter using airborne interception starts to weave when it gets too close to a bomber, and showing that the distance at which this occurs depends on both the absolute and relative speeds of the two aircraft, as well as their minimum angular displacement. Hanbury Brown was then involved in establishing the chain of operational radar stations along the east and the south coasts of England that were to play a vital role during the Battle of Britain.

Radio stars

After the war, at the beginning of 1949, Hanbury Brown joined Bernard Lovell, who was making Jodrell Bank in the United Kingdom a centre for radio astronomy, building a 250-foot paraboloid dish now known as the Lovell radio telescope. With a research student,

Cyril Hazard, Hanbury Brown set about using the existing 66-metre paraboloid dish as an effective radio telescope, designing a narrowed beam (of two degrees) and a primary feed to obtain the shortest possible wavelength (about 1.89 metres). He thus had at his disposal the largest telescope in the world. This enabled him to begin mapping radio sources that were concentrated in the Milky Way and widely distributed throughout our galaxy. Of great interest was the observation that 'bright spots' of radio emissions did not necessarily line up with visible stars. Aptly, these were given the name radio stars. Some radio stars were extragalactic objects – for instance, from the M31 nebula – showing that radio waves are not unique to our galaxy, but can also be found in the Andromeda spiral galaxy, far outside our own.

Radio astronomy using the intensity interferometer

Hanbury Brown's greatest theoretical and experimental contribution to astronomy was his idea of an intensity interferometer, which could be used to give the angular dimensions (the angle subtended) of a source of radio, and later light, emissions. Interferometry instrumentation had been used for some time and consisted of two antennae in the case of the measurement of radio waves. The separation between the antennae was varied, with closer distances between them providing better coherence in the phase and amplitude of the two signals, and greater distances providing greater incoherence. Determining the longest distance at which the signals become mutually incoherent allows for a simple calculation of the angular diameter of the source of the radio waves to be made.

Hanbury Brown's great discovery, in 1952, was that if the radiation received by the two antennae at a particular baseline separation is mutually coherent, then the fluctuations in the intensity or energy of the two signals are also correlated. A brilliant young English mathematician, Richard Twiss, was able to confirm Hanbury Brown's proposal. As Hanbury Brown stated,

> To my joy the mathematics showed that the correlation between their two pictures [due to each of the antennae] is a direct measure of mutual coherence and can therefore be used to find the angular size of the source.[5]

In order to test this, he used two completely independent receivers with their own antennae, covering frequencies around 125 MHz, together with a linear multiplier. With this equipment, the angular size of a radio source could be determined from correlations of the low frequency noise fluctuations recorded by each receiver with the antennae at different distances apart.

---

5   Hanbury Brown 1991, 105.

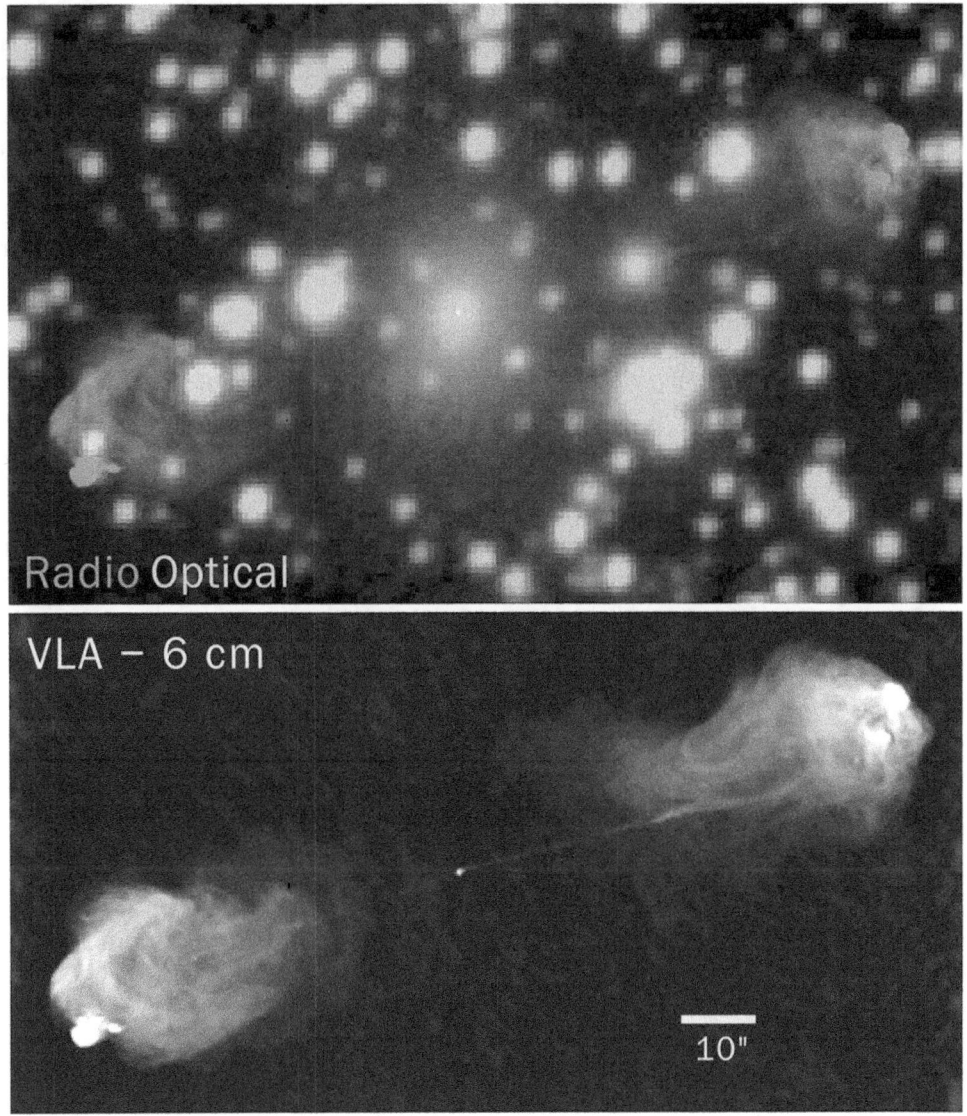

Plate 10.1 The upper panel shows a comparison between the resolution of radio telescope and an optical telescope. Clearly, the former resolves two objects whereas the latter does not. The lower panel shows a very large array (VLA) radio telescope image of two lobes, with material drawn towards a black hole. Image composition and overlay by William Keel. Optical image courtesy of Frazer Owen. VLA image courtesy of NRAO/AUI.

In December 1952, Hanbury Brown reported the size of Cygnus A, the brightest of the radio stars, measured using his intensity interferometer. At the same time, Bernard Mills (Chapter 11) in Sydney measured it with a conventional interferometer. As both reported the same result, the accuracy of the intensity interferometer was confirmed. These results were published back-to-back in *Nature*. We now know why Cygnus A (in the constellation Cygnus) is such an intense radio source, as it was subsequently identified with optics in the 1950s. It is, in fact, a galaxy consisting of billions of stars with the largest black hole yet identified at its centre. As Plate 10.1 shows (upper panel), the finer resolution of radio waves in the electromagnetic spectrum over that of visible light waves means that the angular size of radio stars is thousands of times better resolved than that of visible stars. Plate 10.1 (lower panel) also shows streams of material drawn towards the black hole, with two lobes at the farthest extremities of the material. Amazingly, even in 1952, Hanbury Brown and his colleagues were able to show that Cygnus A was very asymmetrical, subtending about 35 seconds in one direction and two minutes and ten seconds in the other. In other words, it is four times longer in one direction than the other. This has been confirmed with modern instrumentation. Another radio source studied at this time, Cassiopeia A, was determined to be symmetrical at about four degrees angular width and proved to be the brightest extra-solar radio source (at 1 GHz) in the Milky Way. It is now known that it is most likely a supernova remnant.

The stellar interferometer and the Hanbury Brown-Twiss Effect

In 1954, Hanbury Brown and his team, as well as Twiss, were observing Cygnus A with the intensity interferometer when the ionosphere was particularly unstable. It was noted that although the signals were exceptionally noisy, the correlation – the effect measured by the intensity interferometer – was unaffected. Twiss then realised that an optical intensity interferometer should be unaffected by atmospheric turbulence. The principle of the intensity interferometer was extended to the visible part of the electromagnetic spectrum in 1956. Radial antennae were replaced by mirrors, using the reflectors of two standard anti-aircraft search lights, 156 centimetres in diameter, left over from the war to focus light into an area of only 8 millimetres diameter.

The team first chose the star Sirius (Alpha Canis Majoris A), which is bright enough to make preliminary measurements possible. At this time, no direct measurement of the angular diameter of a star had ever been made. The starlight received by the search lights was shown to be maximally correlated at 2.4 metres separation and decreasing to nearly zero at a separation of nine metres, giving a measurement of 0.0063 minutes. This figure compares well with modern measurements and was a triumph for the principle of the intensity interferometer. Unlike conventional light telescopes, the interferometer gave measurements that were independent of ionospheric scintillations. It required only relatively crude light collectors, compared with those used in conventional telescopes; 'their function would be simply to collect light from the star like rain in a bucket and poured it on to a detector'.[6] Furthermore, Hanbury Brown showed that his interferometer

---

6   Hanbury Brown 1991, 119.

had a resolving power hundreds of times greater than the highest value then reported by conventional astronomy, limited only by the electronics available at the time, rather than by the optical techniques used.

The paper by Hanbury Brown and Twiss, Correlation Between Photons in Two Coherent Beams of Light in *Nature*, provided the necessary foundations for the use of intensity interferometry in the light electromagnetic spectrum.[7] It caused a major controversy in the physics world. As Hanbury Brown commented,

> The most common objection to our work was that the time of arrival of one photon at a detector cannot conceivably be correlated with that of another because individual photons are emitted at random times and must therefore arrive at random times.[8]

It was not until much later, with development of quantum optics based on the Hanbury Brown–Twiss Effect, that the physics community came to realise the profound nature of these insights. At the heart of the controversy surrounding the successful development of the intensity interferometer some 60 years ago was the accepted wisdom that photons are particles, which, when in a stream projected at a detector/absorber, exchange energy with it in quanta. What Hanbury Brown and Twiss' critics had not taken on board was that in a beam of light the now enormous number of photons do not preserve their individuality, but act as a wave. So in the Hanbury Brown–Twiss effect, it was the waves collected that were correlated and not individual particles or photons. This was apparent in the critical comment subsequently made in the journal *Nature* that Hanbury Brown and Twiss' experiments could not be reproduced. Hanbury Brown and Twiss attributed this failure to the critical authors using a low intensity light source, a beam, in which the photons were detected as uncorrelated particles. They showed that the wave-like properties are revealed and the correlations obtained if a mercury-vapour lamp is used – a source with millions more photons than in a beam. A fuller account of interferometry and of the sources of this controversy is given in the Appendix.

The stellar interferometer at Narrabri

Hanbury Brown next sought to measure the size of about 200 stars with reflectors several metres in diameter at a baseline of about 200 metres. This was estimated to cost about £70,000 sterling, an enormous amount in 1956. When most of the money for this new intensity interferometer was offered by the head of the physics department at the University of Sydney, Harry Messel, Hanbury Brown found the offer too good to resist. He went to Sydney intending to stay for a year, on leave from Manchester University, and stayed for 27 years! In the first few years, he guided the building of his newly designed intensity interferometer in the Australian bush at Narrabri. The equipment consisted of two telescopes, some seven metres in diameter, that could move on a circular track 183 metres in diameter.[9] Hanbury Brown described, in some detail, the hazards of maintaining

---

7 Hanbury Brown and Twiss, 'Correlation between photons', 1956.
8 Hanbury Brown 1991, 121.

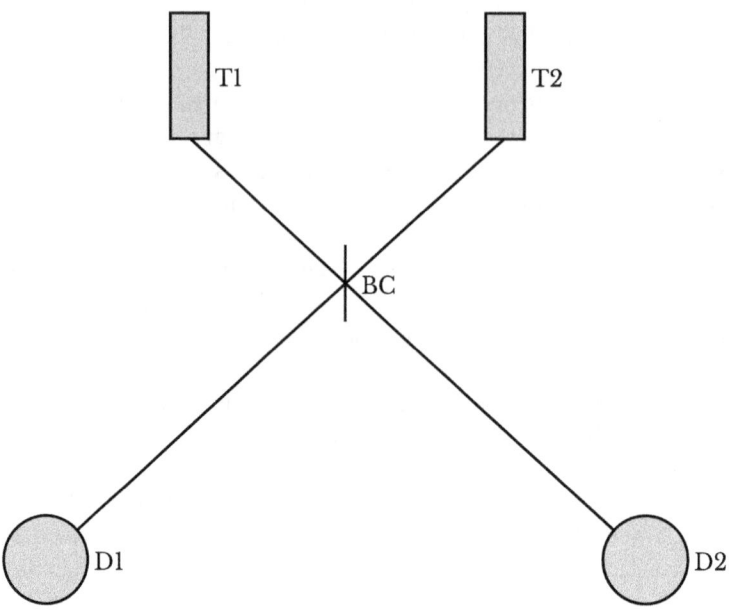

Figure 10.4 Diagram of a classical interferometer. Courtesy of William Tango.

an interferometer in an Australian sheep paddock. These included clambering over a telescope to remove bird droppings from its 250 mirrors, dislodging frogs from the equipment and removing snakes. This was a regular job, especially clearing the droppings as the local birds became accustomed to pecking at the mirrors. In addition, Hanbury Brown had to work through very hot summers and cold nights waiting for the ideal conditions to take measurements. The first star he measured was Vega (Alpha Lyrae) in August 1963. Indeed, this was the first main-sequence star to be measured other than Sirius, which he had measured years earlier at Jodrell Bank. The main program, which was to measure 100 stars, began in June 1965 with Beta Crucis (Mimera; which appears on the Australian flag) and finished with measurement of the coolest star on his list, S. Canis Majoris (Wezem) in 1971.

***

Some 17 years after his death, Hanbury Brown has become a legendary figure, described as 'as giant from a golden period of innovation in astronomy'.[10] I can personally attest to the truth of the final line of his obituary in the journal *Nature*, written by Robert May (Chapter 16) and Bernard Lovell – Hanbury Brown was 'a really lovely man'.[11]

---

9 Hanbury Brown 1991, 126
10 Lovell and May 2002, 34.
11 Lovell and May 2002, 34.

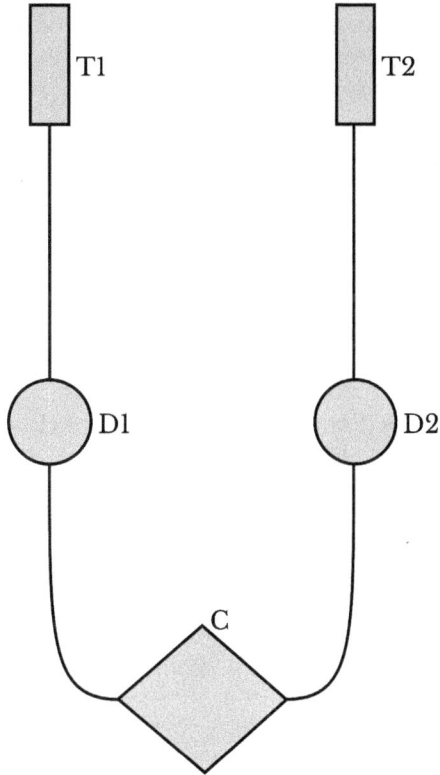

Figure 10.5 Diagram of an intensity interferometer.
Courtesy of William Tango.

Appendix

The original radio intensity interferometer developed by Hanbury Brown was non-controversial; it was based on standard electromagnetic theory and a recently developed theory of noise processes. However, when the technique was used with visible light it caused a major controversy.[12]

Figure 10.4 shows a simplified diagram of a classical interferometer. *T*1 and *T*2 are telescopes, and the light from the two telescopes is combined in a 'beam combiner' (typically a half-silvered mirror). The light is then detected by two photodetectors, *D*1 and *D*2. According to classical wave theory, the light waves interfere at the beam combiner and give rise to a characteristic interference signal when the light is detected. According to quantum mechanics, light is made up of photons that can exhibit particle-like or wave-like properties, depending on the experimental set-up used to detect them. Interference will occur even when the incident beam is reduced in intensity to the point where only one

---

[12] Appendix informed by William Gibson and William Tango.

photon enters at a time. This occurs because the wave-like property of the photon allows it to interfere with itself. Any measurement of the location of the photon in the apparatus will destroy the interference pattern.

Figure 10.5 shows an intensity interferometer. In this case light from each telescope is separately detected by the photodetectors. The electrical signals from the detectors then go to a piece of electronics called a correlator (C), where the signals are combined. According to conventional quantum theory, the intensity interferometer should not work because a photon arriving at a detector must have passed through $T1$ or $T2$ and thus cannot interfere with itself. The fact that the intensity interferometer actually works (gives an interference pattern) appeared to fundamentally challenge the conventional interpretation of one of the foundations of quantum mechanics.

It was not until 1962 that a satisfactory explanation was finally given by Roy Glauber (see Glauber's Nobel Prize lecture for an excellent account). Critics of the intensity interferometer had focused on the 'single photon' case; the Hanbury Brown–Twiss effect can only be observed when there are many photons present. If one treats photons as particles, then, according to quantum statistical mechanics, they obey Bose–Einstein statistics, which means that an arbitrary number can occupy the same quantum state and thus exhibit a 'bunching effect'. This means that when many photons are present, they should not be treated as independent classical particles but as a quantum ensemble. Hanbury Brown and Twiss' stellar intensity interferometer made significant contributions to fundamental astrophysics and, perhaps more importantly, marked the beginning of a new field in physics – quantum optics.

Further reading

Davis, J., and B. Lovell. 'Robert Hanbury Brown 1916–2002.' *Historical Records of Australian Science* 14, no. 4 (2003): 459–83.
Hanbury Brown, R. *Boffin: A Personal Story of the Early Days of Radar, Radio Astronomy and Quantum Optics*. New York; Abingdon, ON: Taylor and Francis, 1991.
Hanbury Brown, R., and R.Q. Twiss. 'A Test of a New Type of Stellar Interferometer on Sirius.' *Nature* 178, no. 4541 (1956): 1046–8.
Hanbury Brown, R., and R.Q. Twiss. 'Interferometry of the Intensity Fluctuations in Lights. I Basic Theory: The Correlation Between Photons in Coherent Beams of Radiation.' *Proceedings of the Royal Society of London. Series A, Mathematical and Physical Sciences* 242, no. 1230 (1957): 300–24.
Hanbury Brown, R., and R.Q. Twiss. 'Interferometry of the Intensity Fluctuations in Lights. II An Experimental Test of the Theory for Partially Coherent Light.' *Proceedings of the Royal Society. Series A, Mathematical and Physical Sciences* 243, no. 1234 (1958): 291–319.
Tango, W.J. 'The Hanbury Brown–Twiss Effect and the Birth of Quantum Optics.' *Australian Physics* 51, no. 4 (2014): 116–21.

11
Radio signals from stars and the invention of the Mills Cross telescope: Bernard Mills

Professor of Astrophysics (1965–1985). Mills was one of the foremost radiophysicists of his generation as a consequence of his design of a radio telescope that came to be known as the Mills Cross. This provided unparalleled accuracy for the determination of the position of radio sources in the heavens and for their subsequent identification by optical astronomy. His research had considerable consequences for cosmology.

In the period from 1959 to 1961, the head of the physics department at the University of Sydney, Harry Messel, a PhD graduate under the great Erwin Schrödinger, of quantum mechanics fame, formed a 'radio astronomy centre'. This had far-reaching consequences for the world of radio astronomy. First, as we have seen, Messel brought Robert Hanbury Brown (Chapter 10) from Manchester by offering him supporting funds to establish a major optical intensity interferometer at Narrabri. Second, he offered to assist with funding Bernard Mills' construction of the large cross-type radio telescope known as the Molonglo Cross, with arms of one mile in length. Hanbury Brown, as we have seen, was expected to be at the School of Physics for a year or two but stayed on for 27 years. Mills stayed on for 25 years. It must have been an extremely supportive department to have retained two such brilliant men. They, together with Ruby Payne-Scott (Chapter 12), made Sydney a mecca for world astronomy for over two decades.

Mills was born in Manly and, like Hanbury Brown (Chapter 10), who was five years his senior, showed precocious gifts in engineering at an early age. He entered the engineering school at Sydney University at 16, in 1937, and subsequently graduated with degrees in both physics and engineering in 1943. His exceptional gifts were recognised by the head of the Radiophysics Laboratory of the Council for Scientific and Industrial Research (CSIR) on the campus of Sydney University, Joseph Pawsey, who instilled in him both a physical grasp and an analytical understanding of radiophysics. During the war years, Mills made significant contributions to the design of a height-determining radar system within the receive-and-display group at the university, a technique that was used after the war at Mascot Airport for determining the altitude of commercial aircraft.

Mills' progress was temporarily arrested when he contracted tuberculosis in 1947. He was lucky to be able to receive injections of penicillin shortly after its introduction by

Figure 11.1 *Dr Bernard Mills, Sydney University, 1960*, Australian News and Information Bureau. National Library of Australia, PIC/10555/1814.

another Australian, Howard Florey, restoring him to normal health in six months. Mills then carried out research on X-rays and developed a resonant-cavity X-ray tube, which gave rise to his first publication in 1950. An earlier cavity tube, the klystron – invented in Manchester during the war by a team headed by yet another Australian, Marcus Oliphant – made a very significant contribution to the success of radar in the later part of the war.

A necessary requirement of undergraduate education in engineering was that part of one's annual holidays was spent working on the shop floor of various industries, obtaining hands-on experience. As a consequence, Mills became quite left-wing in support of the workers he met and joined the Communist Party. I also carried out such hands-on experience as an undergraduate in engineering at Melbourne University and can well understand why Mills went down this political path, given the work conditions I observed. Mills' far left-wing views were consolidated by his future wife, the Russian-born medical student Lerida Karmalsky. He remained a member of the Communist Party until the Russian invasion of Hungary in 1956, five years after Prime Minister Robert Menzies had unsuccessfully attempted to ban the party through a referendum to change the constitution. Mills would have been carefully monitored by the Australian Security Intelligence Organisation, even though he had played an important part in the development of radar during the war. Figure 11.2 shows Mills and Menzies sharing a joke in 1965, nine years after Mills had left the party and 14 years after the failed referendum; presumably any hostilities between the two great men had wound down by this stage and both had mellowed.

An atlas of radio sources in the heavens

In 1951, Pawsey suggested that Mills do some work in radio astronomy, an opportunity Mills jumped at. He was invited to join a new radio astronomy group that had been established at Badgerys Creek (at the time of writing, 2018, Badgerys Creek is appropriately destined to be Sydney's new airport). Mills then used interferometry (see Chapter 10), to discover 77 new and discrete radio sources. He concluded, in 1952, that many of these sources were greatly extended in space, as Hanbury Brown had shown the extended nature of Cygnus A. Furthermore, very strong sources were concentrated in two astronomical areas: one of these sources, designated Class 1, is found within our galaxy; the other source, designated Class 2, radio stars, is found within our Milky Way or outside our galaxy altogether. By 1953, thanks to the work of his group, Mills was able to make the first comparison between optically determined positions of nebulae and maps of radio sources.[1]

Mills' group paid particular attention to Cygnus A, which was also intensely studied at this time by Hanbury Brown's group at Jodrell Bank and Ryle's group at Cambridge. Mills not only worked on Cygnus A at this time, but also on Taurus A, Virgo A and Centaurus A. He found that optical measurements of the angular size of the latter three nebulae were similar to those determined by radio astronomy, providing strong support for the accuracy of the radio method. He also discovered that, in most cases, the nebulae were not stars at all. These research results were published back-to-back with the results

---

1 See Mills 1953.

Figure 11.2 Mills enjoying a moment with the then Australian Prime Minister, Sir Robert Menzies during the official opening ceremony for the Molonglo Observatory on 19th November 1965. The Head of the School of Physics at the University of Sydney, Professor Harry Messel, is on the far right. Photograph commissioned by the University of Sydney, reproduced with permission from the School of Physics.

of Hanbury Brown's group in *Nature* in 1952. Mills' group later published a survey of the radio sky that catalogued 2,270 discrete radio sources.[2]

Implications of the atlas of radio sources for cosmology

Mills' surveys were significantly different from those of Ryle's group in Cambridge (although Ryle was destined to win the Nobel Prize in 1974). Mills put this down to the inadequate resolution of the interferometer used by Ryle at Cambridge in 1950; this led to an incorrect estimation of the number, distribution and identification of radio sources in the so-called Cambridge 2C catalogue of radio emission sites. Mills regarded the

---

2   Mills, Slee and Hill 1958, 1960, 1961 (known as MSH).

number of radio sources identified by Ryle as impossibly high. Ryle rejected this and claimed his group's work gave the most accurate account of radio sources. He went on to argue, in his 1955 Halley Lecture in Oxford, that his group's work had important cosmological implications. Specifically, he claimed that Fred Hoyle's[3] cosmological hypothesis – namely, that the universe cycled through a period of expansion, contraction and renewal known as the Steady State Model – was wrong.[4] To this Mills responded vehemently, stating that 'deductions of cosmological interest derived from its [Ryle's] analysis are without foundation'.[5]

This profound disagreement can be expressed quantitatively by plotting the logarithm of the number of sources (N) against the logarithm of their flux density (S), which produces a slope, in the case of Class 2 sources, of -1.5 (indicating that radio stars, which are relatively weak emitters, are in fact extra-galactic sources). On the other hand, Class 1 sources (within our galaxy at relatively low density but with strong emissions) had a $\log(N)$ versus $\log(S)$ slope of -0.75, consistent with their non-homogeneous distribution in our galaxy. Plotting Ryle's data gave a slope that was substantially steeper than -1.5, indicating a very large number of faint sources. A slope of -1.5 is consistent with Hoyle's theory of a steady state universe, whereas a slope steeper than -1.5 is not. Hence, Ryle's claim in his Oxford lecture that his group's empirical evidence refuted the cosmological hypothesis of a steady state universe, in contra-distinction to the Big Bang Theory, was important. His Cambridge 2C survey, challenged by Mills as incorrect, was then important for distinguishing between cosmological theories.

At that time, Mills received a letter from Fred Hoyle asking for an opinion on Ryle's data, as the latter would not acknowledge that his group's 2C catalogue was in grave error. Indeed, Ryle never publicly retracted his claims, but by 1957 the 2C catalogue was generally recognised as unreliable. Ryle buried the problem by producing a new catalogue, called 3C, that corrected the 2C catalogue and brought the Cambridge observations into line with Mills'. The confusion generated by the 2C catalogue was due to 'the blending of several weak sources' by the inferior interferometer that Ryle used at Cambridge.[6] As for the rival cosmological models, this matter was not settled until 1965, when Penzias and Wilson serendipitously discovered cosmic background radiation, greatly favouring the Big Bang Theory of the origin of the universe.

Engineering the development of radio astronomy

In the early 1950s, Mills recognised the importance of resolution rather than sensitivity in the design of a survey radio telescope. He conceived the idea of placing two linear arrays of antennae at right angles to one another, realising that the combination of phase-reversing switches with a crossed symmetrical array of antennae had the effect of multiplying the two sets of antenna responses together. The resulting narrow pencil-beam response would provide very exact determinations of the positions and angular properties of radio

---

3   Hoyle was the leading mathematical astronomer of his generation.
4   See Ryle 1955
5   Mills and Slee 1957.
6   Frater, Goss and Wendt 2013, 302.

The Search for Knowledge and Understanding

Figure 11.3 A close up view of the prototype Mills Cross at the Potts Hill field station. The prototype cross operated at 97 MHz with a beamwidth of eight degrees. Each arm of the cross was 36 metres in length. CSIRO Radio Astronomy Image Archive (B3064-3).

sources. This idea was tested in 1953 with a 36-metre cross, consisting of arms composed of wooden posts and aerials made of chicken wire (see Figure 11.3). Amazingly, this prototype was able to provide the first radio-continuum detection of the Large Magellanic Cloud. After the success of the prototype, Mills decanted to Badgerys Creek, where the Fleurs field station had been established at a disused Second-World-War air-strip. By 1954, two arms of 450 metres in length were established, forming the Mills Cross, as it became known (see Figure 11.4). This was equivalent to a single dish antenna 450 metres in diameter, large enough to provide greatly improved resolution and reveal the basic spiral form of our own galaxy, together with the tangential directions of its spiral arms.

In 1960, Mills left the CSIR Radiophysics Laboratory and joined the School of Physics at the University of Sydney. With funding from the Head of School, Harry Messel, together with a substantial grant from the US National Science Foundation, the Mills Cross at Fleurs was surpassed by an even larger cross, with arms over a mile long, built by Mills at the Molonglo Radio Observatory near Canberra. The sensitivity of this instrument was about 20 times greater than that of the cross at Fleurs. The Molonglo Cross was operational in 1967. Over a period of 11 years, it achieved remarkable results, including

Figure 11.4 The Mills Cross at the Fleurs field station looking south along the N-S arm. The telescope operated at 85.5 MHz with a beamwidth of 48 arc min. Each arm of the cross was 450 metres in length. CSIRO Radio Astronomy Image Archive (B3476-3).

identifying more than half of the known supernova remnants and pulsars, and providing observations for the production of the Molonglo Reference Catalogue, consisting of more than 12,000 radio sources.

By the late 1970s, computers and electronics had reached a level of sophistication that enabled real-time control of the telescope over periods of 12 hours. This meant that tracking observations could be made with just the east-west arm of the cross, using the rotation of the Earth to synthesise a telescope one mile in diameter. By 1982, a map of, for example, the radio source 1733-565 had sufficiently high resolution to pinpoint its optical counterpart, an elliptical galaxy, despite the high density of foreground stars (see Figure 11.5).

***

The Mills Cross design led to many important discoveries, including identifying individual sources in the Magellanic Clouds and over 2,000 sources across the southern radio sky,[7] as well as providing insights into the physics of normal spiral galaxies. It

---

7   Mills 2011.

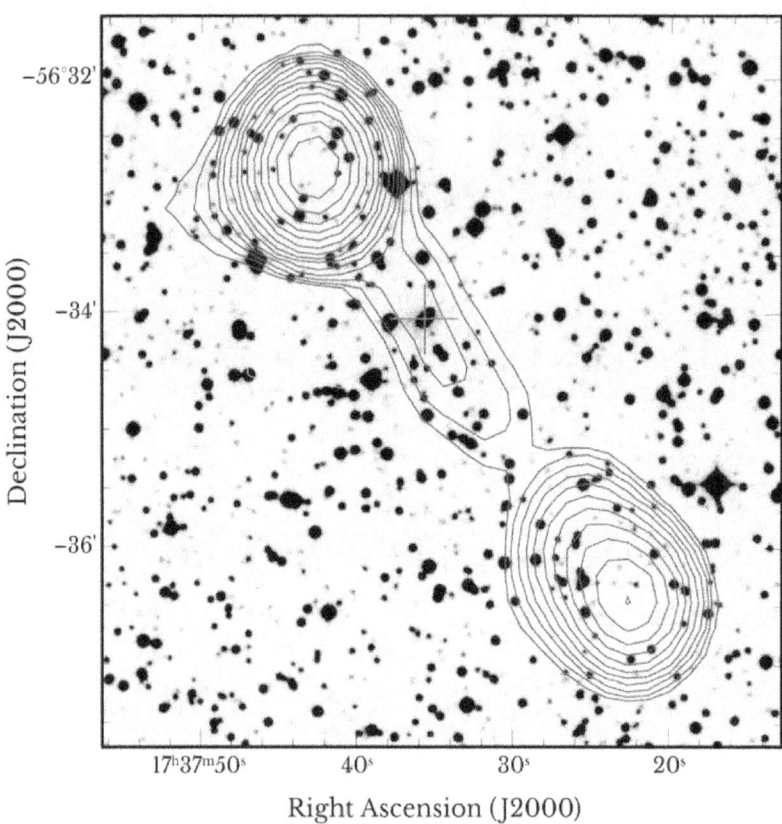

Figure 11.5 Radio contours from the Sydney University Molonglo Sky Survey at 843 MHz overlaid on an optical image of the field from the UK Schmidt IIIaJ survey. The galaxy responsible for the radio emission is marked with a cross. Note that the radio emission extends way beyond the confines of the host galaxy, carried outwards by symmetric jets travelling at a significant fraction of the speed of light. Modified by Richard Hunstead from R.W. Hustead, J.M. Durdin, A.G. Little, J.E. Reynolds and M.J.L. Kesteven, '1733–565: A Compact Radio Galaxy at Low Galactic Latitude,' *Publications of the Astronomical Society of Australia* 4, no. 14 (1982): 447–51. © Cambridge University Press. Reproduced with permission from Cambridge University Press and Richard Hunstead.

contributed in very significant ways to matters of great interest in astronomy.[8] But while Mills' legacy is centred on his capacity for highly original designs and applications of radio telescopes, he was also, as Harry Messel commented at a memorial service, 'the mentor of many well-known researchers'; 'many distinguished astronomers benefited

---

8   Bhathal 2012, 2.20.

from Bernie's astute mind and towering intellect'.[9] In the words of his mentor, Joseph Pawsey, 'Mills' past work "has been outstanding, his contribution has probably been the greatest single factor in giving Australian radio astronomy the high prestige it now enjoys".'[10]

Further reading

Frater, R.H., W.M. Goss and H.W. Wendt. 'Bernard Yarnton Mills 1920–2011.' *Historical Records of Australian Science* 24, no. 2 (2013): 294–315.

Goddard, B.R., A. Watkinson and B.Y. Mills. 'An Interferometer for the Measurement of Radio Source Sizes.' *Australian Journal of Physics* 13, no. 4 (1960): 665–75.

Mills, B.Y. 'On the Identification of Extragalactic Radio Sources.' *Australian Journal of Physics* 13, no. 3 (1960): 550.

Mills, B.Y., E.R. Hill and O.B. Slee. 'The Galaxy at 3.5 m.' *The Observatory* 78 (1958): 116–21.

Mills, B.Y., and O.B. Slee. 'A Preliminary Survey of Radio Sources in a Limited Region of the Sky at the Wavelength of 3.5 m.' *Australian Journal of Physics* 10, no. 1 (1957): 162–94.

Mills, B.Y., O.B. Slee and E.R. Hill. 'A Catalogue of Radio Sources Between Declinations +10° and –20°.' *Australian Journal of Physics* 11, no. 3 (1958): 360–87.

Mills, B.Y., O.B. Slee and E.R. Hill. 'A Catalogue of Radio Sources Between Declinations –20° and –50°.' *Australian Journal of Physics* 13, no. 4 (1960): 676–99.

Mills, B.Y., O.B. Slee and E.R. Hill. 'A Catalogue of Radio Sources Between Declinations –50° and –80°.' *Australian Journal of Physics* 14, no. 4 (1961): 497–507.

Ryle, M. 'Radio Stars and Their Cosmological Significance.' *The Observatory* 75 (1955): 137–47.

---

9 Frater, Goss and Wendt 2013, 310.
10 Pawsey 1960, quoted in Frater, Goss and Wendt 2013, 304.

12
Radio signals from sunspots and the invention of the swept-lobe interferometer: Ruby Payne-Scott

Payne-Scott was a brilliant physicist who, at an early age, played a major role in the establishment of radio astronomy through contributions in engineering and mathematics and, especially, observations on sunspots.

The survival of life on Earth, as well as transient phenomena such as the aurora borealis and magnetic storms, depends on the sun. Research into solar physics was revolutionised by the discovery that sunspots emit radio waves, which can be used to probe the properties of the sun's plasma. Ruby Payne-Scott, over a relatively short period as a research officer on the campus of Sydney University, made fundamental contributions to our understanding of the origins, identity and properties of these radio waves.

Payne-Scott was a brilliant and feisty feminist who did not suffer fools gladly, essential characteristics for a woman in the academic research world in the first half of the 20th century. She was greatly admired by her peers, not least for her unique combination of gifts in the design of astronomical instrumentation, in mathematical analysis and in scientific enquiry. These peers were world leaders in radio astronomy, such as Hanbury Brown (Chapter 10) and Mills (Chapter 11). Payne-Scott, like Mills, was a member of the Communist Party, a commitment made at that time by many who felt deeply about society, but one that brought her to the attention of the Commonwealth Investigation Service and the Australian Security Intelligence Organisation. Fortunately for astronomy, this attention did not interrupt her work, although absurd rules, especially governing the employment of women in Australia, did.

Payne-Scott was born in Grafton, New South Wales, in 1912 to Cyril Payne-Scott, an accountant, and his wife Amy (née Neale), a teacher. At the age of nine, Payne-Scott was sent to Sydney to live with her aunt and attend public primary school. At 13, she entered Cleveland Street High School. She subsequently attended the prestigious Sydney Girls' High School, where she finished her secondary school education with honours in mathematics and botany. Payne-Scott was awarded two scholarships to enter the University of Sydney, where she studied physics, chemistry, mathematics and botany, achieving a Bachelor of Science at 21, in 1933, with first class honours in physics and mathematics. At this time, she was only the third female to ever graduate in physics at the

Figure 12.1 Ruby Payne-Scott at the Potts Hill Reservoir in 1948, when she and Alec Little (centre) were using the recently built swept-lobe interferometer to observe solar radio emissions at 97 MHz. In the background (right) is the famous radio astronomer and electrical engineer 'Chris' Christiansen. CSIRO Radio Astronomy Image Archive (B14315).

university. Payne-Scott then completed a Master of Science in physics in 1936, together with a Diploma of Education in 1938.

In 1939, towards the end of the Great Depression and the beginning of the Second World War, Payne-Scott took full-time employment with Amalgamated Wireless Australasia (AWA) in Sydney, the foremost engineering establishment in communication technology in the country. She quickly developed skills related to radio reception and transmission, as well as small signal visibility on radar displays, becoming an expert in the detection of aircraft using what became known as Plan Position Indicator displays. This led to her recruitment to the Radiophysics Laboratory of the Council for Scientific and Industrial Research (CSIR) to contribute to research on radar. This was housed in the National Standards Laboratory Building, now called the Madsen Building, at the City Road entrance to the University of Sydney.

Joseph Pawsey, head of radar research, soon recognised her brilliance, and by 1942, in the middle of the war, they started collaborating on measurements of extra-terrestrial radio signals, regarded by many as belonging to the realms of science fiction. Their success was such that, towards the end of the war, Payne-Scott, Pawsey and others were able to form the Radiophysics Division of the CSIR in the Madsen Building, creating one of only two such teams in the world devoted to radiophysics at that time. This new discipline was principally involved in determining the origins of cosmic radio signals, which were thought to emanate from the galaxy. Why such excitement over the identification and characterisation of solar radio waves? Because it was soon realised that these waves provided fundamental information concerning the physics of the sun, the importance of which is self-evident.

The team's first measurements were made at the seaside suburb of Collaroy (24 kilometres north of Sydney) and later at Dover Heights in Sydney's Eastern suburbs (17 kilometres from Collaroy) and on the North Head at the entrance to Sydney Harbour, using radar equipment discarded by the Royal Australian Air Force. These sites are on the edges of cliffs, about 85 metres above sea level; they were strategically located there during the war to detect the approach of enemy aircraft. At these locations, as well as at Potts Hill, Payne-Scott made seminal contributions to radio astronomy, to the design of novel instrumentation for recording radio signals and to the analysis of these recorded signals.

The photosphere and sunspots

Sunspots arise from the surface of the photosphere – the visible outer layer of the sun (Figure 12.2). The photosphere is composed of plasma – a mixture of charged positive ions and electrons, together with some neutral atoms, in a magnetic field. This plasma is organised into turbulent cells, each about 1,000 kilometres in diameter, which only last for about ten minutes. While the photosphere is about 5,500 degrees Celsius, the corona is much hotter and is separated from the photosphere by the 2,000-kilometre-thick chromosphere (Figure 12.2). Sunspots – each about 10,000–100,000 kilometres in diameter – appear as dark spots in comparison to their surroundings as a consequence of the reduced temperature of the plasma (to between 2,700 and 4,200 degrees Celsius); the brightness (luminance) varies with temperature changes by about the fourth power.

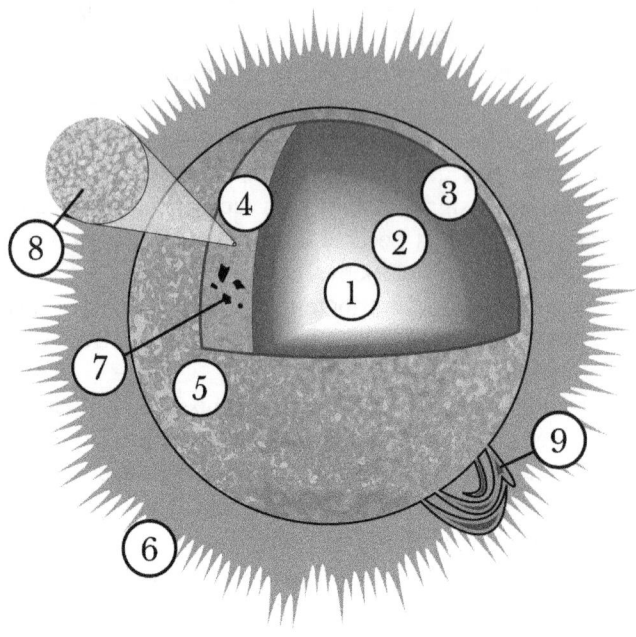

Figure 12.2 The structure of the sun. 1. core; 2. radiation zone; 3. convection zone; 4. photosphere; 5. chromosphere; 6. corona; 7. sunspot; 8. granules; 9. prominence. Modified from sun diagram by Pbroks13, Wikimedia Commons, https://bit.ly/2tAksg9.

Sunspots occur due to intense tubes of magnetic flux emerging from the plasma and subsequently plunging back into it, reducing the convection of the plasma at these sites and so causing a drop in temperature. The emergence of the magnetic flux and its subsequent return to the plasma means that sunspots always appear in pairs. Sunspots can be active for many weeks. They may disappear from view for weeks due to the rotation of the sun over 27 days; their reappearance indicates that they have lasted at least two weeks. One of the largest sunspots ever observed occurred in February 1946, occupying 0.52 per cent of the solar area (Figure 12.3). On 7 April that year, an even larger sunspot was detected, occupying 0.61 per cent. Payne-Scott and her colleagues were lucky enough to be making solar radio measurements at this time. Solar flares – sudden flashes of increased brightness – arise when the plasma reaches enormous temperatures of millions of degrees, resulting in the accelerated ejection of electrons, as well as of protons and heavy ions, at almost the speed of light.

Identification of solar radio bursts

In February 1942, the radar equipment used by the British to detect enemy aircraft was interrupted by noise from an unidentified source, thought at first to be due to the Germans

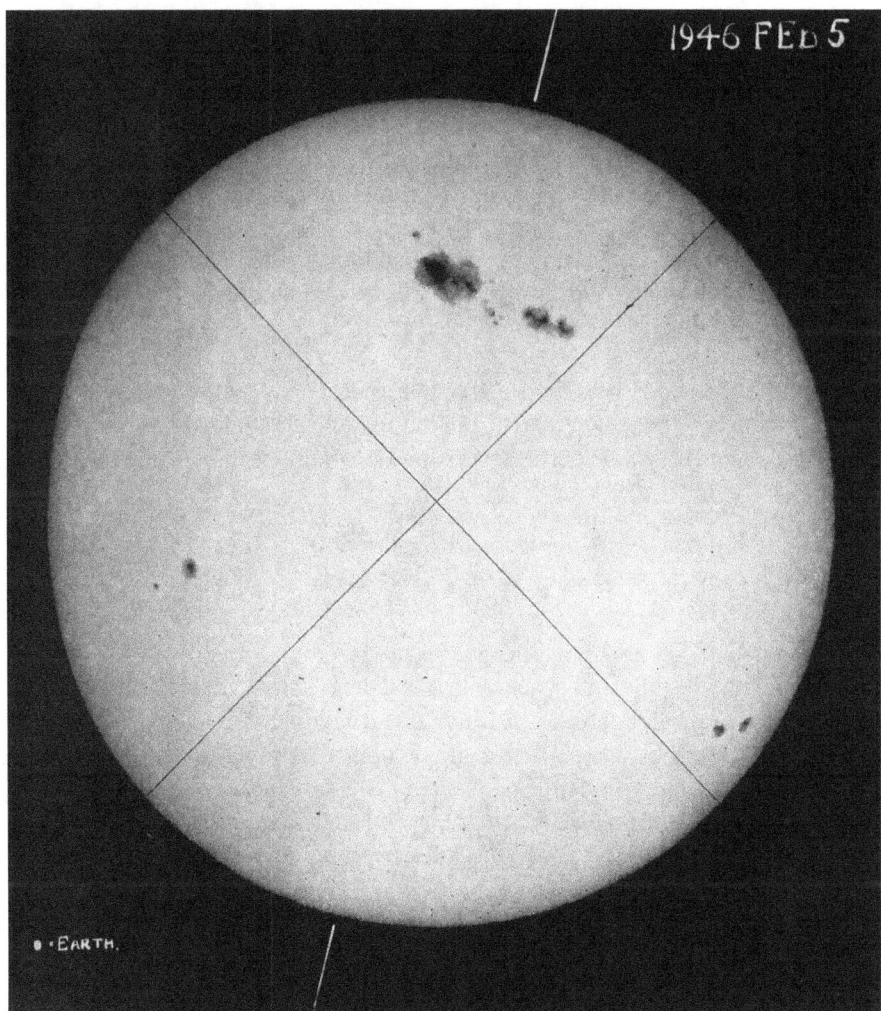

Figure 12.3 An optical image of one of the largest sunspots ever observed, occupying 0.52 per cent of the solar area. Observed at the Royal Greenwich Observatory on 5 February 1946. From E. Appleton and J.S. Hey, 'Solar Radio Noise.- I,' *The London, Edinburgh and Dublin Philosophical Magazine and Journal of Science (Series 7)* 37, no. 265 (1946): 73–84. Reprinted with permission of the publisher, Taylor and Francis Ltd., www.tandfonline.com.

jamming radar reception.[1] Just over three and a half years later, on 3 October 1945, at sea cliffs near Sydney, Payne-Scott and her colleagues detected noise signals on the Eastern horizon at 5:31 am (sunrise). These signals were 27 per cent above the general background noise, rising to 450 per cent higher (equivalent to a flux density of 106 Janskys[2]) nine minutes later, at 5:40 am. They reported: 'We observed, from the direction of the sun, a

---

1 Army Operational Research Group (British) Report No. 275 (Restricted Reports), 13 June 1945.
2 A Jansky is a unit of flux density for electromagnetic radiation.

considerable amount of radiation having the apparent characteristics of fluctuation "noise" when observed on a cathode-ray oscillograph or head-phones.'[3] However, changes in the azimuth (see Chapter 10) of arrival and the intensity of the radiation with variations in the horizontal rotation of the aerial, as well as the elevation of the sun, indicated that the body of the sun was the source of the radiation. Payne-Scott and her colleagues rejected the proposition that the increased noise signals came from interstellar space:

> In view of observations of such intense bursts of radiation from the sun at the wavelengths at which 'cosmic static' is known, it appears desirable to question the suggestion that the latter originates in the interstellar space.[4]

Furthermore, they regarded it as improbable that such bursts 'should originate in atomic or molecular processes, but suggest an origin in gross electrical disturbances analogous to our thunderstorms'.[5] This was the first occasion on which the fluctuations were referred to as 'bursts'.

Solar radio bursts emanate from sunspots

In late 1945, Payne-Scott and her colleagues established that solar bursts of radio waves occur coincidentally in time and space with sunspots.[6] This involved collaboration with Clabon Allen at the Australian National University's Mount Stromlo Optical Observatory. Allen could alert them by phone that a major optical sunspot, or sunspots, had been observed. Through comparisons of radio bursts and visualisations of sunspots, Payne-Scott and her colleagues were able to report that 'it is apparent that the peaks of 1.5-metre radiation coincide with peaks of the sunspot area curve and with the passage of large sunspot groups across the meridian'.[7]

This is clearly shown in Figure 12.4. In the upper graph, the left ordinate indicates the increases in receiver power output relative to the value when the antenna was directed away from the sun, while the ordinate to the right indicates equivalent temperature. The lower graph gives the optical size of sunspots observed by Clabon Allen at the Mount Stromlo Observatory. Both graphs are plotted on the horizontal axis for dates in October 1945. At the bottom are shown major sunspots observed on 5, 11 and 21 October 1945 (barely visible). The coincidental peaks and troughs in the upper and lower graphs show the correlation between the sunspots and the burst radiation. Payne-Scott commented that

> It will be seen that there is good correlation between the two curves [the radio intensity and the sunspot area], particularly between their peaks, the peaks of the radiation curve being sharper than those of the curve for the sunspot area ... the

---

3   Pawsey, Payne-Scott and McCready 1946, 158.
4   Pawsey, Payne-Scott and McCready 1946, 158.
5   Pawsey, Payne-Scott and McCready 1946, 159.
6   Pawsey, Payne-Scott and McCready 1946.
7   Pawsey, Payne-Scott and McCready 1946, 158.

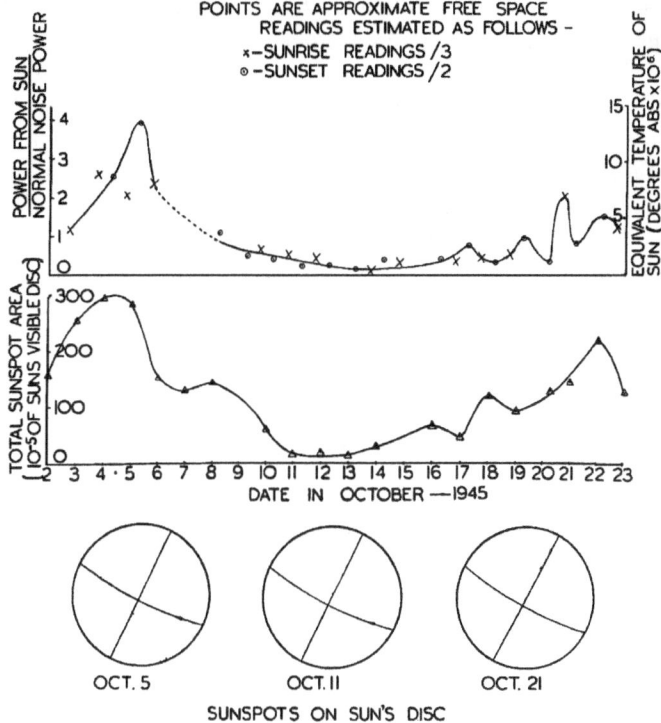

Figure 12.4 This figure, from the first Australian publication on solar radio noise, shows correlations between the size of the optical image of sunspots and the power of the solar radio noise recorded on the same dates in October 1945. The top graph shows the power of the radio noise and the lower graph the optical size of sunspots, as observed at the Commonwealth Solar Observatory at Mt Stromlo on the same date. The bottom figure gives the position of sunspots (barely visible) on the surface of the Sun on the dates specified. Reprinted by permission from Springer Nature: J.L. Pawsey, R. Payne-Scott and L.L. McCready, 'Radio-Frequency Energy from the Sun,' 1946. https://www.nature.com/

sketches of the sun's disc ... show that the peaks coincide with the passage of large optically visible spots across the meridian.[8]

These classical papers were recognised as 'the first direct experimental verification of this effect [solar bursts] ... and obtained a close correlation with sunspot activity'.[9] However, a number of possible caveats to the claim that the radio bursts arose from the sun, and, more specifically, from sunspots, had to be considered before the claim could be accepted.

---

8 Payne-Scott 1945, quoted in Goss 2013, 107.
9 Letter from Bowen to Appleton on 23 January 1946, quoted in Goss 2013, 111.

Perhaps the most important of these was that the bursts arise in the Earth's atmosphere, like the twinkling of stars. However, there were no consistent changes in the bursts as the sun rose from the horizon to its zenith.

A comparison between data collected from antennae at sites positioned on the cliffs at Collaroy and Dover showed that 'in each case the radiating strip has a width considerably less than that of the Sun's disc, being of the order of the size of the sunspot group, and passes through the group'.[10] Later, detailed comparisons between the radio data and the optical data from the observatory at Mount Wilson showed that 'the size of the largest spot in the group is a more certain indication than the size of the whole group of the chance that a noise storm will be associated with the group'.[11] Payne-Scott and colleagues commented on the observations made at both Collaroy and Dover:

> It is highly improbable that variations having such a high degree of correlation at widely separated sites should be due to any effect in the atmosphere, and it seems certain that most of them are extra-terrestrial, and presumably solar, in origin.[12]

They were also observed at similar intensities at both Sydney and Mount Stromlo, 260 kilometres apart. However, it is still not clear whether these bursts arise from the superposition of a number of different sources (for example, sunspots within a particular group) or from a single site (such as a large sunspot within the group).

Characteristics of Type I solar radio bursts and storms

The first radio bursts to be identified lasted for periods as short as a second or as long as several days. Those of short duration were shown to have widely different frequencies and intensities, about an order of magnitude greater than the average, and were later named 'Type I bursts'. Those of long duration possessed a 200-fold range of intensities, from $0.05–10 \times 10^7$ Janskys, and were later named 'Type I storms'. A single spot of at least 0.04 per cent of the sun's surface seemed to correlate best with Type I storms. As such spots were independently correlated with magnetic field strength, they were indicative of strong magnetic fields. Later, Payne-Scott and Little examined thirty Type I storms and showed that they originated high in the solar corona. The change in position of the Type I storms was related to that of the sunspots determined by optical means (Figure 12.5).

Characteristics of Type II solar radio bursts

On 8 March 1947, Payne-Scott and her colleagues observed a spectacular burst with a 60 MHz peak of 1,011 Janskys. It was detected at both Mount Stromlo and Dover Heights observatories, with the former working at 200 MHz and the latter at 60–100 MHz. Such bursts were called 'outbursts' by Payne-Scott but are now referred to as 'Type II bursts'. They

---

10 McCready, Pawsey and Payne-Scott 1947, 368.
11 Goss 2013, 174.
12 McCready, Pawsey and Payne-Scott 1947, 361.

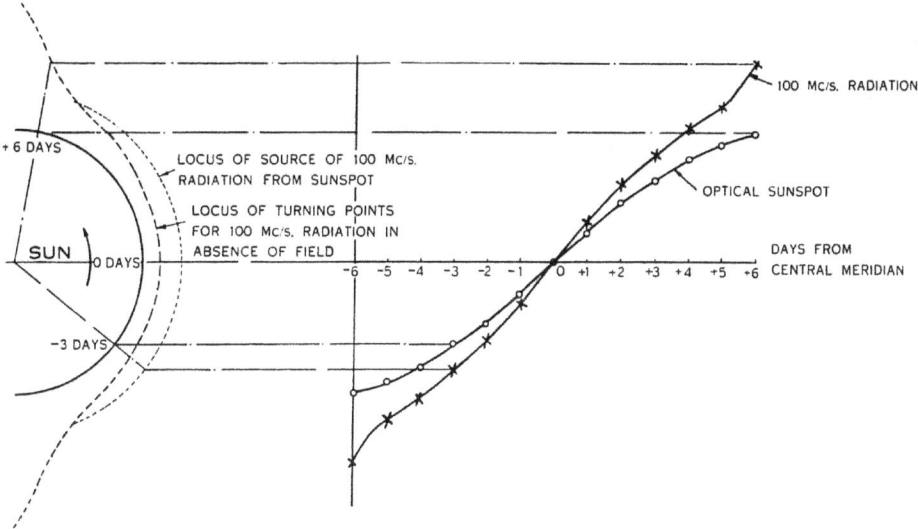

Figure 12.5 This figure shows a plot of the position of 100 MHz radiation (the Type I radio storm; see Table 12.1) and that of the correlated sunspot group during a solar rotation. This kind of plot allowed Payne-Scott and Little (1951) to deduce that the radiation emanated from a site high in the corona, which was located at about 0.3–1.0 x the photospheric radius above the visible surface of the sun. Reproduced from R. Payne-Scott and A.G. Little, 'The Position and Movement on the Solar Disk of Sources of Radiation at a Frequency of 97 Mc/s. II. Noise Storms,' *Australian Journal of Scientific Research A* 4 (1951), with permission from CSIRO Publishing.

possess frequencies as low as 20 MHz (see Table 12.1) and so interfere with broadcasting stations in the same frequency range, a phenomenon that can be used to determine the time of the major flare and to predict the occurrence of a large aurora borealis light event, which, in the case of the 1947 burst, was duly observed on 9 March. Type II bursts are relatively infrequent (perhaps three or four a month) and have their origins in magnetohydrodynamic shockwaves of very high velocity (about 1,000 kilometres per second), which give rise to magnetic storms and very bright aurora light events when they reach Earth.

Characteristics of Type III solar radio bursts

In 1947, Payne-Scott and Little reported observations on radio bursts lasting for only a few seconds, which were associated with a very wide range of frequencies (Table 12.1) that were correlated in time. These were later termed Type III bursts. The emission of these bursts occurred with delays in the sequence of about 200 MHz first, then 75 MHz, and finally 60 MHz. This indicated that the source of the radiation began low in the sun's corona and then progressed to higher levels, from which especially high-intensity emissions occur. It is now known that Type III bursts are associated with very fast streams of electrons moving through the corona at near the speed of light.

Type	Characteristics	Duration	Frequency range	Associated phenomena
I	Short, narrow-bandwidth bursts. Usually occur in large numbers with underlying continuum.	Single burst: ~ 1 second Storm: hours – days	80–200 MHz	Active regions, flares, eruptive prominences.
II	Slow frequency drift bursts. Usually accompanied by a (usually stronger intensity) second harmonic.	3–30 minutes	Fundamental: 20–150 MHz	Flares, proton emission, magnetohydrodynamic shockwaves.
III	Fast frequency drift bursts. Can occur singularly, in groups, or storms (often with underlying continuum). Can be accompanied by a second harmonic.	Single burst: 1–3 seconds Group: 1–5 minutes Storm: minutes – hours	10 kHz – 1 GHz	Active regions, flares.
IV	Stationary Type IV: Broadband continuum with fine structure.	Hours – days	20 MHz – 2 GHz	Flares, proton emission.
	Moving Type IV: Broadband, slow frequency drift, smooth continuum.	30–2 hours	20–400 MHz	Eruptive prominences, magnetohydrodynamic shockwaves.
	Flare Continua: Broadband, smooth continuum.	3–45 minutes	25–200 MHz	Flares, proton emission.
V	Smooth, short-lived continuum. Follows some type III bursts. Never occur in isolation.	1–3 minutes	10–200 MHz	Same as type III bursts.

Table 12.1 Solar Radio Burst Classifications. Sourced from the Commonwealth of Australia (Bureau of Meteorology) 2018.

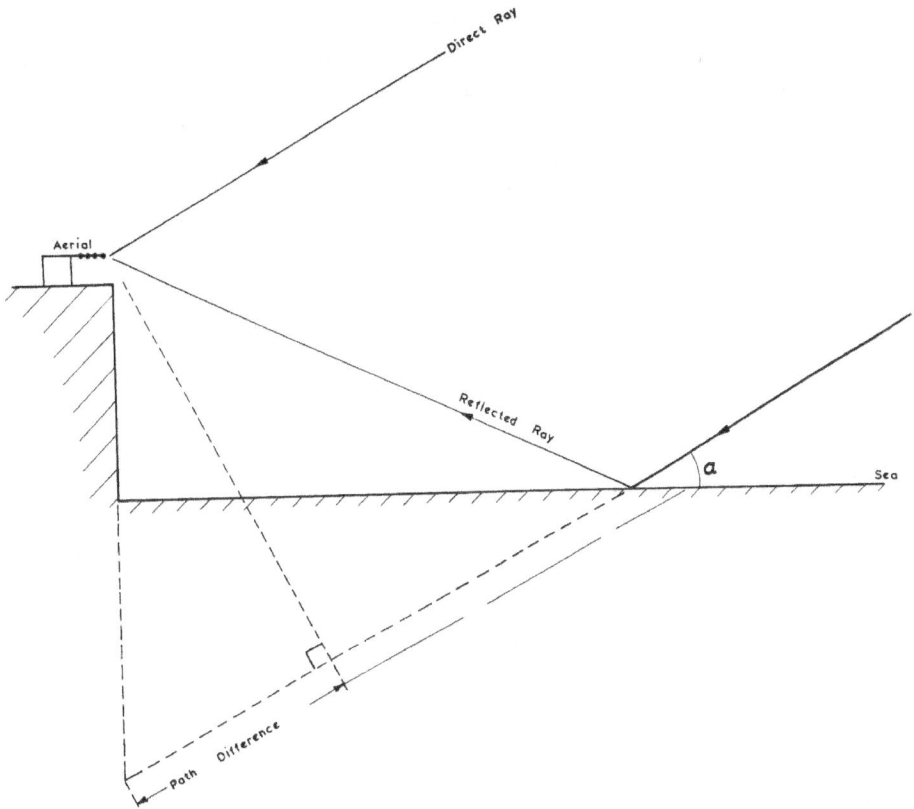

Figure 12.6 Diagram of the sea-cliff interferometer at Dover Heights, showing how the 'direct ray' of a radio source and the 'reflected ray' interfere with each other as the sun rises, with an 'effective' baseline of the interferometer that is twice the height of the sea-cliff. CSIRO Radio Astronomy Image Archive (B1639-4).

Interferometry

The invention of the sea-cliff interferometer by Payne-Scott and colleagues introduced interferometry into radiophysics for the first time, a very important innovation for the future of the discipline. Payne-Scott realised that solar radio wavefronts reflected from the sea below the cliffs around Sydney, where she carried out her observations, travel an additional distance to reach the antennae, compared with wavefronts from the same source that arrive at the antennae unreflected. The length of this additional distance is given by multiplying twice the cliff height by the sine of the angle to the source above the sea (see Figure 12.6). It is equivalent to placing another antenna below the base of the cliff (sea level) at a distance equivalent to the height of the cliff (Figure 12.6). This means the baseline of such a virtual interferometer is equivalent to twice the cliff's height, so that the reflected rays of the radio source interfere with the direct rays to give the interferometer. As Payne-Scott put it,

Briefly, at dawn both direct radiation from the sun and that reflected from the surface of the sea are received, and as the sun rises the receiver output varies sinusoidally as the phase difference between the direct and reflected rays increases; from the times of minima relative to the known time of sunrise, the elevation of the radiating source relative to, say, the centre of the sun can be calculated, while the ratio of the minimum to maximum power gives a measure of the width of the source.[13]

This sea-cliff interferometer has significant advantages over a normal interferometer composed of two separate antennae joined by cables and amplifiers: there is no confusion as to the source because of the sharp horizon and corrections are not required to allow for transmission times between the antennae.

The swept-lobe interferometer and Type IV radio bursts

Perhaps the most remarkable radio-astronomical development led by Payne-Scott was the design, construction and use of the swept-lobe interferometer[14] at 97 MHz, built at the edge of Potts Hill Reservoir in 1948–1949, which enabled imaging of the sun 25 times a second. This allowed the time evolution of moving Type IV solar bursts to be followed (see Table 12.1).[15] The reason for developing such an instrument was that, in Little and Payne-Scott's words, in

> existing interferometers the position of the source is calculated from the interference pattern, which is produced by motion of the source through the lobes pattern of the aerials. But if, as in the case of bursts, the source has a life of only a few seconds, it will not have moved sufficiently during this time to produce the required interference pattern. Consequently, the methods are not directly applicable where the disturbance is of short duration or is rapidly changing its position, and this paper will describe a modified spaced-aerial interferometer which has been built to measure the position and polarization[16] of such a variable component.[17]

Fourier synthesis in radio astronomy

The procedure by which an arbitrary function – say, consisting of repeated square waves or even random noise – can be decomposed into a series of oscillatory components of different amplitude and phase is called Fourier analysis. This analysis replaces the original

---

13 Payne-Scott 1947, 118.
14 The principal beam of a radio antenna's radiation pattern, containing the maximum power, is called the main lobe. The pattern is given by the angular dependence of the radio wave's strength. Other lobes occur at different angles, with lower power, down to zero.
15 Goss 2013, 168.
16 Transverse waves are those that oscillate transverse to the direction of the wave. In an electromagnetic wave like light, the electrical and magnetic fields oscillate perpendicular to each other, with the direction of the electric field defined as the polarisation of the electromagnetic field.
17 Payne-Scott and Little 1951, 'Equipment,' 490.

function with sums of simpler trigonometric functions. It follows that the original function can be resynthesised from its Fourier components. Payne-Scott and her colleagues introduced Fourier synthesis into radio astronomy early in 1946. They showed that their interferometer detected two terms: a steady term and a Fourier cosine series. The complete Fourier spectrum is then obtained from the amplitude and phase recordings from many antennae spacings, allowing determination of the true distribution. Payne-Scott and colleagues commented that,

> since an indefinite number of distributions have identical Fourier components at one frequency, measurement of the phase and amplitude of the variation of intensity at one place at dawn cannot in general be used to determine the distribution over the sun without further information. It is possible in principle to determine the actual form of the distribution in a complex case by Fourier synthesis using information derived from a large number of components. In the interference method suggested here Δ [the phase difference between the direct and the reflected rays from a distant source] is a function of h [the height of the cliff] and λ [the wavelength of the radiation], and different Fourier components may be obtained by varying h or λ.[18]

Payne-Scott's biographer, the radio astronomer Miller Goss, wrote: 'The association of Fourier synthesis and interferometry can be ascribed to Pawsey and Payne-Scott, a major highlight in the development of twentieth century astronomy.'[19]

***

This essay would be incomplete without reference to the humiliating conditions under which Payne-Scott had to work as a woman in the public service. Women in the CSIR were not allowed to smoke, although their male colleagues were; they were expected to wear skirts and not shorts, even when scrambling over astronomical installations; women could not be married while still retaining a permanent position in the CSIR, with sick leave and superannuation benefits, but men could. Payne-Scott fought against these intolerable restrictions again and again: she deliberately smoked when attending meetings called expressly to forbid women from smoking and urged her female colleagues to defy this nonsense;[20] she attended inquisitions concerning the proper behaviour of women in the laboratory and the inappropriateness of wearing shorts,[21] for, as she commented, 'this is absurd. We're climbing up on ladders, up on aerials every day. I'm not going up on a ladder with a skirt on'.[22] But in the end the forces of male chauvinism were too great, and when her marriage was discovered, when she became pregnant, her provident fund contributions were returned with the loss of the CSIR contributions over the years of her service (1946–1950), and she lost all pension rights.[23] It was not until as late as 1966 that

---

18 McCready, Pawsey and Payne-Scott 1947, 367–8.
19 Goss 2013, 123.
20 Commonwealth Scientific and Industrial Research Organisation, 'Ruby Payne-Scott'.
21 Goss 2013, 74.
22 Commonwealth Scientific and Industrial Research Organisation, 'Ruby Payne-Scott'.
23 Commonwealth Scientific and Industrial Research Organisation, 'Ruby Payne-Scott'.

Figure 12.7 Radio astronomers at the 1952 International Assembly of the Union Radio Scientifique Internationale. Front row left to right: Chris Christiansen, F. Graham-Smith, Bernard Mills, S.F. Smerd, C.A. Shain, Robert Hanbury Brown, Ruby Payne-Scott, A.G. Little, M. Laffineur and J.G. Bolton. Second row: J.P. Wild, J.L. Steinberg, J.V. Hindman, F.J. Kerr, C.A. Muller and O.B. Slee. Third row: C.S. Higgins, J.P. Hagen and H.I. Ewen. Back row: J.H. Piddington, E.R. Hill and L.W. Davies. CSIRO Radio Astronomy Image Archive (B2842-43).

women won the right to be both married and a full-time employee in the CSIR, on the grounds of Sydney University.

Payne-Scott's personality was larger than life. She has been described as 'out there', 'a large gestured, loud mouthed excitable person'.[24] She was strong minded, with a no-nonsense disposition and a shrill voice that was most effective in argument.[25] 'I remember well how in discussion, if a contrary point of view started an argument, her voice would rise in pitch and intensity to over-ride and then silence the opposition', one colleague recalled. 'Although such discussions were very wearing, she was always responsive to the logic of an opposing point of view and, if convinced, would readily concede.'[26]

Her much honoured engineering colleague Christianson said 'with deep feeling' that 'she was a *physicist*', in the sense that she was a physicist's physicist, possibly the best

---

24 ABC Radio National, 'Ruby Payne-Scott'.
25 ABC Radio National, 'Ruby Payne-Scott'.
26 Hooker 2004, 165.

of her generation.[27] Astronomy lost a wonderful leader when the rules of the Australian public service forced her to retire. There is a certain irony in the fact that her first-born, Peter, became a great mathematician and her daughter, Fiona, a major artist, perhaps providing some solace to her in isolation from the subject of radio astronomy, to which she had made such revolutionary contributions.

Further reading

McCready, L.L., J.L. Pawsey and R. Payne-Scott. 'Solar Radiation at Radio Frequencies and Its Relation to Sunspots.' *Proceedings of the Royal Society of London. Series A, Mathematical and Physical Sciences* 190, no. 1022 (1947): 357–75.

Pawsey, J.L., R. Payne-Scott and L.L. McCready. 'Radio-Frequency Energy from the Sun.' *Nature* 157, no. 3980 (1946): 158–9.

Payne-Scott, R. 'Bursts of Solar Radiation at Metre Wavelengths.' *Australian Journal of Scientific Research. Series A, Physical Sciences* 2, no. 2 (1949): 214–27.

Payne-Scott, R., and A.G. Little. 'The Position and Movement on the Solar Disk of Sources of Radiation at a Frequency of 97 Mc/s. I. Equipment.' *Australian Journal of Scientific Research. Series A, Physical Sciences* 4, no. 4 (1951): 489–507.

Payne-Scott, R., and A.G. Little. 'The Position and Movement on the Solar Disk of Sources of Radiation at a Frequency of 97 Mc/s. II. Noise Storms.' *Australian Journal of Scientific Research. Series A, Physical Sciences* 4, no. 4 (1951): 508–25.

Payne-Scott, R., and A.G. Little. 'The Position and Movement on the Solar Disk of Sources of Radiation at a Frequency of 97 Mc/s. III. Outbursts.' *Australian Journal of Scientific Research. Series A, Physical Sciences* 5, no. 1 (1952): 32–49.

Payne-Scott, R., D.E. Yabsley and J.G. Bolton. 'Relative Times of Arrival of Bursts of Solar Noise on Different Radio Frequencies.' *Nature* 160, no. 4060 (1947): 256–7.

---

27 Hooker 2004, 161.

Chemistry and geology

13
Photosynthesis and the quantum mechanics of electron transfer: Noel S. Hush

Professor of Theoretical Chemistry (1971–1989); Research Foundation Professor Emeritus (1990–present). Hush developed general quantum theories for the transfer of electrons between atoms or molecules, known as oxidation–reduction reactions. These theories provide an understanding of organic processes such as photosynthesis and cell respiration, as well as inorganic processes in batteries and chemical reactors. Electron-transfer theory has been used to design devices at the molecular level, a significant part of the field of nanotechnology.

I arrived at the University of Sydney 50 years ago to take up a lectureship in physiology when, unbeknown to me, Noel Hush was about to take up the inaugural chair in theoretical chemistry. He invited me to join him for supper and has since been something of a mentor. The inspiration he instils comes from an unrelenting dedication to the understanding of nature, an active commitment that has been maintained for over 70 years. Indeed, recently he has published papers rebutting the mathematical ideas of the great Roger Penrose (a senior colleague of Stephen Hawking) as they pertain to the origins of consciousness. It is this subject that we often discuss over lunch. During a recent meal, he surprised me by relating discussions he had had on that subject in Manchester with a fellow academic, the genius Alan Turing, shortly before Turing's death and at a time when he was revolutionising our understanding of the ideas of 'computer consciousness' and cellular morphogenesis. The image of Sydney as a great university gathers much force when observing Noel Hush going about his research, walking across campus to make contact with other scholars, gently mentoring much younger generations and, more particularly, continuing to make seminal contributions to our understanding of nature.

Hush was born in 1924 in Sydney, where he attended state schools in the 1930s. It is not surprising that he achieved an almost perfect score in the eight subjects of the then intermediate examination. As he commented, 'I was a voracious reader – I devour books. It was really in the vacations that I felt that I learned anything. One could get through an enormous amount of stuff in these vacations'.[1] It was this extensive reading

---

1   Australian Academy of Science, 'Professor Noel Hush'.

Figure 13.1 Professor Noel Hush. Reproduced with permission from Noel Hush.

that undoubtedly led Hush to look for underlying themes in the knowledge he was gaining. He found this in some subjects but not others. As he put it,

> I was always looking for very general patterns. At school I made a nuisance of myself. When they were trying to tell me about Ethelred the Unready and all the problems of the Kings of England I would point out Wells's *A Short History of the World*. The book began with the world five billion years ago. We didn't know exactly how the world began, but it went up through the formation of stars and so on. After a while, you began to get to things coming out of the sea, then they got legs, then they started to write books about philosophy, then they discovered atoms and then it started to be interesting. The book showed an unfolding of almost certainly interpretable complexity modulated by

contingency, although I didn't put it like that. Like the weird business about Ethelred, there was no pattern to school history, it was just one after the other. Ambrose Bierce described history as a lot of untruths about powerful people doing foolish things for no reason at all and having other people die for them. That seemed to summarise history as it was being taught.[2]

The phrase 'then they discovered atoms and then it started to be interesting' showed that Hush was already leaning towards a scientific vocation.

He entered the University of Sydney in 1942, at the age of 17, and found very small staff numbers in the scientific departments, with many away at the war. However, his extensive reading paid off; he had already decided,

> by the time I began my course, that everything was electronic. I also wanted to look at the world at the level of chemistry. You can be doing things at the level of galaxies or the level of molecules or people, or you can go down to the nuclear level. Now you can look at a sub-nuclear level.[3]

Hush settled on the electron level, the level that, among other things, determines the position of elements in the periodic table and governs reactions between molecules to produce new molecules, an area of research in which he was to become a dominant figure on the international stage. Over millennia, chemists had worked out the nature of many chemical processes, developing sophisticated modern industries. Little was understood about why these processes occurred, how to control them and how to use them to invent new technologies beyond imagination. Basic chemical understanding was the critical challenge Hush took up.

Although the science departments at Sydney were small, with very little research going on, Hush had considerable luck during his research period there (1945–1949) in that 'there were a couple of research-active people in that department. One of them had just come back from working with Linus Pauling in California, which was a big thing'.[4] At the time, Pauling was recognised as the greatest living theoretical chemist as a consequence of his application of the relatively new theory of quantum mechanics (especially that due to Schrödinger) summarised in his book *The Nature of the Chemical Bond*. So Hush was working in probably the only Australian department at that time interested in applying quantum mechanical methods to understanding the properties of molecules.

Nevertheless, Hush made a splendid choice of experimental projects for his research. He was introduced to two substances called Wurster's Red and Wurster's Blue, whose magnetic properties were supposed to be capable of being explained by the application of quantum mechanics, at least according to Linus Pauling (see 'Photosynthesis'). Hush showed that this was not the case, but, perhaps more importantly, he was introduced to analogous molecules called quinones (see Appendix). These are of the first importance in biological systems, such as photosynthesis. Their properties were to become of enduring interest to Hush in his study of the transfer of electrons.

---

2   Australian Academy of Science, 'Professor Noel Hush'.
3   Australian Academy of Science, 'Professor Noel Hush'.
4   Australian Academy of Science, 'Professor Noel Hush'.

On completion of this outstanding research during his honours and Master of Science years (1945–49), Hush was appointed to a junior lectureship at Manchester University, the leading department of basic research into physical and theoretical chemistry in Europe at the time. He was invited to Manchester by a precociously brilliant young chemist, M.G. Evans, who died tragically just a few years later. The department had been reinvigorated in the 1930s by one of the great chemistry pioneers, Michael Polanyi, who, with his students Henry Eyring and M.G. Evans, had developed and applied Transition-State Theory to describe how chemical reactions occur. The main idea underpinning this theory was that electrons needed to be treated by quantum mechanics, but after this was done, the motion of atoms could be studied using the old, simple ideas of classical Newtonian mechanics. These sorts of ideas dominate teaching in chemistry to this day, providing the basis of understanding chemical, biochemical and material structures. However, Hush's life's work was to show that this is not always correct, with the exceptions typically being the most interesting cases to study in terms of understanding modern biochemistry and making new nanotechnologies.

At Manchester, Hush met leading theoreticians in quantum mechanics in the United Kingdom. Hush commented that

> within six months of being ... [at Manchester], I was fully acquainted with the theory by which one could actually make [quantum mechanics] calculations. By a strange quirk, the systems on which you could do these calculations most easily were the large hydrocarbons like benzene, naphthalene and these sorts of aromatics. I embarked on quantum investigations of properties and of energetics of electron transfer amongst such species.[5]

Hush enjoyed working with Evans. As Hush related,

> We worked on calculating the energetics of many [chemical] reactions. In particular those involving hydrogen peroxide and its various breakdown products like HO_2, oxygen and the radicals. ... We worked out theoretical interpretations of data for about 80 important reactions.[6]

Today, there is strong activity worldwide to exploit the exquisitely tuned redox properties of naturally evolved metalloenzymes for production of renewable fuels in biochemical cells. For example, hydrogenase for H_2 oxidation and production (and CO-dehydrogenase for CO oxidation and CO_2 reduction).

Quantum mechanics

Newton's classical mechanics describes everyday objects and how they move from place to place. When combined with Maxwell's revolutionary description of light, electricity

---

5   Australian Academy of Science, 'Professor Noel Hush'.
6   Australian Academy of Science, 'Professor Noel Hush'.

and magnetism, classical mechanics was once believed to be able to describe all phenomena. But it was found that these equations could not describe chemical processes. This problem was resolved when Schrödinger showed that light and matter were really just different aspects of the same thing – a thing that gets all mixed up when it comes to atoms and electrons, and their motions. Hush noted:

> Schrödinger says that if you want to know how electrons and atoms move, then you need to solve a wave equation – as you would do if say you poured some sand on a drum top and struck the drum. Waves are set up that tell where the sand goes, but the waves don't tell how the sand got there.[7]

The idea that matter is located at some place in time and then moves to another place sometime later, as a car does, is completely lost. Electrons and atoms can be in more than one place at the same time and can move between places without ever being in the middle. A molecule can have two different shapes at the same time, and molecules can *never* stop moving. The Schrödinger equation is a linear partial differential equation describing the time evolution of the wave function of a system (usually an atom, molecule or subatomic particle). The wave function is the most complete description that can be given of any physical system. Hush set himself the task of working out what the wave function is and what it means for chemistry.

Electron transfer and redox processes

It was clear that chemical processes involving the transfer of electrons could not be described using the 1930s theories established by Evans, Polanyi, Pauling and others. Electrons are part of atoms and are therefore much smaller and lighter, making them more susceptible to quantum mechanics. Hush realised that a quantum treatment of these problems was needed. He commented:

> the combustion of the burning piece of wood involves oxygen from the air being reduced by transferring electrons from the carbon. Also, the production of metallic steel from iron ore occurs through a reaction of the ore with charcoal. Such processes are termed oxidation and reduction reactions and are associated with the transfer of electrons. The reaction can occur very quickly as in a fire or very slowly as in rusting. The transfer of electrons between molecules in chemical reactions is called an "oxidation-reduction" or redox process. The rusting of a metal, whereby it becomes ionic, is due to its loss of electrons so that it becomes oxidized whereas reduction occurs when, for example, haemoglobin in blood takes up an electron from oxygen so as to transport it.[8]

Indeed, the voltage coming from any battery results from redox processes.

---

7   Hush, personal communication, 11 October 2018.
8   Hush, personal communication, 11 October 2018.

A quantitative measure of this redox process is provided by the redox potential, which gives the extent to which a chemical species has taken up electrons. Each such species has a characteristic redox potential, measured in volts; the larger the potential, the greater its tendency to take up electrons. To get the output voltage of a battery, one needs to know the redox potentials of the two electrodes in the battery and the chemical composition. But the principles apply far beyond this application. Hush showed theoretically

> how it was possible to get absolute ion energy values. ... Our results provided fundamental information on reactions of fleeting unstable radicals which were hard to characterise experimentally. There were people out in the industry who would have a radical, like HO_2 [an ion arising from reaction between water and hydrogen peroxide], that would be generated in some way. They would be in the oil industry or in the polymer industry, for example. It would react with a metal ion and induce various types of reaction, such as polymerisation. ... the reaction of [hydrogen peroxide and its various breakdown products] with metal ions was of great importance in many industrial applications.[9]

The central feature of electron-transfer reactions is that they involve two chemical species: one that loses an electron in the process, called the donor, and one that gains the electron, called the acceptor. In the reactions Hush considered, separate donor and acceptor molecules came together during collisions, exchanging electrons as 'ships in the night'. However, in batteries, the donor molecule collides with an electrode to which its electron is passed; the electron flows down a connecting wire and does useful things to a second electrode before being transferred to the acceptor molecule. Hush showed that although the connections, and therefore the details, are different, the intrinsic processes involved are identical. The same applies in photosynthesis and nanotechnology.

Hush's quantum theory for electron transfer

In constructing his theory of electron transfer,[10] Hush's main tasks were to describe what happens when a molecule or system is behaving normally, without undergoing any chemical reaction, what brings the chemical reaction about and how experiments or calculations can be designed to manifest these events. Hush said:

> What a molecule does most of the time is – almost nothing. It just sits there and vibrates as if it were made up of a collection of atomic billiard balls held together by springs. This is boring. If the reactants and products are just boring billiard balls held together by springs using different connections, how do you make one molecule from another?[11]

---

9   Australian Academy of Science 'Professor Noel Hush'.
10 Cotton and Hush 1967; Hush 1958; Hush 1961.
11 Hush, personal communication, 11 October 2018.

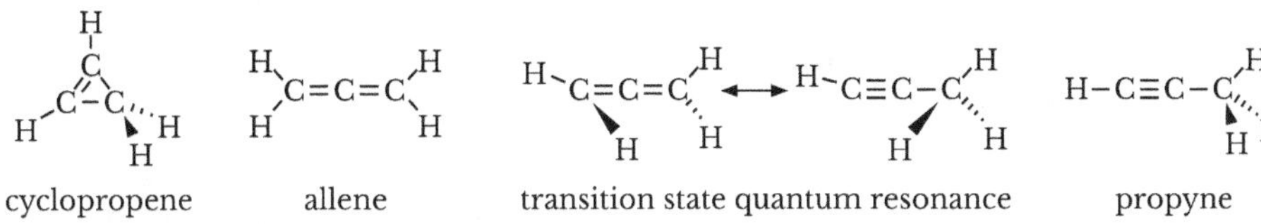

Figure 13.2 The three isomers of C$_3$H$_4$, propyne, cyclopropene and allene differ in the ways bonds are drawn between the C and H atoms. Bonds represent electron pairs and are treated as springs holding the atoms together to form molecules. The single, double and triple carbon–carbon bonds shown indicate that the springs get shorter in length and stronger in force. Isomerisation reactions involve the breaking of bonds and the reformation of others, changing the topology of the spring network, as shown in the transition state connecting allene to propene. In this transition state, the electrons and bonds exist as quantum resonance between the allene and propyne structures, as indicated by the double-headed arrow. Courtesy of Noel Hush.

This is where quantum mechanics comes in. When the springs stretch enough, the molecule becomes not one set of springs or the other, but a simultaneous quantum superposition of both. This is illustrated in Figure 13.2.

From Figure 13.2 it is clear that conversion of allene to propene requires movement of a hydrogen atom from one end of the molecule to the other. Hush stressed the issue of how to define the quantum region in the middle. He commented: 'For most chemical reactions including this one, the quantum region is relatively small and classical ideas like Transition-State Theory work.'[12] However, Hush showed that for electron transfer the quantum region could get tiny, invalidating Transition-State Theory. In effect, for electron transfer, the details of the tiny quantum region control everything. He also showed that the quantum region could get very large and, indeed, encompass the reactants and products. In this case, quantum mechanics again controls everything.

One thing that comes with quantum mechanics is the unification of matter and radiation into a single concept. If quantum mechanics controls chemistry, then light can be used to control quantum chemical process. So the colour of a molecule and its chemical reactivity become correlated, allowing access into the chemistry quantum world through simple laboratory measurements. Hush was the first person to point this out, studying the colour of the world's first commercial synthetic dye – Prussian Blue. Despite being a commercial dye, no one knew how it was able to absorb red light. Hush invented the field known as intervalence charge-transfer spectroscopy,[13] showing how light absorption can, in itself, produce a chemical reaction. He showed how to deduce the electrical conductivity of a solid knowing only its colour and atomic structure.

Knowing where the atoms are: Prussian Blue and the Creutz-Taube ion

Hush's research in the 1940s and 50s was hampered because no one knew where the atoms were located when electron-transfer processes occurred in a solution or in a gas. If

---

12 Hush, personal communication, 11 October 2018.
13 Cotton and Hush 1967.

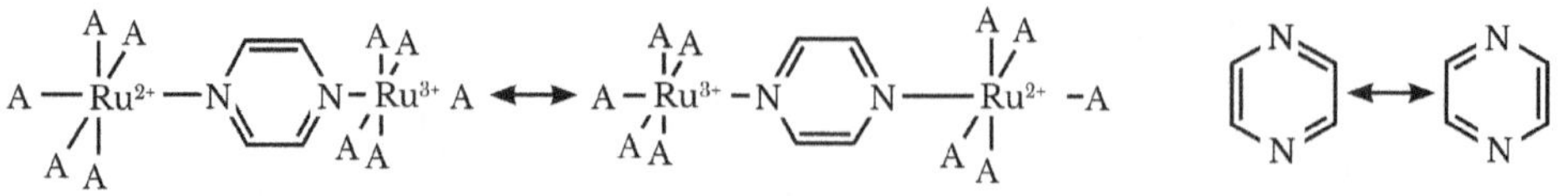

Creutz-Taube ion: a quantum superposition of two chemical structures

A = NH_3

pyrazine: itself also a quantum superposition of two chemical structures

Figure 13.3 The Creutz-Taube ion is a quantum superposition of two classical chemical structures, akin to its inner lingand, pyrazine. The Ru-N bond lengths are much shorter for Ru3+ than for Ru2+. Courtesy of Noel Hush.

one considers the spring model, there are, in these circumstances, no springs holding the two molecules together, so there is no structure. The question then arises: how close does a molecule have to get before there is a collision? Is the relative orientation important? These critical features were simply not known.

In 1967, Prussian Blue allowed Hush to overcome this problem. The dye was crystalline and people knew where the atoms and the springs were. Focusing on such a controlled system produced a major change in thinking.

Simplifying the process even further, in 1969 Carol Creutz and Henry Taube synthesised the Creutz-Taube ion (Figure 13.3), in which all processes of interest occur in an isolated molecule. Nothing could be simpler for understanding the basic processes involved. This led to Taube being awarded the 1983 Nobel Prize. In his Nobel Prize lecture, Taube acknowledged the critical role played by Hush's theory in designing the project and interpreting the results. The Creutz-Taube ion features what people imagined to be a Ru(II) and a Ru(III) centre bridged by a pyrazine ligand. Just like in the allene–propyne example described in Figure 13.2, the geometries and strengths of the springs describing the bonds are different around the Ru(II) and Ru(III) ions, with Ru(III) making shorter and stronger Ru-N bonds.

Modern applications

Little did Hush know in the 1960s how easy it would become, some 50 years later, to understand and control the atomic structure of functional materials. X-ray crystallography opened up biochemical research, allowing the atomic structures of proteins to be determined. Modern nanotechnology allows synthetic devices to be controlled at the atomic level.

Any molecular device that captures solar energy and uses it for constructive purposes will depend, in some way, on Hush's theories. Similarly, any non-metallic or non-semiconductor device conducting electricity will operate according to the rules of electron-transfer theory. Such rules govern the operation of natural photosynthesis, all energy regulation mechanisms in biology, modern photovoltaic cells, photocatalytic converters and organic light-emitting diodes (OLEDs) now used in flexible plastic mobile phone and computer displays. Modern applications are endless.

Photosynthesis

Hush did not know at the time of his Master's research in the 1940s that he would become involved in understanding photosynthesis from the 1980s to the 2000s. Hush gave a delightful description of photosynthesis:

> Natural photosynthetic units consist of a complex of chromophores or pigments and proteins responsible for light absorption and energy reactions. In bacterial photosynthesis, a pigment bacteriochlorophyll molecule is excited by absorption of a photon of light, thence passing this energy on to a 'reaction centre' in which spontaneous electron transfer occurs from a bacteriochlorophyll dimer called the 'special pair', producing charged molecules. Once converted thus into electrochemical energy, a quick chain of redox reactions leads to temporary charge storage on nearby quinones. This energy is then used to produce membrane potentials facilitating cell function. It drives capture of carbon dioxide from the atmosphere and eventually causes conversion of the initial solar energy into stored chemical energy in many forms, including carbohydrates like glucose and starch.[14]

Hush commented further that

> the important reaction centre is in the middle and it is surrounded by a great protein network, like a basket, which we treat rather approximately. The bit in the middle we treat with much more precision. We have to account for the vibrations of this centre,[15]

which, along with the electrons, must be treated quantum mechanically, as the basic processes cannot be described in terms of the language of classical mechanics that is taught in chemistry lectures and used as the basis for understanding most chemical processes.[16]

Hush considered that the task of theoretical chemists is to find out the biochemical structure and the details of how processes such as photosynthesis take place.

> The light harvest and energy conversion machinery displays great symmetry and beauty, but often it is small deviations from perfect symmetry that control function, with complex assemblies of hundreds of chlorophyll molecules, carotenoids and quinones being able to pass solar energy and electrical energy from site to site just as if they had internal wires like those making up power grids, on circuit boards and inside integrated circuits … yet there are no wires, just structured arrays of proteins and organic molecules.[17]

To understand the heart of solar energy conversion during photosynthesis, Hush participated in a large synthetic and experimental effort to make model compounds that showed the principal effects, including intervalence charge transfer.[18]

---

14   Hush, personal communication, 11 October 2018.
15   Australian Academy of Science 'Professor Noel Hush'.
16   Reimers and Hush 2004.
17   Hush, personal communication, 11 October 2018.
18   Hush, Paddon-Row, Cotsaris, Oevering, Verhoeven and Heppener 1985.

The quinones (see Appendix) present in the system play a critical role. They represent a class of organic compounds that are derived from aromatic compounds such as benzene. Remarkably, Hush had the insight to investigate quinone chemistry in his research years at Sydney University.[19] He commented:

> I was presented with a number of possible research projects and one of them was to do with a magnetic molecule. [Leonor] Michaelis was a famous biochemist at the Rockefeller Institute in the US. ... he had published a paper on some peculiar substances which had been synthesised in the 19th century by a German chemist [Casimir Wurster]. The substances were called Wurster's Red and Wurster's Blue. Michaelis got onto these Wurster salts because they were analogous in a way to quinones.[20]

Hush went on to say:

> Michaelis saw that there was a parallel with these salts and proposed an explanation of their magnetic properties in terms of Pauling's 'resonance' theory. ... I was able to devise a molecule which would be a test for his theory. By making it and taking magnetic measurements, I showed that it was not correct. The first paper I ever published was in *Nature* on this work.[21]

In this paper, Hush stated: 'One of their main conclusions was that polymerization of a semiquinone ion of the type depicted ... is impossible when all the amino hydrogens are substituted.'[22] Rather, Hush and his colleagues concluded that 'polymerization of this semiquinone ion occurs in spite of the fact that all the amine hydrogens are substituted'.[23]

Molecular electronics (nanoscience)

It is no exaggeration to say that Noel Hush led development of the theoretical foundations of nanoscience through his application of ideas from electron-transfer theory and photosynthesis to help pioneer the field of molecular electronics.[24] In 1974, Aviram and Ratner proposed that Hush's theories could be applied to design molecules that showed not just conductivity, but also logical functions, like those of silicon integrated circuits. Hush later provided basic understanding of how molecular switches can function. Hush described molecular electronics as using conductive molecules and electronically active, self-assembled molecular scale structures, which include switchable 'wires' made from conductive molecules, carbon nanotubes, semiconductor nanowires and conducting organic or inorganic materials.

---

19 Hughes, Hush and Mellor 1947, 612.
20 Australian Academy of Science 'Professor Noel Hush'.
21 Australian Academy of Science 'Professor Noel Hush'.
22 Hughes, Hush and Mellor 1947.
23 Hughes, Hush and Mellor 1947.
24 Hush 2003.

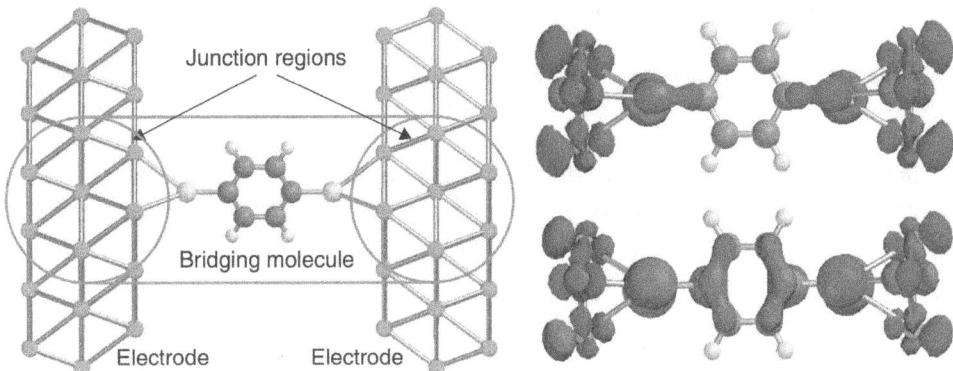

Figure 13.4 Left: sketch of a single 1,4-benzenedithiol molecule chemisorbed between two gold electrodes, with the junction and molecule regions highlighted in red; green - gold, yellow - sulfur, black - carbon, white - hydrogen. Right: molecule orbitals (wave solutions of Schrodinger Equation) depicting different conduction channels through the device. Reproduced from J.R. Reimers, A. Bilić, Z. Cai, M. Dahlbom, N.A. Lambropoulos, G.C. Solomon, M.J. Crossley and N.S. Hush, 'Molecular Electronics: From Basic Chemical Principles to Photosynthesis to Steady-State Through-Molecule-Conductivity to Computer Architectures,' *Australian Journal of Chemistry* 57, no. 12 (2004), with permission from CSIRO Publishing.

A typical scenario for a molecular-electronic device is shown in Figure 13.4, where a chemisorbed 1,4-benzenedithiol molecule is made to span two macroscopic gold electrodes connected to external circuitry. The single molecule bridges the electrodes in a fashion very similar to the way pyrazine bridges the two Ru redox centres in the Creutz-Taube ion (see Figure 13.3). But now the molecular contacts can be directly addressed. A voltage is placed on the electrodes, and the current passing through the single bridging molecule is measured. To calculate the current, Schrödinger's wave equation must be solved. Two sample waves, or conduction channels, are shown in Figure 13.4. The bridging molecule could be expanded to be a piece of material of any dimension, from nano-sized up to centimetres. Some unusual aspects of this quantum conduction are discussed in the Appendix.

Hush's classic 1967 paper on intervalence charge-transfer spectroscopy,[25] which underpins photosynthesis, actually describes the relationship between the colour and conductivity of the metal organic framework (MOF) solid Prussian Blue. The great interest in MOFs over the past 15 years has come about because these half-organic half-inorganic solids allow amazing structures to be synthesised. To do novel things in chemistry one typically needs quantum effects, and to control quantum effects one must first control structure. Over the past decade, Hush has made many significant advances in controlling structures for applications in nanotechnology.[26]

---

25   Cotton and Hush 1967.
26   Reimers and Hush (submitted 2017).

Exposing the heart of the quantum world of chemistry

The advent of quantum mechanics provided basic understanding of chemical processes of general relevance, but this remains a challenge for modern science. Hush summarised:

> In the 1920s and 1930s pioneers like Evans and Polanyi dreamed of making simple theories for chemistry that depicted multitudes of structural, spectroscopic, and kinetic properties. Except for electron transfer, this vision never eventuated. We recently were able to show how it all could be done.[27]

The quantum nature of Hush's theories means that they depict quantum entanglement between electronic and nuclear motions. This weird property, related to the Einstein-Podolsky-Rosen paradox, forms the basis of modern designs for quantum information processors. Hush has analysed chemical reactions to find those most suitable for use in quantum mechanics and concludes that, although 'chemistry is the quantum science, interactions are usually far too strong and uncontrollable for a real device to be made using chemical processes'.[28]

***

Hush has been and remains, at 94 years old, the greatest scientist at the University of Sydney. This perspective is based not only on his being elected to all the world's most prestigious societies and receiving the premier award in chemistry, the Welch Prize, but, more particularly, on the elegance of his penetrating analysis of electron transfer. Hush recognised at an early age that understanding the way in which electrons move between atoms and molecules holds the key to understanding molecular reactions, with all this means for grasping the workings of chemical activity in nature and in the construction of new devices. Clearly, in the age of the 'greenhouse effect', it is of the utmost importance to understand the details of photosynthesis and the way cells utilise electron transfer in the generation of energy. For those of an engineering turn of mind, the ushering in of nanoscience is of particular interest; this development would not have been possible without understanding how to manipulate atoms and molecules to make new devices. This understanding came from deep probing of the mechanisms of electron transfer, led by Hush.

Appendix

Quinones

Quinones are substituted benzenes (Figure 13.5). Benzene exists as a quantum superposition of two chemical structures, whereas oxygen substitution in quinones results in a single classical structure. The bonding pattern makes quinones highly coloured

---

27 Hush, personal communication, 11 October 2018.
28 Hush, personal communication, 11 October 2018.

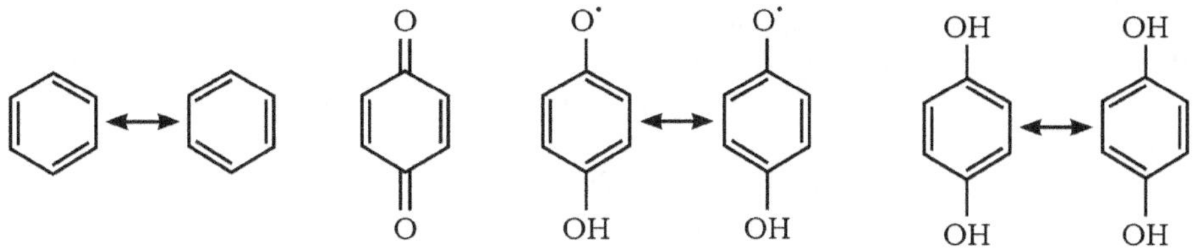

13 Noel S. Hush

| benzene: quantum superposition of two chemical structures | quinone | semiquinone: quantum superposition of two chemical structures | hydroquinone: quantum superposition of two chemical structures |

Figure 13.5 Hush looked at quinones, their colour and their ability to accept electrons throughout much of his career. Courtesy of Noel Hush.

molecules that are good electron acceptors, whereas benzene is colourless and relatively unreactive. Simple chemical reactions widely utilised in biology convert quinones into hydroquinones. Semiquinones were also important to Hush's work, being akin to the Creutz-Taube ion.

Conduction through single molecules

An amazing property of molecular electronics is that conductance is governed by the laws of quantum mechanics, not classical mechanics as is typical for most inorganic semiconductor systems. If the molecular wire is replaced by, say, a line of metal atoms (gold atoms, for example, like to stick together into filaments one atom wide when two pieces of gold are pulled apart), then the conductivity increases in discrete amounts as increasing voltage opens up new discrete channels. The resistance of a metal-filament molecular wire can be expressed as $12.9/nk\Omega$, where n is an integer from 0, 1, 2, … ∞. Intermediate values are not allowed. However, if insulating organic molecules like 1,4-benzenedithiol are used, the conductivity of every open channel is much less. Typical resistances for commonly studied single molecules range from $100\ k\Omega$ to $100\ G\Omega$. For the most conductive molecules, currents of 1,013 electrons per second per molecule can be sustained. Such values are extraordinarily high.

Further reading

Hush, N.S. 'Adiabatic Rate Processes at Electrodes. I. Energy-Charge Relationships.' *The Journal of Chemical Physics* 28, no. 5 (1958): 962–72.

Hush, N.S. 'Adiabatic Theory of Outer Sphere Electron-Transfer Reactions in Solution.' *Transactions of the Faraday Society* 57 (1961): 557–80.

Hush. N.S. 'Intervalence-Transfer Absorption. Part 2. Theoretical Considerations and Spectroscopic Data.' In *Progress in Inorganic Chemistry, Volume 8*, edited by F.A. Cotton, 391–444. New York: Interscience Publishers, 1967.

Hush, N. S. 'An Overview of the First Half-Century of Molecular Electronics.' *Annals of the New York Academy of Sciences* 1006, no. 1 (2003): 1–20.

Hush, N.S., M.N. Paddon-Row, E. Cotsaris, H. Oevering, J.W. Verhoeven and M. Heppener. 'Distance Dependence of Photoinduced Electron Transfer Rates Through Non-Conjugated Bridges.' *Chemical Physics Letters* 117, no. 1 (1985): 8–11.

Reimers, J.R., and N.S. Hush. 'A Unified Description of the Electrochemical, Charge Distribution and Spectroscopic Properties of the Special-Pair Radical Cation in Bacterial Photosynthesis.' *Journal of the American Chemical Society* 126, no. 13 (2004): 4132–44.

Reimers, J.R., and N.S. Hush. 'Adiabatic Electron Transfer Theory.' *Chemical Reviews* (submitted 2017).

Reimers, J.R., A. Bilić, Z. Cai, M. Dahlbom, N.A. Lambropoulos, G.C. Solomon, M.J. Crossley and N.S. Hush. 'Molecular Electronics: From Basic Chemical Principles to Photosynthesis to Steady-State Through-Molecule-Conductivity to Computer Architectures.' *Australian Journal of Chemistry* 57, no. 12 (2004): 1133–8.

14

Discovery of land masses in Antarctica and Precambrian fossils: Tannatt William Edgeworth David

Professor of Geology and Physical Geography (1891–1924). David is known for his discovery of the great northern coal field of New South Wales, of numerous land masses and islands in Antarctica and of the first fossils to be claimed to be Precambrian in the rocks of Central Australia, and for drilling on Funafuti in the Pacific Ocean, supporting Darwin's theory on the origin of atolls. These discoveries and observations led to his recognition as one of the greatest geologists in the world.

It is difficult to escape a *Boy's Own Annual* description of Tannatt William Edgeworth David's adventures in the Hunter Valley, in Antarctica, in Central Australia and on the atoll of Funafuti. They are reminiscent of those of Hanbury Brown, who used himself as a guinea-pig to test radar devices in aeroplanes while preparing for the aerial Battle of Britain in 1940 (Chapter 10). However, David, like Hanbury Brown, was a serious scientist. He made very important geological, meteorological and geographical discoveries during his exploits, all of which make for an extraordinary life.

David was born in 1858 at St Fagans Rectory near Cardiff in Wales, the eldest child of the Rev. William David and Margaret Harriette, a Canadian with French ancestry. David was educated at home before entering Magdalen College School at the age of 12, where, for some six years, he showed excellent scholastic gifts. At 18, he entered New College in Oxford as a classics student. There he gained a First Class in Moderations in 1878, but failed to read for Final Honours due to a nervous breakdown, which was almost certainly precipitated by a loss of faith in the Christian religion and in the theology of the Anglican Church, although he did retain a deep deist commitment. David was expected to enter orders, following in his father's footsteps, so his loss of faith made matters very difficult. His loving family came to the rescue and sent him on a convalescing boat trip to Melbourne via Canada.

David did not take up classics when he returned to Oxford in 1880. He had developed an intense interest in geology, stimulated at Oxford by excellent lectures given by Sir Joseph Prestwich and by the famous John Ruskin. David began taking walks around St Fagans with his relative, William Ussher, a keen amateur in geology. This interest developed rapidly when David started more serious field-work on erratic rocks, which

Figure 14.1 Professor Tannatt William Edgeworth David. Photograph from the University of Sydney Archives (G3_224_1206).

had been transported by glaciers to different areas around Cardiff and left behind on the gradually melting glacial ice. His first paper arose from this work. The Cardiff Naturalists' Society had a discussion meeting in October 1880 concerning several two-ton erratics that were found near Peterson. David determined the positions of six of these and plotted the direction of the glacier's movement, which he gave in a paper entitled 'Evidence of Glacial Action in the Neighbourhood of Cardiff', read at the Society's meeting on 17 November 1881.

Determined to extend his amateur knowledge into a professional career, David attended the Royal School of Mines in London, where he received excellent tutelage and inspiration from Professor W.J. Judd. Such practical experience and expert training placed David in an excellent position to succeed in his application for the newly advertised position of Assistant Geological Surveyor in Sydney, which he took up in 1882 at the age of only 24, sailing on the *Potosi* to return to Australia once more. There David was given the task of carrying out a geological survey of Yass and New England in New South Wales. The Yass region possessed superb exposures of Silurian and Devonian fossil beds; New England possessed immense coal and tin fields, then largely undiscovered.

The geological survey of New South Wales: tin and coal

David's first task was to survey the tin deposits in New England, which he carried out with such thoroughness that both his report of 1884, 'Vegetable Creek Tin-Mining Field, New England District', and a larger memoir in 1887 guided the future mining of the field and £10 million worth of tin was extracted, an immense sum to add to the revenue of the colony.

By 1886, coal had been discovered and mined at Newcastle, on the coast of New South Wales, at Maitland, 38 kilometres northwest of Newcastle, at Greta, 20 kilometres northwest of Maitland, and at Rix's Creek near Singleton. The question posed to David, after his mapping of the tin deposits, was whether the coal discovered at Newcastle, Maitland, Greta and Rix's Creek was part of a vast northern coal field? Although the aforementioned coal beds could be identified on account of very good cliff sections, these sections were not sufficient to support the hypothesis that a great northern coal field existed. The skills of a first-rate geologist were needed to identify data that could support such a proposition.

David made his first discovery in 1886 at Lochinvar, halfway between Newcastle and Singleton. There he discovered that the direction of the angle at which the strata of rock layers inclined to the horizontal, otherwise known as the dip, was easterly, whereas the dip was westerly at Rix's Creek. David determined from this observation that a very large dome had formed between Rix's Creek and Newcastle, with its peak at Lochinvar. This immense coal seam, stretching from Rix's Creek to Newcastle, would now be largely horizontal, having been worn down by forces from a large dome thousands of feet in height over immense periods of time. What become known as the Great Greta Coal Seam was largely hidden up to 1,000 feet below the surface. David was able to trace through a stratum of Muree rock – which is hard conglomerate rock largely impervious to weathering – that occurred about 914 metres above the coal seam. So he could still trace the seam even though no coal was visible at the surface.

Figure 14.2 David, with shouldered pick, and assistant Jack Rourke on 3 August 1886, looking pleased to have uncovered the Greta Coal Seam in Swamp (Deep) Creek near Abermain. Photograph from the University of Sydney Archives (G3_224_1589).

David predicted that the coal seam would be near the surface in the vicinity of the base of the once-existing dome, with outcrops occurring some distance from Lochinvar. To confirm this theory, he went prospecting for surface coal south of Lochinvar. David found lumps of coal at Swamp Creek (sometimes called Deep Creek) near Abermain, where a farmer had reported seeing floating coal pieces. There he and his assistant built a concrete dam and sank a shaft through the outcrop of the coal seam (Figure 14.2). He noted in his diary:

> in portion 15, Parish of Heddon, at point where track crosses creek about a quarter mile above junction of Black Waterhole Creek with Swamp Creek, loose lumps of coal on right bank of creek.[1]

He went on to say that Swamp Creek 'dips about SSW, good coal about 3 feet [1 metre] thick, bottom rather hard coal'.[2] Following this discovery, the Department of Mines reserved

---

1 Branagan 2005, 41.
2 Branagan 2005, 41.

260 square kilometres in the area and put down shafts and bores that showed that the coal seam was about four metres thick. By 1937, the coal seams David had discovered had yielded over £50 million of coal.

David showed that there were three separate seams of coal, one at Greta, one at East Maitland and one at Newcastle. These constituted the great coal fields of Maitland and Greta. He completed this classical mapping exercise in less than two years using the methods of field geology, not the time-honoured approach of prospecting and making discoveries serendipitously. In 1907, David published a detailed summary of his magnificent geological achievement, entitled 'The Geology of the Hunter River Coal Measures'.

Some eight years after leading this geological survey in New South Wales, David had his second great piece of well-earned luck. A Chair of Geology and Physical Geography was established at Sydney; the university was expanding following a very large philanthropic gift – the Challis Bequest. David applied for the Chair and, given his great success in both scholarly and commercial activities following the survey of the Hunter Region, was able to overcome the British academic establishment's choice for that position, taking up his appointment in 1891.

Mount Erebus

In 1907, David was invited to join the very first expedition to Antarctica, led by Sir Ernest Shackleton, several years before the ill-fated attempt by Robert Scott to reach the geographic South Pole. David realised the great opportunity this offered for scientific work on glaciation and mineralogy. He decided to accompany the expedition part of the way and then return to the university, from which he was given a short leave for scientific research. Instead, he was destined to absent himself from the university, without official leave from the Senate, for over a year. This enabled him to journey to the only active volcano in Antarctica, Mount Erebus, and note the geology of its summit at four kilometres, then to sledge over broken sea ice and splintered glacial ice for over 2,000 kilometres to the South Magnetic Pole (see Figure 14.3).

He reached the vicinity of Mount Erebus during March 1908, following a heroic journey, which he described in detail in *The First Journey to the South Magnetic Pole*. His colleagues were a former student and subsequently famous geological explorer (later Sir) Douglas Mawson and Mackay, both much younger than David, who was then 50. Near Mount Erebus, the geologists were excited to discover

> epidote, actinolite, tourmaline and calcite in the form of marble, [which] were abundantly developed in the vicinity of Cape Bernacchi. In the marble cubes of graphite and iron pyrites, together with some tetrahedra of copper pyrites, were observed. In a moraine[3] in this vicinity also a boulder of reef quartz containing iron pyrites was observed. Natrolite was found in seams in boulders of basic lava in a moraine near Mount Larsen. Titanium minerals appeared to be abundant in the

---

3   A moraine is an accumulation of soil and rock debris that accumulates as a consequence of being carried or pushed along by a glacier.

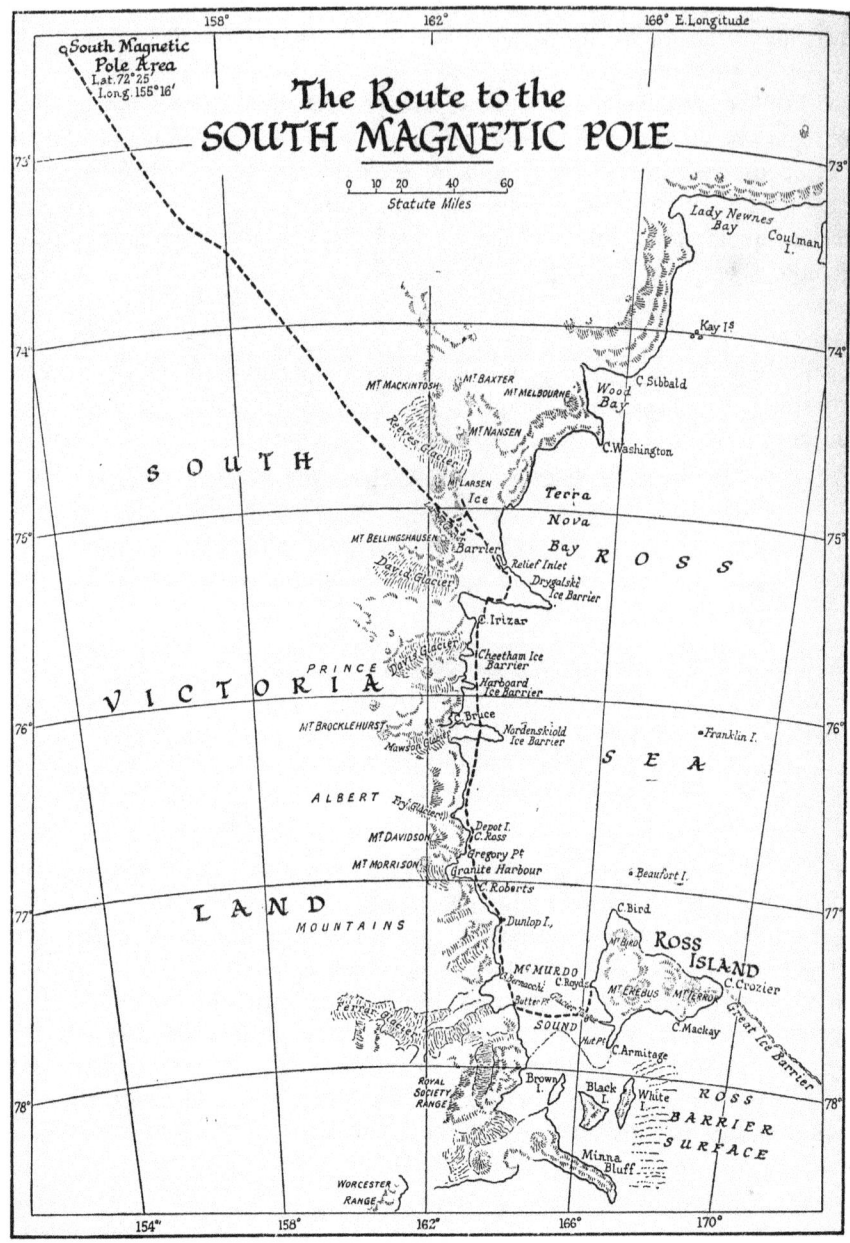

Figure 14.3 Map of the route to the South Magnetic Pole taken by David, Mawson and Mackay. From David 1937. Reproduced with permission from the David family.

eruptive rocks and schists [metamorphic rocks] met with between Granite Harbour and Mount Larsen.[4]

David gave detailed meteorological descriptions of the blizzards and their interactions with the volcano:

> Our actual experience of a heavy blizzard at a level of over 5000 ft. [1,524 metres] on Erebus, as well as our subsequent observations of the height to which the blizzard wind extended, showed that during blizzards the whole atmosphere from sea level up to at least 11,000 ft. [3,352 metres] moves, near Cape Royds from south-east to north-west, and the speed of movement is from forty [64 kilometres] up to over sixty miles [97 kilometres] an hour. The day that we reached the summit of Erebus, March 10, 1908, we found ourselves at the level of over 13,000 ft. [4 kilometres] within the lowest limit of the upper wind. Subsequent observations by us of the point in the steam-cloud over Erebus, where the bend took place at the junction of the lower limit of this current, with the top limit of the middle current, showed that after and during the blizzard the middle-air current, normally blowing from west-south-west, is temporarily abolished, being absorbed by the immense outrushing air stream of the south-east blizzard.[5]

The South Magnetic Pole

Following these geological and meteorological observations, David and his party proceeded on a hazardous journey to the South Magnetic Pole, involving then the longest man-hauled trip ever made, some 2,028 kilometres across glacier tongues, such as the Drygalski Ice Tongue, and along the Antarctic coast, past Victoria Land (Figure 14.3). They claimed Victoria Land for the Crown and then proceeded 2,438 kilometres to the Antarctic plateau, on which they continued for a further 418 kilometres to reach the pole. The party sledged for 10 weeks through the jagged surfaces of screw pack-ice, followed by two weeks of negotiation across 32 kilometres of crevasses, before eventually reaching the pole on 16 January 1909. David described the events:

> We then walked five miles in the direction of the Magnetic Pole so as to place us in the mean position calculated for it by Mawson, 72° 25' South latitude, 155° 16' East longitude. Mawson placed his camera so as to focus the whole group, and arranged a trigger which would be released by means of a string held in our hands so as to make the exposure by means of the focal plane shutter. Meanwhile, Mackay and I fixed up the flag-pole. We then bared our heads and hoisted the Union Jack at 3.30 p.m. with the words uttered by myself in conformity with Lieutenant Shackleton's instructions, "I hereby take possession of this area now containing the Magnetic Pole for the British Empire." At the same time I fired the trigger of the camera by pulling

---

4   Shackleton 1909, 365.
5   Shackleton 1909, 405.

the string. Thus the group were photographed in the manner shown on the plate. The blurred line connected with my right hand represents the part of the string in focus blown from side to side by the wind. Then we gave three cheers for his Majesty the King (Figure 14.4).[6]

The heroic nature of this journey is described in David's 'Narrative of the Magnetic Pole Journey' (part of the second volume of Shackleton's *The Heart of the Antarctic*) as follows:

> If one may be permitted to take a brief retrospect of our journey the following considerations present themselves: The total distance travelled from Cape Royds to the Magnetic Pole and back to our depot on the Drygalski Glacier was about 1260 miles [2,000 kilometres]. Of this, 740 miles [1,190 kilometres] was relay work, and we dragged a weight of, at first, a little over half a ton, and finally somewhat under half a ton for the whole of this distance. For the remaining 520 miles [836 kiolmetres] from the Drygalski Depot to the Magnetic Pole and back we dragged a weight at first, of 670 lb [300 kilograms], but this finally became reduced to about 450 lb [200 kilograms], owing to consumption of food and oil, by the time that we returned to our depot.[7]

Among the geographical discoveries made on this journey were a great mountain range extending from the 82nd parallel, south of McMurdo Sound, to the 86th parallel, trending in a south-easterly direction, and another range preceding south and southwest, with the largest glacier in the world between the two ranges. They also discovered a plateau of 3,352 metres height at latitude 88 degrees South from Cape Adere to the Magnetic Pole.

Reaching the Magnetic Pole, fixed at latitude 72 degrees 25 minutes South, longitude 155 degrees 16 minutes East, necessitated a journey along the coastline of new lands, which were named and claimed for the Crown, such as Victoria Land. David and his colleagues identified new glaciers, ice tongues, peaks and small islands (see Figure 14.3). The geology of this land was described in detail in the scientific report of the expedition. For example, Cape Bernacchi and Victoria Land possess, as David noted, a very interesting geology:

> Cape Bernacchi, a little over a mile north of our previous camp. Here we hoisted the Union Jack just before 10 am and took possession of Victoria Land for the British Empire. Cape Bernacchi is a low rocky promontory, the geology of which is extremely interesting. The dominant type of rock is a pure white coarsely crystalline marble; this has been broken through by granite rocks, the latter in places containing small red garnets. The marble or talc schist contains graphite disseminated through it in small scales. A great deal of tourmaline and epidote are developed in the granite at its point of contact with the calcareous schists. It appeared that the granite had intruded the black tourmaline rocks.[8]

---

6   Shackleton 1910, 310.
7   Shackleton 1910, 333.
8   Shackleton 1910, 269.

Figure 14.4 The South Magnetic Pole. Expedition leader David (centre) does the honours, pulling the string to trigger Mawson's camera for the celebratory photograph. (Alistair Forbes Mackay on picture's left; Douglas Mawson on right.) The trio would be lucky not to perish on the return leg. This photo later figured in a promotional brochure for fund-raising lectures by David, and also appeared on commemorative postage stamps in the 1950s and 1960s. From the *David Family Papers*, National Library of Australia, MS 8890/11/6.

> At lunch time, soon after midnight, we reached some very interesting glacial moraines in the form of large to small blocks, mostly of eruptive rock, embedded in the ice. It was probable, from their general distribution, that they formed part of an old moraine of Mount Nansen, though now about fifteen miles [24 kilometres] in advance of the present glacier front. A conspicuous rock amongst the boulders was a greenish-grey to greenish-black diorite, very rich in sphene. The brown crystals of sphene were frequently intercrystallised with the feldspars, and gave the rock a very pretty appearance. Small fragments of sandstone and clay shale were also represented in these moraines. The larger blocks were up to seven feet [2 metres] in diameter, and formed chiefly of reddish porphyritic granite. We collected a number of specimens from this moraine.[9]

---

9   Shackleton 1910, 295.

David and his colleagues discovered a rare titanium on one of the small islands, which they called Depot Island. David described this discovery as a consequence of the island having

> very little snow or ice upon it, the surface being almost entirely formed of gneissic granite. This granite ... was full of dark enclosures of basic rocks, rich in black mica and huge crystals of hornblende. It was in these enclosures that Mawson discovered a translucent brown mineral, which he believed to be monazite, but which has since proved to be titanium mineral.[10]

Glacial geology

David's interest in glaciation, probably his most enduring passion, began with a paper written in Wales and was rekindled while he was mapping the coal seams in the Hunter Valley. He identified rocks in quarries there as being of glacial origin, belonging to the Cretaceous period, with streaks indicating annual winter and summer deposits. He laid out the evidence for his claim in a paper to the Geological Society of London in 1887, entitled 'Evidence of Glacial Action in the Carboniferous and Hawkesbury Series'. Later visits to the area confirmed that the Carboniferous rocks, or carbon-bearing sediments less than 300 million years old, were of glacial origin, supporting the argument that the Hunter River region was a Carboniferous basin. Some geological colleagues were sceptical about his claim, but their doubts were largely overcome in 1914, when he made a trip from Maitland to Seaham and identified a moraine. His discovery was soon confirmed, providing evidence of a Carboniferous Ice Age. David held that

> among geological problems in Australia, perhaps the phenomena of the three great glacial ages through which Australia has passed in Cambrian [545 million to 490 million years ago], in Permo-Carboniferous [later Carboniferous and early part of the Permian about 300 million years ago], and in late Cainozoic [65 million years ago until today] times, and the allied problem of what influences these ice ages have had upon the distribution of contemporaneous plants and animals, is still the most fascinating that Australian geology has to offer.[11]

Evidence of such glaciation impacted on the theory of continental drift, with similar distributions of glacial rocks from the late Paleozoic (Permo-Carboniferous) period in Australia, India and South America pointing to an earlier conjunction of these continents. David's research on the late Paleozoic ice age led to a 40-page paper on these older glacial deposits in South Africa, India and Australia, providing further evidence for an Indian–Oceanic continent in Paleozoic times. Similarities between Indian and eastern Australian coal fields provided further support. This super continent became known as Gondwanaland; consisting of Australia, Antarctica, Madagascar, Africa and South

---

10 Shackleton 1910, 273.
11 Edgeworth David 1904, quoted in Branagan 2005, 110.

America, Gondwanaland existed some 630 million to 545 million years ago, in the Pre-Paleozoic or Ediacaran era.

The magnificent MacDonnell Ranges in Central Australia (passing through Alice Springs), a spiritual area for the Aboriginal people, became an important location for David's investigations on glaciation during the Carboniferous–Permian period. At the Yellow Rock Horseshoe Bend in the Finke River, boulders and pebbles forming a till conglomerate were identified – excellent evidence for glaciation. Although most geologists put the origin of the tills in the Cretaceous period (141 million to 65 million years ago), David placed them in the late Paleozoic Era – namely, Permo-Carboniferous – like those he had seen in Bacchus Marsh in Victoria, in the Hunter Valley, at Hallett's Cove and in the Inman Valley in South Australia. David also identified glaciation at Mount Kosciuszko that belonged to the Pleistocene (2.6 million to 11,700 years ago) era, through observations of scratched pebbles and polished rocks, as well as of moraines. He established that the lakes there were due to glaciation – the only glacial lakes on the continent. As he reported to the great Aboriginal anthropologist Baldwin Spencer, 'traces of old glaciers there' are 'clear and beautiful'.[12]

Funafuti and the origin of coral atolls

The origin of coral atolls was a matter of some controversy in the late 19th century. Charles Darwin suggested

> an atoll might be regarded as a monument erected by corals to the memory of a buried island, on the shore of which it had begun its existence as a "fringing reef", and had continued to grow upwards as the land beneath it gradually subsided.[13]

In 1897, the Royal Society of London decided to fund an expedition to a coral atoll in the Pacific Ocean for the purposes of boring through the coral limestone to a sufficient depth to determine the kind of rock on which it was established. They chose the Funafuti atoll in the South Pacific Ocean, some 800 kilometres north of Fiji. David was singled out to lead the expedition. He took equipment sufficient to drill to a depth of about 180 metres, the depth at which the basalt basement of the buried island was expected to be reached.

David described the prodigious labour and skill required to achieve the intended drilling depth on such a remote site in an article in the *Daily Telegraph* (16 October 1897). He reported that the required depth set by the Royal Society was achieved, but the predicted basalt had not been found. Further expeditions were then necessary; the third reached over 340 metres, under the direction of A.E. Finckh, on 20 June 1898, but no basalt substratum was reached. Nevertheless, David reported from his own drilling that 'it is tentatively suggested that so far, the evidence of the Funafuti bore ... supports Darwin's theory'.[14] Indeed the

---

12 Branagan 2005, 111.
13 David 1937, 63.
14 'Professor David's Return', 14.

remains of shallow-water marine organisms brought from the bottom of the hole, finally 340 m deep, gave striking support for Charles Darwin's theory that coral atolls had grown progressively on slowly sinking platforms.[15]

It is hard to see how this could be the case, given that the basalt had not been found. Nevertheless, David was elected a Fellow of the Royal Society of London for his leadership, and in 1914 a colleague wrote that 'in geological sciences of all countries, David became known for his research in the Pacific region, where he led a coral boring expedition on the atoll of Funafuti'.[16]

The hypothesis of Precambrian life

The Cambrian period is noted for the preservation of the soft parts of organisms in large sedimentary deposits, indicative of an explosion of diversified life forms. In the Precambrian or Ediacaran period, no life forms had been reliably detected. David set himself the task of reaching back further than the fossiliferous Cambrian period, to the Ediacaran. He studied the ancient Flinders Ranges outside Adelaide in order to determine whether there were other than very primitive life forms present over 545 million years ago. The first task was to clearly delineate the Ediacaran (or Precambrian) from the Cambrian rock in the stratigraphy of the Flinders Ranges. David was able to reach depths that were 1,828 to 3,048 metres lower than the fossiliferous Cambrian limestone in the southern Flinders Ranges. At this depth he thought that he had found and could identify two forms of fossils – arthropods (such as joint-legged crustaceans) and annelids (such as worms) – a discovery that, if true, would have forced palaeontologists to make significant changes to the times at which they believed complex life began on Earth.

David stated that

there is not the slightest doubt, in my opinion, that in pre-trilobite [before the earliest arthropods] and in pre-Archaeocyathinae days [before this extinct group of reef building marine organisms] there was a most wonderful fauna of archi-eurypterids [extinct groups of the largest of all arthropods] distributed throughout the world.[17]

He went on to declare that

the remains in the Adelaide series are often extraordinarily well preserved, even in small details, such as the tiny denticles being traceable and drawable from the extraordinarily enormous casts in the black chert replacing the Upper Torrens limestone. The horizon is more than 12,000 feet [3,657 metres] vertically below the Archaocyathinae limestone.[18]

---

15   Branagan and Vallance 'David, Sir Tannatt William Edgeworth'
16   'Dr Arnold Heim, translated Obituary Notice'.
17   Branagan 2005, 419.
18   Branagan 2005, 420.

This limestone was known not to even contain trilobites, so David's apparent discoveries of more sophisticated species at 3,657 metres below the strata was certainly related to the Precambrian Ediacaran period. These claims, upsetting the accepted scheme of the succession of life forms through the Paleozoic era, were met with extreme scepticism. His old student and colleague from the Antarctica expedition, Douglas Mawson, commented that

> he is doing his best to make a case for his 'fossils'. There may be something in his views but for the most part they are very far-stretched. I have not yet had time to look into the matter in the field. At least he has made a mountain out of a molehill of evidence.[19]

David described the opposition to his ideas as

> sceptics almost everywhere: Mawson, 'Parson' Ward, Dr Whitehouse, (palaeontologist to Queensland Government), Dun (I suspect), E.C. Andrews (Gov. Geologist NSW) and many members of the Royal Society here and of the Linnean Society.[20]

The final blow to his ideas on Precambrian life came in June 1932, when his paper making this claim was rejected by the Royal Society of London. In 1946, 22 years after David died, unequivocal evidence of life forms was discovered in the Precambrian rocks of the Flinders Ranges and, indeed, in Precambrian rocks of other continents. The Ediacaran fossil site in the Flinders Ranges has come to define a new major time division, the first in 120 years and the first based on rocks in the Southern Hemisphere, namely the Ediacaran.

The Geological Map of the Commonwealth

In March 1931, six years after 'retirement', David published his magnificent 'Geological Map of the Commonwealth', which summarises his own geological surveys and those of others, collating material from across the Commonwealth (Figure 14.5). Large geological profiles with, for example, Cretaceous sediments in green and granites in red, provided an authoritative visual summary. This was accompanied by 175 pages of 'Explanatory Notes', which gave a synopsis of Australian geology based on David's own (more than 100) scientific papers and reports. The publication of the map and accompanying notes received great praise. The Government Geologist of New South Wales, E.C. Andrews, commented that it was a colossal task. In particular, 'interpretations of the distribution of Late Precambrian and Palaeozoic Groups – extensive and impressive structures of the Cambrian–Cretaceous'[21] were highlighted for special mention.

***

---

19 Branagan 2005, 418.
20 Branagan 2005, 428.
21 Branagan 2005, 406.

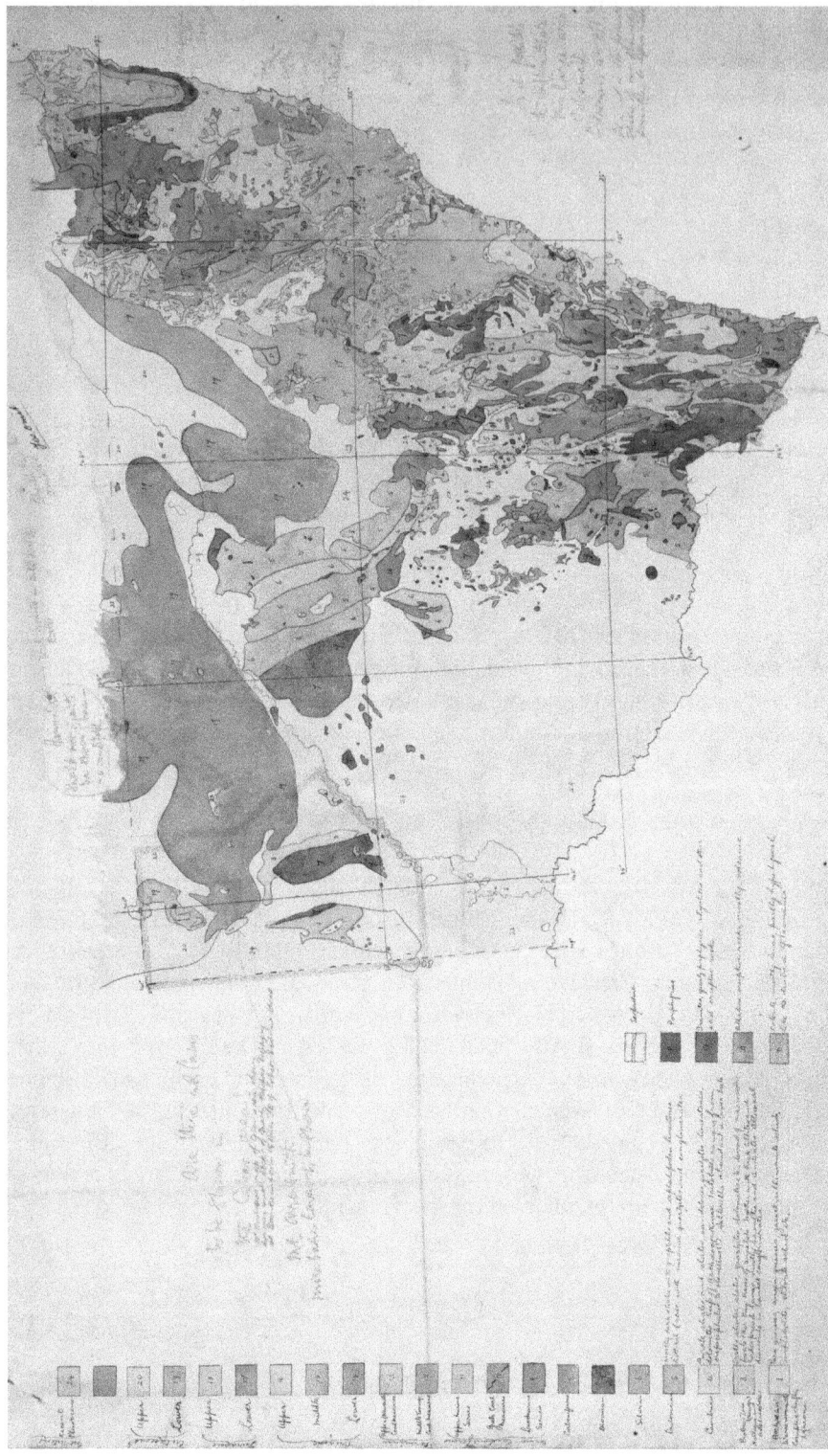

Figure 14.5 David's preliminary plot of the New South Wales section of the Geological Map of the Commonwealth of Australia. National Library of Australia, MAP Edgeworth David Coll/3. Reproduced with permission from the David family.

Figure 14.6 'Famous Australians' 5c stamp. © Australia Postal Corporation 1968.

David remained at the University of Sydney for 43 years, until he died, wearied by the abuses his body had suffered through many adventures. During these years, he vitalised the university, both intellectually and administratively, bringing it fame through his reputation as one of the greatest geologists in the world. This esteem was earnt through his discovery and description of the coal fields in the Hunter Valley and of glaciers and volcanoes in Antarctica, through the drilling of bores in the coral reef atoll of Funafuti to obtain evidence for Charles Darwin's theory of the origin of these structures, and finally, through his work in hunting down evidence for Precambrian life in Central Australia.

In his final address in 1933, on receiving an honorary Doctorate of Science in the Great Hall of the University of Sydney, David said, 'one thing I will stand to, and that is, that all who earnestly pursue truth will find glory and loveliness in this universe.'[22] His loss of faith in Anglican theology as a young man, which had brought him so much distress, was replaced by belief in a deity that was revealed in the 'loveliness of the universe', a universe he strove to understand through scientific work.

> To attain to absolute truth we neither aspire nor desire, content, however faint and weary, to be still pursuing, for in the pursuit itself we find an exceeding great reward.[23]

As his student and fellow explorer Sir Douglas Mawson put it in his Obituary Notes for Fellows of the Royal Society,

---

22 Mawson 1935, 492.
23 Mawson 1935, 499.

for quite two generations past he, by his keen advocacy, ardent enthusiasm, and devotion in the search for truth had been a leading pillar of the scientific community in Australasia.[24]

Further reading

Branagan, D. *T.W. Edgeworth David: A Life*. Canberra: National Library of Australia, 2005.

David, M.E. *Professor David: The Life of Sir Edgeworth David*. London: Edward Arnold, 1937.

Edgeworth David, T.W. The First Journey to the South Magnetic Pole.' In *The Heart of the Antarctic: Being the Story of the British Antarctic Expedition 1907–1909, Volume 2*, chs VI–XIII. London: William Heinemann, 1909.

Mawson, D. 'Sir Tannatt William Edgeworth David 1858–1934.' Biographical Memoirs of Fellows of the Royal Society, 1 December 1935. Accessed 22 March 2018. https://bit.ly/2Sa6ITm.

Shackleton, E.H., *The Heart of the Antarctic: Being the Story of the British Antarctic Expedition 1907–1909*. With an Introduction by Hugh Robert Mill, D.Sc. An Account of the First Journey to the South Magnetic Pole by Professor T.W. Edgeworth David, F.R.S., Volume II, Philadelphia: J.B. Lippincott Company, 1909.

Shackleton, E.H., *The Heart of the Antarctic: Being the Story of the British Antarctic Expedition 1907–1909*. New and Revised Edition with Illustrations in Colour and Black and White. London: William Heinemann, 1910.

---

24 Mawson 1935, 492.

Biology, epidemiology and mathematics

15
Distribution and abundance of species: Louis Charles Birch

Challis Professor of Biology (1960–1985). Birch was one of the 20th century's leading ecologists. He established the importance of the environment in determining the distribution and abundance of species and argued that all species have some form of consciousness.

Of the great early 20th-century philosophers Alfred North Whitehead, Bertrand Russell and Ludwig Wittgenstein, it was Whitehead who had the greatest influence on Charles Birch. Whitehead and Russell were responsible for the magisterial work *Principia Mathematica*, which, following ten years of intellectual labour, sought to place all mathematics on a logical foundation. Russell's student, Wittgenstein, questioned the possibility of this in his *Tractatus Logico-Philosophicus*. Whitehead was clearly a metaphysician; in his later influential works, such as *Science and the Modern World*, and his magnum opus *Process and Reality*, he sought to find a scheme that would reconcile the scientific view of what constitutes the ultimate 'stuff' of the universe with the possession of a mind or consciousness. Whitehead came up with a metaphysical system that had a profound effect on great biologists, such as Birch, C.H. Waddington, Sewall Wright and W.E. Agar, the Professor of Zoology at Melbourne University (1919–1948) at the time Birch studied biology there. Agar's book *A Contribution to the Theory of the Living Organism*, published in 1943, was very much in the tradition of Whitehead's philosophy and had very considerable influence, as I can personally attest after carrying out my first biological research in his department in 1960. Indeed, its influence was so extensive that I formed a group called the 'Athenian Society' (mentioned in the introduction), dedicated to understanding the philosophy of Whitehead, Russell and Wittgenstein.

These similar interests, together with the fact that we had both worked as young students in Agar's department in Melbourne, naturally led to a warm friendship between Birch and myself when we ended up together at the University of Sydney. I came to greatly admire his foundational contributions to ecology, with which this essay is primarily concerned (although other aspects of his contributions to society, philosophy and religion could have been emphasised).

Figure 15.1 Professor Louis Charles Birch. Photograph from the University of Sydney Archives (G77_4_0049).

Whitehead's central idea was, in Birch's words, that 'mentality and physicality are two aspects of the same phenomenon'.[1] Birch added:

> Further, the universe is not made of physical substances like Newtonian billiard balls but of events, and these basic events are experiential. This is the doctrine of internal relations. It destroys the notion of material substances and substitutes that of an event.[2]

'Things' are then replaced by 'processes', hence the title of Whitehead's book, *Process and Reality*. Birch, in adopting Whitehead's philosophy, came to regard 'mind and matter as two aspects of the same thing and experience in some form as a feature of entities that extend into the inanimate world'.[3]

Birch was born in Melbourne in 1918. He began his biological career as a child hunting bugs, as had other great biologists such as Charles Darwin and the Australian immunologist and Nobel Prize winner Macfarlane Burnet. This interest was encouraged by his Irish mother, Nora, who bought him the new and rare book Bullard's *Insects of Australia and New Zealand*. He commented: 'That was tremendously important to help me identify things I found in the field. I became a bug hunter.'[4] Being of an evangelical turn of mind,

---

1 Birch 2004, 3.
2 Birch 2004, 3.
3 Birch 2004, 14.
4 Australian Biography, 'Charles Birch'.

Birch sought to harness his biological interest in a way 'that could be very helpful to the world'.[5] He hit on the idea of doing agriculture at Melbourne University, graduating in this subject when he turned 21, at the outbreak of the Second World War in 1939.

The choice of agriculture as an undergraduate course was most propitious. It provided the young Birch with the knowledge he needed to create the revolution in ecology he was destined to make. As he commented,

> that was probably a good choice because in agriculture I learnt an awful lot of things that I wouldn't have done in a science course. ... Things about soil, about domestic plants and animals, about climatology. A lot of stuff which eventually was going to become very important to me when I decided I was really interested in ecology.[6]

His subsequent career proved this to be true. First, in his experimental research on the rice weevil destroying stored wheat during the Second World War, which gave rise to the concept of the 'intrinsic rate of natural increase' of a species. Next, in 1954, through research with his mentor, Herbert Andrewartha, that led to their foundational work in ecology, determining the effects of the environment, in contrast to those of population density, on *The Distribution and Abundance of Animals* (as their magisterial work was called). Third, by introducing concepts such as meta-populations and the dispersion of populations, as spelt out in his next significant work with Andrewartha, *The Ecological Web*. Finally, in his creation of the subject of ' ecological genetics' with the great geneticist Theodosius Dobzhansky. All of this was carried out in parallel with Birch's very significant impact on the academic discipline of ecology in Australia. In 1954, he introduced animal ecology as an independent discipline at the University of Sydney, after joining the university in 1948. He then established the country's first experimental zoology laboratory, namely the CSIRO Joint Unit in Animal Ecology.

On a more personal level, he retained his evangelical commitments until his death at the age of 91. These took the form of philosophical enquiries into how and when consciousness arises in the evolution of species, a question that led to books such as *Nature and God* in 1965 and *Science and Soul* in 2008, the year before he died.

Identifying the environment as the key factor determining the distribution and abundance of animals

Around the middle of the 20th century, the form that ecology took was dominated by a debate, pursued aggressively by two camps, both led from Australia. On one side were those such as Andrew Nicholson, the head of CSIRO Entomology, who believed that 'populations are self-governing systems. They regulate their densities in relation to their own properties and those of their environments' (by which he meant resources, competitors and natural enemies).[7] On the other hand, Birch and Andrewartha, who was then professor of biology in Adelaide, emphasised the importance of external events,

---

5   Australian Biography, 'Charles Birch'.
6   Australian Biography, 'Charles Birch'.
7   Nicholson 1954, 10.

such as stochasticity and disturbances. They contended that external processes, driven by weather and other types of disturbance, are critical in controlling the numbers and distribution of animals.

At the time of Birch's first research contribution to ecology, the density-dependent view was dominant. Accordingly, the accepted mechanisms responsible for the distribution and abundance of species could be expressed as follows:

> All animal populations are kept in check by factors whose restraint on the growth of a population is directly correlated with the population's density. Only such density-dependent factors can regulate a population. The role of density-independent factors is restricted to determining the level at which the density-dependent factors inhibit further increase. The function of research in population ecology is merely to isolate in each case the limiting factor involved. Failure to find this factor is symptomatic of either sloppy research technique or of inadequate time spent on the project.[8]

As Birch put it:

> That meant that, as the numbers went up under favourable conditions, the animals would become so crowded that the birth rate would drop, the death rate would go up and the numbers would go down. And so, if you asked the question, 'what prevents the species from becoming extinct?' The answer was density regulation: the number wouldn't go right down because, as the animals got to a low density, the pressure on them was decreased.[9]

'This is a plausible mechanism and a modeler's dream but very hard to prove in most cases.'[10]

Birch's opponent, Nicholson, worked from a deductive base – that is, from first principles – and then determined if nature conformed to this. The alternative process of researching nature first to ascertain facts regarding the abundance and distribution of species and then forming principles governing these factors – i.e. the process of induction (see Gaukroger on Francis Bacon in Chapter 9) – was not favoured by density-dependent advocates like Nicholson at all. It is perhaps for this reason that density-dependent advocates preferred to work with species under laboratory-controlled conditions (in Nicholson's case, with blow flies), in which one can fix, for example, the amount of food they receive each day.

In 1954, Birch, together with his mentor Andrewartha, produced the key counter-argument to the prevailing density-dependent orthodoxy, summarising field studies in which no density regulating factors could be found. This summary occupied 750 pages of a sustained polemic – *The Distribution and Abundance of Animals*. This work showed that environmental factors, such as the weather, were critical in regulating numbers, rather than the orthodox argument that populations regulated themselves through competition, for example, for limited resources. As Birch puts it:

---

8   'Book Reviews: The Distribution and Abundance of Animals', 223.
9   Australian Academy of Science, 'Professor Charles Birch'.
10 Meats, 'What Ever Happened'.

Both of us came to the conclusion that the numbers of animals could be determined by almost any component of the environment. One was sometimes more important than others but, in most of the cases that we studied, the numbers were determined very largely by the weather. ... We therefore didn't put emphasis where the central emphasis had been in ecology of the numbers of animals, on the so-called density-dependent factors.[11]

The Distribution and Abundance of Animals established the subfield of density-independent population ecology. The book became 'one of the century's most successful guides to ecology'.[12] It successfully changed the notion that there was 'a balance of nature' arising from a stability engendered by density dependence, a notion that Ehrlich and Birch asserted in 1967 was 'demonstrably false'. Rather,

a realistic basis for building models dealing with the changes of numbers in populations would include the following propositions: (a) All populations are constantly changing in size. (b) The environments of all organisms are constantly changing. (c) Local populations must be recognized and investigated if changes in population size are to be understood. (d) The influence on population size of various components of environment varies with population density, amongst species, among local populations, and through time.[13]

The impact of this work on ecology was enormous, bringing about a paradigm shift in the subject. In 1988, Andrewartha and Birch received the leading recognition in the world for ecology, the Eminent Ecologist Award of the Ecological Society of America. Their citation read:

The Distribution and Abundance of Animals was a landmark synthesis of field population ecology that inspired the generation widely credited with constructing modern ecology.[14]

Theoretical and empirical determination of the effects of an unlimited environment on the intrinsic rate of natural increase of a species

The basic statistic of population ecology and genetics is the 'intrinsic rate of natural increase'. Although the concept was originally introduced by Lotka in 1924 for human populations, it was Birch who gave the idea form and substance, indicating that the concept had far-reaching implications when considering a species' chances to survive and reproduce. Lotka had shown in 1929 that the experimental rate of growth of a human population, or the statistical increase of a population, could be estimated from registers of births and deaths. Birch's elaboration of this concept grew out of his earlier research.

---

11   Australian Academy of Science, 'Professor Charles Birch'.
12   Steffes 2011, 2.
13   Ehrlich and Birch 1967, 106–7.
14   Simberloff 1989, 28–9.

During World War II, I had made laboratory measurements on the influence of temperature and moisture on the chance of grain weevils to survive and reproduce. The objective was a practical one of determining the most favourable environments for the storage of huge quantities of grain stockpiled in Australia during the war years. This meant finding the environments least favourable for the multiplication of the insect pests of stored grain.[15]

The rice weevil in question was *Calandra (Sitophilus) oryzae*, which grew exponentially in numbers when there were no limits on space and resources and no predators – the very conditions that occurred in the large wheat stacks. The increase in numbers is then governed by density-independent mechanisms, so that neither the logistic equations for density-dependent increases (see Chapter 16) nor the predator-prey Lotka–Volterra equations are relevant.

Birch started by defining the 'intrinsic rate of natural increase' as 'the rate of increase per head under specified physical conditions, in an unlimited environment where the effects of increasing density do not need to be considered'.[16] These conditions clearly applied for the grain weevil *Calandra (Sitophilus) oryzae*. As Birch had gathered the birth rates and death rates of these, he could determine their intrinsic rate of increase. This enabled him to give what J.H. Brown and R. May called 'the first quantitative analysis of the demographic behaviour of an animal population, albeit one which was growing exponentially under laboratory conditions'.[17] Birch calculated the intrinsic rate of increase (r) as follows. First, he constructed a life table (see Table 15.1) from data in four experimental papers he had published in 1945 on *Calandra (Sitophilus) oryzae*, together with an estimate of the lifespan of adult females from a different species of flour beetle (*Tribolium confusum*) to give age-specific rates of fecundity (m) and survival (l). Table 15.1, the life table, has columns for age in weeks (x), probability at birth of being alive at x (l_x), age-specific fecundity rate (m_x) and the product of l_x and m_x.

The net rate of reproduction (R_0), the ratio of total female births in two successive generations ($R_0 = N_T/N_0$), is the sum of all the products of $l_x m_x$ for the population (see Table 15.1, which gives $R_0 = 113.56$), where N_0 is the population of animals at the beginning. N_t is the population size at a time t and r is the intrinsic or instantaneous rate of increase (as noted). The differential is $dN/dt = rN$. Therefore $N_t = N_0 e^{rt}$, at time $t = T$. Taking the natural log of both sides gives, at time $t = T$, $T = \ln R_0/r$. T is obtained from the life table (Table 15.1) as the mean of a frequency distribution (namely, $T = \sum x l_x m_x / \sum l_x m_x = 943.09/113.56 = 8.3$ weeks) giving $T = 8.3$ weeks. So $r = 0.57$ per head per week. According to Birch, an r of 0.57 is far too small and arises from the approximate estimate of T from the table. This forced him to use an alternative approach for calculating r, involving a trial and error substitution. This new method involved an approximation to the Lotka equation, which is given in Table 15.2, providing an r of 0.76. Table 3 in Birch's paper gives the percentage contribution of each age group to the value of r when $r = 0.76$. It shows that 85.24 per cent of the intrinsic rate of increase (r) is accounted for

---

15 Birch 1982.
16 Spencer 2015.
17 May, 'Birch, L.C (1948)'.

Pivotal age in weeks (x)	(l_x)	(m_x)	$l_x m_x$
4.5	0.87	20.0	17.400
5.5	0.83	23.0	19.090
6.5	0.81	15.0	12.150
7.5	0.80	12.5	10.000
8.5	0.79	12.5	9.875
9.5	0.77	14.0	10.780
10.5	0.74	12.5	9.250
11.5	0.66	14.5	9.570
12.5	0.59	11.0	6.490
13.5	0.52	9.5	4.940
14.5	0.45	2.5	1.125
15.5	0.36	2.5	0.900
16.5	0.29	2.5	0.800
17.5	0.25	4.0	1.000
18.5	0.19	1.0	0.190
			R_0=113.560

Table 15.1 Showing the life table (for oviposition span) age-specific fecundity rates and the method of calculating the net reproduction rate (R_0) for *Calandra oryzae* at 29 degrees in wheat of 14 per cent moisture content. Sex ratio is equal. Republished with permission of Blackwell Publishing Ltd. from L.C. Birch, 'The Intrinsic Rate of Natural Increase of an Insect Population,' *Journal of Animal Ecology* 17 (1948); permission conveyed through Copyright Clearance Center, Inc.

in the first two weeks of egg laying. The first two weeks of fecundity overwhelmingly determine r even though the adults continue to lay eggs for a period of eight weeks! This age distribution shows that by far the greatest extent of the population is in the egg and larval stages, due to the high value of r. It follows that researchers had been greatly underestimating the population size of the insects because most of them are effectively hidden in the grains in the egg and larval stages.

A further ecological insight was apparent from these calculations – namely, that abiotic (non-biological) environmental factors can have a major effect on populations. Birch calculated that at 23 degrees Celsius, $r = 0.43$, whereas at 29 degrees Celsius, $r = 0.76$. So the intrinsic rate of increase is very temperature sensitive, independent of parasites or a limitation of resources. A common method now used to control for *Calandra (Sitophilus)*

Pivotal age group (x)	l_xm_x	$r = 0.76$		$r = 0.77$	
		$7-rx$	e^{7-rx}	$7-rx$	e^{7-rx}
4.5	17.400	3.58	35.87	3.53	34.12
5.5	19.090	2.82	16.78	2.76	15.80
6.5	12.150	2.06	7.846	1.99	7.316
7.5	10.000	1.30	3.669	1.22	3.387
8.5	9.875	0.54	1.716	0.45	1.5683
9.5	10.780	−0.22	0.8025	−0.32	0.7261
10.5	9.250	−0.98	0.3753	−1.09	0.3362
11.5	9.570	−1.74	0.1755	−1.86	0.1557
12.5	6.490	−2.50	0.0821	−2.62	0.0728
13.5	4.940	−3.26	0.0384	−3.39	0.0337
$\sum_{4.5}^{13.5} e^{7-rx} l_x m_x =$			1108		1047

Table 15.2 Showing the method of calculating r for *Calandra oryzae* at 29 degrees by trial and error substitution in the expression $\sum e^{7-rx} l_x m_x = 1097$. Republished with permission of Blackwell Publishing Ltd. from L.C. Birch, 'The Intrinsic Rate of Natural Increase of an Insect Population,' *Journal of Animal Ecology* 17 (1948); permission conveyed through Copyright Clearance Center, Inc.

oryzae is to change the environmental temperature, for example, to 17.5 degrees Celsius for three days. In summary, Birch's paradigm setting investigations show

> that the intrinsic rate of increase is determined to a much greater extent by the rate of oviposition [egg laying] in the first 2 weeks of adult life than by the total number of eggs laid in the entire life time. … With each successive week, eggs laid make a lessened contribution to the value of r. … The methods of calculation of r provide a means of determining the extent to which the various components – the life table, the fecundity table and the length of the pre- reproductive stages – enter into the value of r.[18]

Defining the 'environment' and developing quantitative measures of its effects on populations

Andrewartha and Birch summarised the complexity of the environmental factors acting on different populations of the same species in *The Ecological Web*. They emphasised their

---

18   Birch 1948.

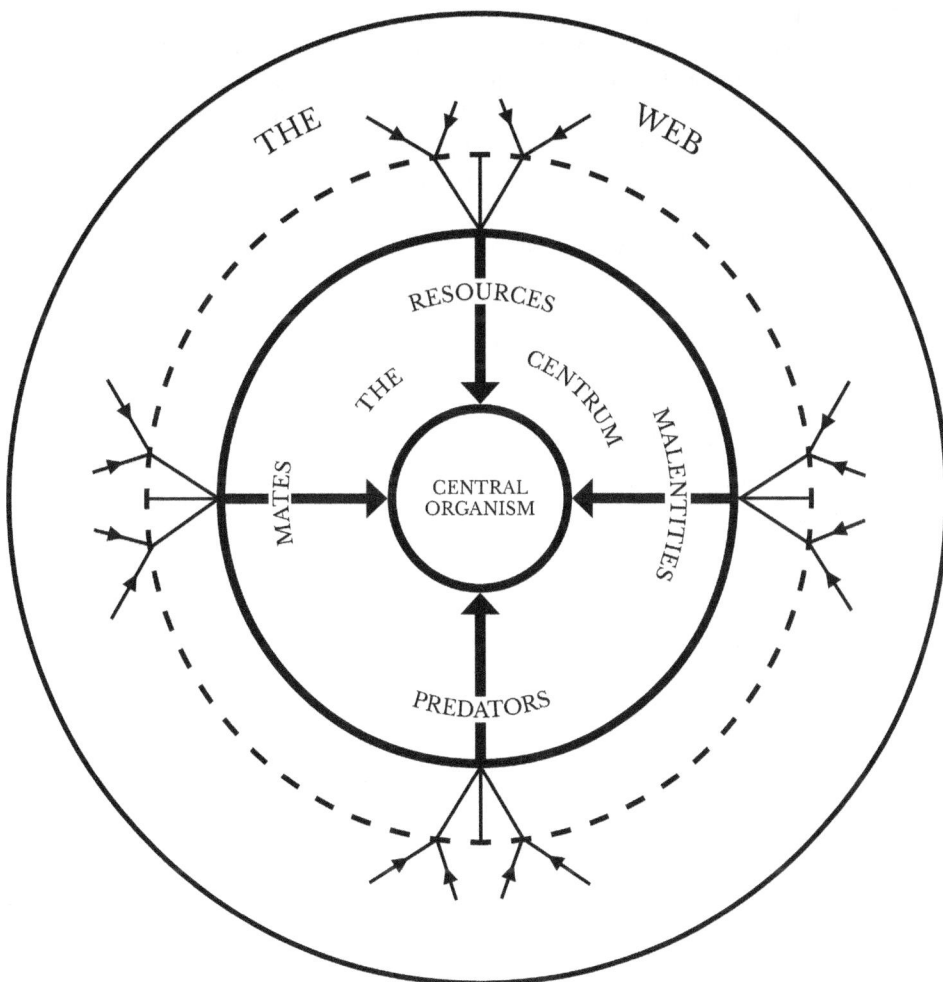

Figure 15.2 The environment comprises everything that might influence the animal's chances to survive and reproduce. Only those 'things' that are the proximate causes of changes in the physiology or behaviour of the animal are placed in the centrum and recognized as 'directly acting' components of the environment. Everything else acts indirectly – that is, through an intermediary or a chain of intermediates that ultimately influences the activity of one or other of the components in the centrum. All of these indirectly acting components are placed in the web. From H.G. Andrewartha and L.C. Birch, *The Ecological Web* (Chicago: University of Chicago Press, 1984). © 1984 The University of Chicago.

own field and laboratory studies on beetles, which Birch had first worked on as a child, as well as on plant feeding thrips, for which Andrewartha had gathered information in his garden over 20 years. As in *The Distribution and Abundance of Animals*, they eschewed the 'excessively abstract' and the 'departure from reality' found in many mathematical modelling exercises. They recognised that the power of the density-dependent approach to determining the abundance of animals is that it lends itself to mathematical modelling

– indeed, to the application of logistic equations (see Chapter 16). In contrast, the realignment of ecology to take into account environmental conditions is not so readily open to quantitative modelling. Birch and Andrewartha proposed to overcome this difficulty by carefully defining what was meant by the term 'environment' and then applying symbolic logic to tease out the important components that impact upon it. They did this in *The Ecological Web*, analysing the environment in terms of 'anything that influences an individual's chance to survive and/or to reproduce.'[19] This book spelt out 'a new theory of the environment' that might be outlined as follows:

> First, an environment is made up of a centrum[20] of directly acting components and a web[21] of indirectly acting components. Second, the centrum of the environment of any animal comprises four divisions or compartments; each division houses a characteristic set of components that we call resources,[22] mates, malentities,[23] and predators.[24] Third, the web comprises a number of systems of branching chains. A link in the chain may be a living organism (or its artefact or residue) or inorganic matter or energy.[25]

These branching chains comprise a large web of environmental factors outside the centrum. This model is depicted in Figure 15.2.

The logistic equations considering only density factors, which so enamoured modellers, were replaced by envirograms.[26] These reflected the centrum/web relationship in the form of a diagram in which the condition of a species arose from the proximate

---

19 Andrewartha and Birch 1984, 5.
20 The centrum of any environment comprises, on logical grounds, four components. The general names are resources, mates, malentities, and predators. There is no directly acting component of the environment that does not fall into one of these categories. From Andrewartha and Birch 1984, 10.
21 'According to the theory of environment, activity in the directly acting components is the proximate cause of the condition of the animal, which reflects its chance to survive and reproduce. But the distal cause of the animal's condition is found in the web, among the indirectly acting components which modified the centrum.' From Andrewartha and Birch 1984, 19.
22 'Food is the most familiar resource. The others are water, oxygen, heat and tokens. Food and water contribute the chemicals from which the body is built; and food, with oxygen, provides energy. Heat, radiant or ambient, that is absorbed by the animal may help keep the body at a temperature that favours a healthy metabolism. … We speak of a token when a caterpillar or a bird, having measured the length of a day, changes its body chemistry to suit the season, preparing for diapause or migration as the case may be. In this instance the length of the day is a token.' From Andrewartha and Birch 1984, 13.
23 Often conceived as 'unfortunate accidents', like small insects drowning in a deep footprint left by a bullock walking across a marsh. A malentity may kill the primary animal and even eat it, but this behaviour is not selective. The animal may be eaten along with some other sort of food that is sought.' From Andrewartha and Birch 1984, 14.
24 Distinguished from a malentity, in as much as the former treats the primary animal as a food source. The predator usually shows some adaptation that equips it for feeding on the primary organism. From Andrewartha and Birch 1984, 14.
25 Andrewartha and Birch 1984, 3–5.
26 'A modifier may be one or several steps removed from the centrum, and the pathway from a particular modifier to its target in the centrum may be joined by incoming pathways from other modifiers that may be behind or alongside the first one. To indicate the degree of indirectness in the action of a modifier, we call one that is n steps away from its target a "modifier of the nth order". The envirogram is a graphic representation of these pathways.' From Andrewartha and Birch 1984, 19.

causes of the centrum, which acted directly on the populations, and the more distal components, forming a web acting on the population through modulation of the centrum. Envirograms gave substance to the web, showing lines joining boxes that represent all the things that affect some central organism through the centrum (Figure 15.3). Each organism, at any time, has its own envirogram. These called for specific definitions of 'niche',[27] 'habitat',[28] and 'demographics', as well as 'aggressive malentities' and 'stochastic malentities'.

This approach arose from Birch's rejection of the mathematical models of the 1950s, which he argued had no contact with reality; he claimed that the logical schemes did. Birch was completely cognisant of the logistic curves beloved of the modellers, but rejected these curves in favour of estimating growth rates directly from empirical data summarised in life tables, a method still in popular use today. His ideas were further clarified by the logician Susan Norton in an appendix to *The Ecological Web*. Factors that modify the directly acting components in the centrum constitute a web of influences spreading out around the centrum (see Figure 15.2). Importantly, the environment considered here does not act on a population but on individuals. These individuals exert influences on each other, so that the environment of the individual includes not only that defined above, but also that supplied by other individuals.

Meta-populations, and their dispersion and regulation by environmental and genetic factors

The concept of a 'meta-population' arose from studies on what appears, at first, to be a single population but turns out to be a set of local populations, each best suited to a particular area, with free migration between populations. The idea was first enunciated by Birch and Andrewartha in their concept of 'the dispersion of populations', which emphasised how extinction of a subpopulation of a species in one area could be compensated for by migration of another subpopulation into the vacated area. The existence of 'multi-partite populations' – that is, populations dispersed into different habitats with free migration between them – helps explain why it is so difficult for species to become extinct. Indeed, the subpopulations of a species may be genetically different, having evolved to best suit the environment provided by a particular area. Nevertheless, if a local extinction occurs, migration from another local population can fill the niche.

---

27 'A niche is a quality of the animal which determined how the animal responds to its environment – for example, the ability to live on a particular sort of food or to co-exist with a particular sort of predator. For every component of the environment there is a corresponding niche. In a nutshell, the habitat makes the environment; the niches of the animal are its response to the environment.' From Andrewartha and Birch 1984, xiii.
28 'A "habitat" is a place that might be habitable for the animal whose ecology is being studied. The boundaries of the habitat and the qualities that determine the boundaries are fixed arbitrarily by the ecologist.' From Andrewartha and Birch 1984, xiii.

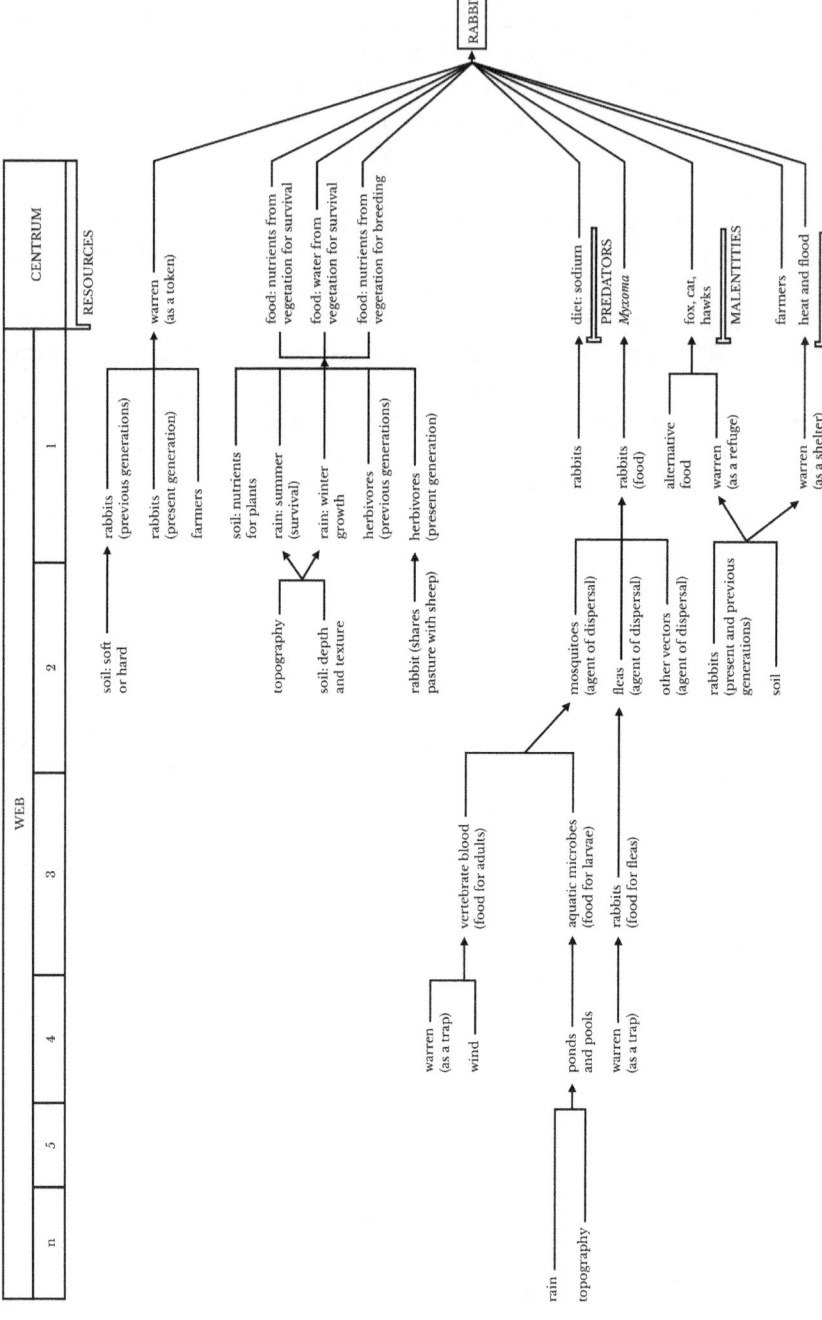

Figure 15.3 The envirogram of the European rabbit in Australia. From H.G. Andrewartha and L.C. Birch, *The Ecological Web* (Chicago: University of Chicago Press, 1984). © 1984 The University of Chicago.

Birch studied such dispersions in the Queensland fruit fly as it spread south. As he described it,

> the Queensland fruit fly was spreading south – populations, even small ones, began to establish themselves in southern Victoria. So I made a study of the birth rates and death rates under different conditions, and I found that the populations that managed to get south were changed populations; they had evolved to suit that environment better.[29]

In recent times, the idea of what are now called 'meta-populations' has been shown empirically to hold for the dispersion of populations in many instances. It has great significance in planning conservation strategies, particularly in the context of the ecology of landscapes.

Ecological genetics

Birch became interested in the relationship of ecology to evolution and, in 1960, went to the great American geneticist Theodosius Dobzhansky to learn more about evolution, which he did through field trips to places as far away as Brazil. Birch realised from these experiences that

> with fast-growing populations like insects, particularly, you can get through many generations in a relatively short period of time, and opportunities for evolutionary change are significant. Well, having demonstrated that there was evolutionary change, I became interested in relating evolution to ecology.[30]

This led Birch to form a new sub-field in ecology – ecological genetics. This sub-field subsequently became a central pillar of what would be known as the Modern Synthesis in evolutionary biology – the joining of Mendelian genetics with Darwinian evolution.

Science and the spiritual

The majority of Birch's nine books were not directly concerned with ecology, but rather with the relationship between scientific enquiry and the spiritual, as indicated by titles such as *Nature and God*, *On Purpose*, *Regaining Compassion: Humanity and Nature*, and his final book, published a year before he died, *Science and Soul*. To this end, he became Vice Chairman of the Science, Technology and Environment Unit of the World Council of Churches (1970–1984). These concerns also extended to his founding the Social Responsibility in Science movement in Australia in the 1960s. It is interesting that the great Bob May (Chapter 16) commented 'it is this movement to which I owe my

---

29 Australian Academy of Science, 'Professor Charles Birch'.
30 Australian Academy of Science, 'Professor Charles Birch'.

subsequent career'.[31] These contributions were recognised by the award of the Templeton Prize, the foremost award in the area of science and religion, to Birch in 1990.

***

Birch was one of the great figures of mid-20th-century ecology, playing a leading role, with his close colleague Herbert Andrewartha, in establishing the importance of the environment in determining the distribution and abundance of species. In so doing, they helped lay the foundations for our understanding of how deterioration in the present environment is affecting humans and other species. Birch's ecological work dovetailed with his philosophical and religious leanings, which, in his many books, became a search for the origins of consciousness. He came to attribute consciousness, in some form, to all species. This led to a strong commitment to organisations concerned with the preservation of species and a reverence for life.

Further reading

Andrewartha, H.G., and L.C. Birch. *The Distribution and Abundance of Animals*. Chicago: University of Chicago Press, 1954.
Andrewartha, H.G., and L.C. Birch. *The Ecological Web*. Chicago: University of Chicago Press, 1984.
Birch, L.C. 'The Intrinsic Rate of Natural Increase of an Insect Population.' *Journal of Animal Ecology* 17, no. 1 (1948): 15–26.
Hanski, I., and M. Gilpin. 'Metapopulation Dynamics: Brief History and Conceptual Domain.' *Biological Journal of the Linnean Society* 42, no. 1–2 (1991): 3–16.

---

31   May, 'Birch, L.C. (1948)'.

16
Biodiversity, the spread of diseases and mathematical predictions: Robert May

Bachelor of Science (1956); PhD (1959). May is one of the most distinguished graduates of Sydney University. He carried out theoretical work in physics and was awarded the university's first personal professorship in 1972. Theoretical physics provided mathematical skills that enabled him to become a foundation figure in theoretical ecology throughout the 1970s and 80s, and later in theoretical studies of biodiversity and the spread of diseases.

In 1981, I received a letter from the head of graduate studies at Princeton University congratulating me on being awarded a personal professorship at the University of Sydney. This letter was from Robert May, who had received the first such professorship some years earlier. Unfortunately, our academic paths at Sydney never crossed. This was a great pity, for as May was writing his great population biology monograph *Stability and Complexity in Model Ecosystems*, I was writing a Physiology Society monograph, *Autonomic Neuromuscular Transmission*, some 100 metres away from May's office (that is the distance between the physics school and the old medical school at Sydney). There were difficult and unsolved mathematical problems in my monograph, which would undoubtedly have profited from the application of May's extraordinary gifts.

May's interest in animal population dynamics was fostered by Charles Birch, professor of biology at Sydney (Chapter 15). As May commented,

> The first thing I did in ecology is one of the most important things I have done. ... Professor Charles Birch was head of biology at Sydney and a wonderful man. He was one of the founders of Social Responsibility in Science in Australia. ... When I had this insight about stability and complexity, I immediately went to Professor Charles Birch because he was the co-author of what was then the world's leading text on ecology – Andrewartha and Birch. ... he said, '... My friend Ken Watt, whose book you've just read [*Ecology and Resource Management*] would really love that. You write it up and send it to him and come and give a seminar in biology'. So I did all that and I had a nice letter from Ken Watt, who wrote 'This is a milestone in ecology'.[1]

---

1 Australian Academy of Science, 'Lord Robert May'.

Figure 16.1 Robert McCredie May, Baron May of Oxford, by Norman McBeath. © Norman McBeath / National Portrait Gallery, London.

Following this auspicious beginning, May went on to Princeton, initially for a short time to work with the then leading theoretical ecologist Robert MacArthur. But this was to become a permanent sojourn when he became professor of zoology there in 1973.

May's early and very influential research papers, which emanated from his work at Sydney (sometimes overlapping with that in Princeton), included those on complexity and stability in ecological populations. These papers showed how chaos can arise in such communities and provided the development of the now famous May–Wigner theorem relating complexity and stability in ecological populations ('Will a Large Complex System be Stable?', which was followed by May's monograph on this subject *Stability and Complexity in Model Ecosystems*). Furthermore, contrary to then accepted ideas, May showed that overlap of different species in a particular niche is not much affected by variations in their environment ('Niche Overlap as a Function of Environmental Variability'). Finally, he provided solutions for ecological equations that had, on previous occasions, been discarded as unstable but were actually stable limit cycles or oscillations ('Limit Cycles in Predator-Prey Communities').

Niche overlap as a function of environmental variability

The concept of an ecological niche involves consideration of how a population (such as parasites) fares in relation to competitors, as well as the availability of resources. Growth is associated with scarcity of pathogens and abundance of resources, with such growth providing the opportunity for the population to change its environment. This can happen through, for example, restricting some resources for other populations, consuming prey and, in turn, providing food for predators. Niche overlap occurs between different species that compete for the same resources.

Robert MacArthur, May's first publishing collaborator and mentor at Princeton, introduced statistical methods into the description of niches. For example, a bell-shaped normal distribution could be used in some cases to give the occurrence of prey of a certain size, taken as the food of another species. The normal distribution gives the form of the niche. In Figure 16.2, the middle distribution is for a species that competes with the species on its left and right, as indicated by the overlaps between the distributions. The extreme distributions are for species that do not overlap with each other, so the niche overlap is greatest for the middle species.

A number of interesting observations on the overlap of the niches of different species of birds were made in the 1960s. These observations suggested some kind of regularity – the overlap between niches was about equal to the variability in the niches of each of the species. For example, different congeneric species of hawk, each competing for the same food but preferring different weights of food, were found to overlap in their food preference to about the same extent as the separation of their average weight of food preference. To put it another way, if the average preferred weights of food for particular species are distributed as bell-shaped normal distributions, then the mean of these will be separated by distances d, where d is roughly the standard deviation of the distribution (called w), as shown in Figure 16.2. That is, the mean weight is separated by about one standard deviation. To emphasise the possible generality of the relation between d and w, consider a number of species of tropical ant bird that each forage for ants, on average, at different heights. Again, it is found that the separation of the mean heights is roughly equal to the standard deviation of the heights.

Observations of this kind, with the regularity of $d/w \approx 1$, indicate that there may be a restriction on the extent of niche overlap. A further important observation is that bush-land bird communities in the Sierra Nevada show packing of different species (that is, d size) that is about equal to the packing in forest-foliage guilds of birds, even though the microenvironment is likely to be much more stable in the forest than in the Sierra Nevada. This suggests the possibility that the relation $d/w \approx 1$ might, very surprisingly, be independent of the extent of changes in the environment. In this case, not only is the mean food weight of neighbouring species different by an amount that is about equal

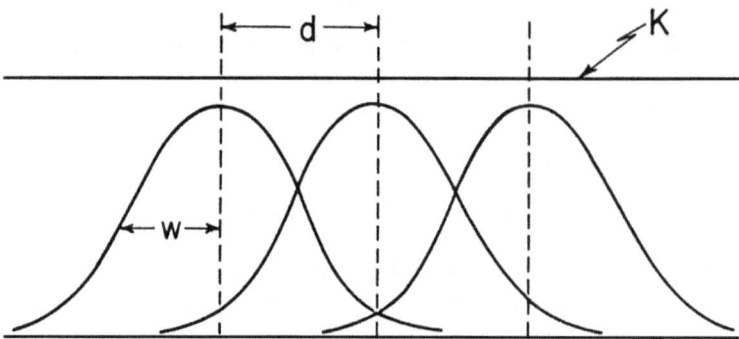

Figure 16.2 The curve labeled K represents some resource continuum – say, amount of food as a function of food size – that sustains various species whose utilisation functions, characterised by a standard deviation w and a separation d are shown. From May and MacArthur 1972. Reproduced with permission from the May and MacArthur families.

to the standard deviation in the food weight eaten by the individual species, it is also independent of changes in the environment. The relation $d/w \approx 1$ is then an inherent property of species competing for the same resource (in this case, food). May set out to investigate whether such a relationship could be predicted by a theory that might provide insights into the mechanisms responsible for the relationship. The theory that he and his mentor, Robert MacArthur, developed showed that

> there is an effective limit to niche overlap in the real world, and this limit is insensitive to the degree of environmental fluctuation, unless it be very severe [greater than 30 per cent].[2]

May and MacArthur formulated a model in which n different species compete for a resource. They defined an $n \times n$ matrix (A), the competition matrix, with elements α_{ij} equal to the strength of the competition between the ith and jth species. In the deterministic case, in which the properties of the environment remain constant,

$$\alpha_{ij} = [\alpha]^{(i-j)^2}$$

where $\alpha = \exp(-d^2/4w^2)$, and d and w are as in Figure 16.2. Analysis then showed that this system is stable for all non-zero values of d/w, with the stability being governed by the minimum eigenvalue of matrix A, as illustrated in Figure 16.3.[3] This result is unrealistic; it indicates that an arbitrarily large number of species can be packed into an environment, yet the system remains stable.

---

2 May and MacArthur 1972, 1109.
3 For an understanding of eigenvalues consult www.sosmath.com.

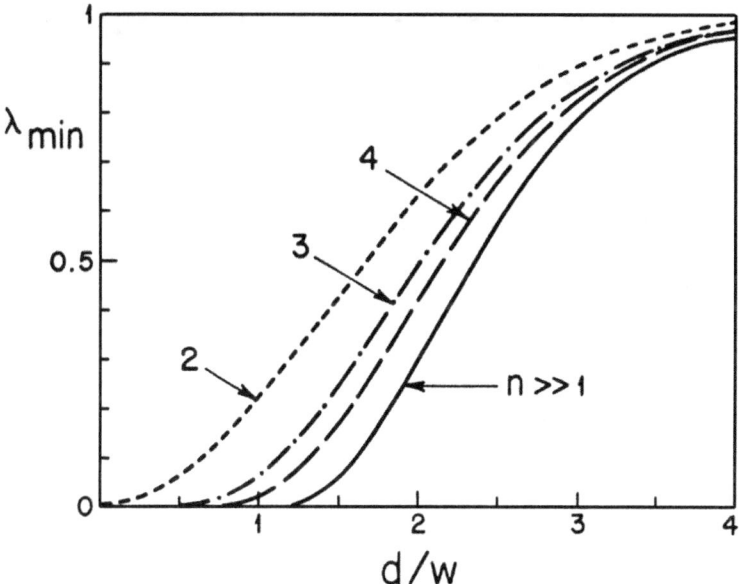

Figure 16.3 The minimum eigenvalue of the stability matrix is plotted as a function of niche overlap, given by d/w for an n-species guild, where n = 2, 3, 4 and $n \gg 1$. From May and MacArthur 1972. Reproduced with permission from the May and MacArthur families.

May and MacArthur then considered what happens in the more realistic case where there are random environmental fluctuations. This was modelled by allowing the line given by K in Figure 16.2 to vary in a random fashion, achieved by introducing 'white noise' with standard deviation σ into the system. So systems with eigenvalues close to zero become unstable, meaning species that are too close together cannot continue to co-exist. Specifically, stability requires that the smallest eigenvalue (λmin) is/ greater than $\sigma^2 / \bar{k}$, where $\bar{k}$ is a constant, so that each value of sigma imposes a lower limit on d. This is shown in Figure 16.4, where lines separate the stable zones (on the right) from the unstable zones (on the left) for various numbers of species. The significant result is that these lines are close to vertical until sigma becomes very large, indicating the ratio d/w is not sensitive to the degree of environmental fluctuation over a wide range. In fact, this ratio is approximately one, as is observed ecologically.

Limit cycles in predator/prey communities

Cycles in the size of populations of lemmings were thought, in the 1950s, to occur as a consequence of the lemmings acting as predators on a prey identified as their food. Another example of oscillatory behaviour is that of the lynx and hare populations observed by the Hudson Bay Trading Company: the hare populations reached a constant

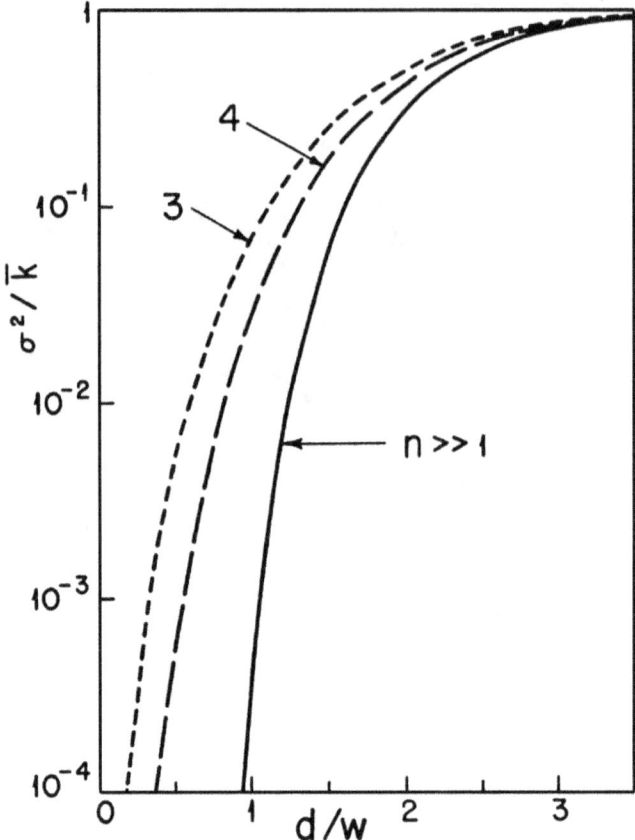

Figure 16.4 The closest niche overlap, d/w, consistent with community stability in a randomly varying environment whose fluctuations are characterised by a variance (relative to the mean) of $\sigma^2/\bar{k}$. The variance is plotted on a logarithmic scale to emphasise that, over a wide range, it has little influence on the species packing distance for n > 2. From May and MacArthur 1972. Reproduced with permission from the May and MacArthur families.

maximum, to within a factor of two, over nine cycles or 100 years, indicating extraordinary stability. Mathematical descriptions of predator/prey behaviour up to May's work in 1972 had involved different formulations of the effects of the limitation of resources or the effects of the density of populations on the birth rate of prey, together with concomitant changes in the reproduction of predators and in the saturation of their appetites. May showed that all such theoretical descriptions possess either a point of stable equilibrium or a stable limit cycle (see Figure 16.5). In particular, these oscillations in populations vary between limits that are dependent on the parameters of the model, and not on the initial perturbations, such as those due to the environment (see Figure 16.5B).

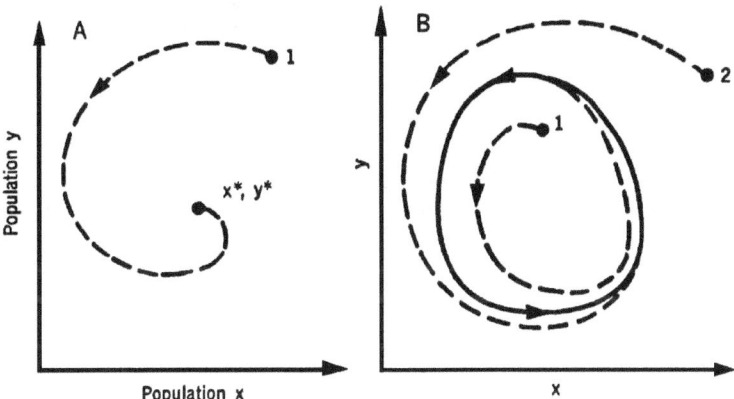

Figure 16.5 Depiction of the 'phase space' of two species with populations x and y; each point in the plane corresponds to some particular value of the two populations. In A the point x^*, y^* is a stable equilibrium point; if the populations are displaced from it (for example, to point 1), they tend, in time, to return, as exemplified by the dashed line. In B the solid curve is a stable limit cycle. In equilibrium the two populations cycle around and around this trajectory, exhibiting well-defined and periodic oscillations in population numbers; if displaced, either inside (for example, to point 1) or outside (for example, to point 2) their stable limit cycle, they tend to return to it, as illustrated by the dashed lines. Republished with permission of the American Association for the Advancement of Science from R.M. May, 'Limit Cycles in Predator-Prey Communities,' *Science* 177, no. 4052 (1972); permission conveyed through Copyright Clearance Center, Inc.

May considered a community comprising one prey species and one predator species, whose populations at time t are x(t) and y(t) respectively. A general model for the dynamics of the system may be written:

$$\frac{dx}{dt} = xg(x, y) \qquad (1a)$$

$$\frac{dy}{dt} = yh(x, y) \qquad (1b)$$

A typical example from the ecological literature is a pair of equations (an elaboration of the Lotka–Volterra equations) where the rate constants and their definitions are given by Rosenzweig.

$$\frac{dx}{dt} = rx\left(1 - \frac{x}{K}\right) - ky\left(1 - e^{-cx}\right) \qquad (2a)$$

$$\frac{dy}{dt} = -by + \beta y\left(1 - e^{-fx}\right) \qquad (2b)$$

The first term in equation 2a is the prey birth rate, which includes a stabilising density-dependent factor of the conventional logistic type – namely, of the form:

$$xnext = rx\left(1 - \frac{x}{K}\right)$$

where r is a constant. If no predators were present, this factor would lead to a stable equilibrium ($x = K$). The second term in equation 2a represents the prey-loss rate due to predation and is of a form suggested on empirical grounds. This predation rate is proportional to x for small values of x, but saturates to a constant k for large values of x, this being a destabilising element of the overall system. The second term on the right in equation 2b describes the relation between prey abundance and predator birth rate. The form of many of these interaction terms is determined by the observed properties of real predator/prey communities. The Lotka–Volterra system of equations corresponds to the singular limiting case obtained by the use of greatly simplified forms of all terms in equations 2a and 2b, as given by:

$$\frac{dx}{dt} = rx - kyx \qquad (3a)$$

$$\frac{dy}{dt} = \beta yx - by \qquad (3b)$$

The great mathematician A.N. Kolmogorov proved, in 1936, that models such as those given by equations 1a and 1b, and therefore the specific example given in equations 2a and 2b, possess either a stable limit cycle or a stable equilibrium point. May discovered this 'significant, and much neglected, theorem of Kolmogorov', which indicated that models that have been discarded as unstable do, in fact, show a stable cycle in population numbers.[4]

Nonlinear dynamics of single populations: chaos theory

A large number of orchard and crop pests breed on a seasonal basis, with no overlap between successive generations. These can provide a great deal of data concerning the average and maxima of distinct populations, which is fortunate as it is clearly of economic importance to understand the determinants of changes in such populations. Another area of observation in which there is much data relates to changes in the populations of bacterial, viral and protozoan infections. This leads to enquiries concerning non-seasonal oscillations in the occurrence of diseases such as childhood measles and rubella. In this context, it is important to be able to predict the consequences of particular immunisation programs on the frequency of infections. May commented:

---

[4] May, 'Limit Cycles in Predator-Prey Communities', 1972, 901.

One of the things I stumbled upon fairly early on, but not right at the beginning, concerned some of the very simple equations for populations of animals that had discrete non-overlapping generations. For example, relating the number of fish born this year in spring and the knapweed gall-flies hatched this year in Wytham Wood, with the same number next year. How is the number this year ... related to the number last year ... You don't treat time as continuous, unlike nearly all of the physical sciences. You use much neglected difference equations. I got interested in trying to understand what happened when the equations could give you stable solutions. Where the population tended to grow when it was at low density and decline if it was at too high a density (and ate itself out of house and home). So there would be some balance point, such that, if you fluctuated above or below, you would come back to that same point. What happened if the boom and bustness got too steep so that that point wasn't stable and, instead of it being like a ball at the bottom of the cup, it was like a ball on top of a billiard cue? What I could see was at first you would start getting the thing going in deterministic cycles – up, down, up, down. Then they would bifurcate to give you up down, different up, different down, up down. I could see this cascade of period-doubling bifurcations coming to a point where it just went bonkers and it just looked like random noise. I wanted to write a paper on it, but first I wanted to know what happened in the noisy-looking region.[5]

A model that seeks a relationship between discrete generations must take into account that relatively small populations (low N) will tend to increase from one generation to the next, while larger populations (large N) will tend to decrease. The tendency to get larger at low densities and smaller at higher densities, perhaps following a boom and bust scenario, must be taken into account.

When there is no overlap between successive generations we best describe them not by differential equations with continuous time, but by equations with discrete times – the so-called logistic difference equation[6] – so that in this case:

$$N_{t+1} = N_t(a - bN_t) \quad (1)$$

where N_{t+1} is the magnitude of the population in generation time $t+1$ and N_t is the magnitude of the population in the preceding generation time t. If we put $N = aX/b$ into equation 1, we get:

$$X_{t+1} = aX_t(1 - X_t) \quad (2)$$

If X_t exceeds one then successive iterations will give X_{t+1} approaching $-\infty$, so the population X becomes extinct. If, on the other hand, X_t reaches $1/2$, then at X_{t+1} we have a maximum value of $a/4$ (note that the steepness of the hump in the above equation is a; see Figure 16.6). Therefore, the equation exhibits non-trivial behaviour only if a is less

---

5 Australian Academy of Science, 'Lord Robert May'.
6 See also May, 'Limit Cycles in Predator-Prey Communities', 1972.

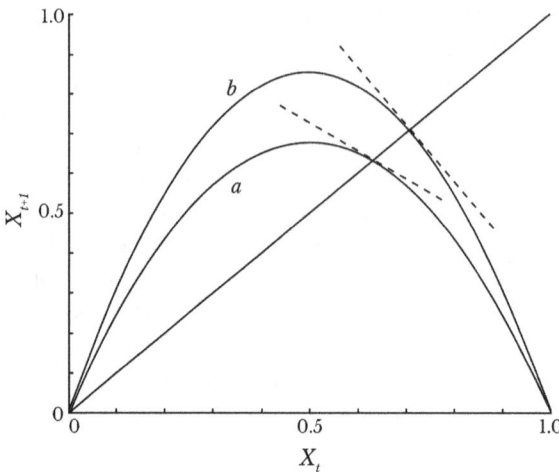

Figure 16.6 A typical form for the relationship between X_{t+1} and X_t described in the text. The curves are for equation 2 with $a = 2.707$ (a) and $a = 3.414$ (b). The dashed lines indicate the slope at the 'fixed points' where the curve intersects the 45° line: for the case 'a' this slope is less steep than $-45°$ and the fixed point is stable; for 'b' the slope is steeper than $-45°$, and the point is unstable. Reprinted by permission from Springer Nature: R.M. May, 'Simple Mathematical Models with Very Complicated Dynamics,' 1976. https://www.nature.com/

than four. However, if a is smaller than one, then successive iterations will lead to $X = 0$. Thus, extinction will only be avoided if a is less than four but greater than one. Putting it differently, because a gives the steepness (or tangent) of the hump, as a increases the hump becomes steeper. All of this is illustrated in Figure 16.6.

The power of the logistic equation to provide for the wide range of observed changes in discrete populations over time is beautifully illustrated in a description of the phenomena by May in his 1985 Croonian Lecture to the Royal Society, their premier lecture. Figure 16.7 shows how the logistic equation describes a wide range of changes from stable to unstable and chaotic conditions. Figure 16.7a provides a graphical representation of the relationship between X_{t+1} and X_t when $a = 2.4$; it also shows the line $X_{t+1} = X_t$, giving a possible equilibrium point (A), which, in this case, crosses the curve at $X_t = X^*$. The equilibrium point X^* may be approached from any starting point for X_t – that is, successive generations approach X^*. The population size (X_t) changes in time as shown in Figure 16.7b, where equilibrium is clearly reached (in this case at $X_t = 0.6$) in a short time. If a increases to 3.4 (from 2.4), the angle of the tangent at the possible equilibrium point A steepens, so that successive generations (X_{t+1}) are no longer converging on A. Rather, two stable points of period two appear, the point A now being unstable, as shown in Figure 16.7c. This bifurcation leads to an oscillation of period two, shown in Figure 16.7d. Increasing a by successively smaller amounts leads to further bifurcations. Following the period doubling, there is a period four, then eight, then successive values up to $2n$, until the system breaks down into apparent chaos, as shown in Figure 16.7f. This is summarised in Figure 16.8, which shows how X_t breaks into successive bifurcations as a increases, until it reaches a value of 3.8495, called the point of accumulation, when the chaotic regime is reached.

Thus, if a is not increased to 3.99, then successive generations do not converge on the stable position A or on a stable oscillation, but continue in an apparently random fashion, not visiting the same values in any periodic fashion at all. This kind of behaviour was termed 'chaotic' by Jim Yorke in 1975. Interestingly, while Yorke first discovered this behaviour, he did not realise that it grew out of the cascade of period doublings that May had discovered. As May described it, 'I didn't know the second bit [the chaotic bit] and he didn't know the first, period-doubling bit.'[7] May wrote a very influential paper, 'Simple Mathematical Models with Very Complicated Dynamics', in which he gave an overall picture of how such logistic equations could predict the progression from equilibrium to period doublings to chaos.

Stability in multi-species community models

In his 1958 monograph *The Ecology of Invasions by Animals and Plants*, Charles Elton, the founder of modern ecology, commented that simple predator/prey systems in the laboratory oscillate violently and simpler communities on islands are likewise quite unstable. On the other hand, rainforest communities that are of great 'trophic web' complexity seem to be very stable. This led to the conclusion that complexity leads to stability in ecosystems. Another foundation figure in ecology, Evelyn Hutchinson, supported this idea, commenting in 1959 that 'oscillations observed in arctic and boreal fauna may be due in part to the communities not being sufficiently complex to damp out oscillations'.[8] On the other hand, discussions concerning pest control at this time brought attention to observations that lead to the opposite conclusion – namely, that complex prey/predator systems can often be less stable than simpler ones. For example, complex systems such as those involving several species of Lepidoptera, together with their parasites are not as stable as simpler systems. Indeed, introduction of new species, such as the Oriental chestnut blight *Endothia parasitica*, the European gypsy moth and the Japanese beetle, into existing trophic webs in North America certainly did not enhance stability of the webs. On the other hand, a trophic system may be severely compromised by the removal of a single species, as happened to an intertidal community of marine invertebrates, leading, in two years, to the reduction of a 15-species trophic web to one that contained only eight species.

Collectively, the above ecological observations point to considerable nonlinear dynamics. May made perhaps his most important contributions in theoretical ecology as a consequence of his analysis of the underlying causes of these dynamics. His theoretical investigations showed that systems of large numbers of predators and prey are, in fact, less stable, and never more stable, than simple two-species systems. Specifically, May's

---

7   Australian Academy of Science, 'Lord Robert May'.
8   Hutchinson 1959, 150.

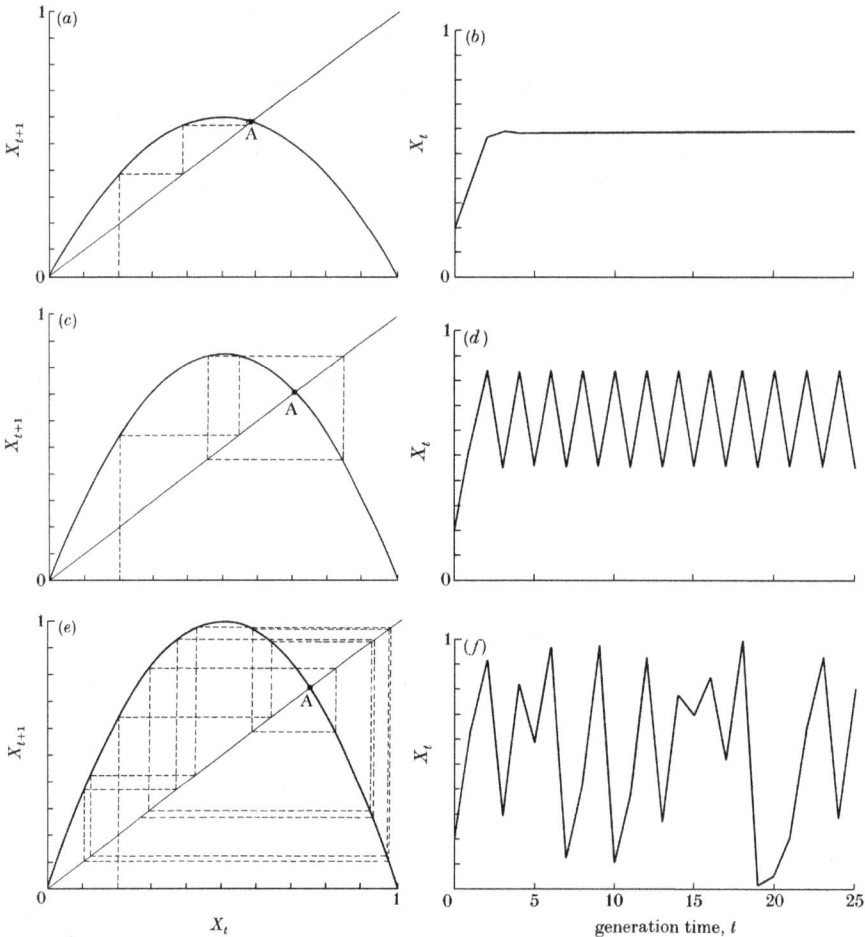

Figure 16.7 (a) The solid curve depicts the relation between X_{t+1} and X_t described by equation (2), with a = 2.4. The intersection between this curve and the 45o line (Xt+1 = Xt) gives the potential equilibrium point, A. As discussed in the text, the dashed lines represent the trajectory of a population whose initial value is as shown. In this case, A is a stable point. (b) The population trajectory, Xt, is shown as a function of generation time, t, corresponding to (a) i.e. equation (2) with a = 2.4. (c) As for (a), except here a = 3.4 in equation (2). The system now settles to a stable two-point cycle. (d) The population trajectory corresponding to (c) (i.e. equation (2) with a = 3.4), illustrating clearly the way the system settles to a stable cycle. (e) Similar to (a) and (c), except now a = 3.99. The system settles neither to a stable point nor to a stable simple cycle, but rather wanders, apparently erratically. (f) The population trajectory corresponding to (e) (i.e. equation (2) with a = 3.99), illustrating the 'chaotic' or apparently random behavior. Republished with permission of the Royal Society of London from R.M. May, 'The Croonian Lecture, 1985: When Two and Two Do Not Make Four – Nonlinear Phenomena in Ecology,' *Proceedings of the Royal Society B* 228, no. 1252 (1986); permission conveyed through Copyright Clearance Center, Inc.

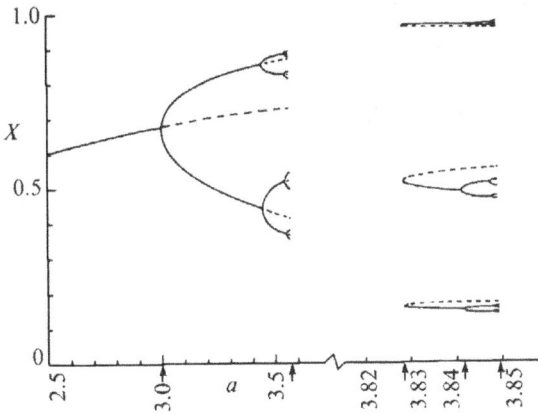

Figure 16.8 This figure illustrates some of the stable (continuous line) and unstable (broken line) fixed points of various periods that can arise by bifurcation processes in equation 2. To the left, the basic stable fixed point becomes unstable and gives rise by a succession of pitchfork bifurcations to stable harmonics of period $2n$; none of these cycles is stable beyond $a = 3.5700$. To the right, the two period 3 cycles appear by tangent bifurcation; one is initially unstable; the other is initially stable, but becomes unstable and gives way to stable harmonics of period $3 \times 2n$, which have a point of accumulation at $a = 3.8495$. Note the change in scale on the 'a' axis, needed to put both examples on the same figure. There are infinitely many other such windows, based on cycles of higher periods. Reprinted by permission from Springer Nature: R.M. May, 'Simple Mathematical Models with Very Complicated Dynamics,' 1976. https://www.nature.com/

analytical investigations showed there are sharp transitions from stability to instability. He commented:

> At that time there was a belief articulated by one of the founding fathers of theoretical ecology, Evelyn Hutchinson at Yale. He was building on ideas by Elton and later work by Robert MacArthur at Princeton. The idea was that complicated ecosystems – ecosystems with more species and more interactions among them – would, by virtue of that complexity, be more stable. … Ken Watt set that out [in his book]. Then, very commonsensically, he said, 'It's pretty contrary to common experience.' Elton gave a series of arguments. One was that mathematical models for two-species systems are characteristically unstable. I thought, 'That's not an argument. That's only half an argument. Let me look at not "one predator one prey." Let me look at "N predator N prey."' I immediately could see that the corresponding system would be less stable.[9]

May considered a large trophic web of many species, in which the population of any particular species, by itself, is stable. He concluded that the larger system will be unstable (i.e. some species will die out) if the interaction between the different species is too high (excessive web connectance, or large C) or the actual strength of these interactions is too high (too large α). He commented that

> roughly speaking ... within a web species which interacts with many others (large C) should do so weakly (small α), and conversely those which interact strongly should do so with but a few species.[10]

Indeed, in 1968 Margalef commented on this in his *Perspectives in Ecological Theory*:

> From empirical evidence it seems that species that interact feebly with others do so with a great number of other species. Conversely, species with strong interactions are often part of a system with a small number of species.[11]

A further prediction of May's model is that communities of species with a particular number of interactions (C), each with average strength (α), will have higher stability (that is, the species will not die out) if the community is arranged into groups, something that is observed in nature.

The key theorem to emerge from May's analytical work on this model is now known as the May–Wigner stability theorem, an understanding of which requires knowledge of matrix algebra (see 'Further reading'). The theorem states the following: consider n species that may interact with each other, such that any one of these species may interact with any of the $n-1$ remaining species. If a species interacts with another, it may do so with a strength of interaction that follows a normal distribution with mean zero and variance α. In this case, we may write down the values of α^2 for each of the n^2C interactions among the n species (there being $n^2 - n^2C$ zero interactions and n^2C non-zero interactions), where C is the extent of connectance of the n species; C is a measure of the number of non-zero interactions, expressed as a percentage. This forms an $n \times n$ matrix, possessing n^2C elements, each with their α^2 and $n^2 - n^2C$ elements each having a value of zero (call this matrix B). Now consider the set of difference equations of the form $X_{t+1} = BX_t$. Let $P(n, \alpha, C)$ be the probability that the difference equation is stable (this will be the case if the dominant eigenvalue of the system is less than one, otherwise species will die out.) In 1972, May showed that:

- If $\alpha^2 nC < 1$, then $P(n, \alpha, C)$ approaches one as n approaches ∞, so the system is stable.
- If $\alpha^2 nC > 1$, then $P(n, \alpha, C)$ approaches zero as n approaches ∞, so the system is unstable.

The two different systems, designated (α_1, C_1) and (α_2, C_2), will have similar stability if $\alpha^2_1 C_1 = \alpha^2_2 C_2$. It follows that a large set of interacting species (large C) will need the

---

9   Australian Academy of Science, 'Lord Robert May'.
10 May, 'Will a Large Complex System be Stable?', 1972, 414.
11 May, 'Will a Large Complex System be Stable?', 1972, 414.

strength of interaction between species to be relatively small (small α) if they are to have similar stability to a small system of interacting species (small *C*) that have relatively high interaction strengths (large α).

May regarded this as one of his most important contributions. As he said:

> To cut a long story short, I proved a rather nice theorem. That is, a generalisation of a physics theorem due to Wigner. I am delighted that my name is now coupled – it is the May–Wigner theorem. He proved it for special kinds of symmetrical matrices. But I said, 'Let's imagine an ecosystem in which each species by itself would be stable. So, I'll put minus one down the diagonal to say that in unit time, left alone, each species would recover from a disturbance. Now I'll start connecting them at random and putting other elements in the matrix. I'll put plus or minus to give predator/prey, competitors or mutualists. I'll let them be of different strengths but, on average, some strength – let's call it alpha [α]'. I proved an interesting generalisation of Wigner's theorem that said: 'Such a system will remain stable, stabilised by the intraspecific effects, provided that the average number of species a species is connected to, times the square on the strength, is less than one. One is the normalising time to recover. Otherwise, the system will collapse, if "N" is big'. That turns the whole thing on its head and resets the agenda for ecology.[12]

And indeed, May's early work, reviewed in this essay, much of which was carried out or initiated in Sydney, did 'reset the agenda for ecology'.

***

May's contributions while at the University of Sydney were just one part of an amazing career that took him from Princeton to a Royal Society Professorship at Oxford, to Chief Scientist advising the government of the United Kingdom, to being made Lord May of Oxford and President of the Royal Society, and finally, to receiving the highest accolade in the gift of the Queen, the Order of Merit. But one's lasting memory of May is the beautiful mathematics he conceived in his quest to illuminate fundamental problems in ecology.

Further reading

Andrewartha, H.G., and L.C. Birch. *The Distribution and Abundance of Animals*. Chicago: University of Chicago Press, 1954.

DeBach, P., and E.I. Schlinger, eds. *Biological Control of Insect Pests and Weeds*. New York: Reinhold Publishing, 1964.

Elton, C.S. *The Ecology of Invasions by Animals and Plants*. London: Methuen, 1958.

Hastings, H.M. 'The May–Wigner Stability Theorem for Connected Matrices.' *Bulletin of the American Mathematical Society* 7, no. 2 (1982): 387–8.

---

12 Australian Academy of Science, 'Lord Robert May'.

Hutchinson, G.E. 'Homage to Santa Rosalia, or Why Are There So Many Kinds of Animals?' *The American Naturalist* 93, no. 870 (1959): 145–59.

Li, T., and J.A. Yorke. 'Period Three Implies Chaos.' *The American Mathematical Monthly* 82, no. 10. (1975): 985–92.

MacArthur, R.H. *Geographical Ecology: Patterns in the Distribution of Species*. New York: Harper and Row, 1972.

Margalef, R. *Perspectives in Ecological Theory*. Chicago: University of Chicago Press, 1968.

May, R.M. 'Limit Cycles in Predator-Prey Communities.' *Science* 177, no. 4052 (1972): 900–2.

May, R.M. 'Will a Large Complex System be Stable?' *Nature* 238, no. 5364 (1972): 413–4.

May, R.M. 'Simple Mathematical Models with Very Complicated Dynamics.' *Nature* 261, no. 5560 (1976): 459–67.

May, R.M. 'The Croonian Lecture, 1985: When Two and Two Do Not Make Four – Nonlinear Phenomena in Ecology.' *Proceedings of the Royal Society of London. Series B, Biological Sciences* 228, no. 1252 (1986): 241–66.

May, R.M., and R.H. MacArthur. 'Niche Overlap as a Function of Environmental Variability.' *Proceedings of the National Academy of Sciences USA* 69, no. 5 (1972): 1109–13.

Rosenzweig, M.L. 'Optimal Habitat Selection in Two-Species Competitive Systems.' *Fortschritte der Zoologie* 25, no. 2–3 (1979): 283–93.

Smith, L.B., and C.H. Hadley. 'The Japanese Beetle.' *United States Department of Agriculture Circular* 363 (1926).

Turnbull, A.L., and D.A. Chant. 'The Practice and Theory of Biological Control of Insects in Canada.' *Canadian Journal of Zoology* 39, no. 5 (1961): 697–753.

Watt, K.E.F. *Ecology and Resource Management: A Quantitative Approach*. New York: McGraw-Hill, 1968.

17
Malignant melanoma, rubella hearing loss and mathematical correlations: Henry Oliver Lancaster

Foundation Chair of Mathematical Statistics (1959–1978). Lancaster discovered the relationship between a pregnant mother being exposed to the rubella virus in her first trimester and her child being born deaf. He also revealed the relationship between malignant melanoma and exposure to ultraviolet light from the sun. He further developed, initially through research involving haematological counting and amoebic surveys, profound insights into the chi-square test for correlations, on which he became the world authority.

Some decades ago, I was carrying out research in my laboratory in the basement of the old medical school, with a sign on the door reading 'DO NOT ENTER', when there was a very loud knock. Before I could jump up, an elderly gentleman in a formal suit entered, thrust a pen into my hand and rather gruffly ordered me to place my signature among many others on the inside cover of the handbook of the Australian Academy of Science, to which I had recently been elected. This was my introduction to Oliver Lancaster, who had retired from the Chair of Mathematical Statistics two years earlier. It was only later that I realised his abrupt style was due to his attempts to overcome a fearful stutter that he had borne since he was child. He invited me to his room in the basement of the Fisher Library, where we discussed the history of science and, in particular, the proofs of his magnum opus, *Expectations of Life*. There I got to know a gentle man, entirely dedicated to the well-being of humanity, to which he made such profound contributions.

Lancaster was born in Sydney in 1913 and spent his childhood in the New South Wales country town of Kempsey, where his father, Llewellyn, practised medicine and his mother, Edith, was a nurse. Lancaster displayed mathematical skills at an early age, entertaining his father's professional friends with prodigious feats of mental arithmetic, although this precociousness was curtailed by the emergence of a serious stutter at the age of five. This affliction narrowed the extent of his success in public presentations, such as the *viva voce* in medical examinations, a problem that he only partly overcame later in life. Nevertheless, his scholarly activity flourished. His mathematical skills came to the fore at the schools he attended in rural Kempsey, so much so that he received a distinction in the Leaving Certificate Examination when he was 16. His ability was also reflected in successes in the New South Wales Chess Championship, including a victory against

Figure 17.1 Professor Henry Oliver Lancaster in 1978. Reproduced from E. Seneta and G.K. Eagleson, 'Henry Oliver Lancaster 1913–2001,' *Historical Records of Australian Science* 15, no. 2 (2004), with permission from CSIRO Publishing.

a young graduate in chemistry, J.W. Cornforth, who was later a Nobel Laureate. There was a wonderful photograph of the young Lancaster and Cornforth at their match, with the future great radio astronomer Bernard Mills watching over them, which Lancaster was proud of but which is now lost.

Lancaster's father was anxious that his son should acquire a secure income on leaving school, a concern that was particularly pressing during the Great Depression. So Lancaster took up an appointment as trainee with the Mutual Life and Citizens Company (MLC), while maintaining his interest in mathematics by attending evening courses in economics at the University of Sydney. He eventually transferred to a full-time arts course, doing exceptionally well, with a high distinction in Mathematics I. However, the deteriorating economic conditions did not favour someone looking for a position as a professional mathematician, so Lancaster changed his career path once more. At 18, he enrolled in medicine at the university, boarding in Manly with the financial support of his mother, Edith, in Kempsey. He subsequently graduated MB BS at the early age of 24, in 1937. Lancaster became a pathologist and senior medical officer at Sydney Hospital, which was affiliated with Sydney University – a most propitious time to arrive there, for a group of young neuroscientists of genius, including future Nobel Prize winners, were working together in the Kanematsu Pathological Institute at the hospital. They were led by (the future Sir) John Eccles (Nobel Laureate 1963), (Sir) Bernard Katz (Nobel Laureate 1972) and Stephen Kuffler (regarded as the founding father of neuroscience). Although Lancaster did not participate in their experiments, he later said 'the two years 1938 and 1939 were perhaps the happiest in his life'.[1] It was during this period that Lancaster realised that pathological studies, involving haematological counting and amoebic surveys, required deeper statistical analysis than had been previously used. This led him to read Udny Yule's *Introduction to the Theory of Statistics,* which introduced him to the chi-square test for correlations (see Appendix) and led him to the realisation that 'I would need to resume part of my mathematical studies'.[2] He had already determined that the chi-square test would become an enduring passion, bringing together his mathematical and epidemiological abilities. This was to have profound impact on public health.

With the outbreak of the Second World War in 1939, Lancaster left pathology at Sydney Hospital and joined the Australian Imperial Forces as a medical officer in pathology, first in the Middle East, at Alexandria in Egypt then at Nazareth, and then, in early 1942, with the 117th Australian General Hospital in Townsville. His interest in eosinophilia, and its possible cause through hookworm infestation and intestinal protozoan infections, led to a paper in the *Medical Journal of Australia* in 1944, the first of more than 50 papers he published on medical statistics and epidemiology[3] in that journal over the succeeding years. By this time, he was working as a pathologist at Port Moresby and Lae with the Australian New Guinea Administrative Unit. There is a beautiful pencil sketch of Lancaster by the noted artist Nora Heysen, showing him carrying out pathological work at a microscope (Figure 17.2). Given the workload in

---

1   Seneta and Eagleson 2004, 227.
2   Lancaster 1996, 14.
3   Epidemiology is the study and analysis of the patterns, causes and effects of the health and disease conditions in defined populations. It is the cornerstone of public health and evidence-based practice, identifying risk factors for disease and targets for preventive health.

Figure 17.2 Pathologist (Major Henry Lancaster), 1944, by Nora Heysen. Pencil 55.9 x 38.4 cm. Australian War Memorial (ART22670).

New Guinea after Australia had repelled the Japanese attack along the Kokoda track, it is surprising that Lancaster managed to find an outlet for his mathematical proclivities by enrolling as an external student in second year Honours mathematics.

At the end of the war, now aged 33, Lancaster's growing distinction in mathematical epidemiology ensured the success of his application for a lectureship in medical statistics at the School of Public Health and Tropical Medicine, affiliated with the University of Sydney. At this time, he took on the Herculean task of placing all medical statistics relating to diseases in Australia into coherent order through publications in the *Medical Journal of Australia*.

Discovery of the relationship between malignant melanoma and exposure to sunlight

The relationship between skin cancer and exposure to ultraviolet radiation from the sun is taken as given nowadays; children are shielded from this source of cancer by their parents. Lancaster's discovery, with its momentous implications for public health, took place through the application of classical epidemiological statistics in the mid-1950s. In 1956, he published in the *Medical Journal of Australia,* the final article in a series that unequivocally established that melanoma was correlated with the extent of exposure to sunlight, showing this relationship through consideration of the frequency of this type of cancer in different Australian states at different latitudes; those states nearest the equator were shown to have the highest incidence of malignant melanoma.

The suggestion of a relationship between melanoma and sunlight first appeared in a paper in 1954, in which Lancaster gave a general overview of the medical statistics on all cancers in Australia. In that work, he drew attention to the fact that while other researchers

> have devoted special attention to the effects of trauma and sunlight on the carcinomata of the skin, they do not comment on the possibility sunlight might produce malignant melanomata.[4]

He went on to comment that

> There is a tendency for it [melanoma] to occur on those parts exposed to the sun. This may account for the very striking differences in incidence between Australia, England and Wales. Thus, there were in 1951, 112 male and 137 female deaths from melanoma of the skin in England and Wales, compared with 61 and 49 deaths in Australia in the same year, in other words, only about twice the deaths in five times the population.[5]

Further, he provided an explanation for why

> death rates are usually about 50 per cent higher in the males than in the females in Australia. This is perhaps related to the greater exposure of the male to the weather,

---

4 Lancaster, 'The Mortality in Australia from Cancer', 1954, 94.
5 Lancaster, 'The Mortality in Australia from Cancer', 1954, 96.

either due to his occupation or in sport, and the greater tendency to neglect among elderly males.[6]

By 1956, Lancaster had firmed his opinion that malignant melanoma is causally related to sunlight exposure. The medical statistics considered in his 1956 paper are confined to what he calls 'Europeans'– hence the title 'Some Geographical Aspects of the Mortality from Melanoma in Europeans'. He pointed out that

> as the fair races differ from the dark-skinned races in their reaction to sunlight and in the incidence of melanoma, the study has been confined to the relatively fair-skinned types, who may be collectively referred to as Europeans.[7]

The frequencies are given for deaths from melanoma

> per million persons per annum for the individual States in the years 1950 to 1953 as follows: Queensland 23, New South Wales 15, Western Australia 15, South Australia 12, Victoria 8, and Tasmania 8. For Australia as a whole, the rate is 14. The corresponding figures for England and Wales and for Scotland are 7 and 5 respectively.[8]

So the death rates for the United Kingdom are far lower. Furthermore, 'the figures by state in Australia are of interest for they are in the same order as the capital cities as one passes from the tropical north to the south'.[9] Finally, the largest number of malignant melanoma cases reported annually from the two largest Sydney hospitals was on average 40, whereas the number from the largest hospital in Melbourne was only 12. So crude death rates due to malignant melanoma are related to the distance of the population centres from the equator. Sunlight is then the most likely causal agent for this most deadly of cancers.

The series of papers by Lancaster in the *Medical Journal of Australia* (1954 and 1956) relating malignant melanoma to sunlight were summarised in a clinical survey with Janet Nelson. Lancaster and Nelson first pointed out how far the medical statistics on malignant melanoma pursued by Lancaster had changed the perspective on its origin. The 1940s perspective had been summarised by Blum, who claimed, in the most frequently cited survey by Australian clinicians, that it is the thickening of the horny layer of the skin that is important in

> three different ways: (a) by changes in the absorbing components, e.g. the accumulation of melanin; (b) by thickening, which results from epidermal hyperplasia; and (c) by alteration of the scattering characteristics.[10]

None of these refers to sunlight. But now Lancaster and Nelson could produce evidence (see Table 17.1) that showed that 62 per cent of malignant melanoma patients had a red skin

---

6   Lancaster, 'The Mortality in Australia from Cancer', 1954, 93.
7   Lancaster 1956, 1082.
8   Lancaster 1955, 929.
9   Lancaster 1955, 929.
10 Blum 1945, 503.

Characteristic	Melanoma	Skin cancer	Other cancer
Hair colour:			
Black	13.9	16.8	21.4
Brown	44.5	46.8	49.1
Fair	24.8	23.1	19.1
Red	16.8	13.3	10.4
Skin colour:			
Olive	8.1	4.6	16.8
Medium	15.0	23.1	20.2
Fair	76.9	72.3	63.0
Skin texture:			
Fine	83.8	76.9	70.5
Coarse	16.2	23.1	29.5
Eye colour:			
Brown	19.7	17.3	36.4
Hazel	19.7	16.8	17.3
Blue	41.6	43.4	31.2
Green-grey	19.0	22.5	15.1
Reaction to sun:			
Red	62.4	53.8	36.4
Brown	37.6	46.2	63.6

Table 17.1 A comparison of cancer patient skin types (per cent). From H.O. Lancaster and J. Nelson, 'Sunlight as a Cause of Melanoma: A Clinical Survey,' *Medical Journal of Australia* 44, no. 14 (1957): 452–6. © 1957 The Medical Journal of Australia. Reproduced with permission.

reaction to sunlight, 54 per cent of skin cancer patients had this reaction and only 36 per cent of patients with all other cancers had the reaction. This allowed them to conclude that

> those who produce little pigment in the skin are more prone to melanoma than those who produce pigment readily, and that sunlight appears to be as important in the production of the melanoma of the skin as it is in the production of basal cell carcinoma and other skin cancers.[11]

---

11 Lancaster and Nelson 1957, 452.

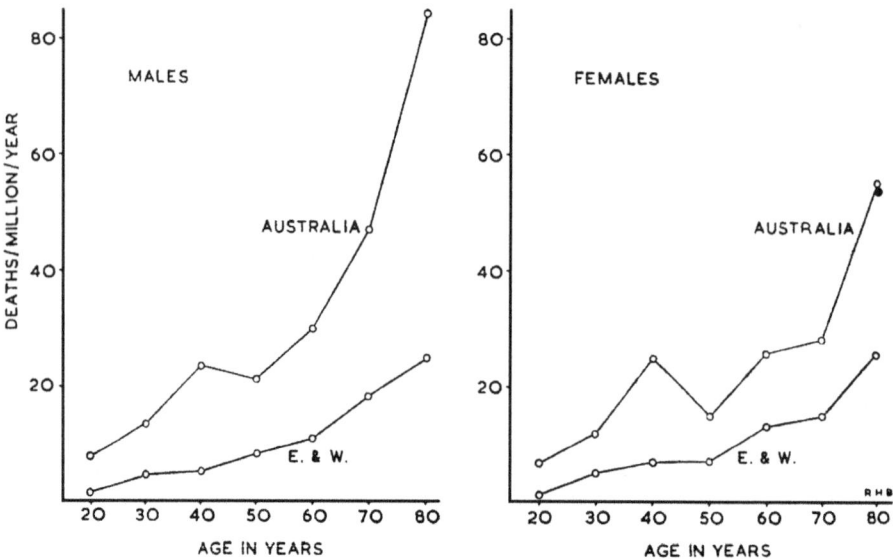

Figure 17.3 A comparison of the mortality from melanoma in Australia, 1951 to 1953 with that in England and Wales, 1950 to 1953. From H.O. Lancaster, 'Some Geographical Aspects of the Mortality from Melanoma in Europeans,' *Medical Journal of Australia* 43, no. 26 (1956): 1082–7. © 1956 The Medical Journal of Australia. Reproduced with permission.

Lancaster was able to clearly show graphically (see Figure 17.3) and by means of statistical tables of death rates from melanoma (see Table 17.2) that sunlight is a major contributor to the incidence of malignant melanoma. He was then able to state that 'vital statistics ... suggested that the latitude (and so probably the ultraviolet light dosage) was important in producing melanoma'.[12] He concluded his studies with the comment that melanoma is

> caused by exposure to the ultra-violet light of the sun, and that some skin types are less susceptible to damage by such exposure. Melanoma tends, therefore, to occur in the fair or red headed types with fair skin, and to be more frequent in those who have been exposed to excessive doses of sunlight.[13]

These papers amount to 'great success stories for statistical analysis, in being definitive and totally convincing in their conclusions, and impinging directly on public health'.[14] But this was just the first of Lancaster's triumphs for the benefit of public health. The other was the association between a pregnant mother being exposed to rubella virus in her first trimester and her child being born deaf.

---

12 Lancaster and Nelson 1957, 455.
13 Lancaster and Nelson 1957, 455.
14 Seneta and Eagleson 2004, 232.

State	Latitude (South) of its capital	Melanoma deaths per million		
		Males	Females	Persons
Queensland	27	28	17	23
Western Australia	32	13	17	15
New South Wales	34	17	13	15
South Australia	35	15	10	12
Victoria	38	8	8	8
Tasmiania	43	7	9	8
Australia	35	16	12	14

Table 17.2 Mortality from melanoma in Australia. From H.O. Lancaster, 'Some geographical aspects of the mortality from Melanoma in Europeans,' *Medical Journal of Australia* 43, no. 26 (1956): 1082–7. © 1957 The Medical Journal of Australia. Reproduced with permission.

Discovery of the relationship between the rubella virus and deaf-mutism

In 1941, the Sydney ophthalmologist W.M. Gregg reported that many cases of cataracts in children seemed to be related to maternal rubella in the first trimester of pregnancy. He attributed this to a highly virulent type of rubella that occurred in Australia from 1938 to 1941, due to a mutation of the rubella virus to a strain capable of this kind of action (teratogenic). Lancaster was inspired to follow up on Gregg's observations, pursuing a rigorous statistical approach after realising, when passing the New South Wales Institution for the Deaf and Blind on his way to the university each morning, that the data required for an appropriate study might be readily available there. He discovered that the institution had kept impeccable records on admissions since 1861. However, even though the International Statistical Institute had stated at its St Petersburg meeting in 1872 that there was a need to collect and analyse epidemiological data relating to blindness and deaf-mutism, nothing appeared to have been done about it. Perhaps the nearest effort to following the suggestion of the Statistical Institute was the work of the statistician C.H. Wickens, who suggested in 1927, that

> the age incidence of deaf-mutism varies in such a manner that it is apparent that the cause of the disability is of variable intensity, and there is some evidence to suggest that the increase in incidence of deaf-mutism at certain ages synchronises with the occurrence of epidemic diseases such as scarlet fever, diphtheria, measles and whooping cough,[15]

These suggestions, although interesting, were very wide of the mark.

---

15   Wickens 1924–7.

Lancaster first showed in 1951, using data from the Institution for the Deaf and Blind, that there had been severe outbreaks of the rubella virus in 1898–1899 in both Australia and New Zealand. Furthermore, while the prevalence of blindness increased with age in the general population, this was not the case with deaf-mutism, which reached sudden peak values for those born in the years 1896 to 1900 – that is, covering the period of outbreak of the rubella virus. Even if the collection of data were separated by as much as 12 years – for example 1911, 1921 and 1923 – the statistical results still pointed to an event that took place during a period in the mother's first trimester. As Lancaster stated,

> analysing the figures for New South Wales in more detail, we find that there were 70 births of the deaf in 1899 but only 15 in 1898 and 16 in 1900. This great excess of births of the deaf in 1899 as compared with the numbers in the previous and following years can be explained only by presuming an epidemic cause acting from without. Thus we should regard such a finding as very unlikely on the hypothesis that the cause was genetic and hence that each of the events – the births of the deaf – was independent.[16]

Similar results were observed for other comparatively isolated communities with relatively small populations, such as Iceland. While the number of children born deaf was around two or fewer per year in most years in Iceland, there was a large peak of ten deaf children in 1941. At about this time, Iceland recorded an epidemic of rubella, suggesting again some dependence of deafness on the appearance of the rubella virus in mothers during their pregnancy.

Lancaster concluded that his medical statistics had shown that others were incorrect in postulating a unique rubella virus giving rise to deafness and, indeed, in claiming to be able to show how the unique virus spread throughout the world. Rather, Lancaster said, it was the distinctive nature of relatively isolated communities like Australia, New Zealand and Iceland that gave rise to the epidemiological pattern. Indeed, with the improvement in public hygiene in the relatively non-isolated communities of England and Wales, in which rubella had been continuously endemic, females were now able to reach adulthood without infection, which exposed unborn children to the same risk of rubella as those in isolated communities. So the epidemics of deafness in Australia in children in 1899, 1916, 1924, 1925 and then 1938 to 1941 were all associated with previous epidemics of rubella.[17] Specifically, for example, in the case of the 1899 epidemic, Lancaster was able to show that there had been an epidemic of rubella about six months before by collecting historical data from each of the Australian states. As Lancaster summarised,

> further census and institutional data have been analysed. The only country other than Australia and New Zealand that experienced deafness on a severe epidemic scale has been Iceland. Other countries investigated include the United Kingdom, the United States of America, Italy and Sweden. No dramatic episodes have been noted in these countries although the institutional data shows sporadic cases to have occurred

---

16 Lancaster 1951, 1430.
17 Lancaster 1951, 1432.

recently in the United States, in England and Sweden. The importance of isolation in lengthening the time between epidemic waves of rubella has been stressed.[18]

Therefore, in addition to showing that rubella was likely a major cause of childhood deafness, Lancaster had demonstrated a new principle in epidemiology:

> the normal textbook model of infectious diseases should be modified so that the population is not represented by one homogeneous unit but by a number of isolates or sub-units, which are relatively isolated from one another.[19]

In the case of deafness due to rubella, it was a 'feature of the population that was important not that of the virus'.[20]

The chi-square test for goodness-of-fit

Lancaster's epidemiological insights involved detailed analysis of tables consisting of the joint occurrences (frequencies) of, say, exposure to sunlight (that is, latitude) and the incidence of malignant melanoma. These are referred to as contingency tables; this example provides a two-way contingency table. The question immediately arises as to whether the two variables (latitude and malignant melanoma) are independent of each other – that is, they are not correlated, and hence there can be no causal connection between them. The usual way to assess such independence is to use a chi-square goodness-of-fit statistic. It was natural then that Lancaster's prodigious mathematical mind should come to dwell on this statistic, so much so that his work on the chi-square test became his greatest contribution to mathematical statistics, and he was recognised as the foremost authority on this test. For a formal description of this statistic see the Appendix.

A specific quantitative example should make the use of this statistic clear. Consider data from a study of the relationship between serum cholesterol and systolic blood pressure in 1,237 individuals without heart disease, given in Table 17.3 that is from Cornfield.[21] In the example, consider the denominators from this table that are the numbers considered in each category. The null hypothesis is that there is no relationship between cholesterol and blood pressure.

Now consider the first group in each variable. If the variables are independent we would expect $319 \times 408 / 1329 = 97.9$ in the first cell so the first value to calculate in the chi-square test statistic is $(119 - 97.9)^2 / 97.9 = 4.55$. The sum of this calculation of all the cells is the test statistic which approximately has a chi-square distribution under the hypothesis of independence, with a number of degrees of freedom of (number of rows $-$ 1)(number of columns $-$ 1) $= (4-1)(4-1) = 9$. If the test statistic is so large that it is improbable according to the chi-square distribution, that is, if the chance of obtaining such a high value for a chi-square variable with nine degrees of freedom (the p-value) is small,

---

18 Lancaster, 'The Epidemiology of Deafness', 1954, 23.
19 Lancaster, 'Deafness Due to Rubella', 1954, 323.
20 Lancaster, 'Deafness Due to Rubella', 1954, 324.
21 Cornfield 1962.

Serum cholesterol, mg/100cc	Blood Pressure, mm Hg				
	Total	<127	127–146	147–166	167+
Total	92/1329	20/408	28/555	20/224	24/142
<200	12/319	2/119	3/124	3/50	4/26
200–219	8/254	3/88	2/100	0/43	3/23
220–259	31/470	8/127	11/220	6/74	6/49
260+	41/286	7/74	12/111	11/57	11/44

Table 17.3 Ratio of number of new events in 6 years to number exposed to risk: by initial systolic blood pressure and serum cholesterol. Republished with permission of the Federation of American Societies for Experimental Biology from J. Cornfield, 'Joint Dependence of Risk of Coronary Heart Disease on Serum Cholesterol and Systolic Blood Pressure: A Discriminant Function Analysis,' *Federation Proceedings* 21, no. 4 (1962): permission conveyed through Copyright Clearance Center, Inc.

then there is evidence against the hypothesis of independence. In the above example the sum of these values is 25.21, giving a p-value of .003, so there is strong evidence against independence.

Lancaster's first unique contribution to this subject came in 1949 and was concerned with the ' decomposition' of the chi-square goodness-of-fit statistic. Pearson's chi-square test for independence of values in a contingency table (of s columns and r rows) is the sum of the squared standard deviations of the cell frequencies in the $r \times s$ table from their expected value. More formally, supposing independence of the values of the cells, these should be distributed as a chi-square variable with $(r-1)(s-1)$ degrees of freedom. If the chi-square statistic calculated for a contingency table is sufficiently large, then the probability (p) of independence is correspondingly low, but this does not give us any indication of where in the contingency table the independence hypothesis fails. Lancaster set out to address this in his first mathematical statistics paper in 1949. Here he showed how to decompose a single global chi-square with multiple degrees of freedom into mutually independent components, each of which is distributed as a chi-square with one degree of freedom and available for testing. Lancaster's detailed method is given in the Appendix.

***

Lancaster made extraordinarily important contributions in three areas. Firstly, in medical and public health statistics, where he showed that rubella was the cause of deaf-mutism in children whose mothers were exposed to the virus in their first trimester. He also discovered that malignant melanoma, the worst of all cancers, was largely due to exposure to high levels of ultraviolet radiation from the sun. This is a topic of special interest to me, having recently developed an early stage malignant melanoma as a consequence of bathing and surfing without protection from the sun for months each year as an adolescent, some 65 years ago. My typical Australian adolescent experience occurred well before Lancaster established that sunlight exposure could lead to malignant melanoma.

Lancaster's second important contribution was in mathematical statistics, which I have briefly alluded to in the context of his research on the chi-square test for determining independence of data in contingency tables and looking for correlations between items of data. This related to his work on the tabulations involved in medical and public health statistics. As he said,

> It was the blood counting statistical test that led me to the theory of chi-squared and has really introduced me to a lifelong interest in a particular branch of mathematical statistics.[22]

So the chi-square analysis of cross-tabulated categorical tables became the major theme of his mathematical contributions.

There was also a third area in which Lancaster made very important contributions towards the end of his life. He said in his own autobiographical sketch that

> my chief interest at this stage was in the survey of world mortality. I want to complete a project which I had in mind for many years, indeed from the time I was working on Australian mortality[23]

(and from which he had made over 50 contributions to the *Medical Journal of Australia*). He continued:

> I took advantage of the London libraries to prepare for the survey. The survey needed to bring together the official statistics, demography, some mathematical ideas on epidemiology and laboratory research.[24]

The result was a 605 page book entitled *Expectations of Life: A Study in the Demography, Statistics and History of World Mortality*. This extraordinary work of scholarship and statistical bibliography, accompanied by 2,800 references, was published in 1990. It was described in a *Nature* review as, 'a magisterial survey'[25] and a very suitable way for this extraordinary man to complete his life's work.

Appendix

The chi-square distribution

In statistics, the chi-square distribution with k degrees of freedom is the distribution of a sum of the squares of k independent standard normal random variables. In order to calculate this statistic, consider a contingency table, which is a table in matrix format that displays a (multivariate) frequency distribution of the variables. The chi-square

---

22 Seneta and Eagleson 2004, 231.
23 Seneta 2002, 392.
24 Seneta 2002, 392.
25 Seneta and Eagleson 2004, 237.

correlation (goodness-of-fit) statistic for an $r \times s$ contingency table (that is, of r rows and s columns) is the sum of the squared standard deviations of cell frequencies from their expected values. Under the hypothesis of independence, the chi-square is asymptotically distributed as a chi-square variable with $(r-1)(s-1)$ degrees of freedom. If the cell frequencies in the table of interest are given by $\{f_{ij}, i = 1, ..., r, j = 1, ..., s\}$ and their expected values by $\{e_{ij}, i = 1, ..., r, j = 1, ..., s\}$, then the chi-square statistic is calculated as:

$$\chi^2 = \sum_{i=1}^{r} \sum_{j=1}^{s} \frac{(f_{ij} - e_{ij})^2}{e_{ij}}$$

Lancaster's method of decomposition of the chi-square statistic

The following example from Lancaster's 1949 paper gives a decomposition of the statistic in the case of testing for goodness-of-fit where the method is generalised to contingency tables.

> The partition of chi-square is useful in the following type of case which arises frequently in bacteriology. Constant amounts of liquid suspension of a bacterial culture are mixed with an equal quantity of disinfectant solution of known concentration, and a plate is poured with the number of colonies developed being noted. For each plate the concentration of disinfectant used is given by some series such as $r, r^2, r^3 ...$, where 'r' is some factor such as 2 or 1.5. In such a case the following results might be obtained: the number of colonies (a_i) developing in successive plates are 427, 440, 422, 409, 310, 302 .... We are interested in finding the point at which the disinfectant begins to inhibit growth. It is convenient now to write the cumulative sums which are 427, 867, 1361, 1783, 2192, 2502, 2804 ... and their differences which are –13, –121, 95, 147, 642, 690.... That is $\{a_1+a_2+...+a_{k-1} - (k-1)a_k\}$. We may then display a partition of chi-square by means of a table where the successive chi-square of the exact partition are given by:
>
> $$\chi_k^2 = n\frac{\{a_1 + a_2 + ... + a_{k-1} - (k-1)a_k\}^2}{ak(k-1)}$$
>
> where there are n categories and $a = a_1+a_2+...+a_n$. The chi-squares of the approximately equivalent binomial partition are given by:
>
> $$\chi_k^2 = \frac{\{a_1 + a_2 + ... + a_{k-1} - (k-1)a_k\}^2}{(a_1 + a_2 + ... + a_k)(k-1)}$$
>
> The total chi-square may be obtained by the usual formula:

$$\chi^2 = \sum_{i=1}^{n} \frac{\left(a_i - \frac{a}{n}\right)^2}{\frac{a}{n}} = 73.474$$

We can now formulate a table consisting of three columns.

Binomial partition	Exact partition	The value of k
0.195	0.211	2
5.379	6.092	3
1.687	1.877	4
2.465	2.697	5
32.947	34.298	6
28.299	28.299	7
70.973	73.474	

Table 17.4. Partition of chi-square. From H.O. Lancaster, 'The Derivation and Partition of Chi-Square in Certain Discrete Distributions,' Biometrika 36, no. 1–2 (1949): 117–29, by permission of Oxford University Press.

The comparison in each case is that between plate k and the plate preceding it. In those cases where the null hypothesis is not true this discrepancy between the two methods will be very high.[28]

Further reading

Lancaster, H.O. 'The Mortality in Australia from Cancer (Concluded).' *Medical Journal of Australia* 2, no. 3 (1954): 93–7.
Lancaster, H.O., and J. Nelson. 'Sunlight as a Cause of Melanoma: A Clinical Survey.' *Medical Journal of Australia* 44, no. 14 (1957): 452–6.

---

28 Lancaster 1949.

Neuroscience, neurology and respiratory medicine

18
Seeing the world in three dimensions depends on identified neural mechanisms: Peter Bishop

Professor of Physiology (1954–1967). Bishop was the foremost neuroscientist elucidating the neural requirements for seeing the world in three dimensions – that is, stereopsis arising from binocular vision. He and his colleagues identified the 'binocular neurons' in the cortex that allow for stereopsis, moving our capacity to see depth from the realm of the mystical, as claimed by great physicists such as Wheatstone and Helmholtz, to that of experimental investigation.

Like Hanbury Brown (Chapter 10) and Mills (Chapter 11), Peter Bishop wanted to be an electrical engineer. But his mother deflected him into doing medicine at Sydney University. Nevertheless, he found an outlet for his interest in engineering through medical research.

Bishop had a revelatory experience while taking an anatomy course in his third year:

> I will never forget the fascination of actually holding a human brain in my hands and realizing that it once belonged to a person like myself with the same sorts of thoughts and feelings as I had. This experience had a tremendous impact on me, and from then on I never questioned that I would try to make a career in brain research.[1]

Indeed, the relationship between brain and mind remained a subject of fascination for Bishop until the end of his life. In 1939, while still a 22-year-old undergraduate in medicine, he published a short article in the *Sydney University Medical Journal* entitled 'The Nature of Consciousness'. I had also become interested in the neural basis of consciousness after completing degrees in electrical engineering and zoology at Melbourne University in 1968. I serendipitously came across Bishop's youthful article and was determined to work in future at Sydney University, arriving there shortly after Bishop had discovered the neural basis of stereopsis. Thirty-four years later, at 85, Bishop acommented to me that his steadfast aim had been, and was still, to understand the neural foundations of consciousness. He did not achieve this, but he did discover the neural foundations of our capacity to see the world in three dimensions.

---

1   Bishop 1996, 83.

Figure 18.1 Professor Peter Bishop © University of New South Wales and Teaching Hospitals, Department of Medical Illustration. Reproduced with permission.

Bishop's introduction to visual science

In 1968, Helmholtz, who, together with Clerk Maxwell, was one of the two greatest physicists of the 19th century, stated with respect to stereopsis:

> We come now to the question of how it is possible for two flat images on the retina, each from a different perspective and each representing only two-dimensions, can combine so as to present a single solid image of three-dimensions? The combination of these two sensations into a single perceptual image of the external world must therefore be produced, not by any anatomical mechanism of sensation, but by a mental act.[2]

Nearly 100 years later, in 1951, one of the two greatest neuroscientists of the 20th century, Charles Sherrington, stated that

> It is much as though the right and left eye images were seen each by one of two observers and the minds of the two observers were combined into a single mind. It is as though the right eye and the left eye perceptions are elaborated singly and then psychically combined to one. The synthesis is a mental one.[3]

By the 1960s, stereopsis – that is, binocular depth perception – was formally considered to involve a mental act and not to have a neural basis. Bishop showed that this was not the case.

After finishing medicine, Bishop obtained a Sydney Graduate Committee Scholarship in 1946 in order to hone his surgical skills at Queen Square in London. It was there that Bishop saw the power of 'modern' electrical engineering equipment, casually wandering into a laboratory where electroencephalogram recordings were being made from the scalp in response to stimulation of the ulnar nerve in the arm. He was hooked. Using electrophysiological techniques, he could marry his early enthusiasm for engineering with research on the workings of the brain, and perhaps even contribute to an understanding of the neural underpinnings of consciousness. So in 1947, Bishop entered laboratories at University College London, which constituted one of the two main settings of neurophysiological research in Great Britain, the other being at Cambridge. There he met J.Z. Young, B. Katz and A.V. Hill, three well-chosen mentors (the last two were independently awarded Nobel Prizes).

This was the beginning of Bishop's lifelong research on the visual system. He decided to measure the different classes of axons in the optic nerve between the eye and other parts of the brain, such as the lateral geniculate nucleus. These classes are distinguished by the velocity of conduction of action potentials travelling along the axons. In order to measure this velocity, he needed to build appropriate amplifiers for recording the electrical signs of action potentials propagating along the nerves. He also needed to build equipment that could stimulate the nerves and display the electrical activity on a cathode-ray oscilloscope tube. His design of a directly coupled amplifier, published in the *Review*

---

2   Helmholtz 1995, 185.
3   Sherrington 1940, 273.

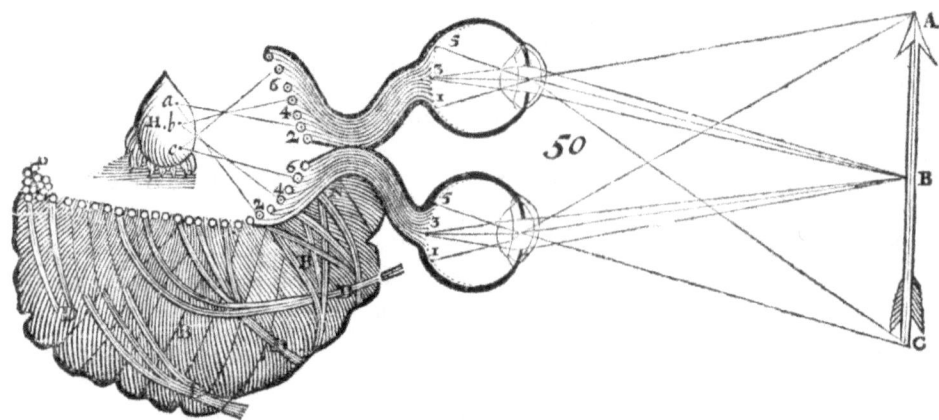

Figure 18.2 Descartes' idea of vision, showing the function of the eye and the brain (pineal gland, H) joined by optic nerve axons (6, 4, 2), on which Bishop carried out his first research. Rene Descartes, *Renati Des-Cartes Tractatus de homine et de formatione foetus quorum prior notis perpetuis Ludovici de La Forge, M.D., illustratur*, 1677, p. 124. Den Haag, Koninklijke Bibliotheek, Nationale bibliotheek van Nederland, shelfmark: 232 L c[1]. Image produced by ProQuest as part of *Early European Books* (www.proquest.com). Published with permission of ProQuest. Further reproduction is prohibited without permission.

of Scientific Instruments, meant that his first contribution to research was as an engineer, not a physiologist!

Neurophysiology of the optic nerve

Bishop's first recordings involved placing electrodes in the lateral geniculate nucleus, which allowed him to observe potentials that reflect synaptic transmission between axons in the optic nerve and nerve cells or neurons in this nucleus. Descriptions of these synaptic potentials were given in Bishop's first neurophysiological paper, published in the prestigious *Proceedings of the Royal Society of London*.

Following this auspicious beginning of his career in brain research, the 34-year-old Bishop was awarded a senior lectureship at the University of Sydney, allowing him to pursue both teaching and research. To this end, he recruited an outstanding group of medical students who were allowed to take a year off from their studies to pursue research. These included Richard Gye, subsequently a neurosurgeon and Dean of the School of Medicine; Jim Lance, a future professor of neurology; Jim McLeod, a great neurologist who was destined to become a world authority on multiple sclerosis (Chapter 19); and Bill Levick, a student with remarkable analytical gifts (he was awarded the University Medal in mathematics in 1952 and in medicine in 1956), destined to be a Fellow of the Royal Society of London, like Bishop himself, and to discover some of the unique properties of neurons in the retina.

With this gifted group, Bishop established that axons of the optic nerve are of the same class as those found in nerves in the peripheral nervous system, then designated class A. The field potentials due to the currents recorded in the lateral geniculate nucleus on stimulating the optic nerve were shown to be of three different components: a slow potential, due to synaptic transmission between the optic nerve and the neurons of this nucleus; a potential arising from where axons leave neurons of the nucleus to invade the cerebral cortex; and a third potential, due to invasion by action potentials of the junction between the processes (dendrites) and cell bodies of neurons. Bishop was assisted in this work by a new recruit, Liam Burke, who succeeded Bishop as professor of physiology at Sydney after he left to take up the position of professor of physiology at the Australian National University. Liam Burke was still carrying out research on the nervous system in the medical school when he died in 2018, at the age of 95.

The neurophysiological basis of stereopsis

In 1964, Bishop turned his attention to the central problem of his research life – the neural basis of stereopsis. There is no better description of the challenges that such research presented than that given in his own words:

> In the late 1960s I became interested in stereopsis, which is the ability to see in depth, to see that one object is further away than another object. We started single cell recording from the cerebral cortex – the visual parts at the back of the brain, the occipital lobe. Hubel and Wiesel had already done this as well. What was new was the realisation that the two eyes send impulses up to the brain that, by coming together on a single cell in the striate cortex, could form the basis for stereopsis. We started by studying the properties of the receptive fields. A receptive field is that little patch in the visual world – the outside world – that each cell keeps a watch on. Each cell is concerned with a little area in the visual world – that is its receptive field. The reason why the impulses from similarly placed receptive fields in the two eyes can provide for stereopsis is because each eye, being horizontally separated in the head, sees an object from a slightly different point of view so giving a small horizontal shift in the similarly positioned receptive fields.[4]

To identify this horizontal disparity, one must determine a reference surface for each eye that allows the relative positions of imaged points on each retina to be ascertained. Thus, some imaged points that do not correspond are identified by being closer to this reference plane than a companion image in the other eye.[5] The disparities occur because the observed points arising from an object give a range of different retinal image locations. Neurons in the visual cortex that receive inputs from both eyes are sensitive to these disparities and fire action potentials accordingly, providing a biological measure of depth. The properties of such disparity determining neurons in the visual cortex are as follows: first, each binocular neuron must fire impulses in relation to the extent of the disparity of the two receptive fields that give rise to our sense of a particular depth; second, in order to

---

4   Australian Academy of Science, 'Professor Peter Bishop'.
5   Blakemore 1969.

ensure that a range of horizontal disparities can be identified, a group of binocular neurons should show the same range of different receptive field disparities.

In order to carry out this kind of research, the optics of the eye needed to be known with an exceptional degree of accuracy. Bishop set out to develop a self-consistent mathematical description of the eye. He achieved this with his colleague Vakkur in 1963, determining the relationship between the visual axis (a line that passes through the centre of the pupil and the centre of the *area centralis*) and both the optic disc (the point of exit of axons leaving the eye) and the centre of the *area centralis* (the point of highest density of visual receptors). In addition, consideration had to be given to the so-called position of paralysis – namely, the position that the eyes take up when the experimental animal, usually a cat, is anaesthetised. Bishop also recruited Tetsuro Nikara and Jack Pettigrew, an honours student still doing medicine, to join him in researching the problem of how projections from the two eyes interact on single cells in the visual part of the cortex. To their surprise, they found, using electrophysiological techniques, that most cells in this part of the cortex are sensitive to horizontal disparities of a kind expected to underlie stereopsis.

Horace Barlow, working at Cambridge University and the University of California, was also interested in the neural basis of binocular vision in the late 1960s, at the time Bishop and his colleagues were working on the project. Barlow had suggested that in binocular vision there are neurons that fire impulses in relation to the same features of an object detailed in the retinal images of each eye. Bishop's group tested this idea in 1984 using a Risley counter-rotating prism. This prism allowed separation of the normally corresponding receptive fields in each eye, enabling them to visually stimulate these independently of each other. Thus, the positions of these receptive fields could be moved in small increments. This prism was adapted and placed in front of the eyes of the experimental cat so that small variations could be obtained in the disparity of positions of the two receptive fields of a binocular neuron in the visual cortex, one for each eye. In this way, Bishop and his colleagues were able to test the proposition that the receptive fields in each eye that excite a binocular neuron in the cortex do so in response to the same feature of an object. This elegant experiment showed, in quantitative detail, that the two receptive fields are always identical, supporting Barlow's suggestion that the binocular cells could be considered to be feature detectors. Indeed, every sub-region of the two receptive fields under investigation possesses similar attributes. It is important to emphasise that monocular 'form perception' does not play a necessary part in stereopsis. As far back as 1960, Julesz had already shown, that one can perceive depth between random dot stereograms even though these possess no form, as only horizontal disparities exist between the sets of dots.

Depth encoded by binocular neurons then depends on the horizontal disparities of their receptive fields in each eye. Each depth is determined with respect to the fixation point. It surprised Bishop to discover that many of the neurons recorded in the visual cortex responded to vertical retinal image disparities. What could that be about? Why should there be vertical receptive field disparities between the two eyes as well as the well-researched horizontal disparities? The probable answer was provided by Longuet-Higgins and Mayhew in 1982. They proposed that horizontal disparities provide depth with respect to the fixation point, whereas vertical disparities give the distance and

Figure 18.3 Peter Bishop in the laboratory. Reproduced with permission from the Bishop family.

direction of the fixation point itself. This produces a scaling of binocular vision that gives absolute distance. In one of his last papers, published in 1994, Bishop supported this interpretation.

The intense interest in stereopsis in both the Sydney and Berkeley groups, led by Bishop and Barlow respectively, gave rise to tension between them concerning the allocation of priority for the discovery of the neural basis of binocular depth discrimination. This tension arose partly due to the honours student Jack Pettigrew, who had worked on the problem in Bishop's laboratory and then transferred to Barlow's laboratory to carry out further research. In hindsight, Bishop was exceptionally generous in saying that

> The work of the Sydney and Berkeley groups, together with further observations from the Canberra laboratory, particularly those concerning the position disparity tuning curves of striate neurons (Bishop et al., 1971), formed the basis of the neural theory of binocular depth discrimination described by Bishop (1973).[6]

***

Bishop's attempt to identify the neural basis of consciousness was ultimately unsuccessful. As he commented at the end of his career,

> the brain is unquestionably the last frontier. We seem to know most things about the physical world now. We haven't quite got to integrating gravity with the other atomic forces, but it won't be long, I think, before that can be done. But the brain, the nature of consciousness, is a very, very tough problem.[7]

Nevertheless, he was primarily responsible for bringing our wonderful capacity to see the world in depth, rather than as a two-dimensional sheet, from the realm of the psychic into the realm of neuroscientific enquiry. There is no doubt that

> this adds up to a remarkable achievement. For one who did not have the chance to start research work until the age of 30 to become a world leader in his field and to inspire so many others along the way, there must be intrinsic magical ingredients.[8]

These ingredients included

> intellectual honesty and the total commitment to the scientific method for the advancement of knowledge ... it is these characteristics that has set the man apart and made him so greatly admired in the world of science.[9]

The comments made by his close friend, the future Prime Minister of Australia Gough Whitlam, when they were still undergraduates at Sydney University proved to be prescient:

---

6 Bishop and Pettigrew 1986, 1593.
7 Australian Academy of Science, 'Professor Peter Bishop'.
8 Lance 1986, 433.
9 Henry 1986, 437.

he will not have much patience with the routine of the general practitioner or the hypocrisy of the specialist. He will probably be happiest in a research job, for which his intellectual ability, eagerness and independence should pre-eminently fit him.[10]

As the citation declared when he received the Australia Prize,

Professor Bishop had been a major contributor to sensory neurophysiology in Australia, by attracting and training the brightest graduates around the world, by building on the strengths of others and combining it with original insights and research, and by contributing to the policies and distribution of medical research funding in Australia. He is known as one of the three or four world leaders in visual science.[11]

Further reading

Australian Academy of Science. 'Professor Peter Bishop, Visual Neurophysiologist.' Interviews with Australian Scientists. Accessed 13 September 2016. https://bit.ly/2SA6SZ0.

Bishop, P.O. 'Peter O. Bishop.' In *The History of Neuroscience in Autobiography, Volume 1*, edited by L.R. Squire, 80–108. Washington, DC: Society for Neuroscience, 1996.

Bishop, P.O., and J.D. Pettigrew. 'Neural Mechanisms of Binocular Vision.' *Vision Research* 26, no. 9 (1986): 1587–1600.

Helmholtz, H. von. *Science and Culture. Popular and Philosophical Essays*. Translated by D. Cahan. Chicago: University of Chicago Press, 1995.

Sherrington, C.S. *Man on His Nature*. Cambridge: Cambridge University Press, 1940

---

10   Lance 1986, 431.
11   Science.gov.au, 'Professor Peter Bishop'.

19
Delaying nerve degeneration, inherited diseases and multiple sclerosis: James McLeod

Professor of Neurology (1978–1997). Recognised as a world leader in nerve regeneration as well as in optimising conditions for delaying nerve degeneration in both inherited diseases of the peripheral nervous system and diseases of the central nervous system such as multiple sclerosis.

When I arrived in the medical school occupying the Anderson Stuart Building at the University of Sydney to take up a lectureship at the end of 1968, I was guided to a room in the basement that was destined to be my laboratory and office for nearly 40 years. It was next to the mortuary, where cadavers were frequently delivered for anatomical studies by medical students on the floors above. I did not realise at the time that the nerves of these cadavers, if the deceased had passed away less than 24 hours earlier, could be used in transplant operations on patients that had lost function in one or more of their peripheral nerves. Regeneration could be promoted in the nerves that lie outside the brain and spinal cord (hence the term 'peripheral') if they had been damaged through a physical lesion, such as a shrapnel wound inflicted in the Vietnam War, or through a disease such as leprosy or, indeed, if they had degenerated as a consequence of a genetic disorder.

When I entered my office for the first time, I found that it was already occupied by a senior lecturer and his research assistant. They were recording the velocity of the conduction of impulses in the peripheral nerves of rats that were being used to test the efficacy of regeneration transplants before the technique could be used on patients. The senior lecturer was James (Jim) McLeod, who was later appointed by the university to the first established professorship in neurology in Australia as a consequence of his leadership in research on acquired and inherited diseases of the peripheral nervous system, as well as in the clinical treatment of degenerating nerves in the central nervous system, as occurs in multiple sclerosis (MS).

McLeod was born in Sydney in 1932 and entered Sydney University's Faculty of Medicine in 1949, at a very fortunate time, when Professor Peter Bishop (Chapter 18) was establishing the physiology department as a world centre for neurophysiology and Professor Frank Cotton was providing physiological foundations for sports medicine. The former guided McLeod in his first research on nerves; well before he graduated

Figure 19.1 Professor James McLeod. Reproduced with permission from the Faculty of Medicine and Health, University of Sydney.

in medicine in 1959, McLeod joined Bishop's research group, working alongside future leaders in neurology and neurosurgery such as Richard Gye and James Lance. This early experience ensured that, after being awarded a Rhodes Scholarship to Oxford in 1953, McLeod would continue his research into nerve function, in this case on referred pain. In addition, as a consequence of being exposed to Frank Cotton's experiments on optimising the performance of rowers as an undergraduate, McLeod excelled in this sport, joining the crew that won the 100th Oxford and Cambridge Boat Race in 1954. After graduation, he honed his experimental skills on peripheral nerve function and disorders, taking a Nuffield Fellowship to the Institute of Neurology in London in 1964 and subsequently becoming a fellow in neurology at Harvard. This provided intensive preparation for his celebrated experimental and clinical contributions to our understanding of nerve function.

Successful regeneration of nerves following war injuries and in diseases like leprosy

In the early 1970s, McLeod led a team that was concerned with optimising the chances of successfully promoting nerves to grow after they had been severely damaged. At this time, there was a pressing need to assist the wounded from the Vietnam War with lesions to peripheral nerves such as the sciatic (for controlling the legs) and the ulnar (for the arm). McLeod began investigations of lesioned sciatic nerves in rats, and later monkeys, using the most complete set of techniques available for providing a quantitative measure of the degree of nerve regeneration through a lesion. These included electrical measurements of impulse conduction through the regenerated region, histological measures of the extent of nerve axon growth and, most importantly, measures of the extent to which the animal could now use the limbs controlled by the originally lesioned nerve. Regeneration was promoted using allografts – lengths of nerves from another animal of the same species – which were inserted into gaps at the site of the lesion. McLeod observed that the success of these allografts was facilitated by the use of immunosuppressive agents such as azathioprine. This agent increased the number of regenerating axons in a graft, as well as the velocity of impulses through the graft. The success of the animal experiments was repeated when the allograft technique with immunosuppression was used to promote peripheral nerve regeneration in humans. Furthermore, continual immunosuppression therapy had no deleterious effects once the regeneration was complete. This was a triumph of translation from animal experimentation to the alleviation of human suffering.

The question McLeod then posed was whether this approach would be successful in treating peripheral nerves that had degenerated in leprosy patients. Such degeneration leads to loss of normal sensation in limbs and ulceration. Indeed, severe burns and loss of parts of the limb may follow due to the subject's failure to quickly withdraw their limbs from accidental contact with fire or other potential sources of injury. Up until the 1980s, a leprosarium existed to look after the large number of Aboriginal people in the Kimberley suffering from leprosy, a disease ultimately caused by their contact with Europeans. There was no known way of treating such sensory disabilities at the time McLeod's team began their clinical investigations. The medial and ulnar nerves in the arm, at the elbow, are sites of major degeneration in leprosy. So McLeod and his colleagues attempted to restore sensation of the arms by promoting axon regeneration in these nerves.

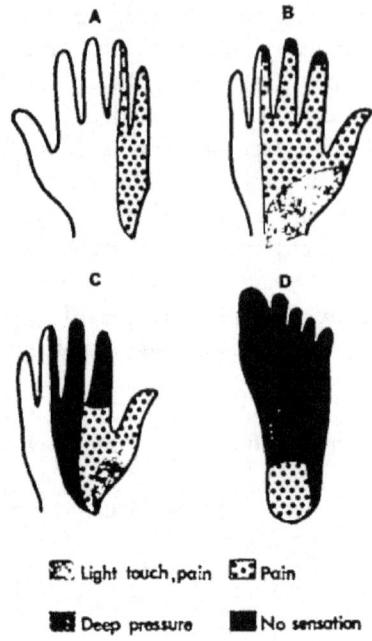

Figure 19.2 Charts of sensory findings in 4 patients with leprosy following nerve grafting, selected to illustrate quality of results obtained. A, Patient 8, graft XI, good results; B, Patient 1, graft 1, fair result; C, Patient 2, graft II, fair result; Patient 5, graft V, poor result. From J.G. McLeod, J.C. Hargrave, R.S. Gye, J.D. Pollard, J.C. Walsh, J.M. Little and G.C. Booth. 'Nerve Grafting in Leprosy.' *Brain* 98, no. 2 (1975): 203–12, by permission of Oxford University Press.

This involved freeze-drying a nerve allograft, then inserting it into the degenerating region of the medial and ulnar nerves of the leprosy sufferer. Next, the patient was treated with the immunosuppressant drug azathioprine for a period of six months – a procedure that had proved so successful in the nerve injury experiments. The clinical results were spectacular, with the capacity to detect harmful stimuli restored for more than three years following the surgery in over 40 per cent of patients (see Figure 19.2).

Treatment for chronic inflammatory demyelinating polyneuropathy (CIDP)

Chronic inflammatory demyelinating polyneuropathy (CIDP) is now the most common treatable neuropathy (a damaged or diseased peripheral nerve) in the Western world. It was first delineated in the late 1970s by McLeod and his colleagues, who established a line of treatment that largely followed from their earlier experiments in nerve regeneration. They distinguished CIDP from a well-known nerve disease that gives rise to Landry-Guillain-Barré syndrome, which is characterised by a lack of control over movements, limb weakness, paralysis of respiration and tremors of the head. Although frightening for the subject when it occurs, Landry-Guillain-Barré syndrome is an acute disorder that remits and generally does not return. CIDP has similar symptoms but a completely different time course; unfortunately, it recurs throughout the lifetime of the subject. McLeod showed that there is a slowing of impulse velocity in the nerves controlling muscle function and in the sensory nerves in Landry-Guillain-Barré syndrome and CIDP. This decrease in velocity is due to demyelination of the axons (that is, loss of the myelin sheath around each axon), reduction in axon diameter and even loss of some axons from the nerve.

McLeod and his colleagues searched for clues to the basis of the demyelination. First, they discovered that 35 per cent of patients with CIDP

> gave a history of preceding infection or some other possible antecedent precipitating event and there was a significantly higher titre for cytomegalovirus antibody in the serum of patients with CIDP than in controls.[1]

Next, they found that CIDP had definite associations with the human leukocyte antigen (HLA) gene complex, encoding the major histocompatibility complex (MHC) cell surface proteins responsible for regulation of the immune system. Specifically, HLA-AW30 and HLA-AW31 showed a direct association with CIDP. Indeed, 38 per cent of CIDP patients were positively typed for these, compared to only four per cent of normal subjects. In contrast, Landry-Guillain-Barré syndrome did not have such associations. This discovery led to the hypothesis that CIDP is most likely an autoimmune disease, in which the body's immune system is turned against some of its own cells. Such autoimmune pathogenesis might then be responsible for other demyelinating diseases, such as MS.

This finding also suggested that CIDP and MS might be arrested using immunosuppressive drugs, as these had been very effective in nerve regeneration procedures. McLeod's group tested this hypothesis in the early 1980s by clearing autoimmune antibodies from the blood of CIDP patients. Such plasma exchange was shown to be an effective therapy in experiments with animal models of inflammatory neuropathy, and carrying out plasma exchange on patients with CIDP provided considerable clinical improvement in many of them. There was enhanced action potential conduction and less axonal degeneration than in patients who did not respond to the plasma exchange. The exchange was shown to decrease myelin antibodies and was especially efficacious when combined with immunosuppressive drugs. Careful clinical, histological and electrophysiological analyses of animal models and of humans suffering from CIDP established a manageable approach to this most common of treatable neuropathies.

---

1   McCombe, Pollard and McLeod 1987, 1617.

Identifying the genetic basis of Charcot-Marie-Tooth disease (CMTD)

Charcot-Marie-Tooth disease (CMTD) is the most common of all inherited demyelinating diseases of the peripheral nerves – that is, of neuropathies. It is a motor and sensory neuropathy, involving the nerves that control muscle and those that convey sensations. McLeod's group established that CMTD was a heterogeneous group of disorders. They were able to characterise the different homogeneous disease subgroups by combining careful clinical studies, electrical recording of conduction velocities and histology of biopsy material. At the same time, in the mid- to late-1970s, they made an intense study of the best animal model of inherited demyelinating neuropathy, the Trembler mouse, which provided genetic insights into the origin of CMTD. The Trembler mouse drags its limbs and develops tremors about ten days after birth. It has a peripheral neuropathy with a three-fold loss of myelinated axons; the axons remaining in the sciatic nerve are of small-diameter and conduct long-latency impulses with reduced amplitude. Conduction fails completely during trains of impulses (see Figure 19.3) and is very sensitive to changes in temperature.

The description of neuropathy in an animal with a chronic demyelinating disorder laid the groundwork for subsequent enquiry into the genetic basis of the disorder and its possible relationship with CMTD. The gene involved, found by Garth Nicholson in McLeod's laboratory, is on a chromosome analogous to human chromosome 17. The gene encodes the myelin protein PMP22, which is expressed by Schwann cells that make abnormal myelin sheaths around the axons, hence the demyelination and loss of axons in CMTD, as well as in the Trembler mouse. Another common hereditary neuropathy, called 'hereditary neuropathy with liability to pressure palsies', was found to be associated with a deletion in the PMP22 gene region, and hence failure of Schwann cells to adequately myelinate axons, in 25 per cent of patients. These discoveries focused continuing experimental work on the failure of Schwann cells to make myelin protein PMP22 as a cause of demyelinating diseases of the peripheral nervous system.

The treatment of multiple sclerosis (MS) with vitamin D and leukocyte extracts

In the 1980s, McLeod's team carried out painstaking epidemiological studies on the geographical incidence of MS in major cities of Australia such as Perth, Newcastle and Hobart, and in North Queensland. This work revealed that MS is more likely to follow a progressive course in the southern cities than in the north, with the former identified as high-frequency zones compared with the latter median-frequency zones (5 to 29 cases per 100,000 population). Thus, they established that there is a latitudinal gradient for MS, with the frequency decreasing closer to the equator. The obvious environmental factor contributing to this gradient is the extent of sunlight, which determines the level of a subject's vitamin D. This latitudinal gradient was later extended to other autoimmune diseases, with the result that a standard component of treatment now involves supplementing vitamin D.

Given McLeod's team's experience with chronic relapsing polyneuropathy, it was natural for them to enquire whether a central demyelinating disease such as MS might have analogous origins. Both of these involve destruction of myelin sheaths by mononuclear

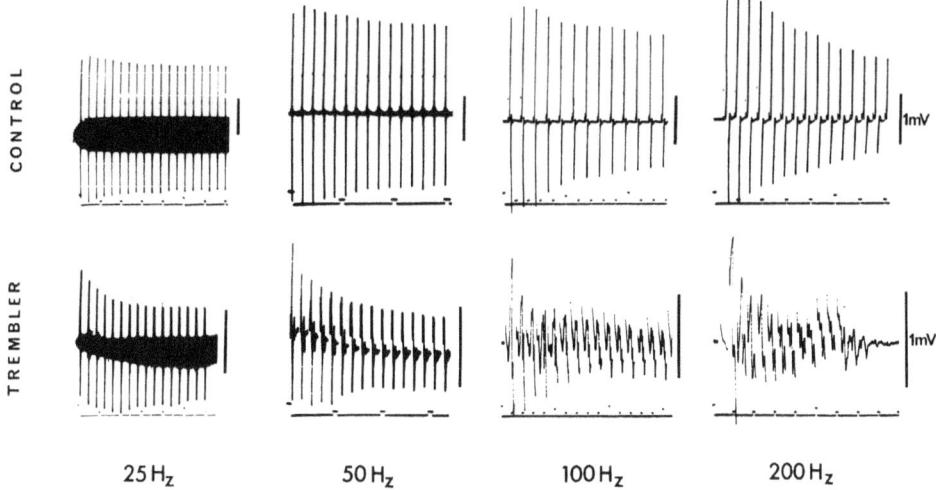

Figure 19.3 Effect of trains of impulses on the amplitude of compound nerve action potential of sciatic-tibial nerves of control and Trembler mouse. Reproduced from P.A. Low and J.G. McLeod, 'Refractory Period, Conduction of Trains of Impulses, and Effect of Temperature on Conduction in Chronic Hypertrophic Neuropathy,' *Journal of Neurology, Neurosurgery and Psychiatry* 40, no. 5 (1977): 439, with permission from BMJ Publishing Group Ltd.

lymphocytes, so they have a strong association with HLA and autoimmunity. This was supported by the presence of antibodies to myelin and to the central myelinating cells, the oligodendrocytes (the central equivalent of the peripheral Schwann cell), in the blood of MS patients. This observation suggested that a form of plasmapheresis might be effective, as it had been for chronic relapsing neuropathies. Plasmapheresis is a technique for isolating cells from blood plasma after it has been removed from a patient, and then transfusing only the cells back into the patient.

Animals can provide good models for demyelinating diseases if they are injected with peripheral nerves from another animal. In this case, an antibody attack is mounted; this attack does not discriminate between the foreign nerves and the animal's own nerves, giving rise to what is called experimental allergic neuritis (EAN). McLeod's team used plasmaphersis on EAN animals two weeks after such injection. These animals developed less severe weakness, demyelination and action potential reduction than the control EAN animals. Following the animal proof in principle of the technique of plasmarphersis, McLeod's team turned to optimising the effects of plasmapheresis in human cases of MS by incorporating a leukocyte extract called transfer factor. This approach was found to be effective in subsequent large-scale clinical immunotherapy trials. Observations were made every six months during a two-year prospective double-blind trial using transfer factor obtained from the leukocytes of family members. Steady improvement was noted after 18 months in patients with moderate MS, although without reversing the progressive nature of the disease. As well as bringing relief to many patients, this work laid the foundations for more effective immunotherapy using beta-interferon rather than transfer factor.

***

McLeod was a world leader in the clinical treatment of neuropathies and MS for more than two decades while Bushell Professor of Neurology at the University of Sydney. He fostered skills in clinical assessment, electrophysiological measurements of nerve conduction and histological determinations of nerve demyelination and deterioration. This allowed him and his team to make seminal contributions to the alleviation of human suffering by establishing the efficacy of nerve allografts and immunosuppression in promoting nerve regeneration in neuropathies, pioneering the use of plasma exchange in inherited neuropathies and establishing the importance of vitamin D, together with plasmapheresis incorporating transfer factor, a forerunner of beta-interferon, in the treatment of MS.

Further reading

Hammond, S.R., J.G. McLeod, K.S. Millingen, E.G. Stewart-Wynne, D. English, J.T. Holland and M.G. McCall. 'The Epidemiology of Multiple Sclerosis in Three Australian Cities: Perth, Newcastle and Hobart.' *Brain* 111, no. 1 (1988): 1–25.

Low, P.A., and J.G. McLeod. 'Refractory Period, Conduction of Trains of Impulses, and Effect of Temperature on Conduction in Chronic Hypertrophic Neuropathy.' *Journal of Neurology, Neurosurgery and Psychiatry* 40, no. 5 (1977): 434–47.

McLeod, J.G., J.C. Hargrave, R.S. Gye, J.D. Pollard, J.C. Walsh, J.M. Little and G.C. Booth. 'Nerve Grafting in Leprosy.' *Brain* 98, no. 2 (1975): 203–12.

Pollard, J.D., J.G. McLeod, P. Gatenby and H. Kronenberg. 'Prediction of Response to Plasma Exchange in Chronic Relapsing Polyneuropathy.' *Journal of the Neurological Sciences* 58, no. 2 (1983): 269–87.

Pollard, J.D., J.G. McLeod and R.S. Gye. 'Regeneration Through Peripheral Nerve Allografts.' *Archives of Neurology* 28, no. 1 (1973): 31–7.

Stewart, G.J., J.D. Pollard, J.G. McLeod and C.M. Wolnizer. 'HLA Antigens in the Landry-Guillain-Barré Syndrome and Chronic Relapsing Polyneuritis.' *Annals of Neurology* 4, no. 3 (1978): 285–9.

20
Asthma risk factors identified as allergens and genetic predispositions: Ann Janet Woolcock

Woolcock revealed the importance of allergens in the environment, such as dust mites, together with genetic predisposition, in the initiation and exacerbation of asthma; delineated important physiological and pathological differences between asthma and chronic obstructive pulmonary disease (COPD); led research into the critical importance of the small airways in the development of COPD; and introduced effective means of monitoring and facilitating recovery from asthma, especially in children.

In 2000, I contracted a lung infection that reached a stage at which my doctors brought in Ann Woolcock to provide advice on treatment. I remember her as a kind, considerate, no-nonsense person, traits she no doubt developed from her earliest experiences in research and practice with the New Guinea highlanders. Indeed, I identified with the prone patient being cared for by Ann in Figure 20.3, as she bent over me with a concentrated expression, determining the clinical signs of my ailment, which was soon to be alleviated following her advice.

Ann's devotion to the understanding and treatment of lung diseases arising from allergens[1] is legendary. One in nine Australians suffers from asthma,[2] and the prevalence is about three times higher in children than in adults. Severe asthma remains a lethal condition, causing about 455 deaths per year in Australia, compared with 1200 deaths from road traffic accidents each year. For decades, Woolcock was the leading researcher

---

1   Allergens are types of antigens that produce an abnormally vigorous immune response in which the immune system fights off a perceived threat that would otherwise be harmless to the body. Such reactions are called allergies. Allergens can have a variety of sources, such as dust mite excretion, pollen, pet dander or even royal jelly. Food allergies are not as common as food sensitivity, but some foods, such as peanuts (a legume), nuts, seafood and shellfish, are the cause of serious allergic reactions in many people.
2   Asthma is a common long-term inflammatory disease of the airways of the lungs. It is characterised by variable and recurring symptoms, reversible airflow obstructions and bronchospasm. Symptoms include episodes of wheezing, coughing, chest tightness and shortness of breath. Asthma is caused by a combination of complex and incompletely understood environmental and genetic interactions. These factors influence both its severity and its responsiveness to treatment.

Figure 20.1 Professor Ann Janet Woolcock. Reproduced with permission from the Woolcock Institute of Medical Research.

studying the causes and causal mechanisms of this disease and developing means of ameliorating it.

The eldest of four children, Woolcock was born in December 1937 in Reynella, South Australia, where her father and mother ran the general store. There she attended the public primary school. She then went to Adelaide for secondary education at Walford Church of England Girls Grammar. After completing medical school at the University of Adelaide, she elected to pursue research in respiratory medicine at the University of Sydney. Here she carried out clinical and physiological enquiries on the functioning of the lungs (Figure 20.2), with special reference to airway function, a subject she pursued until the end of her life. She was mentored in Sydney by Professor Ruthven Blackburn, who later became her husband. He guided her to a position in the Page Chest Pavilion of Royal Prince Alfred Hospital, where she met John Read, the professor of respiratory physiology and medicine, who introduced her to research on asthma.

Upon completing postgraduate work on this subject, she was awarded an Asthma Foundation of New South Wales scholarship in 1966 to continue her research at McGill University in Montreal. Her ground-breaking work on the function of the small airways was undertaken in Montreal with Peter Macklem and other eminent researchers. Woolcock maintained a close relationship with the Asthma Foundation for the rest of her life, reporting many of her results at their scientific meetings and in their publications. She was a talented and enthusiastic public speaker and educator about asthma.

She was appointed senior lecturer in medicine at Sydney University in 1973, where she remained as an academic for the rest of her life, building a powerful team of researchers that established the major role of allergens in asthma, developed standard tests for ascertaining the extent of asthmatic conditions and designed an 'asthma action plan', involving pharmalogical intervention, for optimising the amelioration of the condition, using corticosteroids and anti-allergic beta agents.[3]

Distinguishing between asthma and chronic obstructive pulmonary disease

In her earliest epidemiological studies in 1965–6, Woolcock worked in the western and eastern highlands of Papua New Guinea with a team including her future husband Ruthven Blackburn. Supported by the US National Institute of Health and the University of Sydney, this team explored the nature of the chronic lung disease that was unique to that environment and frequently misdiagnosed.[4] There was evidence of bronchitis,[5] bronchiolitis, emphysema, parenchymal fibrosis and dense pleural adhesion in the few autopsy specimens available.[6] While there were elements of obstructive lung disease

---

3 Beta-agonists, or beta-adrenergic agonists, are medications that relax the muscles of the airways so that they widen, allowing for easier breathing. They are a class of sympathomimetic agents that act upon the beta adrenoceptor. In general, pure beta-adrenergic agonists have the opposite function of beta-blockers.
4 Buist 2003.
5 Bronchitis causes a cough that often brings up mucus (the inflamed bronchial tubes prodce a lot of mucus). It can also cause shortness of breath, wheezing, a low fever and chest tightness. There are two main types of bronchitis: acute and chronic. Chronic bronchitis is one type of COPD.
6 Woolcock, Blackburn, Freeman, Zylstra and Spring 1970.

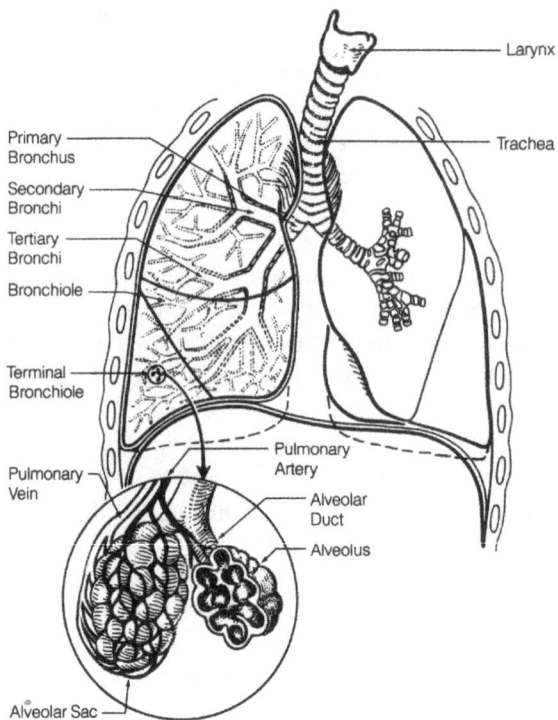

Figure 20.2 A diagram of the bronchi, bronchioles and in the enlargement the lung parenchyma (consisting of aveoli and aveolar ducts at the end of the respiratory bronchioles involved in gas transfer). Modified from National Cancer Institute Visuals Online (visualsonline.cancer.gov): AV-0000-4101.

present, there was also evidence of pulmonary restriction. Respiratory infections in childhood were rife, raising the hypothesis that repeated infective insults to the developing lung in childhood were setting the stage for much more severe damage in later life. Woolcock commented on the living conditions of the highlanders:

> in the New Guinea highland population, there is extreme overcrowding in the huts, and the smoke of the wood fires (used to keep the people warm in the cold mountain nights) contains aldehydes, which is extremely irritating. Respiratory infections are common from infancy onward, and chronic bronchiolitis has been demonstrated pathologically. Asthma is, however, very rare in this population, and it seems unlikely that it plays any role in the development of a disease in New Guinea.[7]

---

7   Woolcock, Blackburn, Freeman, Zylstra and Spring 1970, 589.

Figure 20.3 Ann Woolcock and Ruthven Blackburn performing an electrocardiograph on a villager in Pompomere, Eastern Highlands, Papua New Guinea. c. 1966. Reproduced with permission from the Blackburn family.

Woolcock argued that a change in the New Guinea highlanders' lifestyle was imperative if the high rates of morbidity were to be avoided, but that such development might be two-edged. When she first went to Papua New Guinea, no asthma could be detected in the eastern highlands or in the Baiyer river district in the western highlands, as already noted. Several years later, following a degree of Westernisation of these tribal environments, the prevalence had risen dramatically, with Woolcock now recording that 0.6 per cent of the children and 7.3 per cent of the adults had asthma. This sudden appearance of asthma was correlated with[8]

> modifications to the traditional lifestyles by the recent introduction of blankets and changes in sleeping environment that promote a more fertile environment for growth and multiplication of mites.[9]

So the morbidity and mortality of the highlanders was substantially increased, not only because of the COPD identified some ten years earlier, but because of the introduction of

---

8   Turner, Dowse, Stewart, Alpers and Woolcock 1985.
9   Dowse, Turner, Stewart, Alpers and Woolcock 1985.

asthma. Woolcock had identified the probable causes of the increased frequency of these conditions and the likely source of the diseases.

Identifying asthma in children as an allergy disease involving genetic predispositions

In the early 1970s, Woolcock noted a contrast between the lack of asthma in the highland children of New Guinea and the Aboriginal children of Central Australia, on the one hand, and the high levels of asthma in Eastern Sydney, where 12 per cent of children had asthma and 30 per cent showed signs of wheezing, on the other. She traced these differences to allergens – antigens that produce excessively high and uniquely provocative (rather than protective) immune responses. She reasoned that New Guinea and Aboriginal children are less allergic and so have less reaction to allergens when given a skin test. She also noted that as the children grew older they responded to the skin test like Caucasians. This later acquisition of atopy[10] – that is, the genetic tendency to develop allergic diseases – did not have anything like the effect of acquiring atopy as a child, protecting the mature-age New Guinea and Aboriginal populations. Clearly, if one could delay the onset of atopy in Caucasians then asthma would be greatly diminished. Woolcock commented that

> throughout the 1980s a big controversy raged about whether asthma caused allergy or allergy caused asthma, or whether they were two phenomena in the community that happened to be related. It was clear to me by 1990 that allergy is the highest risk factor. If you do a logistic analysis on all this epidemiological data from children, there is no escaping that the major risk factor and therefore cause of asthma is being allergic. It is allergens.[11]

What had brought about this conviction? Woolcock and her colleagues undertook a large population study of 2,363 school children in New South Wales (Belmont and Wagga Wagga) between 1982 and 1984. The extent of asthma among these children could be measured objectively using the 'histamine inhalation test' described in the next section. It became evident that allergic (skin test) sensitisation was the most important risk factor for asthma.[12]

A breakthrough occurred about this time in Woolcock's laboratory when the faeces of the house dust mite were identified as a major allergen, as was already suspected.[13] This prompted Woolcock and her colleagues to consider whether strong correlations existed between asthma, allergic reactions and the presence of mites in the children's homes. A correlation was ascertained between atopy, established with a skin prick test, respiratory illness, determined by clinical observations such as wheezing, and the histamine inhalation test, which quantitated bronchial hyper-responsiveness (see next section).[14] Current

---

10   Atopy refers to the genetic tendency to develop allergic diseases, such as allergic rhinitis, asthma and atopic dermatitis (eczema). Atopy is typically associated with heightened immune responses to common allergens, especially inhaled and food allergens.
11   Australian Academy of Science, 'Professor Ann Woolcock'.
12   Salome, Peat, Britton and Woolcock 1987, 271–81.
13   Voorhorst, Spieksma-Boezeman and Spieksma 1964, 329–34.

asthma in the children, measured by wheezing frequency, hay fever and bronchial hyper-responsiveness, was found to be directly correlated with large skin weals in response to house dust extracts in skin tests, establishing atopy in these children. Furthermore, dust mite sensitivity in children showed the strongest independent association with current asthma.[15] The mite allergen in the homes was identified as the causative factor; this was shown to have four times higher density in the home than in public places and buildings outside the home.[16]

Removing mite populations from the home commended itself as an intervention to prevent asthma and cut down on attacks, but although

> we know that allergen avoidance works ... in the real world people are exposed to a lot of allergen all the time, and reducing it in a house and keeping it out (particularly in Sydney) is very difficult. It is in your clothes and everywhere ... the most important thing is the right treatment – which has to be begun early until control of the asthma is achieved, and then keep going. That means people taking inhaled corticosteroids[17] if they have persistent asthma.[18]

The airway hyper-responsiveness test

In 1984, Woolcock's research team established that those with asthma have abnormal airways,[20] indicated by hyper-responsiveness to inhaled stimulants, such as histamine. In this case, the airways narrow to a much greater extent than those of normal subjects. This was quantitated for both normal and asthmatic patients by measuring forced expired volume in one second following inhalation of histamine at a particular concentration (see Figure 20.4). The concentration was increased until a plateau was reached in the forced expired volume for both normal and mildly asthmatic subjects, and until the expired volume had dropped by 60 per cent in other asthmatics. The observations showed that the asthmatics did not reach a plateau at all, but rather exhibited greater sensitivity to histamine, as indicated by the higher slopes of their curves.[21] The results were taken to suggest that 'asthmatics lack a normal mechanism that inhibits severe airway narrowing during histamine challenge',[22] meaning that the technique of measuring airway hyper-responsiveness could provide a quantitative measure of the extent of asthma. By applying

---

14 Bronchial hyper-responsiveness is defined as an increase in sensitivity to a wide variety of airway-narrowing stimuli. Most patients with asthma and COPD exhibit such an enhanced sensitivity. It is a state characterised by easily triggered bronchospasm (contraction of the bronchioles or small airways). In asthma, it tends to be reversible with bronchodilator therapy, although this is not the case in COPD.
15 Peat and Woolcock 1991, 573–81.
16 Green, Marks, Tovey, Toelle and Woolcock 1992.
17 Corticosteroids are a class of steroid hormones that are produced in the adrenal cortex of vertebrates, as well as the synthetic analogues of these hormones.
18 Australian Academy of Science, 'Professor Ann Woolcock'.
20 Smith 2014, 320.
21 Woolcock, Salome and Yan 1984.
22 Woolcock, Salome and Yan 1984, 71.

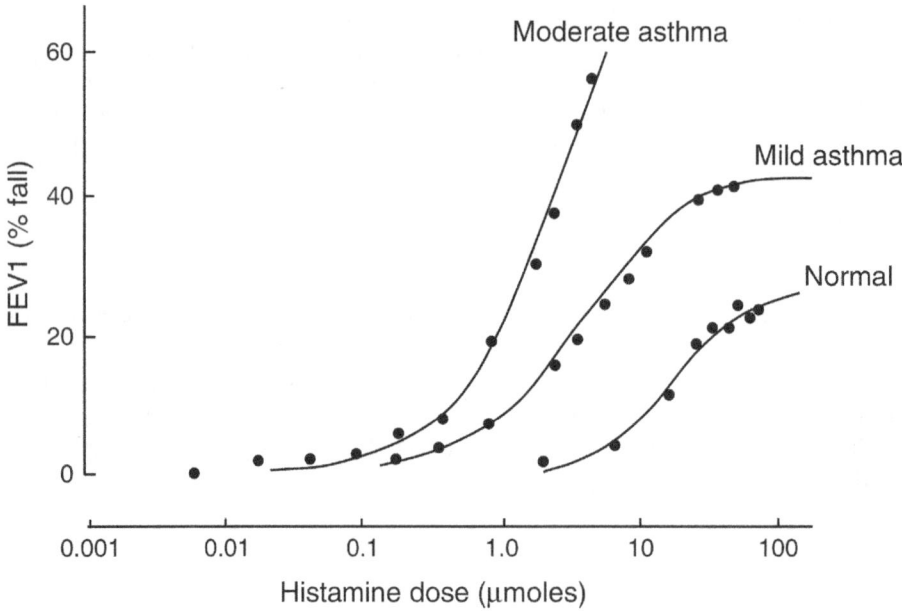

Figure 20.4 In a normal person, increasing concentrations of histamine lead to a fall in lung function that reaches a plateau, whereas in a person with asthma this fall does not reach a plateau. Reproduced from B. Smith, 'Ann Janet Woolcock (1937–2001),' *Historical Records of Australian Science* 25, no. 2 (2014), with permission from CSIRO Publishing.

the technique to 50 subjects with different degrees of respiratory disorder, a direct correlation was found between symptom severity and histamine concentration over a hundredfold range of concentrations.[23] This provided the kind of simple, portable, rapid test that Woolcock had sought for asthmatics.

Bronchial hyper-responsiveness, a form of late-phase airway hyper-responsiveness, refers to an increase in sensitivity of these airways to a range of constrictor agents. Woolcock and her colleagues studied such hyper-responsiveness in a large population from Busselton in Western Australia, using the test they had devised.[24] They showed that the dose/response curves for those with COPD overlapped with the curves for those suffering from asthma, although the mean values for the two groups were significantly different. Thus, a significant proportion of each group suffered from bronchial hyper-responsiveness, which was shown to be prominent in asthmatics.[25] Population health surveys carried out in Busselton over 18 years showed that patients with asthma experienced a greater decline in their forced expiratory volume in one second compared with those without asthma (a rate of 50 millilitres per year compared with 35 millilitres per year).

---

23 Yan, Salome and Woolcock 1983.
24 Yan, Salome and Woolcock 1985.
25 Peat and Woolcock 1991.

Direct measures of the extent and distribution of airway closure became possible when single positron emission computed tomography (SPECT) became available.[26] SPECT scans showed that this method of determining airway hyper-responsiveness provided a reliable, rapid and safe technique for measuring the extent of patients' asthma, as well as a means for following the recuperation of patients receiving corticosteroid treatment. It also indicated that the extent of pulmonary elastic recoil determines airway closure in healthy subjects, and that this is lost in asthmatic patients, probably secondary to allergic inflammation.[27]

Identifying abnormal airway smooth muscle as a major contributor to asthma

Speaking at an asthma workshop just over a year before she died, Woolcock commented:

> throughout the 1990s, it became clear, with the advent of the longer-acting β-agonists, that there are in fact two abnormalities in everybody with asthma, that is, virtually everyone: the allergic inflammation [treated with corticosteroids] and abnormal behaviour in their airway smooth muscle [treated with beta-agonists].[28]

As she put it,

> There are many new theories about how the smooth muscle is controlled by ordinary tidal breathing … Actually, just our tidal breathing as we sit here now is enough to stretch the smooth muscle and the airways. If we stop doing that, the smooth muscle undergoes less and less hysteresis and gets stiffer and stiffer unless it is kept going by some means. It can go into the state of latch bridge … where the thing is contricted [sic] to its minimum size and all the bridges are acting so slowly it is stuck. To open it and pull it back to its original length takes a lot of force, a lot of stretching and probably a lot of beta agonists.[29]

However, airway hyper-responsiveness to histamine may not reflect deterioration of normal smooth muscle. In a series of ingenious experiments, Woolcock and her colleagues measured the inhaled histamine dose at which a 20 per cent reduction in forced expiratory volume occurred in patients who subsequently underwent thoracotomy. The in vitro responses of the bronchial and parenchymal tissue[30] (see Figure 20.2), obtained through the thoracotomy, showed little variation in responses to applied histamine despite large variations in the histamine inhalation test.[31] It is now conjectured that airway hyper-responsiveness has a

---

26   King, Eberl, Salome, Young, and Woolcock 1998.
27   Allergic inflammation is an important pathophysiological feature of several disabilities or medical conditions including allergic asthma, atopic dermatitis, allergic rhinitis and several ocular allergic diseases.
28   Smith 2014.
29   Australian Academy of Science, 'Professor Ann Woolcock'.
30   Bronchi are airways in the respiratory tract that conducts air into the lungs. The first bronchi to branch from the trachea are the right main bronchus and the left main bronchus. Lung parenchyma is the portion of the lung involved in gas transfer, the alveoli, alveolar ducts and respiratory bronchioles.
31   Vincenc, Black, Yan, Armour, Donnelly and Woolcock 1983.

number of origins, one of which involves enhanced proliferation of the pro-inflammatory airway smooth muscle phenotype.[32]

***

Woolcock had an immense influence, not only on our understanding of the origins and practical treatment of asthma, but also by mentoring future generations of epidemiologists and researchers concerned with infectious lung diseases, such as Professor Judy Black and a future Dean of Medicine, Professor Steven Leeder. Leeder commented that

> She had a team around her who used to regularly curse her demands, but were as loyal as if they were wired into her, largely teams of women, a few men but mainly women – just extraordinary. And she was incredibly loyal to them. When things were going wrong or they were unwell or something, Ann would be their staunch advocate. She had this sort of mother hen thing.[33]

Ann was a driving force in asthma epidemiology, which

> brought her great international distinction and respect. It also emphasised the relevance of population health studies to the practice of clinical medicine and she never lost an opportunity to make population health relevant to the individual.[34]

Her individualised management plans for asthmatics were

> probably her greatest achievement and her idea has now been copied worldwide. It is probably the most important therapeutic advance for asthma since the introduction of steroids, and all it took was common sense, which Ann had in abundance.[35]

Ann's life in science and academic medicine 'left an unrivalled legacy that will continue to inspire respiratory scientists and clinicians'.[36] She died from cancer in 2001, at the early age of 64.

> Despite her frantic schedule, she never gave up clinical medicine and she was still doing her outpatients clinics in the last month of her life, farewelling some of the patients she had looked after for nearly 30 years.[37]

The memory of her contributions to medical science is now enshrined at the University of Sydney in the best way possible – in the Woolcock Institute of Medical Research, devoted

---

32 Doeing and Solway 1985.
33 Smith 2014, 325.
34 Smith 2014, 318.
35 Macklem 2001, 1041.
36 Jenkins 2001, 160.
37 Jenkins 2001, 160.

to respiratory research, which now employs more than 130 researchers and support staff. Today it is considered one of the top six such institutes worldwide.[38]

Further reading

Dowse, G.K., K.J. Turner, G.A. Stewart, M.P. Alpers and A.J. Woolcock. 'The Association Between Dermatophagoides Mites and the Increasing Prevalence of Asthma in Village Communities Within the Papua New Guinea Highlands.' *Journal of Allergy and Clinical Immunology* 75, no. 1 (1985): 75–83.

Green, W.F., G.B. Marks, E.R. Tovey, B.G. Toelle and A.J. Woolcock. 'House Dust Mites and Mite Allergens in Public Places.' *Journal of Allergy and Clinical Immunology* 89, no. 6 (1992): 1196–7.

King, G.G., S. Eberl, C.M. Salome, I.H. Young and A.J. Woolcock. 'Differences in Airway Closure Between Normal and Asthmatic Subjects Measured with Single Photon Emission Computed Tomography and Technegas.' *American Journal of Respiratory and Clinical Care Medicine* 158, no. 6 (1998): 1900–6.

Peat, J.K., and A.J. Woolcock. 'Sensitivity to Common Allergens: Relation to Respiratory Symptoms and Bronchial Hyperresponsiveness in Children from Three Different Climate Areas of Australia.' *Clinical and Experimental Allergy* 21, no. 5 (1991): 573–81.

Salome, C.M., J.K. Peat, W.J. Britton, and A.J. Woolcock. 'Bronchial Hyperresponsiveness in Two Populations of Australian Schoolchildren. I. Relation to Respiratory Symptoms and Diagnosed Asthma.' *Clinical Allergy* 17, no. 4 (1987): 271–81.

Turner, K.J., G.K. Dowse, G.A. Stewart, M.P. Alpers and A.J. Woolcock. 'Prevalence of Asthma in the South Fore People of the Okapa District of Papua New Guinea. Features Associated with a Recent Dramatic Increase.' *International Archives of Allergy and Immunology* 77, no. 1–2 (1985): 158–62.

Vincenc, K.S., J.L. Black, K. Yan, C.L. Armour, P.D. Donnelly and A.J. Woolcock. 'Comparison of In Vivo and In Vitro Responses to Histamine in Human Airways.' *American Review of Respiratory Diseases* 128, no. 5 (1983): 875–9.

Woolcock, A.J., C.R. Blackburn, M.H. Freeman, W. Zylstra and S.R. Spring. 'Studies of Chronic (Nontuberculous) Lung Disease in New Guinea Populations. The Nature of the Disease.' *American Review of Respiratory Disease* 102, no. 4 (1970): 575–90.

Woolcock, A.J., C.M. Salome and K. Yan. 'The Shape of the Dose-Response Curve to Histamine in Asthmatic and Normal Subjects.' *American Review of Respiratory Disease* 130, no. 1 (1984): 71–5.

Yan, K., C.M. Salome and A.J. Woolcock. 'Prevalence and Nature of Bronchial Hyperresponsiveness in Subjects with Chronic Obstructive Pulmonary Disease.' *American Review of Respiratory Diseases* 132, no. 1 (1985): 25–9.

Yan, K., C.M. Salome and A.J. Woolcock. 'Rapid Method for Measurement of Bronchial Responsiveness.' *Thorax* 38, no. 10 (1983): 760–5.

---

38 Mellor 2006, 262.

Epilogue: Knowledge and understanding

This work has two goals, as set out in the introduction: first, to give a scholarly account of some of the great achievements of this University and second to illuminate what is meant by gaining new knowledge and understanding. I will draw on what I learnt from the work of the scholars and researchers described in this book, together with, in many cases, personal discussions concerning their search for understanding.

It seems that knowing something new, gained through experience, in the natural sciences generally refers to learning or establishing new facts.[1] This is evident in the facts determined by the astronomers Hanbury Brown, Mills and Payne-Scott concerning the magnitude of stars and the position of radio signal sources in the heavens. It is also evident in the chemical measurements made by Hush in establishing electron transfers during photosynthesis. The physical and chemical sciences lend themselves to quantitative judgements that are taken to establish new facts. In the medical sciences, emphasis is placed on correlations, such as those discovered by Bishop between binocular vision and the activity of a class of neurons in the cortex, by Woolcock between asthma and mites in the environment and by McLeod between immunosuppressive drugs and the efficacy of allografts in nerve regeneration. Correlations are perhaps most evident in Lancaster's work; he established correlations between malignant melanoma and ultraviolet radiation and between hearing loss and rubella infection, which he formalised as the leading mathematician on the chi-squared test. In the biological sciences, Birch also emphasised correlations between the abundance and distribution of species, on the one hand, and changes in the environment, on the other. Powerful mathematical theories relating to these were subsequently developed by May. In a social science like economics, the principal concern is establishing correlations, typified by Hogan's work probing the basis of instabilities in financial institutions.

Knowing something new, gained through experience, in the humanities – the possession of new information[2] – seems to shift from the quantitative to the qualitative. It is evident in Trendall's identification of the artists responsible for thousands of red-figure

---

1   Elgin 2007.
2   Hacker 2013, 154.

pots, in Clunies Ross' elucidation and classification of Icelandic sagas and poetry, in Ward's gathering of documents from British and Australian sources to build a narrative concerning the development of federation and in Gaukroger's gathering material from an enormous range of sources to reveal the foundations of science. In jurisprudence, it is evident in Tay's collection of evidence on the workings of the 20th-century Russian and Chinese constitutions to argue against the incursion of autocracy and in Stone's study of the procedures of judges and the contemporaneous morals of society to ascertain whether the former reflects the latter. Some regard this shift in emphasis from quantitative to qualitative judgements as a basis for deriding the disciplines of these scholars, an attitude which is misplaced.

But what of knowledge in philosophy? Does such a notion exist? I don't think it does, at least not on the model of scientific knowledge. This has been quite erroneously used to deny philosophy's central place in universities. Wittgenstein emphasised that the principal role of philosophy is to remove conceptual confusions leading to logically incoherent claims, which so often arise in other disciplines. This especially holds at present for my own subject of neuroscience, concerned as it is with the relationship between human behaviour and the workings of the brain.[3] Price clears away deep confusions in physics concerning notions of time and causality and Armstrong is especially concerned with an attempt to solve what he sees as a classical philosophical problem – namely, that of the relationship between brain and mind, for which he provides a materialist solution. I will leave it to the reader to determine whether the conception of philosophy as a critical and elucidatory discipline is more powerful than the idea that it achieves new knowledge.

Understanding seems to be different from knowledge and is certainly held to be of higher value.[4] Natural scientists are concerned with understanding various phenomena, such as sunspots, radio sources, asthma, nerve degeneration and stereopsis. In some cases, where there is substantial comprehension and knowledge of the connections between parts of the phenomena, theories and models may be developed, such as those for biodiversity and the spread of disease formulated by May. These models and theories are representations of the phenomena under investigation, so they must respond to the facts.[5] However, clearly understanding these phenomena involves more than developing a representation of the facts and their interconnections that pertain to the model or theory. It must, in some way, be connected to the person who is seeking understanding. What might this connection be? From my observations of many of the researchers who figure in this work, I think that, for them, understanding consisted of coming to *grasp* how the different components in the representation relate to each other in a coherent way.[6] Such grasping is not merely synonym for understanding, but rather a belief that they could see the causal relations involved in the phenomenon, what it is about one element in the representation that causes another element to change in some way and, in particular, what enabled them to explain the phenomenon under investigation.[7]

---

3   Bennett and Hacker 2003; Bennett and Hacker 2013.
4   Gardiner 2012; Pritchard 2008; Pritchard 2009.
5   Newman 2012; Newman 2017.
6   Kvanvig 2009.
7   Hacker 2013, 3.

Can the work of our five great scholars in the humanities – Trendall, Clunies Ross, Ward, Tay and Stone – be said to create representations that imply causal relationships that allow for analysis of the kind we have come to expect in the natural sciences? I don't think so, but that is unimportant. In their case, meaning is attached to human behaviour and to social practices and institutions – an entirely different enterprise to that of the natural sciences. Indeed, interpretation of social phenomena can only be evaluated in terms of 'internal coherence and fit with the behaviour and avowals of the participants'.[8] Neither causal explanations nor inductive regularities leading to predictions are especially relevant in history and jurisprudence, although there is a special need to avoid any preconceptions and to have no axes to grind. There does not seem to be a single methodological procedure that is used across the humanities, a conclusion often used to downgrade their importance, particularly in relation to the natural sciences. However, this claim is turned on its head below, where it is argued that statements in the natural sciences often include terms that need clarification through methodologies that lie outside of these sciences.

I have tried to relate, to the best of my knowledge, the paths taken by the eminent scholars and researchers at Sydney in their search for knowledge and understanding. The question one must now ask is: to what extent are their claims to understanding justified? There is a limit to the domains of natural sciences – not all forms of understanding are scientific. The works of Trendall, Clunies Ross and Ward in the humanities are not scientific, nor are those of the philosophers Price and Armstrong, or of Gaukroger in the history and philosophy of the natural sciences. Nor, for that matter, are those of the mathematicians May and Lancaster, since they do not have to face the tribunal of experimental testing – of experience – and so cannot be confirmed or invalidated by experience, but only by proof. The claim that all real knowledge comes from scientific enquiry is erroneous; the understanding of key terms, such as truth and causality, that are used in scientific enquiry is found outside such enquiries. The function of these terms is clarified by the description of 'language games' (as Wittgenstein specified), which are not themselves a part of science. It is not possible to draw a clear demarcation between the descriptive statements of science, on the one hand, and the kinds of statements that involve terms that characteristically lie outside of natural science, on the other.

Given that we live in a world that can be described by statements of fact, we have the urge to go down the path of understanding them. This involves a search for covariance between some of these facts, a hunt for what we call causal relationships. In attempting an investigation, what criteria do we use to choose the facts, or the documents, we consider relevant? Clearly that is up to the investigator, whose knowledge or ignorance of the relevant facts and documents comes into play – a subjective process that will vary between investigators. Gaukroger points out the extent of this variation in considering the lengths to which 17th-century scientists went to marshal facts in support of a microcorpuscular theory of nature, an effort that collapsed in the 18th century when faced with newly discovered facts in physiology.

Even if the world was deterministic, we would need to use probabilities for we have no handle on the whole array of facts that might be considered causal. There is a need to make explicit the extent to which human behaviour and psychology play a part in the choice of

---

8   Martin 2017, 241.

facts. Without this, we will not be persuaded of the correctness of the understanding we have grasped. As Price puts it,

> causal reasoning too depends on the stand point of creatures engaged in a certain kind of journey ... in which ... their choices determine what path they take through a tree of branching possibilities.[9]

The use of this one term, 'causes', takes us out of the realm of natural science, as does the use of many other terms. It is only by probing the limitations that such terms place on us (whether in the sciences or the humanities) and identifying the prejudices that we bring to the exercise that we can hope to enhance our understanding.

---

9   Price 2007, 265.

References

ABC Radio National. 'Ruby Payne-Scott – Radio Astronomer.' The Science Show. Accessed 3 August 2018. https://ab.co/2N9IkAf.
Andrewartha, H.G., and L.C. Birch. *The Distribution and Abundance of Animals*. Chicago: University of Chicago Press, 1954.
Andrewartha, H.G., and L.C. Birch. *The Ecological Web*. Chicago: University of Chicago Press, 1984.
Armstrong, D.M. *Perception and the Physical World*. London: Routledge and Kegan Paul, 1961.
Armstrong, D.M. *A Materialist Theory of the Mind*. London: Routledge and Kegan Paul; New York: Humanities Press, 1968.
Armstrong, D.M. *Belief, Truth and Knowledge*. London: Cambridge University Press, 1973.
Armstrong, D.M. *Nominalism and Realism, Volume 1: Universals and Scientific Realism*. Cambridge, UK: Cambridge University Press, 1978.
Armstrong, D.M. *The Nature of Mind and Other Essays*. St. Lucia: University of Queensland Press, 1980.
Armstrong, D.M. 'The Causal Theory of the Mind.' In *The Nature of Mind and Other Essays*, edited by D.J. Chalmers. Ithaca, NY: Cornell University Press, 1981.
Armstrong, D.M. 'An Intellectual Autobiography.' *Quadrant* 27, no. 1–2 (1983): 98–102.
Armstrong, D.M. 'An Intellectual Autobiography: Part II.' *Quadrant* 27, no. 3 (1983): 68–78.
Armstrong, D.M. *A Combinational Theory of Possibility*. Cambridge, UK: Cambridge University Press, 1989.
Armstrong, D.M. *Truth and Truthmakers*. Cambridge, UK: Cambridge University Press, 2004.
Aroney, N. 'Julius Stone and the End of Sociological Jurisprudence: Articulating the Reasons for Decision in Political Communication Cases.' *University of New South Wales Law Journal* 31, no. 1 (2008): 107–35.
Aspromourgos, T. 'Warren Pat Hogan, 1929–2009.' *Economic Record* 86, no. 273 (2010): 289–93.
Australian Academy of Science. 'Lord Robert May, Physicist and Ecologist.' Interviews with Australian Scientists. Accessed 6 January 2017. https://bit.ly/2X67Cnr.
Australian Academy of Science. 'Professor Ann Woolcock (1937–2001), Medical Scientist.' Interviews with Australian Scientists. Accessed 15 January 2018. https://bit.ly/2TSWTun.
Australian Academy of Science. 'Professor Charles Birch (1918–2009), Ecologist.' Interviews with Australian Scientists. Accessed 5 January 2017. https://bit.ly/2Ij2iK1.
Australian Academy of Science. 'Professor Noel Hush, Theoretical Chemist.' Interviews with Australian Scientists. Accessed 24 March 2017. https://bit.ly/2SHrKhj.
Australian Academy of Science. 'Professor Peter Bishop, Visual Neurophysiologist.' Interviews with Australian Scientists. Accessed 13 September 2016. https://bit.ly/2SA6SZ0.

References

Australian Biography. 'Charles Birch.' Accessed 4 January 2017. https://bit.ly/2GJXj2E.

Avey, A.E. *Handbook in the History of Philosophy*. New York: Barnes and Noble, 1954.

Bacon, J., K. Campbell and L. Reinhardt, eds. *Ontology, Causality and Mind: Essays in Honour of D.M. Armstrong*. Cambridge, UK: Cambridge University Press, 1993.

Ball, D., and K. Tamura, eds. *Breaking Japanese Diplomatic Codes: David Sissons and D Special Section During the Second World War*. Canberra: ANU Press, 2013.

Barnes, G. 'The "Discourse of Counsel" and the "Translated" *Riddarasögur*.' In *Learning and Understanding in the Old Norse World: Essays in Honour of Margaret Clunies Ross*, edited by J. Quinn, K. Heslop and T. Wills, 375–98. Turnhout, BE: Brepols Publishers, 2007.

Batten, J.A., and W.P. Hogan. 'A Perspective on Credit Derivatives.' *International Review of Financial Analysis* 11, no. 3 (2002): 251–78.

Beasley, B. '*Expressivism, Pragmatism and Representationalism* Book Review.' *Dialogue: Canadian Philosophical Review* 54, no. 3 (2015): 573–6.

Bennett, M.R. *History of the Synapse.* Sydney: Harwood Academic, 2001.

Bennett, M.R. 'The Discovery of a New Class of Synaptic Transmitters in Smooth Muscle 50 Years Ago and Amelioration of Coronary Artery Thrombosis.' *Acta Physiologica* 207, no. 2 (2013): 236–43.

Bennett, M.R. 'Founding the Brain and Mind Research Institute.' The University of Sydney. Accessed 2 April 2018. https://bit.ly/2GMk31O.

Bennett, M.R., and P.M.S. Hacker. *Philosophical Foundations of Neuroscience*. Oxford: John Wiley and Sons, 2003.

Bennett, M.R., and P.M.S. Hacker. *History of Cognitive Neuroscience.* Oxford: John Wiley and Sons, 2013.

Bhathal, R. 'Bernard Mills and Australian Radio Astronomy.' *Astronomy and Geophysics* 53, no. 2 (2012): 2.19–2.21.

Birch, L.C. 'The Intrinsic Rate of Natural Increase of an Insect Population.' *Journal of Animal Ecology* 17, no. 1 (1948): 15–26.

Birch, L.C. 'This Week's Citation Classic.' *Citation Classics* Commentaries, 17 May 1982. Accessed 5 January 2017. https://bit.ly/2GRXSaT.

Birch, L.C. 'Why I Became a Pan-Experientialist.' BiosferaNoosfera, 23 December 2004. Accessed 5 January 2017. https://bit.ly/2GRYixZ.

Bishop, P.O. 'Peter O. Bishop.' In *The History of Neuroscience in Autobiography, Volume 1*, edited by L.R. Squire, 80–108. Washington, DC: Society for Neuroscience, 1996.

Bishop, P.O., and J.D. Pettigrew. 'Neural Mechanisms of Binocular Vision.' *Vision Research* 26, no. 9 (1986): 1587–600.

Blakemore, C. 'Binocular Depth Discrimination and the Nasotemporal Division.' *Journal of Physiology* 205, no. 2 (1969): 471-97.

Blum, H.F. 'The Physiological Effects of Sunlight on Man.' *Physiological Reviews* 25, no. 3 (1945): 483–530.

Boardman, J. 'Obituary: Professor A.D. Trendall.' *The Independent*, 25 November 1995.

Bogdan, R.J., ed. *D.M. Armstrong*. Dordrecht, NL: D. Reidel Publishing Company, 1984.

'Book Reviews: *The Distribution and Abundance of Animals*, by H.G. Andrewartha and L.C. Birch.' *New Zealand Journal of Forestry* 9, no. 2 (1964): 223.

Branagan, D.F., and T.G. Vallance. 'David, Sir Tannatt William Edgeworth (1858–1934).' Australian Dictionary of Biography. Accessed 22 March 2018. http://adb.anu.edu.au/biography/david-sir-tannatt-william-edgeworth-5894.

Branagan, D. *T.W. Edgeworth David: A Life*. Canberra: National Library of Australia, 2005.

Buist, A.S. 'Similarities and Differences between Asthma and Chronic Obstructive Pulmonary Disease: Treatment and Early Outcomes.' *European Respiratory Journal, Supplement* 21, no. 39 (2003): 30s–35s.

Burtt, E.A. *The Metaphysical Foundations of Modern Science*. London: Kegan Paul, 1925.

References

Burtt, E.A. *The Metaphysical Foundations of Modern Physical Science*. Garden City, NY: Anchor Books, 1954.

Cambitoglou, A., ed. *Studies in Honour of Arthur Dale Trendall*. Sydney: Sydney University Press, 1979.

Cambitoglou, A., and A.D. Trendall. *Apulian Red-Figured Vase-Painters of the Plain Style*. Rutland, VT: The Archaeological Institute of America, 1961.

Campbell, K. 'David Malet Armstrong (8 July 1926–13 May 2014).' *Australasian Journal of Philosophy* 92, no. 3 (2014): 617–8.

Cercignani, C. *Ludwig Boltzmann*. Oxford: Oxford University Press, 1988.

Chrucky, A. 'An Interview with Professor David Armstrong.' Digital Text International. Accessed 14 September 2016. https://bit.ly/2Ij6ARD.

Clark, C.M.H. *A History of Australia*. Carlton: Melbourne University Press, 1962.

Clunies Ross, M. *Skáldskaparmál: Snorri Sturluson's Ars Poetica and Medieval Theories of Language*. Odense, DK: Odense University Press, 1987.

Clunies Ross, M. *Prolonged Echoes. Old Norse Myths in Medieval Northern Society. Volume 1: The Myths*. Odense, DK: Odense University Press, 1994.

Clunies Ross, M. *Prolonged Echoes. Old Norse Myths in Medieval Northern Society. Volume 2: The Reception of Norse Myths in Medieval Iceland*. Odense, DK: Odense University Press, 1998.

Clunies Ross, M. 'From Near and Far.' *Adelaidean*, 20 September 1999. Accessed 7 December 2016. https://bit.ly/2UZBWOH.

Clunies Ross, M. 'The Conservation and Reinterpretation of Myth in Medieval Icelandic Writings.' In *Old Icelandic Literature and Society*, edited by M. Clunies Ross, 116–39. Cambridge, UK: Cambridge University Press, 2000.

Clunies Ross, M, ed. *Old Norse Myths, Literature and Society*. Odense, DK: University Press of Southern Denmark, 2003.

Clunies Ross, M. *A History of Old Norse Poetry and Poetics*. Cambridge, UK: D.S. Brewer, 2005.

Clunies Ross, M. *The Cambridge Introduction to the Old Norse-Icelandic Saga*. Cambridge, UK: Cambridge University Press, 2010.

Cohen, F.S. 'The Province and Function of Law: Law as Logic, Justice and Social Control.' *The Yale Law Journal* 59, no. 1 (1949): 177–81.

Cohen, H.F. 'Two New Conceptions of the Scientific Revolution Compared.' *Historically Speaking* 14, no. 2 (2013): 24–6.

Commonwealth Scientific and Industrial Research Organisation. 'Ruby Payne-Scott [1912–1981].' CSIROpedia. Accessed 3 August 2018. https://bit.ly/2SVx6Vg.

Cornfield, J. 'Joint Dependence of Risk of Coronary Heart Disease on Serum Cholesterol and Systolic Blood Pressure: A Discriminant Function Analysis.' *Federation Proceedings* 21, no. 4 (1962): 58–61.

David, M.E. *Professor David: The Life of Sir Edgeworth David*. London: Edward Arnold, 1937.

Davis, J., and B. Lovell. 'Robert Hanbury Brown 1916–2002.' *Historical Records of Australian Science* 14, no. 4 (2003): 459–83.

DeBach, P., and E.I. Schlinger, eds. *Biological Control of Insect Pests and Weeds*. New York: Reinhold Publishing, 1964.

Doeing, D.C., and J. Solway. 'Airway Smooth Muscle in the Pathophysiology and Treatment of Asthma.' *Journal of Applied Physiology* 114, no. 7 (1985): 834–43.

Dowse, G.K., K.J. Turner, G.A. Stewart, M.P. Alpers and A.J. Woolcock. 'The Association Between Dermatophagoides Mites and the Increasing Prevalence of Asthma in Village Communities Within the Papua New Guinea Highlands.' *Journal of Allergy and Clinical Immunology* 75, no. 1 (1985): 75–83.

'Dr Arnold Heim, Translated Obituary Notice.' *Neue Zürcher Zeitung*, 6 September 1934.

Edgeworth David, T.W. 'The Aims and Ideals of Australasian Science, Inaugural Presidential Address.' *Transactions of the Australasian Association for the Advancement of Science* X (1904): 1–43.

References

Edgeworth David, T.W. 'The First Journey to the South Magnetic Pole.' In *The Heart of the Antarctic: Being the Story of the British Antarctic Expedition 1907–1909, Volume 2*, Chs VI–XIII. London: William Heinemann, 1909.

Ehrlich, P.R., and L.C. Birch. 'The "Balance of Nature" and "Population Control".' *The American Naturalist* 101, no. 918 (1967): 97–107.

Elgin, C. 'Understanding and the Facts.' *Philosophical Studies* 132, no. 1 (2007): 33–42.

Elton, C.S. *The Ecology of Invasions by Animals and Plants*. London: Methuen, 1958.

Evans, M.G., N.S. Hush and N. Uri. 'The Energetics of Reactions Involving Hydrogen Peroxide, Its Radicals, and Its Ions.' *Quarterly Reviews, Chemical Society* 6, no. 2 (1952): 186–96.

Forbush, E.H., and C.H. Fernald. *The Gypsy Moth: Portheria Dispar (Linn.)*. Boston: Massachusetts Board of Agriculture, 1896.

Frater, R.H., W.M. Goss and H.W. Wendt. 'Bernard Yarnton Mills 1920–2011.' *Historical Records of Australian Science* 24, no. 2 (2013): 294–315.

Gardiner, G. 'Understanding, Integration and Epistemic Value.' *Acta Analytica* 27, no. 2 (2012): 163–81.

Gaukroger, S. *Descartes, An Intellectual Biography*. Oxford: Clarendon Press; New York: Oxford University Press, 1995.

Gaukroger, S. *Francis Bacon and the Transformation of Early-Modern Philosophy*. Cambridge, UK: Cambridge University Press, 2001.

Gaukroger, S. *Descartes' System of Natural Philosophy*. Cambridge, UK; New York: Cambridge University Press, 2002.

Gaukroger, S. *The Emergence of a Scientific Culture: Science and the Shaping of Modernity, 1210–1685*. Oxford: Clarendon Press, 2006.

Gaukroger, S. *The Collapse of Mechanism and the Rise of Sensibility: Science and the Shaping of Modernity, 1680–1760*. Oxford: Oxford University Press, 2010.

Gaukroger, S. *The Natural and the Human: Science and the Shaping of Modernity, 1739–1841*. Oxford: Oxford University Press, 2016.

Gil, L.I.R., L.O. Gonzalez, S.C. Agra and P.D. Santomil. 'The Effect of Credit Derivatives Usage on the Risk of European Banks.' *Revista de Economía Mundial* 40, no. 40 (2015): 197–220.

Goddard, B.R., A. Watkinson and B.Y. Mills. 'An Interferometer for the Measurement of Radio Source Sizes.' *Australian Journal of Physics* 13, no. 4 (1960): 665–75.

Goss, W.M. *Making Waves. The Story of Ruby Payne-Scott: Australian Pioneer Radio Astronomer*. Berlin; New York: Springer, 2013.

Green, W.F., G.B. Marks, E.R. Tovey, B.G. Toelle and A.J. Woolcock. 'House Dust Mites and Mite Allergens in Public Places.' *Journal of Allergy and Clinical Immunology* 89, no. 6 (1992): 1196–7.

Gross, E., W.P. Hogan and I.G. Sharpe. 'Market Information and Potential Insolvency of Australian Financial Institutions.' *Australian Economic Papers* 27, no. 50 (1988): 44–64.

Hacker, P.M.S. *The Intellectual Powers*. Oxford: Wiley-Blackwell, 2013.

Hammond, S.R., J.G. McLeod, K.S. Millingen, E.G. Stewart-Wynne, D. English, J.T. Holland and M.G. McCall. 'The Epidemiology of Multiple Sclerosis in Three Australian Cities: Perth, Newcastle and Hobart.' *Brain* 111. no. 1 (1988): 1–25.

Hanbury Brown, R. *Boffin: A Personal Story of the Early Days of Radar, Radio Astronomy and Quantum Optics*. New York: Taylor and Francis, 1991.

Hanbury Brown, R., and R.Q. Twiss. 'A Test of a New Type of Stellar Interferometer on Sirius.' *Nature* 178, no. 4541 (1956): 1046–8.

Hanbury Brown, R., and R.Q. Twiss. 'Correlation Between Photons in Two Coherent Beams of Light.' *Nature* 177, no. 4497 (1956): 27–9.

Hanbury Brown, R., and R.Q. Twiss. 'Interferometry of the Intensity Fluctuations in Lights. I Basic Theory: The Correlation Between Photons in Coherent Beams of Radiation.' *Proceedings of the Royal Society of London. Series A, Mathematical and Physical Sciences* 242, no. 1230 (1957): 300–24.

Hanbury Brown, R., and R.Q. Twiss. 'Interferometry of the Intensity Fluctuations in Lights. II An Experimental Test of the Theory for Partially Coherent Light.' *Proceedings of the Royal Society. Series A, Mathematical and Physical Sciences* 243, no. 1234 (1958): 291–319.

Hanski, I., and M. Gilpin. 'Metapopulation Dynamics: Brief History and Conceptual Domain.' *Biological Journal of the Linnean Society* 42, no. 1–2 (1991): 3–16.

Hastings, H.M. 'The May-Wigner Stability Theorem for Connected Matrices.' *Bulletin of the American Mathematical Society* 7, no. 2 (1982): 387–8.

Helmholtz, H. von. *Science and Culture. Popular and Philosophical Essays*. Translated by D. Cahan. Chicago: University of Chicago Press, 1995.

Henry, G.H. 'Peter Bishop: The Canberra Years.' In *Visual Neuroscience*, edited by J.D. Pettigrew, K.J. Sanderson and W.R. Levick, 434–7. Cambridge, UK: Cambridge University Press, 1986.

Hogan, W.P. 'Capacity Creation and Utilisation in Pakistan Manufacturing Industry.' *Australian Economic Papers* 7, no. 10 (1968): 28–53.

Hogan, W.P. 'Some New Results in the Measurement of Capacity Utilisation.' *American Economic Review* 59, no. 1 (1969): 183–4.

Hogan, W.P. 'Quicksands of Policy Making.' *Australian Economic Papers* 18, no. 33 (1979): 384–96.

Hogan, W.P., and I.F. Pearce. *The Incredible Eurodollar*. London; Boston: Allen and Unwin, 1982.

Hogan, W.P., and I.G. Sharpe. 'Regulation, Risk and the Pricing of Australian Bank Shares 1957–1976.' *Economic Record* 60, no. 1 (1984): 34–44.

Hogan, W.P., and I.G. Sharpe. 'Market Information and Potential Insolvency of Australian Financial Institutions.' *Australian Economic Papers* 27, no. 50 (1988): 44–64.

Hogan, W. P., and I.G. Sharpe. 'Prudential Supervision of Australian Banks.' *Economic Record* 66, no. 2 (1990): 127–45.

Hooker, C. 'The Sun, Ruby Payne Scott and the Birth of Radio Astronomy into the New Century.' In *Irresistible Forces: Australian Women in Science,* 158–66. Carlton: Melbourne University Press, 2004.

Hope, A.D. *The Wandering Islands*. Sydney: Edwards and Shaw, 1955.

Hughes, G.K., N.S. Hush and D.P. Mellor. 'Polymerization of a Semiquinone Ion.' *Nature* 159, no. 4044 (1947): 612.

Hush, N.S. 'Adiabatic Rate Processes at Electrodes. I. Energy-Charge Relationships.' *The Journal of Chemical Physics* 28, no. 5 (1958): 962–72.

Hush, N.S. 'Adiabatic Theory of Outer Sphere Electron-Transfer Reactions in Solution.' *Transactions of the Faraday Society* 57 (1961): 557–80.

Hush. N.S. 'Intervalence-Transfer Absorption. Part 2. Theoretical Considerations and Spectroscopic Data.' In *Progress in Inorganic Chemistry, Volume 8*, edited by F.A. Cotton, 391–444. New York: Interscience Publishers, 1967.

Hush, N. S. 'An Overview of the First Half-Century of Molecular Electronics.' *Annals of the New York Academy of Sciences* 1006, no. 1 (2003): 1–20.

Hush, N.S., M.N. Paddon-Row, E. Cotsaris, H. Oevering, J.W. Verhoeven and M. Heppener. 'Distance Dependence of Photoinduced Electron Transfer Rates Through Non-Conjugated Bridges.' *Chemical Physics Letters* 117, no. 1 (1985): 8–11.

Hutchinson, A. 'The Province of Jurisprudence (Really) Redetermined.' Comparative Research in Law and Political Economy, Research Paper No. 21/2008. Accessed 29 March 2018. https://bit.ly/2Gu7GbI.

Hutchinson, G.E. 'Homage to Santa Rosalia, or Why Are There So Many Kinds of Animals?' *The American Naturalist* 93, no. 870 (1959): 145–59.

Irvine, A. 'David Armstrong and Australian Materialism.' *Quadrant Online*, 1 March 2014. Accessed 14 September 2016. https://bit.ly/2Ed152G.

Jenkins, C. 'Ann Janet Woolcock AO, FFA, MB BS, MD, FRACP.' *Medical Journal of Australia* 175, no. 3 (2001): 160.

References

Johnson, R. 'Trendall, Arthur Dale (1909–1995).' Australian Dictionary of Biography, Obituaries Australia. Accessed 21 March 2018. https://bit.ly/2GsEQby.

Johnston, R.A. 'The Monetary System in Transition.' *RBA Bulletin* (November 1985): 1–8.

Johnston, R.A. 'The Role of a Central Bank.' *RBA Bulletin* (February 1986).

Kamban, G. *The Virgin of Skalholt*. Translated by E. Ramsden. Boston: Little, Brown and Co., 1935.

Kamenka, E., and A.E. Tay. 'Socialism, Anarchism and Law.' In *Law and Society: The Crisis in Legal Ideals*, edited by E. Kamenka, R. Brown and A.E. Tay, 49–80. London: Edward Arnold, 1978.

Kamenka, E., and A.E. Tay. 'Social Traditions, Legal Traditions.' In *Law and Social Control*, edited by E. Kamenka and A.E. Tay, 3–26. London: Edward Arnold, 1980.

Kamenka, E., and A. Ehr-Soon Tay. '"Transforming" the Law, "Steering" Society.' In *Law and Social Control*, edited by E. Kamenka and A.E. Tay, 105–16. London: Edward Arnold, 1980.

Kamenka, E., and A.E. Tay, 'Legal Entities, Property and the Collapse of Communism.' *India Socio-Legal Journal* 19, no. 1, Special Issue on Legal Persons and Legal Personality (1993).

Keuls, E.C. '*The Red-Figured Vases of Apulia, Volume 1: Early and Middle Apulian*, by A.D. Trendall and Alexander Cambitoglou.' *American Journal of Archaeology* 84, no. 1 (1980): 110–2.

King, G.G., S. Eberl, C.M. Salome, I.H. Young and A.J. Woolcock. 'Differences in Airway Closure Between Normal and Asthmatic Subjects Measured with Single Photon Emission Computed Tomography and Technegas.' *American Journal of Respiratory and Clinical Care Medicine* 158, no. 6 (1998): 1900–6.

Kirby, M. 'Julius Stone and the High Court of Australia.' *University of New South Wales Law Journal* 20, no. 1 (1997): 239–46.

Kvanvig, J. 'The Value of Understanding.' In *Epistemic Value*, edited by A. Haddock, A. Millar and D. Pritchard, 95–111. New York: Oxford University Press, 2009.

Laker, J.F. 'Ideas and Issues in Financial Regulation.' Australian Prudential Regulation Authority, 26 November 2013. Accessed 8 March 2018. https://bit.ly/2TSCOV2.

Lancaster, H.O. 'The Derivation and Partition of Chi-Square in Certain Discrete Distributions.' *Biometrika* 36, no. 1–2 (1949): 117–29.

Lancaster, H.O. 'Deafness as an Epidemic Disease in Australia: A Note on Census and Institutional Data.' *British Medical Journal* 2, no. 4745 (1951): 1429–32.

Lancaster, H.O. 'Deafness Due to Rubella.' *Medical Journal of Australia* 2, no. 9 (1954): 323–4.

Lancaster, H.O. 'The Epidemiology of Deafness Due to Maternal Rubella.' *Acta Genetica* 5, no. 1 (1954): 12–24.

Lancaster, H.O. 'The Mortality in Australia from Cancer (Concluded).' *Medical Journal of Australia* 2, no. 3 (1954): 93–7.

Lancaster, H.O. 'Geographical Aspects of Melanoma.' *The Lancet* 266, no. 6896 (1955): 929.

Lancaster, H.O. 'Some Geographical Aspects of the Mortality from Melanoma in Europeans.' *Medical Journal of Australia* 43, no. 26 (1956): 1082–7.

Lancaster, H.O. *Some Recollections of Henry Oliver Lancaster*, edited by R. Lancaster. Mosman, NSW: H.O. Lancaster, 1996.

Lancaster, H.O., and J. Nelson. 'Sunlight as a Cause of Melanoma: A Clinical Survey.' *Medical Journal of Australia* 44, no. 14 (1957): 452–6.

Lance, J.W. 'Peter Bishop: The First 65 Years.' In *Visual Neuroscience*, edited by J.D. Pettigrew, K.J. Sanderson and W.R. Levick, 430–3. Cambridge, UK: Cambridge University Press, 1986.

Lauzon, A.M., and J.G. Martin. 'Airway Hyperresponsiveness: Smooth Muscle as the Principal Actor.' *F1000research* 5 (2016): 306.

Li, T., and J.A. Yorke. 'Period Three Implies Chaos.' *The American Mathematical Monthly* 82, no. 10. (1975): 985–92.

Lindow, J. *Handbook of Norse Mythology*. Santa Barbara; Oxford: ABC-CLIO, 2001.

Lodewijks, J. 'A Conversation with Warren Hogan.' *Economic Record* 83, no. 263 (2007): 446–60.

Lovell, B., and R.M. May. 'Obituary: Robert Hanbury Brown (1916–2002).' *Nature* 416, no. 6876 (2002): 34.

References

Low, P.A., and J.G. McLeod. 'Refractory Period, Conduction of Trains of Impulses, and Effect of Temperature on Conduction in Chronic Hypertrophic Neuropathy.' *Journal of Neurology, Neurosurgery and Psychiatry* 40, no. 5 (1977): 434–47.

MacArthur, R.H. *Geographical Ecology: Patterns in the Distribution of Species*. New York: Harper and Row, 1972.

Macklem, P. 'Ann Woolcock 1937–2001: An Appreciation.' *American Journal of Respiratory and Critical Care Medicine* 163, no. 5 (2001): 1041.

Malm, M. 'The Notion of Effeminate Language in Old Norse Literature.' In *Learning and Understanding in the Old Norse World: Essays in Honour of Margaret Clunies Ross*, edited by J. Quinn, K. Heslop and T. Wills, 305–20. Turnhout, BE: Brepols Publishers, 2007.

Margalef, R. *Perspectives in Ecological Theory*. Chicago: University of Chicago Press, 1968.

Martin, M. *Verstehen: The Uses of Understanding in Social Science*. Oxford: Routledge, 2017.

Mawson, D. 'Sir Tannatt William Edgeworth David 1858–1934.' Biographical Memoirs of Fellows of the Royal Society, 1 December 1935. Accessed 22 March 2018. https://bit.ly/2Sa6ITm.

May, R.M. 'Limit Cycles in Predator-Prey Communities.' *Science* 177, no. 4052 (1972): 900–2.

May, R.M. 'Will a Large Complex System be Stable?' *Nature* 238, no. 5364 (1972): 413–4.

May, R.M. 'Simple Mathematical Models with Very Complicated Dynamics.' *Nature* 261, no. 5560 (1976): 459–67.

May, R.M. 'The Croonian Lecture, 1985: When Two and Two Do Not Make Four – Nonlinear Phenomena in Ecology.' *Proceedings of the Royal Society of London. Series B, Biological Sciences* 228, no. 1252 (1986): 241–66.

May, R.M. 'Birch, L.C (1948): "The Intrinsic Rate of Natural Increase of an Insect Population".' 100 Influential Papers Published in 100 Years of the British Ecological Society Journals. Accessed 5 January 2017. https://bit.ly/2V3Lo3D.

May, R.M., and R.H. MacArthur. 'Niche Overlap as a Function of Environmental Variability.' *Proceedings of the National Academy of Sciences USA* 69, no. 5 (1972): 1109–13.

McCombe, P.A., J.D. Pollard and J.G. McLeod. 'Chronic Inflammatory Demyelinating Polyradiculoneuropathy: A Clinical and Electrophysiological Study of 92 Cases.' *Brain* 110, no. 6 (1987): 1617–30.

McCready, L.L., J.L. Pawsey and R. Payne-Scott. 'Solar Radiation at Radio Frequencies and Its Relation to Sunspots.' *Proceedings of the Royal Society of London. Series A, Mathematical and Physical Sciences* 190, no. 1022 (1947): 357–75.

McLeod, J.G., J.C. Hargrave, R.S. Gye, J.D. Pollard, J.C. Walsh, J.M. Little and G.C. Booth. 'Nerve Grafting in Leprosy.' *Brain* 98, no. 2 (1975): 203–12.

McNaughton, K. 'The Athenian Society.' The University of Melbourne. Accessed 23 March 2018. https://bit.ly/2N8mZqQ.

McPhee, I. 'Arthur Dale Trendall 1909–1995.' *Proceedings of the British Academy* 97 (1998): 501–17.

Meats, A. 'What Ever Happened to Andrewartha and Birch.' ResearchGate. Accessed 3 March 2017. https://bit.ly/2X6n56T.

Mellor, L. *150 Years, 150 Firsts: The People of the Faculty of Medicine*. Sydney: Sydney University Press, 2006.

Mellor, L. 'Bishop, Peter Orlebar.' Faculty of Medicine Online Museum and Archive, 2008. Accessed 13 September 2016. https://bit.ly/2GsI3rt.

Mills, B.Y. 'The Radio Brightness Distributions over Four Discrete Sources of Cosmic Noise.' *Australian Journal of Physics* 6, no. 4 (1953): 452–70.

Mills, B.Y. 'On the Identification of Extragalactic Radio Sources.' *Australian Journal of Physics* 13, no. 3 (1960): 550.

Mills, B.Y., E.R. Hill and O.B. Slee. 'The Galaxy at 3.5 m.' *The Observatory* 78 (1958): 116–21.

Mills, B.Y., and O.B. Slee. 'A Preliminary Survey of Radio Sources in a Limited Region of the Sky at the Wavelength of 3.5 m.' *Australian Journal of Physics* 10, no. 1 (1957): 162–94.

References

Mills, B.Y., O.B. Slee and E.R. Hill. 'A Catalogue of Radio Sources Between Declinations +10° and –20°.' *Australian Journal of Physics* 11, no. 3 (1958): 360–87.

Mills, B.Y., O.B. Slee and E.R. Hill. 'A Catalogue of Radio Sources Between Declinations –20° and –50°.' *Australian Journal of Physics* 13, no. 4 (1960): 676–99.

Mills, B.Y., O.B. Slee and E.R. Hill. 'A Catalogue of Radio Sources Between Declinations –50° and –80°.' *Australian Journal of Physics* 14, no. 4 (1961): 497–507.

Mills, E. 'Engineer a Star of Astronomy.' *Sydney Morning Herald*, 21 May 2011. Accessed 9 August 2018. https://bit.ly/2N9O6lp.

Mumford, S. *David Armstrong.* Stocksfield, UK: Acumen, 2007.

Newman, M. 'An Inferential Model of Scientific Understanding.' *International Studies in the Philosophy of Science* 26, no. 1 (2012): 1–26.

Newman, M. 'Theoretical Understanding in Science.' *British Journal for the Philosophy of Science* 68, no. 2 (2017): 571–95.

Nicholson, A.J. 'An Outline of the Dynamics of Animal Populations.' *Australian Journal of Zoology* 2, no. 1 (1954): 9–65.

North, J. 'Understanding the Time-Asymmetry of Radiation.' PhilSci Archive, 2003. Accessed 2 April 2018. http://philsci-archive.pitt.edu/4958/.

Oakeshott, N. 'From Lenormant to Trendall.' In *Studies in Honour of Arthur Dale Trendall*, edited by A. Cambitoglou, 1–7. Sydney: Sydney University Press, 1979.

Pálsson, H. 'Review Article: *Prolonged Echoes. Old Norse Myths in Medieval Northern Society, Vols 1 and 2*, by Margaret Clunies Ross.' *Northern Studies* 36 (2001): 131–40.

Pawsey, J.L., R. Payne-Scott and L.L. McCready. 'Radio-Frequency Energy from the Sun.' *Nature* 157, no. 3980 (1946): 158–9.

Payne-Scott, R. 'Solar and Cosmic Radio Frequency Radiation: Survey of Knowledge Available and Measurements Taken at Radiophysics Laboratory to December 1, 1945.' *CSIR Radiophysics Laboratory Report* SRP 501/27 (1945).

Payne-Scott, R. 'A Study of Solar Radio Frequency Radiation on Several Frequencies during the Sunspot of July–August, 1946.' *CSIR Radiophysics Laboratory Report* RPL 9 (1947).

Payne-Scott, R. 'Bursts of Solar Radiation at Metre Wavelengths.' *Australian Journal of Scientific Research. Series A, Physical Sciences* 2, no. 2 (1949): 214–27.

Payne-Scott, R., and A.G. Little. 'The Position and Movement on the Solar Disk of Sources of Radiation at a Frequency of 97 Mc/s. I. Equipment.' *Australian Journal of Scientific Research. Series A, Physical Sciences* 4, no. 4 (1951): 489–507.

Payne-Scott, R., and A.G. Little. 'The Position and Movement on the Solar Disk of Sources of Radiation at a Frequency of 97 Mc/s. II. Noise Storms.' *Australian Journal of Scientific Research. Series A, Physical Sciences* 4, no. 4 (1951): 508–25.

Payne-Scott, R., and A.G. Little. 'The Position and Movement on the Solar Disk of Sources of Radiation at a Frequency of 97 Mc/s. III. Outbursts.' *Australian Journal of Scientific Research. Series A, Physical Sciences* 5, no. 1 (1952): 32–49.

Payne-Scott, R., D.E. Yabsley and J.G. Bolton. 'Relative Times of Arrival of Bursts of Solar Noise on Different Radio Frequencies.' *Nature* 160, no. 4060 (1947): 256–7.

Peat, J.K., and A.J. Woolcock. 'Sensitivity to Common Allergens: Relation to Respiratory Symptoms and Bronchial Hyperresponsiveness in Children from Three Different Climate Areas of Australia.' *Clinical and Experimental Allergy* 21, no. 5 (1991): 573–81.

Pirsig, R.M. *Zen and the Art of Motorcycle Maintenance.* New York: HarperCollins, 2006.

Pollard, J.D., J.G. McLeod, P. Gatenby and H. Kronenberg. 'Prediction of Response to Plasma Exchange in Chronic Relapsing Polyneuropathy.' *Journal of the Neurological Sciences* 58, no. 2 (1983): 269–87.

Pollard, J.D., J.G. McLeod and R.S. Gye. 'Regeneration Through Peripheral Nerve Allografts.' *Archives of Neurology* 28, no. 1 (1973): 31–7.

References

Poole, R. '*Prolonged Echoes: Old Norse Myths in Medieval Society. Vol. 2: The Reception of Norse Myths in Medieval Iceland* and *Old Icelandic Literature and Society* (review).' *Parergon* 18, no. 3 (2001): 162–6.

Pound, R. *Social Control Through Law*. New Haven, CT: Yale University Press, 1942.

Price, H. *Facts and the Function of Truth*. Oxford: Basil Blackwell, 1989.

Price, H. *Time's Arrow and Archimedes' Point*. Oxford: Oxford University Press, 1996.

Price, H. 'Boltzmann's Time Bomb.' *The British Journal for the Philosophy of Science* 53, no. 1 (2002): 83–119.

Price, H. 'Truth as Convenient Friction.' *Journal of Philosophy* 100, no. 4 (2003): 167–90.

Price, H. 'Recent Work on the Arrow of Radiation.' *Studies in History and Philosophy of Science Part B – Studies in History and Philosophy of Modern Physics* 37, no. 3 (2006): 498–527.

Price, H. 'Causal Perspectivalism.' In *Causation, Physics and the Constitution of Reality*, edited by H. Price and R. Corry, 250–92. Oxford: Clarendon Press, 2007.

Price, H. 'Does Time-Symmetry Imply Retrocausality? How the Quantum World Says "Maybe".' *Studies in History and Philosophy of Science Part B – Studies in History and Philosophy of Modern Physics* 43, no. 2 (2012): 75–83.

Price, H. *Expressivism, Pragmatism and Representationalism*. Cambridge, UK: Cambridge University Press, 2013.

Pritchard, D. 'Knowing the Answer, Understanding and Epistemic Value.' *Grazer Philosophische Studien* 77, no. 1 (2008): 325–39.

Pritchard, D. 'Knowledge, Understanding and Epistemic Value.' *Royal Institute of Philosophy Supplements* 64 (2009): 19–43.

'Professor David's Return.' *Daily Telegraph*, 16 October 1897.

Raschella, F.D. 'Old Icelandic Grammatical Literature: The Last Two Decades of Research (1983–2005).' In *Learning and Understanding in the Old Norse World: Essays in Honour of Margaret Clunies Ross*, edited by J. Quinn, K. Heslop and T. Wills, 341–72. Turnhout, BE: Brepols Publishers, 2007.

Reimers, J.R., A. Bilić, Z. Cai, M. Dahlbom, N.A. Lambropoulos, G.C. Solomon, M.J. Crossley and N.S. Hush. 'Molecular Electronics: From Basic Chemical Principles to Photosynthesis to Steady-State Through-Molecule-Conductivity to Computer Architectures.' *Australian Journal of Chemistry* 57, no. 12 (2004): 1133–8.

Reimers, J.R., and N.S. Hush. 'A Unified Description of the Electrochemical, Charge Distribution and Spectroscopic Properties of the Special-Pair Radical Cation in Bacterial Photosynthesis.' *Journal of the American Chemical Society* 126, no. 13 (2004): 4132–44.

Reimers, J.R., and N.S. Hush. 'Adiabatic Electron Transfer Theory.' *Chemical Reviews* (submitted 2017).

Rice, H. 'Price, Huw, *Facts and the Function of Truth* Book Review.' *Mind* 99, no. 394 (1990): 301–5.

Rosenzweig, M.L. 'Optimal Habitat Selection in Two-Species Competitive Systems.' *Fortschritte der Zoologie* 25, no. 2–3 (1979): 283–93.

Russell, B. *The Autobiography of Bertrand Russell*. London: Allen and Unwin, 1967–9.

Russell, B. *Marriage and Morals*. London: Allen and Unwin, 1972.

Ryle, M. 'Radio Stars and Their Cosmological Significance.' *The Observatory* 75 (1955): 137–47.

Salome, C.M., J.K. Peat, W.J. Britton and A.J. Woolcock. 'Bronchial Hyperresponsiveness in Two Populations of Australian Schoolchildren. I. Relation to Respiratory Symptoms and Diagnosed Asthma.' *Clinical Allergy* 17, no. 4 (1987): 271–81.

Schreuder, D.M., and B.H. Fletcher. 'Foreword.' In *The State and the People: Australian Federation and Nation-Making 1870–1901*, by J.M. Ward, edited by D.M. Schreuder, B.H. Fletcher and R. Hutchinson. Annandale, NSW: The Federation Press, 2001.

Schreuder, D.M., B.H. Fletcher and R. Hutchinson. 'Editors' Introduction.' In *The State and the People: Australian Federation and Nation-Making 1870–1901*, by J.M. Ward, edited by D.M. Schreuder, B.H. Fletcher and R. Hutchinson. Annandale, NSW: The Federation Press, 2001.

References

Science.gov.au. 'Professor Peter Bishop (Australia) 1993 Australia Prize (Sensory Perception).' Australia Prizes 1990–1999 Recipients. Accessed 23 August 2018. https://bit.ly/2GKGYuG.

Seneta, E. 'In Memoriam. Emeritus Professor Henry Oliver Lancaster, AO, FAA.' *Australian and New Zealand Journal of Statistics* 44, no. 4 (2002): 385–400.

Seneta, E., and G.K. Eagleson. 'Henry Oliver Lancaster 1913–2001.' *Historical Records of Australian Science* 15, no. 2 (2004): 223–50.

Shank, J.B. 'Stephen Gaukroger. *The Natural and the Human: Science and the Shaping of Modernity, 1739–1841.*' *The American Historical Review* 122, no. 5 (2017): 1678–9.

Sherrington, C.S. *Man on his Nature*, 2nd ed. Cambridge, UK: Cambridge University Press, 1951.

Simberloff, D. 'Eminent Ecologist: Herbert G. Andrewartha and L. Charles Birch.' *Bulletin of the Ecological Society of America* 70, no. 1 (1989): 28–9.

Smith, B. 'Ann Janet Woolcock (1937–2001).' *Historical Records of Australian Science* 25, no. 2 (2014): 313–36.

Smith, C.U.M. 'How the Modern World Began: Stephen Gaukroger's *Descartes' System of Natural Philosophy.*' *Journal of the History of the Neurosciences* 14, no. 1 (2005): 57–63.

Smith, L.B., and C.H. Hadley. 'The Japanese Beetle.' *United States Department of Agriculture Circular* 363 (1926).

Spencer, J. '"The Intrinsic Rate of Natural Increase of an Insect Population", L.C. Birch (1948).' UNM Grad Core Ecology, 10 October 2015. Accessed 5 January 2017. https://bit.ly/2SUVjeo.

Steffes, D.M. *The "Eco-Worldview" of Charles Birch: Biology, Environmentalism and Liberal Christianity in the 20th Century*. Charleston, SC: Proquest, UMI Dissertation Publishing, 2011.

Stevens, G. 'The Inaugural Warren Hogan Memorial Lecture.' Reserve Bank of Australia, 8 December 2011. Accessed 8 March 2018. https://bit.ly/2UXWxTu.

Stewart, G.J., J.D. Pollard, J.G. McLeod and C.M. Wolnizer. 'HLA Antigens in the Landry-Guillain-Barré Syndrome and Chronic Relapsing Polyneuritis.' *Annals of Neurology* 4, no. 3 (1978): 285–9.

Stone, J. 'Cross Examination by the Prosecution at Common Law and Under the Evidence Act, 1898.' *Law Quarterly Review* 51 (1935): 443–67.

Stone, J. *The Province and Function of Law: Law as Logic, Justice and Social Control – A Study in Jurisprudence*. Sydney: Associated General Publications, 1946.

Stone, J. *Legal System and Lawyers' Reasonings*. Stanford: Stanford University Press, 1964.

Stone, J. *Human Law and Human Justice*. Stanford: Stanford University Press, 1965.

Stone, J. *Social Dimensions of Law and Justice*. Sydney: Maitland Publications, 1966.

Stone, J. *Letters to Australia: The Radio Broadcasts (1942–1972). The 1940s, Volume 1 and 2*. Sydney: Sydney University Press, 2014.

Tango, W.J. 'The Hanbury Brown–Twiss Effect and the Birth of Quantum Optics.' *Australian Physics* 51, no. 4 (2014): 116–21.

Tay, A.E. 'Law in Communist China Part I.' *Sydney Law Review* 6, no. 2 (1969): 153–72.

Tay, A.E. 'Smash Permanent Rules: China as a Model for the Future.' *Sydney Law Review* 7 (1976): 400–23.

Tay, A.E. 'Law, the Citizen and the State.' In *Law and Society: The Crisis in Legal Ideals*, edited by E. Kamenka, R. Brown and A.E. Tay, 1–17. London: Edward Arnold, 1978.

Tay, A.E. 'Marxism, Socialism and Human Rights.' In *Human Rights*, edited by E. Kamenka and A.E Tay, 104–12. London: Edward Arnold, 1978.

Tay, A.E. 'The Sense of Justice in the Common Law.' In *Justice*, edited by E. Kamenka and A.E Tay, 79–96. London: Edward Arnold, 1979.

Tay, A.E., and E. Kamenka. 'Editors' Introduction: Law, Lawyers and Law Making in Australia.' In *Law Making in Australia*, edited by E. Kamenka and A.E. Tay, 20–38. London: Edward Arnold, 1980.

Tay, A.E, and E. Kamenka. 'New Legal Areas, New Legal Attitudes.' In *Law Making in Australia*, edited by E. Kamenka and A.E Tay, 247–62. London: Edward Arnold, 1980.

References

Tay, A.E., and E. Kamenka. 'Marxism, Socialism and the Theory of Law.' *Columbia Journal of Transnational Law* 23, no. 2 (1985): 217–49.

Tönnies, F. *Gemeinschaft und Gesellschaft.* Leipzig, DE: Fues's Verlag, 1887.

Tönnies, F. *Community and Association (Gemeinschaft und Gesellschaft).* Translated and supplemented by C.P. Loomis. London: Routledge and Kegan Paul, 1955.

Trendall, A.D. *Paestan Pottery: A Study of the Red-Figured Vases of Paestum.* London: Macmillan, 1936.

Trendall, A.D. *Handbook to the Nicholson Museum.* Glebe, NSW: Australasian Medical Publishing, 1945.

Trendall, A.D. *Handbook to the Nicholson Museum*, 2nd ed. Glebe, NSW: Australasian Medical Publishing, 1948.

Trendall, A.D. *The Red-Figured Vases of Lucania, Campania and Sicily.* London: University of London, Institute of Classical Studies, 1983.

Trendall, A.D. *The Red-Figured Vases of Paestum.* London: British School at Rome, 1987.

Trendall, A.D. *Red Figure Vases of South Italy and Sicily.* London: Thames and Hudson, 1989.

Trendall, A.D., and A. Cambitoglou. *The Red-Figured Vases of Apulia, Volumes 1 and 2.* Oxford: Oxford University Press, 1982.

Trendall, A.D., and A. Cambitoglou. *First Supplement to 'The Red-Figured Vases of Apulia'.* London: University of London, Institute of Classical Studies, 1983.

Trendall, A.D., and A. Cambitoglou. *Second Supplement to 'The Red-Figured Vases of Apulia'.* London: University of London, Institute of Classical Studies, 1991.

Trendall, A.D., and T.B.L. Webster. *Illustrations of Greek Drama.* New York: Phaidon, 1971.

Tulinius, T.H. 'Political Echoes: Reading *Eyrbyggja Saga* in Light of Contemporary Conflicts.' In *Learning and Understanding in the Old Norse World: Essays in Honour of Margaret Clunies Ross*, edited by J. Quinn, K. Heslop and T. Wills, 49–62. Turnhout, BE: Brepols Publishers, 2007.

Turnbull, A.L., and D.A. Chant. 'The Practice and Theory of Biological Control of Insects in Canada.' *Canadian Journal of Zoology* 39, no. 5 (1961): 697–753.

Turner, K.J., G.K. Dowse, G.A. Stewart, M.P. Alpers and A.J. Woolcock. 'Prevalence of Asthma in the South Fore People of the Okapa District of Papua New Guinea. Features Associated with a Recent Dramatic Increase.' *International Archives of Allergy and Immunology* 77, no. 1–2 (1985): 158–62.

Turner, M., and A. Cambitoglou. *Corpus Vasorum Antiquorum, Red Figure and Over-Painted Pottery of South Italy.* Sydney: The Nicholson Museum, the University of Sydney, 2014.

Vincenc, K.S., J.L. Black, K. Yan, C.L. Armour, P.D. Donnelly and A.J. Woolcock. 'Comparison of In Vivo and In Vitro Responses to Histamine in Human Airways.' *American Review of Respiratory Diseases* 128, no. 5 (1983): 875–9.

Voorhorst, R., M.I. Spieksma-Boezeman and F.T. Spieksma. 'Is a Mite (Dermatophagoides Sp.) the Producer of House-Dust Allergen?' *Allergie und Asthma* 10 (1964): 329–34.

Ward, J.M. *Earl Grey and the Australian Colonies, 1846–1857: A Study of Self-Government and Self-Interest.* Carlton: Melbourne University Press, 1958.

Ward, J.M. *Empire in the Antipodes: The British in Australasia, 1840–1860.* London: Edward Arnold, 1966.

Ward, J.M. *British Policy in the South Pacific, 1786–1893: A Study of British Policy in the South Pacific Islands Prior to the Establishment of Governments by the Great Powers.* Westport, CT: Greenwood Press, 1976.

Ward, J.M. *Colonial Self-Government: The British Experience, 1759–1856.* London: Macmillan, 1976.

Ward, J.M. *James Macarthur, Colonial Conservative, 1798–1867.* Sydney: Sydney University Press, 1981.

Ward, J.M. *The State and the People: Australian Federation and Nation-Making 1870–1901.* Edited by D.M. Schreuder, B.H. Fletcher and R. Hutchinson. Annandale, NSW: The Federation Press, 2001

References

Watt, K.E.F. *Ecology and Resource Management: A Quantitative Approach*. New York: McGraw-Hill, 1968.

Whitehead, A.N., and B. Russell. *Principia Mathematica*, Volumes 1–3. Cambridge, UK: Cambridge University Press, 1910–3.

Wickens, C.H. *Census of the Commonwealth of Australia, Taken for the Night Between the 3rd and 4th of April, 1921*. Melbourne: Government Printer, 1924–7.

Wind, E. *Art and Anarchy*. Evanston, IL: Northwestern University Press, 1985.

Wittgenstein, L. *Philosophical Investigations*. Translated by G.E.M. Anscombe. Oxford: Basil Blackwell, 1953.

Woolcock, A.J., C.R. Blackburn, M.H. Freeman, W. Zylstra and S.R. Spring. 'Studies of Chronic (Nontuberculous) Lung Disease in New Guinea Populations. The Nature of the Disease.' *American Review of Respiratory Disease* 102, no. 4 (1970): 575–90.

Woolcock, A.J., C.M. Salome and K. Yan. 'The Shape of the Dose-Response Curve to Histamine in Asthmatic and Normal Subjects.' *American Review of Respiratory Disease* 130, no. 1 (1984): 71–5.

Yan, K., C. Salome and A.J. Woolcock. 'Prevalence and Nature of Bronchial Hyperresponsiveness in Subjects with Chronic Obstructive Pulmonary Disease.' *American Review of Respiratory Diseases* 132, no. 1 (1985): 25–9.

Yan, K., C. Salome and A.J. Woolcock. 'Rapid Method for Measurement of Bronchial Responsiveness.' *Thorax* 38, no. 10 (1983): 760–5.

Zwölfer, H. 'The Structure of the Parasite Complexes of Some Lepidoptera.' *Zeitschrift fur Angewandte Entomologie* 51 (1963): 346–57.

Index

Aboriginal peoples 43, 57
acceptor molecule 206
aesthetics 157
air interception radar 163
airway function 301
  pro-inflammatory airway smooth muscle phenotype 308
aldehydes 302
Allen, Clabon 188
allene 207
allergens 299
  skin test 304
Andromeda spiral galaxy 166
animal populations
  density-dependent 236
  density-independent 237
anomalous societies 45–46, 50, 60
antennae 163, 188
Apulian vase painting 10
Aquinas, Thomas 155
Aristotle 149, 155
aromatic hydrocarbons 204
arrow of time 130, 133
assertoric language 128
asthma 299
  anti-allergic beta agents 301
  asthma action plan 301
  forced expired volume 305
  histamine inhalation test 304
  sensitivity to histamine 305
  wheezing 304
Athenian Society 233
atoms 204
atopy 304; *see also* allergens

aurora borealis 183
Australian colonies 41
  history 43
Australian New Guinea Administrative Unit 265
Australian Security Intelligence Organisation 183
autoimmune disease 295
  azimuth tube 164

Bacon, Francis 149–151
Badgerys Creek 175
Battle of Britain 164
beetles 241
behavioural dispositions 128, 140
belief 143
bell krater 13, 15, 20, 21, 23
benzene 204
beta agonists 307
Beta Crucis (Mimera) 170
biopsy material, research using 296
black holes 168
boffin, origin of word 161
Bologna 155
Boltzmann probabilities 131
brain 140, 281
  brain state 140
  central state 141
  cerebral cortex 285
  occipital lobe 285
  physical workings 141
  striate cortex 285
bronchial hyper-responsiveness 304, 306
bronchiolitis 301
bronchitis 301

Index

cancer 267
  skin cancer 267
  red skin reaction 268
  pigment 269
  basal cell carcinoma 269
Cassiopeia A 168
cathode-ray oscilloscope tube 283
causality 126, 128, 132–134, 273
  perspectival 132, 133
cellular morphogenesis 201
Centaurus A 175
centrum, environmental 242
Charcot-Marie-Tooth disease 296
chemical reactions 203
chi-square tests 265, 273–274, 275–277
  contingency table 273
  hypothesis of independence 274
  degrees of freedom 273
  decomposition 274, 276
  mutually independent components 274
  standard normal random variables 275
  multivariate 275
  goodness-of-fit 276
chlorophyll molecules 209
chromophores 209
chronic inflammatory demyelinating neuropathy 294
church and science 153–155
ciphers and codes 14
cognition 152, 155
  affective states 153
Colonial Office 44, 45, 47, 48, 48, 53, 54, 59
colonies 45, 47, 50, 51, 53, 54, 55, 57, 60
  executive councils 50
  governors 44
  provinces 47
  union of 51, 54
combustion 205
common law 81
Commonwealth Investigation Service 183
communal ethos 149
Communist Party 175, 183
computer consciousness 201
conflict 80
  conflicting interests 82
consciousness 126, 141, 233, 281
conservativism 56, 57, 59, 60
Constitution, Australian 55, 56, 57, 59, 60
  racial aspects 57
convicts and transportation 46, 51, 55, 58, 59
corona, solar 185

corpuscularism 156
corticosteroids 301
cosmic background radiation 177
cosmic radio signals 185
cosmology 29
Council for Scientific and Industrial Research (CSIR) 173, 185
  covariance 127
  Creutz-Taube ion 208
  cryptography 13
  Cygnus A 168, 175
  cytomegalovirus antibody 295

damper 129, 130, 134
  anti-damper 129, 130
deafness 270–273
declarative theory 84
democracy 58, 60
demographic behaviour in animals 238; *see also* animal populations
Descartes 151–153
direct realism 143
disposition 142, 143
Durham Report 47
dust mites 304
duties and tariffs *see* tariffs

ecology 233
  animal ecology 235
  ecological genetics 235
  ecological web 242
Edda 30–35
education to uplift the masses 60
egg laying 239
  oviposition 240
electrical conductivity 207
electrical engineering 281, 283
electroencephalogram 283
electromagnetic spectrum 128, 168
electron 203
  donor molecule 206
  electron transfer 206
  energetics 204
electrophysiological brain techniques 283
elevation measurement 163
emancipists 46, 48
emphysema 301
enclaves of justice 81
energy 128, 129
entropy 131, 133
  gravitational entropy 131

Index

envirograms 242
environment 127, 130, 235, 237
  environmental factors 236
eosinophilia 265
epidemiology 265, 272, 304
epistemology 132, 152
ethics 126
Eureka Stockade 54
events, experiential 234
evolution 245
exclusivists 46, 48
executive governments 46
experimental allergic neuritis 297
explanatory matter theory 156
extinction 236

federation 41, 51–57, 60
  conventions 56
First Nation peoples 45
folk psychology 143
Fourier synthesis 195
free trade 46, 47, 51, 54
freedom of expression 82
fruit flies 245

galaxy 168, 178, 185
  elliptical galaxy 179
Galileo 151
geometrical principles in philosophy 153
Germanic peoples
  religion and culture 27
gods 29, 32, 39
gold 54, 55
Greek vases 6

habitat 243
'headless woman' magic trick 140
heliocentrism 152
hereditary neuropathy 296
histamines 305
hookworm infestation 265
Hoyle, Fred 177
human nature 81
humanities 157
Humean world 134
hydrostatic mechanisms 151

Iceland 272
'illusory reference' judgements 82, 84
  competing reference 83, 85
  meaningless reference 83

indeterminate reference 85
immunosuppressive agents 293
induction 151, 236
  eliminative induction 151
industrial power 57
inference 151
inherited demyelinating neuropathy 296
inherited diseases 291
insects in population research 245
intensity interferometry 161
intentions 141
interference pattern 194
intervalence charge-transfer spectroscopy 207
intervalence 209
intrinsic rate of natural increase 235, 237

Jodrell Bank 165, 175
judgements, legal 81
judicial choice 83
judicial creativity 84
jurisprudence 79, 81, 85
justice 79, 81
  balancing tests 81
  connective analysis of language 85

Karmalsky, Lerida 175
Kokoda track 267

labour 56
Landry-Guillain-Barré syndrome 295
language games 126, 127, 134
larval stages 239
legal activism 81
legal concepts 82
legal formalism 83
legal formulations 83
legal positivism 81, 84, 84, 85
legal premise 82, 83
legends 9
legislature 48
lekythoi 3, 19
leprosy 291, 293
liberal conservativism 56, 57, 59, 60
life tables 243
linguistic behaviour 126, 127
logic 81, 83
logistic equation 238
London krater 16
lung diseases 299
  dense pleural adhesion 301

Index

Magellanic Clouds 178, 179
Magna Graecia 5, 9, 12, 14
magnetic field 185
  magnetic flux 186
magnetic storm 183
magnetohydrodynamic shockwaves 191
major histocompatibility complex 295
male chauvinism 195
malentities 242
  aggressive malentities 243
  stochastic malentities 243
Maori 43–45
  chiefs 44
  tribes 43, 44
materialism 139
matter theory 156
meaning 126
medical statistics 267
melanoma 267
mental states 141
Menzies, Robert 175
mercantilist policy 47
Messel, Harry 178
metalloenzyme 204
metaphysical 139, 151
meta-populations 235
micro-corpuscularism 149
microscopic observations 149, 152
Milky Way 175
Mills Cross 178
  phase-reversing switches 177
  symmetrical array 177
mind 139, 140, 233, 281
minimal intervention 43–45, 60
molecule 203
  molecular electronics 210
Molonglo Cross 173
Molonglo Reference Catalogue 179
mononuclear lymphocytes 296
monotheistic religion 27
morality 81
  moral considerations 81
  morally autonomous 81
  placement problems 126
motion 152
Mount Stromlo Optical Observatory 188
multiple sclerosis 291, 296–297
  latitudinal gradient 296
  transfer factor 297
  beta-interferon 297
mutually incoherent signals 166

myths 9, 10, 27, 30, 37–38, 39

naiskos 13
nanoscience 210
  carbon nanotubes 210
  nanowires 210
nanotechnologies 204
Narrabri 169
nationalism 55, 60
natural philosophy 148
  natural philosopher 149
naturalisation 157
  naturalisation of the human 157
naturalism 125–126, 139
  object naturalism 125, 126, 127
  subject naturalism 126
nerve
  action potentials 283
  allografts 293
  axons 283
  degenerating nerves 291
  demyelination 295
  impulse conduction 293
  impulses 291
  lesioned sciatic nerve 293
  medial-ulnar nerve 294
  myelin protein PMP22 296
  myelin sheaths 296
  optic nerve 283
  peripheral nerves 291, 293
  regeneration 291, 293
  Schwann cells 296
  velocity of conduction 283
  velocity of the conduction 291
neurons 284
Nicholson Museum 3, 10, 12–13
Handbook of the Nicholson Museum 12
non-semiconductor device 208
normative justice 81, 127
null hypothesis 273

Old Norse-Icelandic 30
  myth 32, 33
  religion 29, 39
  literature 27
oligodendrocytes 297
organic light-emitting diodes 208
oscilloscope 163
oxidation 205

Paestum 8, 10

Index

parenchymal fibrosis 301
parenchymal tissue 307
pathology 265
  amoebic surveys 265
  haematological counting 265
  pathological studies 265
Pawsey, Joseph 173, 185
perception 141
philosophical anthropology 157
philosophy 233
  particulars 139
  processes 234
  things 142
photocatalytic converters 208
photon 169
photosphere 185
photosynthesis 203, 206
photovoltaic cells 208
physical lesion 291
physicalism 139
physics 139
Plan Position Indicator 185
plasma 183, 185
plasmapheresis 297
plenum 152
poetry 27, 39
  skaldic 30, 32, 33, 39
  Eddic 30, 32, 39
polymerisation 206
polytheistic religion 27, 30
population density 235
  abiotic environmental factors 239
populations
  local populations 243
  dispersion 243
  multi-partite populations 243
  niche 243
potentialities 149
Potts Hill 185
pragmatism 81
  pragmatic theory 128
precedent 81
pre-Christian 27, 30, 32, 35, 40
predators 238, 242
probabilities 126, 126, 128, 132
  probabilistic 132
propene 207
protectionism 47
protozoan infection 265
Prussian Blue 207, 208
public health 270

pulmonary restriction 302
pulsar 179

quantitative modelling 242
quantum entanglement 212
quantum mechanics 134, 203
quantum optics 169
quasar 161
quinones 203, 209

radar 161, 185
  radar stations 165
  SV Mark II 165
radicals 59, 59, 206
radio astronomy 161, 165, 173
  Cambridge 2C catalogue 176
  Class 1 175
  Class 2 175
  extragalactic sources 177
  radio sources 177
  radio telescope 166
  strong sources 175
  weak emitters 177
radio waves 161, 183
radiophysics 185
reaction centre 209
red-figure pottery 5, 8–13, 14–17
  red-figure technique 5
redox 204, 205
reduction 205
reductionism 149
reflectors 168
representation 127–128, 127
  e-representation 127, 127
  i-representation 127, 127
representationalism 126, 126, 127, 134
representative government 48, 59, 60
  referendum 56
reproductive stages 240
resonant-cavity X-ray tube 175
  klystron 175
resources 238, 242
Respiratory infection 302
respiratory medicine 301
responsible government 46, 47, 48, 50, 59
retarded waves 128
revenue collector 57
rice weevil 235, 238
Risley counter-rotating prism 286
rubella virus 270–273
Ryle 175, 176

sagas 27, 30, 35–37, 38, 39
  contemporary sagas 36, 39
  family sagas 36, 39
  kings' sagas 36, 39
  knights' sagas 36
  legendary sagas 39
  sagas of the old time 35
  skald 32, 33, 40
sea-cliff interferometer 193–194
Second Law of Thermodynamics 131
self-governing systems 235
self-government 46, 47–50, 51, 60
semiquinone 210
senses and sensation 142
sensible qualities 143
  secondary qualities 143
shrapnel wounds 291
single positron emission computed tomography 307
social mores and conventions 81
society 58, 79
  social compact 81
sociological 79, 81, 82
solar radiation 128, 188
  advanced radiation 128, 129
  retarded radiation 128, 129
  solar bursts 188, 188
  solar radio waves 185
  Type I bursts 190
  Type I storms 190
  Type II bursts 190
  Type III bursts 191
  Type IV bursts 194
Stargate Doughnut 133, 134
stars 161
  radio stars 166, 175
  angular size 166
Steady State Model 177
stereopsis 281, 283
  binocular depth perception 283
  depth 285
  absolute distance 288
stochasticity 236
strict legalism 84
subatomic particles 205
submarine 164
suffrage 58, 59, 60
sunspots 183, 185
supernova remnant 168, 179
swept-lobe interferometer 194
symmetry 128

asymmetry 129, 131
  asymmetry of radiation 130
synaptic transmission 284

tariffs 47, 51, 53, 55
Taurus A 175
temporal asymmetry 129, 130, 132, 133
theology 155
thrips 241
token/token identity 140
Townsville 265
Transition-State Theory 204
transportation 46, 48, 51, 51, 53, 54, 55, 57, 59
treatable neuropathies 295
Treaty of Waitangi 43, 45
Trembler mouse 296
truth 120–125, 126, 128, 149
  truthmaker 145
type/type identity 140

ulceration 293
ultraviolet radiation 267
universals 139
universities 155
University of Sydney 57, 60, 61

values 83, 126, 127, 139
valve 163
vase painting
  geometric style 15
  Morellian technique 6–8, 9, 11, 12
  motifs 16
  ornate style 15
  plain style 15
Vega (Alpha Lyrae) 170
Virgo A 175
visual system 283
  area centralis 286
  binocular neuron 285
  field potentials 285
  horizontal disparity 285
  horizontal shift 285
  optic disc 286
  position disparity tuning curves 288
  position of paralysis 286
  receptive fields 285
  retina 284
  retinal image locations 285
  three-dimensions 283
  vertical disparities 286
  visual axis 286

Index

vitamin D 296
volute krater 15, 16, 26

Ward 41–61
waves 169
  electromagnetic waves 128
  wave equation 205

wave function 205
White Australia Policy 57

Yggdrasill 29, 35

www.ingramcontent.com/pod-product-compliance
Lightning Source LLC
Chambersburg PA
CBHW081144230426
43664CB00018B/2794